The survival of the Habsburg Empire

The survival of the Habsburg Empire

Radetzky, the imperial army and the class war, 1848

Alan Sked

Longman
London and New York

Longman Group Limited London

Associated companies, branches and representatives
throughout the world

Published in the United States of America
by Longman Inc., New York

© Longman Group Limited 1979

First published 1979

ISBN 0 582 50711 1

British Library Cataloguing in Publication Data

Sked, Alan
   The survival of the Habsburg Empire.
   1. Italy – History – Revolution of 1848
   2. Austria. Army – History
   I. Title
   945'.08   DG553   78–41021

   ISBN 0-582-50711-1

Printed in Great Britain by
J. W. Arrowsmith Ltd., Bristol

For My Mother and Father

CONTENTS

Introduction

'The Habsburg Monarchy', according to A. J. P. Taylor,[1]* 'was the toughest organisation in the history of modern Europe.' No other dynasty 'stood up so long to such battering from so many sides. The Habsburgs rode out the storm of the Reformation; withstood the impact of the Turks; challenged Louis XIV; and survived the French Revolution.' Yet in 1848 it seemed that the Habsburg Monarchy would collapse: Metternich was forced to resign; the Emperor fled twice from his capital and was eventually persuaded to abdicate; Italy and Hungary prepared to cast off the yoke of Habsburg hegemony; and even in Germany it seemed temporarily possible that Habsburg leadership would be eclipsed. That the dynasty succeeded in overcoming these challenges was due simply to force of arms. And it was the military achievements of one commander in particular Field Marshal Count Radetzky, which made the survival of the Habsburg Empire possible. In the words of William Roscoe Thayer:[2]

If ever a soldier deserved the gratitude of his sovereign, that man was Radetzky. Though driven from Milan by the surprising insurrection of March 1848, he lost neither head nor heart. He rallied his fugitive troops in the Quadrilateral, checked the onslaught of the elated Italians, waited, stubbornly waited, for reinforcements which might never reach him; was unmoved by news of the general dissolution of the government at Vienna and of the Emperor's flight; and when the time came, he turned and crushed his foe. Verona was a mighty fortress and Mantua was well-nigh impregnable but without the determination in Radetzky's heart, Verona and Mantua and Italy itself would probably have been lost forever to Austria. And not only Italy, the Habsburg dynasty and the existence of its polyglot Empire, held together by the balancing of mutual antagonisms, depended on Radetzky's rock-like stability.

The Field Marshal's contribution was therefore a decisive one. If he had failed to defeat the Italians, the Habsburgs would have had to surrender their Italian territories and to have reached an accommodation with the representatives of nationalist Germany and Hungary. Under these circumstances their Empire could only have survived – if it could have survived at all – in a radically different form.[3] This is really what Grillparzer meant when he wrote in his ode to Radetzky that 'In thy camp is Austria', and the point was recognised among others by the Baroness Blaze de Bury, who in her reminiscences of 1848/9 published in 1850 declared:[4] 'The proof of the importance of Radetzky's Italian Campaign lay in the discouragement which which the revolutionists were seized, upon the news of his successes. When the entrance into Milan of

* Notes to this chapter are on pp. 247–8.

the Austrians was known in Paris, you would have thought the republicans had heard their death-knell. And perhaps they had! Custozza may have been to revolutionary rule what Leipsic was to the Empire, *le premier coup de cloche*.' In fact, there was no 'may' about it. Radetzky's victories in Italy heralded the triumph of the counter-revolution, not only in the Habsburg Empire but in Europe as a whole.

How then had the old man done it? Today most historians would ascribe his successes primarily to the military incompetence of his opponents,[5] a judgement which in no way need detract from his own high qualities of generalship. But at the time of course, this was not at all clear. Radetzky, it was claimed, had been able to keep his army together while the rest of the Empire collapsed because of his military reforms in the Vormärz period; because of his unique qualities of leadership; and because of his willingness at crucial times to disobey his civilian superiors. Indeed, it was claimed, that, had Radetzky been listened to before 1848, the revolutions would never have broken out in the first place!

Radetzky's alleged disobedience was given currency by a well-known *mot* of Prince Schwarzenberg: 'The Monarchy has been preserved by the insubordination of three generals: Radetzky, who opposed the projects of Hummelauer; Jellačić, who braved at the same time the Court at Innsbruck and the Ministry at Pesth; and Windischgraetz who refused to obey Count Latour.'[6] However, it was the military memoirs which were published after 1848, and, in particular, the official military history of the 1848 campaign which established the view that the army before 1848 had had a viewpoint of its own which had been rejected at the Empire's peril. The army's case consisted of the following elements: first, that the Field Marshal's warnings of impending revolution were written off as alarmist and exaggerated by the civilian authorities;[7] secondly that the powers demanded by the army in northern Italy were conceded too late by these authorities;[8] thirdly that the troop strength demanded by the army in Italy was resisted by the same authorities;[9] and fourthly, that the army was denied civilian support on account of the lassitude of Austrian officials and the treason of most Italian ones.[10] In particular, according to the official history, the army was opposed by the most influential representatives of the Italian people:[11] 'most actively involved in the clamour against the military were the nobles and the priests, the latter making extensive use of the confessional and pulpit to preach war against Austria'.

How accurate the army's point of view was will become apparent as a result of this study. Yet it has not been the primary aim of my work to examine the military viewpoint; nor have I limited myself to tackling the questions raised by it. I have attempted, rather, to answer some fundamental questions about Radetzky's army in 1848. To what extent could it hold together? How could it eventually take control of events? What were its relations with the civil authorities? To what extent did it have a policy of its own and to what extent could it implement it? In this way, it is hoped that the book will not merely show how Radetzky was able to survive the challenge of 1848 but will also illuminate other aspects of nineteenth-century history – in particular the social history of the Austrian army and the social history of the Risorgimento.

The reader will soon discover that what I have written is no old-fashioned military history and that for a 'fife and drum' account of events in 1848–9 he will have to look elsewhere.[12] For this I make no apology whatsoever. My aim was not to show where any regiment was to be found on any given day but to analyse events from certain defined perspectives. Thus I have divided my research into three parts. The first is sociological and examines the problems faced by the army before and during 1848. The second is political and is devoted primarily to the question of civil–military relations. The third deals with what, for want of a better expression, may be termed the 'social psychology' of the revolutionary crisis – in other words, an investigation of which groups were involved and of what roles they were thought to be playing by the army. This part also examines the political results of that social psychology.

There are some aspects of this approach, however, which, perhaps, deserve an explanation. As far as the sociology is concerned, I should emphasise that my aim was not to give a comprehensive account of every social institution of the Austrian army. For example, I have not examined in detail every aspect of its judicial system. My aim was rather, to investigate the ways in which the army was held together. For instance, what made the men obey orders? To what extent were they prepared to do so during the revolution and for what reasons? How many, in fact, deserted? I have examined the officer corps from the same perspective. But since it has been a traditional belief of military historians that the cohesion of the officer corps is of crucial importance in wartime (see, for example, John Keegan's recent confirmation, *The Face of Battle*, p. 192, that the battle of Waterloo was won on the playing fields of Eton) I have paid it special attention. In fact, I have made a rather exhaustive study of the type of officer who was trained to represent the best that the army could offer – the graduate of the Wiener Neustadt Military Academy. The result of my research – this is to say of investigating military–social relations from the standpoint of cohesion – is, I believe, that it is possible to form a fairly vivid picture of how the Austrian army really functioned.

It is not, I think, necessary to explain the significance of civil–military relations. My main intention here was the traditional one of investigating how military and political decisions are actually arrived at; in this particular case, how the decisions which determined the course of events in Italy in 1848 were reached on the Austrian side. My interpretation of the 'social psychology' of the revolution, on the other hand, might perhaps be considered controversial. Certainly it will offend historians who read the history of the nineteenth century (and of almost every other century for that matter) in terms of 'the rise of the bourgeoisie'. I do not, in fact, attempt to deny that the bourgeoisie were rising; I simply point out that in Italy in 1848 the people who were making policy decisions thought in terms of a completely different social structure, one in which the pre-industrial relationships were those which merited the most attention. The picture of society which determined the view point of the Austrian military mind was, therefore, one on nobles, peasants and kings and the bourgeoisie figured only (and rightly in my opinion) in so far as its *propriétaires non-nobles* took their lead from the nobility. However, I am in danger now of anticipating my conclusions – always a bad policy for authors writing introductions. The point I wish to make at this stage is merely that the decisions of the Austrian army in Italy in 1848–9 cannot be understood without a knowledge of its mental framework.

So much then for my approach to my subject and what I believe are its advantages. It will no doubt be asserted that it encompasses a corresponding disadvantage. That is to say, there will be critics who will resent the fact that the book has not been written as a continuous narrative. The obvious answer to this objection is simply that history does not always lend itself to narrative. Besides, it will be readily apparent that for two-thirds to three-quarters of the present study it proved possible to marry analysis and narrative quite happily.

My work for the most part has been based on primary sources. Secondary sources have also been utilised, but there is surprisingly little in English, German, French, Italian or Hungarian on the matters treated in the book. The Austrian army in the Vormärz period attracted little contemporary notice[13] and has attracted almost none since. Moreover, what work has been done on Radetzky has been distinctly hagiographical.[14] Italian historians, on the other hand, have always preferred to look on the Risorgimento in a positive light (i.e. as the development of Italian national consciousness) rather than in the context of ridding Italy of the Austrians. Thus, my own task in writing this book was not so much one of 'setting the record straight' – so often the real task of historians – but one of establishing a record. I say *a* record rather than *the* record, since no doubt I have made numerous mistakes and others will want to set my record straight. Nonetheless, I have tried to get at the truth. Many of the documents I should like to have consulted – police records, military court records, the archives of the viceregal chancellery, to name only a few – were destroyed in Vienna in 1927 or in Milan in 1944. However, I have tried to piece the picture together as meaningfully as possible.

My final task is to thank a number of people who encouraged me to undertake this research or who sustained me in my efforts once I started. In particular, I would like to thank Mr A. J. P. Taylor who supervised the Oxford doctoral thesis out of which this book grew. I would also like to thank Mr Norman Stone of Jesus College, Cambridge, who reconciled me to working in Vienna, and Professor Herbert Matis and family as well as Frau Eugenie Back who made life in Vienna so much more enjoyable than it might otherwise have been. My thanks are also due to Dr Maria Voinovich whose archival assistance proved indispensable and to Professor Michael Howard of All Souls College, Oxford, who has always encouraged my research. I also wish to thank my friends Bani and Sebastiano Brandolini and Vivina Berla who helped me translate some tricky north Italian dialect while, finally, I have to record a debt of gratitude to the secretaries of the International History Department of the London School of Economics who were kind enough to prepare my manuscript for publication. The responsibility for whatever errors it may still contain is mine alone.

Alan Sked
London, 1978

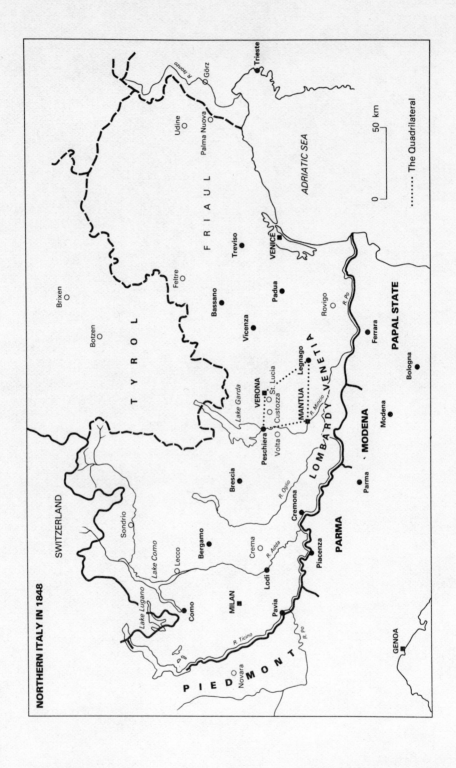

NORTHERN ITALY IN 1848

SWITZERLAND

TYROL

Brixen ○

Botzen ○

Sondrio ○

Lake Lugano

Lake Como

Lake Garda

Como ●

Lecco ○

Bergamo ●

Crema ○

R. Adda

R. Oglio

Brescia ●

Peschiera ○

Volta ○

Custozza ○

VERONA ●

St. Lucia ○

Legnago ●

MANTUA ○

R. Mincio

Feltre ○

FRIAUL

Udine ○

Palma Nuova ○

R. Isonzo

Görz ○

Trieste ●

Bassano ●

Vicenza ●

Padua ●

Treviso ●

VENICE ■

Rovigo ○

ADRIATIC SEA

50 km

0

...... The Quadrilateral

MILAN ■

Pavia ●

Novara ○

R. Ticino

Lodi ○

Cremona ●

R. Po

PIEDMONT

Piacenza ●

PARMA

Parma ●

MODENA

Modena ●

LOMBARDY-VENETIA

Ferrara ●

Bologna ●

PAPAL STATE

GENOA ■

R. Po

Part I

Life in the Austrian army, 1815–1848

Chapter 1

The Austrian officer corps, 1815–1848

Recruitment

We swear a solemn oath to God Almighty to be loyal and obedient to our most excellent Prince and Lord, Ferdinard the First, Emperor of Austria; moreover to obey our generals and other superiors; to honour and protect them; to execute their orders and commands in all matters; against any enemy whatsoever; wherever the imperial will of His Majesty may command; on land and on water; by day and by night; in fights, battles, skirmishes and enterprises of any kind; in short, in any place, at any time; and in all circumstances to behave bravely and manfully; never to desert our colours or standards; never to enter into the slightest understanding with the enemy; to conduct ourselves like true warriors always in accordance with the articles of war; and to live and die in this way with honour. So help us God! Amen!

The oath taken by every Austrian soldier.

The Austrian army had no uniform system for recruiting and training officers. During the period 1815–48 the officer corps consisted of veterans from the Napoleonic Wars, graduates of the various military training institutions, individuals who had been made regimental cadets and then officers by colonels-proprietor of regiments, volunteers who had become cadets and then officers and, finally, a very few former non-commissioned officers who had been promoted from the ranks. Since the first-mentioned group diminished steadily in size and since the military training establishments had a limited output,[1*] the main reservoir of aspiring officers was the civilian population.

The military training schools[2]

Austria had two military *Hochschulen* – the Military Academy at Wiener Neustadt and the Engineering Academy in Vienna. There were also cadet training schools at Ollmütz, Graz and Milan, a Pioneer School at Tulln[3] and a Mining School at Hainburg. However, only Wiener Neustadt and the Engineering Academy produced graduates who became officers immediately. The others turned out cadets.[4] The Engineering Academy, not surprisingly, provided mainly for the technical corps, while Wiener Neustadt supplied the infantry and cavalry. By 1815 the latter had secured the reputation of being the

---

first military training school in the land, and for reasons outlined below a 'Wiener Neustadt man' was held to be an immediately distinguishable creature, someone who stood out among his fellow officers. He was supposed to represent the cream of the corps – rather in the way in which an English public schoolboy was once held to represent all that was best in the English education system – and like an English public schoolboy he could expect to get a top job once he graduated – perhaps even a general staff job.[5] That is not to say, however, that the Wiener Neustadt graduate represented the social élite of the military. The true aristocrat entered the army as a regimental cadet through the *Inhaber* system which will be explained later.

The Wiener Neustadt Military Academy was founded in 1769 by Maria Theresa especially for the children of poor subalterns. This changed in time and gradually it became a foundation for the sons of well-paid generals and staff officers.[6] Fenner von Fenneberg, for example, wrote[7] that he was educated there at the state's expense 'although he held not the slightest claim according to the regulations of the foundation'. His father, however, was a *Feldmarschalleutnant*.[8] It was the same in all the other military training institutions. They were full of the sons of high-ranking officers, and the private middle-class or noble pupils were always in the minority.[9] The nobility, in fact, did not see the point in paying 750 fl. rhennish per year to educate their sons in a place like Wiener Neustadt; poorer parents could not afford to. The result was that the institutions concerned became available for the army to train a hereditary military caste. If there were always pupils to take up the private places, it can only be assumed that these were the sons of fathers who held eccentric views on education or who lacked the right connexions.

Materially speaking, the pupils were not badly off. The intentions of the great Empress had included 'the arrangement in principle to pay full intention to the usual demands of pupils for a material life so that those in the institution would miss as little as possible of what they had learned to regard in their parents' houses as a normal way of life'.[10] There was, therefore, adequate comfort, good service and quite opulent food – a four-course meal at noon and a three-course one in the evening consisting of 'good, simple, well-prepared healthy food'.[11] By 1848, however, this style of life had long been under attack. Wits had it, that what a colonel deemed a luxury was regarded by a Wiener Neustadt pupil as a necessity of life. A memorandum, written by the directors of the Academy in the 1830s, therefore, adopted the following viewpoint:[12] 'This looking after everything in the smallest detail is far above the position the majority of students knew before they entered the Academy and far above the circumstances in which they will probably find themselves after they graduate.' It continued: 'The pupil, too richly fed and cared for through seven or eight years, and accustomed to no restrictions, is, after graduation, only first capable of adjusting to modest circumstances after bitter experience.' The directors, however, had been somewhat less than honest when they referred to the lack of restrictions. The truth, in fact, was that Wiener Neustadt pupils could not have been more restricted had they been members of an Austrian leper colony.

Pupils entered at the age of ten to eleven and remained there until they were seventeen to eighteen years old. Each year's intake was kept apart from those of any other; they were not allowed to meet at meal times or during recreation periods; and it was even forbidden to watch the others from a classroom window. Professor Speer, one of the more lively teachers, was moved to ask on one occasion, 'Who then have the higher classes depraved?'[13] Everything was seclusion and restriction: 'Here everything [was] forbidden which [was] not specifically allowed.'[14] Free movement inside the institution was also forbidden. During the day, pupils, save for a few leisure hours, were not permitted to leave their places. If they did so, they were punished. All movement had to be carried out in military formation (column rows) and single pupils would always be accompanied by a servant or a supervisor.[15] Every hour of the day had prescribed subjects – even the revision hours, no matter whether the pupil needed revision or not. In every classroom a sergeant was always present to watch over the boys, and their behaviour was also observed by patrolling inspection officers through the classroom windows from the corridor.

Recreation hours, which were few enough, were spent in the beautiful Academy parks, where they were divided up into seven groups (one year separated from the next) and taken away to separate clearings. There all they could do was walk around one of two paths.[16] For the first half-hour they were marched in formation, but then they could break ranks:

After which the rows were formed again on more liberal principles, guided by personal inclination. Arm in arm with their chosen friends, and chattering freely, the boys now pursued their way. This was the time at which were laid the foundations of friendships, sometimes to endure for life, for the formation of these 'voluntary ranks' though often the result of mere chance, was apt to crystallise, so that A and B as well as C and D came to 'walk together' almost as regularly as any 'arry and 'arriet.'[17]

In September, the holiday month, on special request, 'country walks' were permitted. It all depended on how well the pupil was doing at the time. If the request was granted, the pupils of a given year who had won this concession would be taken for a picnic by an officer and two sergeants. However, if the directors were 'liberal' the last three *Faschingstage* might bring a change and the pupils might arrange concerts, lectures and a play for themselves. Very, very rarely, there might even be a visit to the civic theatre, but even then it was an unusual occasion: they would be the only ones in the theatre: there would be no orchestra; the play would be more than usually censored – the boys were not to be excited by emotions, especially love – and the leading lady would be boringly respectable, pursued perhaps by a hero, who, having crushed the villain and surmounted innumerable obstacles, would then be rewarded with a victory garland or a good book.[18] However, at a time when there were fewer theatres about, when schoolchildren were rarely taken to them, and when one of these visits would certainly be the first these boys experienced, such trips were just worthwhile.

There were other restrictions on leisure hours. Smoking, like fighting, had to take place in the toilets, because 'against this sin a constant warfare was waged'.[19] Draughts and innocent society games might be allowed, but reading matter was carefully supervised. Books had to be given a *placet*; novels being unconditionally forbidden, although Cooper's *Last of the Mohicans* and *Pathfinder* enjoyed a conditional tolerance if given by a relative. The directors attempted instead to develop their pupils' imaginations with a couple of old volumes of the *Penny Magazine* and by arranging that during the holiday month, tales from *A Thousand and One Nights* were read out to the younger boys.

Contacts with the outer world also came under tight control. Pupils and relatives were given a rule-book covering cases 'in which pupils come into contact with parents, relatives, strangers',[20] and leave during the holiday month was in principle never approved, 'since experience proves almost without exception how disadvantageously the effects of leave impress the pupils'.[21] Contact was limited, therefore, to talking with relatives in a communal 'talk-room' or to 'eating out'.

The first was limited to one hour of a given day at a time when there were no lessons, the second to Sundays or holidays. 'Eating out' took place between 11.30 a.m. and 7.30 p.m. To be allowed to eat out the pupil had to have a good report in moral and religious studies: those whose report read 'excellent' received this privilege once every three weeks; 'good' signified once every six weeks; 'average' meant once every three months, and below 'average' meant never at all. It made not the slightest difference if a pupil excelled in all other subjects but did badly in his religious study – he just did not see his relatives. Moreover, the same lot befell pupils whose parents were either too poor or lived too far away to able to visit Wiener Neustadt.

The strict separation of classes was maintained outside the walls of the Academy too. Pupils of different classes could not be taken out to eat by the same person on the same day, because according to Rule 10 of the rule-book pupils of different years might not 'go anywhere at all together, eat out as guests together, or meet in any other way'.[22] Broad hints were given about behaviour outside: Rule 17 read, 'travel by train is strictly prohibited as are visits to coffee houses';[23] and worse still, among objects forbidden to be bought for the boys were 'sweets, hot drinks, novels and books unsuited for young people'. By the last rule, things particularly prohibited included, 'hammers, files and the like', and yet Rule 28 could still read: 'Although there is no intention to exercise any influence on the expression of pupils to parents, it is nevertheless necessary that all outgoing letters be seen by the company commander in order to prevent any damaging correspondence'. The same rule also extended an invitation to receivers of letters 'composed in a spirit other than the Academy's' to denounce the pupil concerned to the Academy directors.

Where there were rules there were also punishments for breaking them. Wiener Neustadt had three degrees of punishment.[24] The first was known as 'the marble': it was awarded for a dirty collar or unpolished button and meant that the guilty boy was shut upright for two hours in a marble niche behind a panel door. The second was known as 'the lock-up': any pupil who underwent this punishment would be dressed in the worst possible clothes, chained to a bed in a tiny room which was illuminated night and day by an oil-lamp, and left there for two days to a week; he would have no blankets, even in winter, a sentry would patrol outside day and night and he would be fed on bread and water. The 'third degree' meant a flogging: this was used in extreme cases; the pupil concerned would be stripped to his underwear and flogged by a drummer using a pickled rod; after each stroke he had to offer the drummer his thanks.

The results of this kind of policy will be discussed presently, but first it should be remembered that the boys were there to study. According to von Fenneberg, who went through the Academy between 1830 and 1837, he had to take exams in forty-four subjects, 'gymnastic skill and exercises, fencing, dancing, riding and swimming not included'.[25] Subjects which were included were:

religion, German, Latin, French, Italian, Czech, Hungarian, German *Rechtschreibung*[26] rhetoric, poetry, logic, metaphysics, world history, geography, statistics, military geography, the history of war, the history of the art of war,[27] algebra, arithmetic, geometry, trigonometry, practical surveying terrain, higher geometry, physics, mechanics, mathematical geography, permanent fortification, field fortification, weapons, artillery,[28] tactics, strategy, service regulations, cavalry regulations, exercise regulations, training of soldiers, the exposition of the articles of war, private, public and common law, civic and street building, calligraphy, freehand and situation drawing.

A great deal of emphasis was laid on maths and this was linked to practical experiments in surveying and field work which proved very popular and interesting. One reason for this was that in spring the boys were taken outside[29] and allowed to build small fortifications and examine how these were connected to weaponry. Often quite large models were constructed for difficult topics.

Languages also took up a great deal of time but there was 'a decided preference for French'.[30] Only a few who were not native Hungarians or Bohemians or Italians learned the languages of these peoples to the extent 'that they could even express themselves moderately in them'.[31] The blame lay partly in the extraordinary limitations of time, partly because of the difficult idioms of Hungarian and Czech: yet, because the pupils had the privilege of chosing in which regiment they wished to serve, only those who desired to join a non-German regiment had an incentive to study languages other than German.

The teaching, it should be noted, was not really of a very high standard.[32] Patronage played a very important role in appointments, so that it was easy to slip an unqualified 'favourite' into a teaching post. These people could then use their predecessors' notes. Often they would come in from the ranks and 'for the most part first had to learn in the school itself the science or language they were supposed to teach'. Moreover, since Wiener Neustadt was further away than the Engineering Academy, more difficult to reach and taught less specialised subjects, fewer visiting professors called there to judge the level of its teaching. Nor did appointed 'favourites' stay long enough to acquire a certain level of ability in their subjects. After six years they would return to active service with a higher rank. According to von Fenneberg, the history professor used only two dull books and often fell asleep; when he did teach, his history had a decidedly dynastic bias – the Austrian armies, for example, never being allowed to lose the wars against the French. The professor of strategy and tactics merely made his pupils learn a series of questions and answers off by heart. One 'favourite' first of all lectured on service regulations, then passed on to drawing and surveying and finally taught the history of war. The professor of Hungarian spoke only broken German and was openly abused by his pupils in class. 'You're not worth lecturing to', he told one class, and told another, 'It is a matter of complete indifference to me whether you get good reports or bad, whether you learn anything or not – I'll still draw my pay and allowances.'

Looking at all the evidence, therefore, it is hard to decide whether Wiener Neustadt thought of itself as a sort of public school, a training school for officers, a monastery or a gaol. It managed, certainly, to combine aspects of all four. Yet least of all was it a training school for officers, a criticism which was heard on many occasions.

Maria Theresa had wondered in 1769 whether it would not be more practical to devise a 'shorter and more colourful course for the young men'.[33] Joseph II was less polite. Wiener Neustadt, he said, should be put 'on a more military footing'. Its job should be one of training 'intelligent officers for the army'. He wanted the higher classes of the Academy to frequent the army's manœuvres and see what an army life was all about. He wanted veterans to be employed by the Academy, people who could tell the boys 'of battles and sieges in which they took part'. He died, however, and no changes took place. Only a few summer days in the final year were worthy of the name of soldiering.

Perhaps the antagonism between what was required of the Academy and what it provided can best be seen in the regulation concerning riding lessons for the sixth- and seventh-year students. Those students who failed to get a good monthly report in some or other subject were banned from riding for at least a month until a better report was given. However, considering the number of students and the number of subjects, it was not always possible to examine every student in every subject every month and the restriction could last for a very long time. Indeed, as far as the less gifted pupils were concerned, their whole riding course was restricted to a few months. And yet riding was much more important to a future officer than excellence in spherical trigonometry.[34]

This lack of a purely military training was not compensated for by brilliance acquired in other subjects. There were simply too many of them for a pupil to gain a high level of expertise in any one in particular. In any case, 'only those who were completely incapable failed to qualify as an officer in some way or another'.[35] Stupid students were sent into the army as cadets.[36] There was no incentive to think. What knowledge was gained, was gained cramming (von Fenneberg had to learn by heart no less than fifty-two narrowly written pages of instruction for the strategy and tactics' class) and memory learning, a curse which marred bright and dull alike, was all that was needed to pass examinations.

There was also a total lack of inspired teaching. This is not another reference to the men involved, but a criticism of the attitudes which lay behind the teaching. No attempt was made to give the pupils a self-consciousness of their role in what might have been presented to them as a glorious and honourable body of fighting men. Their imagination and spontaneity remained completely undernourished, their sense of phantasy entirely untapped by their masters. As a result, the pupils displayed, 'a complete indifference' when leaving the Academy as to 'whether they entered Heaven or the Austrian army, just so long as they attained an officer's uniform and the longed-for freedom'.[37]

Yet who could blame them? They had been locked up for seven years in Wiener Neustadt. They had met no one else during these seven years save their fellow prisoners – perhaps sixty boys in the same year. They simply did not know how to meet other people after that. They had no other criteria about how to judge people from any other way of life except vague memories of home up to the age of ten. Moreover, they would have nothing else to talk about for years to come except their Academy training. So they were not likely to attract many other sorts of people anyway. As soon as they set foot outside the Academy on the other hand they were immersed in a different world.[38] They did not even know their way to the train station and had to be guided there. They had never seen a train before and when they arrived at their destination they had no idea about what to do next, save ask a military policeman.[39]

Worst of all, of course, was their affect on the army. They had never given a command before and they could now abuse that privilege. Their *Flegeljahre*[40] which by now should have been nearing their end, were in fact, just about to begin, the first intentions of these new officers being naturally to make up for their long years of spiritual repression. On the other hand they now found that they had no money to spend and that army conditions differed greatly from those to which they had long been accustomed. All in all, therefore, the transition from being a relatively comfortable, if spiritually repressed Academy pupil to becoming a free but decidedly poor subaltern[41] brought with it all sorts of psychological strains and problems which naturally affected everybody.

They could be overcome to some extent if fellow officers who had completed the process of adjustment saw fit to dispense some sympathetic advice. However, very often a Wiener Neustadt man made up for his deficiencies in knowledge and maturity by assuming an air of false self-confidence. It came off, no doubt, with other Wiener Neustadt men, people who shared the same complexes and had been victims of the same repression,[42] but from many other officers and men it could hardly have commanded respect. Von Fenneberg said[43] that out of the 90–100 officers turned out each year by Wiener Neustadt and the Engineering Academy, perhaps there were 'only eight to ten who [were] gifted with the talent and will-power to continue their studies on the basis of what they had learned and qualify as versatile, all-round useful officers'. 'The rest' he wrote, 'remain[ed] conceited, pitiable, knowalls, or better, half-knowalls, who relying on their painstaking education, intend[ed] everywhere to lay down the law and in this manner only all too often [brought] to notice in a lamentable fashion their ignorance and arrogance. The phrase *ex omnibus aliquid, ex toto nihil* never suited anybody better. . . .'

This criticism, however, can be mitigated to some degree. For all its faults, Wiener Neustadt did provide a graduate of an intellectual standard which was higher than that of other officers. The 'comprehensive' curriculum did provide some basis for future study which could train these men for the highest posts in the service. Moreover, they were not the only ones who had still to undergo a practical training as subalterns – all the products of all the training schools had to do that. Yet when all is said and done, one still feels that if these pupils were the best, the general standard of officer must needs have been low.

Curiously enough, some aspects of the system practised at Wiener Neustadt might have been better applied to the pupils at the cadet schools or the Pioneer School at Tulln. There, boys, at the end of their school careers, became imperial cadets[44] and as such had to work their way up from the ranks before they were promoted officers. While undergoing this process, therefore, they had every opportunity to acquaint themselves with the practical requirements of an officer's life, but some academic training while they were still in these military training institutions might have served them very well.

The boys (all of whom had to be the sons of army officers[45]) entered these cadet schools at the age of fourteen and wore the uniform of the regiments to which they had been assigned. They were immediately formed into companies governed by army regulations and trained as soldiers. Life differed from the Wiener Neustadt pattern in many ways: they were subjected to the full rigour of military discipline (corporal punishment), but there was no question of being shut away from the outside world and the inmates were allowed an independence more appropriate to their years.[46] In material respects, care was taken to see that they were not spoiled, and when they entered the army it was not so much a process of transition as a continuation of an accustomed way of life. In other words, they entered the army with a realistic knowledge of what was expected of soldiers. However, since only ten or twenty individuals entered the army each year after graduating from these institutions, they lacked the numbers and intellectual training to make a very great impact upon the army although they became good company officers.[47]

Regimental cadets and expropriis-gemeine[48]

The vast majority of officers were recruited in a manner altogether different from those discussed already. They were the people who entered the army by becoming regimental cadets. To do this they needed only a certain amount of money and social connexions which included an *Inhaber*. Because the sum of money involved was relatively small – 37 fl. C.M.[49] by way of *Montursgeld*[50] – all regiments had a large number of cadets and entry was much sought after. For example, in 1841, the 3rd Infantry Regiment had 42 and the 18th and 33rd regiments had 33 each.[51] Many regiments had more than 70 regimental cadets in their lists and very few had less than 20.[52] Entry into cavalry regiments was admittedly less easy. More money was required for these – 60–70 fl. rhennish – the pretensions of the cavalry, the élite social corps of the army, being higher than those of the infantry regarding uniform and weapons. The regimental cadet system proved useful in several ways. It enabled foreigners to enlist[53] and in 1848–9 provided an unusual service for Hungarian freedom-fighters who wished to escape the wrath of the Dictator Windischgraetz – they merely joined his army.[54] As a method of recruiting and training officers on the other hand, it had many obvious drawbacks.

'There were cadet schools',[55] wrote von Angeli but added, 'Regimental cadets had to pick up what they could as they served their way up from the ranks.' Von Fenneberg, who held a low opinion of cadets in general, maintained that their knowledge was restricted (apart from service regulations) to 'situation drawing, terrain study, knowledge of weapons, history and geography.'[56] Regimental cadets, in fact, were not expected to be very bright. Attendance at cadet school was often voluntary and the institution served less to instruct the cadets than to keep them out of mischief. Many cadets were, therefore, encouraged to attend the schools in each regiment which were set up to instruct the men. Yet despite four years' attendance at various regimental schools, not a great deal was absorbed. Time was expected to be the real instructor, and since it took on average seven years before cadets became officers,[57] it was assumed that most of the practical side would be learned in due course. The whole process, however, was a highly questionable one and people insisted on asking questions, sometimes even the right ones.

One man who did so was the Archduke Maximilian d'Este, the Archduke after the death of the Archduke Charles, who was most interested in military matters. Maximilian was something of an expert in fortification works, but he also wrote valuable analyses of the problems facing the Austrian army and in one very long essay, entitled *Ursachen unserer unglücklichen Feldzüge*[58] (Causes of Our Unhappy Campaigning) he stated quite explicitly that the main fault of the Austrian army was 'the bad selection and training of our officer corps. Every officer of the army', he continued, 'denies this contention out of vanity and attributes as causes the lack of freedom, bad pay and the rough and wild nature of the common soldiers who have no disposition for training and no heart to respond to feelings of pride and ambition. . . . But . . . these reasons they offer are totally without foundation.' There then followed what one suspects was a very realistic description of most cadets:

They are youths of twelve to eighteen, mainly those who were too lacking in talent, too slovenly and too wild to do well at school or were unable to hope to secure an honourable position in civilian life. The parents just say: 'the lad is fit for nothing, he will have to be a soldier'. Through the intercession of friends he is taken on by an infantry regiment as a cadet: he enters it without any kind of training, without any desire to become trained, but merely with an inordinate desire to be able quickly to play the role of officer. The greatest part of the cadets take up the colours with no other aim in mind than the expectation to secure respect as a military man, but not of course, at the expense of their other expectations of leading a fanciful life or by purchasing their pleasures through effort.[59]

Yet this was only the beginning of the problem. The bad cadet became a bad infantry officer at which point, thanks perhaps to his 'mighty officer friends', he might be promoted a staff officer, and if his regiment just happened to do well before the enemy, although no thanks were due to him, he might even be promoted general. The army, according to Maximilian, could lose wars, not to mention lives, in this way. He recommended, therefore, that all imperial officers should be examined: 'His Majesty', he wrote, 'could very easily convince himself of the ignorance of the officer corps in warfare if he visited the army and requested regimental commanders and their staff officers to give their subordinate officers an explanation of some subject or another or if the regimental and staff officers were examined by one or several men more learned in warfare especially appointed to do so.' The results, he predicted, would be astonishing but helpful, the more so if every officer seeking promotion were made to sit an exam. This applied especially to staff officers, because, according to the Archduke, 'all our staff officers are fools'.

Clearly, Maximilian had the lowest possible opinion of the Austrian army and in his essay he condemned it absolutely. 'No one', he wrote, 'could believe how weak in knowledge and how bereft of honour many of our generals are, what shocking almost incredible mistakes are made by them.' The officer corps as a whole, he described as thoroughly degenerate:

Knowing their weaknesses they live on a good footing with their subordinates in order to receive no reproach from them, and they pass over their errors in silence. . . . The officers become hardened to these qualities which savour of spinelessness and cowardice and it becomes their way to be capable of any offence. They become so dishonourable that they laugh at any order which reminds them of their duties; they openly make fun of one order after another, mock any noble-minded man and are unashamed enough, in the presence of the very men who are under them, to address these same men with phrases designed to lessen their good will and devotion to the monarch. So, for example, a few years ago in the Rhine Army, the intelligence of the enemy was openly praised and it was maintained that we were in no position to mess about with them, and today the same kind of speeches will be heard too often in officer society and in the presence of subordinates. . . .

It was quite a condemnation and, in Maximilian's view, the result of a system of recruiting and training officers which had barely anything to recommend it.

This was a great pity, for as the Archduke concluded: 'A well-organised army is the support of the state and people should take special care in present times to ensure that more upright, honest and judicious men are maintained in the army. It is well known that the pernicious democratic spirit is growing and that the various clubs are restless in their endeavours to spread their branches into the army as well.'

Promotion

Promotion during this period came to be summed up in the expression *Inhaberswirtschaft*. Basically this meant that all officers beneath the rank of major could only be promoted by the colonel-proprietor or *Inhaber* of their regiment. The system was almost as old as the Austrian army itself and originated in the seventeenth century when the Emperor had had to bargain with the nobility for every man and every penny in order to raise an army. Compromise agreements were reached; someone would promise, in return for money, to raise a regiment for the Emperor, but would generally add the proviso that he be made colonel-proprietor of the regiment for life. Then when the founder of the regiment died, someone else, usually a famous soldier, would take over command of the regiment along with the same rights which had previously been exercised by its founder. In the course of time these 'rights' became very profitable, although by the nineteenth century the Austrian government had taken steps to limit them. For example, at the beginning of the century, the *Inhaber* of a regiment was entitled to the full pay of a colonel of the regiment plus the full pay of a commander of a *Leibcompanie* and *Leibbatallion*. He did not in fact fulfil any of these functions himself – they were executed by a colonel, captain second class and major respectively – but he did draw the pay. The Archduke Charles, as Minister for War during part of the Napoleonic Wars, abolished this privilege.

In the period 1815–48 the most important right retained by the *Inhaber* was the *jus gladii et aggratandi* in regimental legal judgements; promotion of officers from the ranks of ensign[60] to captain inclusive also lay within his power, but an arrangement had been reached with the *Hofkriegsrath* (Imperial War Council) whereby six places in every regiment had to be reserved for Wiener Neustadt graduates while the Hofkriegsrath also retained the option of appointing officers, to every third regimental place which became vacant.[61] All field officers, as well as those of still higher grades in the general army, were nominated by the Crown, and according to regulations, commissions from the ranks of ensign or coronet to captain inclusive could be obtained by seniority only, no rise by purchase being permitted.[62]

The *Inhaber* himself was most often a general or *Feldmarschalleutnant* and unless the regiment of which he was proprietor already held the name of a distinguished member of some princely house – e.g. the Czar of Russia – it would adopt the name of its proprietor as its own.[63] When the *Inhaber* of a regiment was indeed a distinguished foreigner[64] he would usually forgo the customary rights pertaining to his proprietorship, as otherwise he would have at the same time to subject himself to the orders of the Hofkriegsrath. Occasionally, however, such a person might still exercise a little influence and the Duke of Wellington, for example, who in 1818 was nominated *Inhaber* of the 42nd Infantry, was held to have once applied to the second or 'real' proprietor of that regiment, General Mesemacre, to assist in the advancement of a young Englishman.[65]

Since the *Inhaber* of a regiment would most usually be found at one end of the Monarchy while his regiment was at another, the more day-to-day duties of commanding the regiment were carried out by the regimental colonel who was the real commander. In his particular competence lay the creation and promotion of regimental posts from sergeant downwards, the distribution of fourteen-day passes within the regimental area, the granting of several months' or indefinite leave to the men, the transfer of officers from one garrison to another in so far as troops of his own regiment were to be found in both places, transfers to and from regimental battalions and companies, and the administration of the regimental fund, for which, however, he had to give no exact account but which covered items such as the pay of regimental medical, spiritual and legal staff.[66] He was also responsible in infantry regiments for overseeing the making of uniforms, since by this date uniforms no longer came in sizes small, medium and large, but arrived in the form of material which had to be tailored up to size.[67] The *Inhaber* restricted his duties to matters of personnel and law.

Promotion inside a regiment was supposed to go according to seniority and this was 'strictly and repeatedly' ordered by the government. However, the system was subject to 'grave abuse'[68] by the colonels-proprietor, and given their rights it is difficult to see how things could have been otherwise. There is no doubt that the Hofkriegsrath did try to improve the situation – when news leaked out in the German press that it was attempting to abolish *Inhaber* rights or at least severely to reduce them, this occasioned 'common joy in the Austrian army',[69] – but the system constituted an extremely powerful vested interest and resisted such pressure successfully. The most the Hofkriegsrath could do was to suspend for an indefinite period of time the rights of individual *Inhabers* who had too glaringly overstepped the mark.[70]

The primary source of abuse was nepotism and patronage. 'Nepotism', wrote von Fenneberg, 'rules here in its whole fearful power'.[71] The result was that many extremely worthy officers and cadets remained unpromoted for years because the mighty everywhere could pull important strings and monopolise advancement:[72] 'At present, in peacetime, with the army overflowing with young officers who have no intention of leaving the service or asking to be pensioned off on grounds of age or infirmity, an officer of the line can wait twenty or twenty-one years before he is promoted from lieutenant to a real captain.' Von Angeli, curiously enough, was even more critical.[73] According to him, '. . . The overwhelming majority of officers had to wait twenty-five to thirty years to become a captain second class.'

Life for the well placed and the wealthy, on the other hand, was very different:[74] '. . . With some favour', wrote von Fenneberg, 'nothing is easier than to be made captain within six to eight years and one can count many captains and staff officers of twenty-five or twenty-six years who do not really belong to the great houses, but who are no strangers to the lower nobility or aristocracy of wealth. Money is the social lever with which they can turn the world itself upside down and how much easier it is as a result to overstep a completely worthy officer and promote a high noble or rich man in his place.' One example of this was Baron Sternbach. The Baron was a cadet with the rank of corporal, a young but very limited knight of fortune according to von Fenneberg.[75] His captain, aristocratically minded but middle class, suggested he be promoted sergeant, a request which was turned down by the regimental commander on the ground that the Baron still had a lot to learn before he would be able to fill such a post properly. Three months later the cadet won a family legal case and secured an income of 20,000 fl. per year. The regimental colonel duly changed his mind about the promotion and two months thereafter the 'limited and ignorant' Baron was made an officer over the heads of much more suitable candidates. Such stories were legion, many apocryphal:[76]

A story was told and might almost be true of a youth who in the course of one dinner – a particularly excellent dinner no doubt and well watered with champagne – advanced from the rank of cadet to that of captain, three Excellencies in turn having vied with each other in thus proving their appreciation of the cuisine to his father the host. This fortunate lad ate his soup as cadet, the fish course as sub-lieutenant, the roast as full lieutenant, while at dessert the Excellency who had started the movement cried out, 'Hang it all – I'll take him back as a captain.'

There were also variations on this theme. Mollinary, for example, was offered his imperial cadetship at Tulln because his commander wished a place to be vacant into which he could appoint a nephew.[77] The commonest case occurred, however, when a number of *Inhabers* conspired together to promote their favourites. Some lucky man would enter one regiment as a cadet, be transferred after a few weeks to another regiment as a lieutenant and after a few months' leave for a third regiment as an *Oberleutnant*. In this way it was not unusual for relatives of the aristocracy or plutocracy to cover the distance from cadet to captain in a time which for ordinary mortals would scarcely be sufficient to cover the stages of cadet to second lieutenant. Count Kalman Hunyadi, for example, entered a hussar regiment at the age of sixteen as a lieutenant and by the age of thirty was a full colonel – that is, in fourteen years he covered nine ranks. He died a general of the cavalry.[78] In other cases more care was taken to hide the strings being pulled and Count Grünne, for example, was much more circumspect in his arrangements. Having no wish to let it be seen that he had given his a son a lieutenancy in a friend's regiment, he bought the boy, who had graduated from Tulln, an *ex-officio* cadet place in the guards. This appeared a bit more democratic, but in fact was not. There was no question that the boy would have to compete with the other cadets. The arrangement really meant that the young man could appear in splendid uniform in Vienna and escape the cavalry and stall duties undertaken by his Tulln contemporaries in Croatia or Galicia. It was only a matter of time before he was transferred to a hussar regiment as an officer.[79]

One way to gain promotion was simply to buy a commission and it was legally permitted to purchase those of ensign in the infantry and lieutenant in the cavalry,[80] which sold for about 2,000 and 3,000 fl. respectively.[81] It was, however, possible in spite of a great number of ordinances decreeing the opposite, to buy and sell commissions of all ranks, a practice made possible by a system known as 'convention'. As Minister for War the Archduke Charles had tried to abolish this system, but he himself had had to backtrack because he did not wish to put an end to a useful supply of better-educated and ambitious officers. He was quoted as saying that the army could have little success with an officer who wanted to sell his commission anyway, and it was just as well to let him go.[82] Probably the strongest motive in changing the Archduke's mind was the fact that the system carried on in any case. At work once more was the very powerful influence of the *Inhaber*, because, as von Fenneberg points out,[83] a 'convention' could only take place with an *Inhaber*'s consent.

A 'convention' in the Austrian army was a mutual agreement between two officers of unequal rank or between a cadet and an officer. According to this agreement the officer of higher rank retired from the service in return for a certain cash sum and surrendered his place to the man who paid him. This was obviously against all the rules and regulations and was only made possible if the regimental colonel and colonel-proprietor had promised their assent beforehand, because otherwise there was no assurance that the vacant place would be given to the man who paid the money. However, if the colonel and the *Inhaber* liked the young man who had made the convention, they would report that the other officer involved, although frequently still young, had developed some physical defect and would register him sick for nine months. As sick, the man would have no duties, draw his full pay for nine months and would come to an understanding with his doctors who would compose a long imaginary history of illness about some disease or other which he had never contracted. He would then be declared a semi-invalid and be timeously pensioned off, while the other participant in the convention, having paid the agreed lump sum, would be promoted by the *Inhaber* to the vacancy occasioned by the first man's retirement. There were often agents who arranged such deals and their services were eagerly sought after. Prices paid in such arrangements were high and the Duke of Blacas, for example, paid Rittmeister von Matusch of the Tuscan Dragoons no less than 13,000 fl. C.M. (£1,300) for his voluntary retirement. Von Fenneberg said that he knew captains who could have served another twenty years in war or peace but who chose to retire on lump sums plus their pension of 600 fl.[84]

That, then, was the system as far as it affected the minority of officers who could look forward to a career of promise. To others who waited a quarter of a century to become second-class captains, the perspective was a different one. The key to their system of promotion was their 'record of conduct' or *Konduitenlist*. These were kept about every officer by his immediate superior and were transmitted at certain periods of every year to the Imperial War Council in Vienna. Similar records of conduct were made for the non-commissioned officers by their immediate superiors in conjunction with the company captain, and privates were treated in a similar if more general manner. An ordinance of Maria Theresa directed that every conduct record should be communicated to the individual affected by it, to give him, at his discretion, the opportunity to expostulate, but in practice this was rarely attended to. The point about these conduct records was this: although they were for the most part hardly more than a formality, they could become 'an instrument of great individual oppression'.[85] The *Inhaber* would promote on the basis of these, men whom personally he rarely knew. Likewise, the Hofkriegsrath would take it for granted that the record was a statement of the truth. However, in certain cases, the colonels and staff-officers who had composed these records would have done so in such a way as to secure the advancement of their relatives and friends.

The tone of a regiment was much influenced by the personal temperament of its commander, and if this were arbitrary or suspicious, 'an insidious and malicious spirit [might] be engendered among the officers generally, of which the effect [was] to place them all at their colonel's will'.[86] The colonel's opinion might be swayed by petty motives or private suggestions and if so, other officers were hardly likely to risk his displeasure or jeopardise their own future prospects by opposing his views on the record of a fellow officer. In this way, therefore, it was easy for a colonel to evade the order of seniority or to bring in *Einschube*,[87] and such irregularities would be justified by statements in the conduct records sent to the Hofkriegsrath saying that the officer passed over was, from want of talent or for some other reason, unfit for the higher position. Should the unlucky officer not agree to acquiesce quietly in these arrangements, the fault of insubordination might well be added to that of stupidity in his next report or he might even be compelled to retire on the pension list for life. Turnball cites[88] one case in which an officer who felt aggrieved about his lack of promotion secured a private audience with the Kaiser and lodged an official complaint. The Emperor expressed himself 'astonished' that the man should presume so much, but ordered an investigation nonetheless. Eventually the officer was shown his record of conduct and it transpired that the record appended to his name was in fact the record of a completely different officer. The man returned in triumph to his regiment – but a few months later was ordered on the pension list for life. The notions of the Emperor regarding subordination were such that he rarely viewed with complacency a complaint, however just, of an officer against his superior.

A colonel-proprietor could pass over a man for the same appointment up to six times if he thought ill enough of his qualities. But in that case, after the third, fourth, fifth and sixth times, he was obliged to inform the man concerned why he had failed to be selected. Another rule held that if a man were passed over more than six times, proceedings were to be taken against him on the grounds that this conduct must be so bad as to be 'unimprovable'.[89]

What then were the results of the system as a whole? Most obviously it gave rise to what was called *Konkretualstatus*, which meant that the rank numbers of officers were recognised only by their own regiment. This had to be so because not only could differences in rank of people of the same age inside one regiment be quite remarkable but also because it often happened that the captains of one regiment held much more recent promotions than the *Oberleutnants* in another. So, for example before van Angeli[90] was transferred in 1849 to the 37th Hungarian Infantry he was the fifth youngest second lieutenant of the 10th Ruthenian Infantry. After his transfer he became the eighth eldest first lieutenant. This was only because of the different promotion policies inside the two regiments, but von Angeli says he was looked upon as someone's protégé and there was no use trying to explain otherwise as a discussion of the subject merely caused too much pain for those who had been passed over and now had to wait again.

Another obvious result of the system was – and it could scarcely be otherwise – that (in the words of von Angeli)[91] '. . . among the officer corps the most profound bitterness was felt against a system which openly opposed all logical and radical demands'. It was the officer corps after all which was the butt of the arbitrariness of as many colonels as there were regiments. 'Yet nothing', wrote von Angeli, 'could be more unjust than such a verdict.'[92] He seems to be trying to have things both ways: either there was bitterness or there was not.

Still, his assertion that there were mitigating factors rings true to some extent.

For a start, long use had removed the harshness of the system; in a way the officers even supported it. Thus[93]

although there was scarcely a single person who did not have good cause for complaint against the privileges of *Inhabers* it was still the case that it was extremely rare for an officer to apply for a transfer to another regiment on these grounds. Much more often was the case of officers turning down promotion or other advantages if it meant a transfer was also involved. The regiment was in the most literal sense one great tightly-knit family, the officers' true home to which he felt closely bound, whose fate was his own.

So most officers spent their whole career in the one regiment and it was not rare for them to be under the same colonel since their years as cadets or *knabenhäuser* pupils. Under such circumstances, despite all trials, perhaps some sort of bond did indeed develop – perhaps the men did come to view their officers as part of the 'regimental inventory', as von Angeli said. On the other hand, what was the point in asking for a transfer to another regiment if a bad record of conduct would also be transferred? Most likely the new *Inhaber* would also be a good friend of the old one. Seen in this light, it may be said that an officer, at least to some extent, had to love his regiment whether he liked it or not, because whether he liked it or not, he was more or less stuck with it.

Probably it was this kind of resignation to one's fate which mitigated the system's effects more than anything else. The years of peace, too, had put a limit to soldierly ambition and no one expected the Metternich system to come to a sudden end:[94] 'The great majority had learned a long time ago to resign themselves and found their aim in life in securing a comfortable old age as the conclusion of strict and certain fulfilment of duty.' A captain's pension supplied a modest but carefree income in their declining years – even in the big cities – and if years were spent securing it, the aim in life on which their eyes had been set since the day they enlisted was, for most of them, nonetheless fulfilled.

Pay and problems

If an ensign who had died during the reign of the Empress Maria Theresa had suddenly come back to life in the first half of the nineteenth century, he would have found that lots of things had changed. But not all. His rate of pay would have been almost exactly the same, even though its purchasing power would have been considerably reduced. According to Radetzky,[95] during the reign of Maria Theresa a subaltern could save two-thirds of his pay and keep one-third to live on. During the Vormärz period his whole salary did not meet two-thirds of his expenses and the lines of Ferdinand von Saar's 'Pincelliade' were only too true:

'Kadettenjahre voller Müh' und Plagen,
 Ein Leutnantsdasein mit geringsten Sold,
 Der Beutel leer und hungrig stets der Magen –
 Nicht alles, was da eitel glänzt ist Gold.'

The pay scales of an Austrian officer were as follows:[96]

Rates of pay for officers in the Austrian army (per month)

1. Infantry

(*a*) In the German and Italian provinces

Rank	Fl.	£	s.	d.
Colonel	149	15	16	7
Lieutenant-Colonel	110	11	13	9
Major	79	8	7	10
First Captain	71	7	10	10
Second Captain	39	4	2	10
First Lieutenant	26	2	15	3
Second Lieutenant	22	2	6	9

(*b*) In the Hungarian provinces

Rank	Fl.	£	s.	d.
Colonel	138	14	13	3
Lieutenant-Colonel	102	13	16	11
Major	73	7	15	1
First Captain	65	6	17	10
Second Captain	36	3	16	6
First Lieutenant	25	2	13	1
Second Lieutenant	21	2	4	7

(*c*) In Galicia

Rank	Fl.	£	s.	d.
Colonel	145	15	8	1
Lieutenant-Colonel	107	11	7	4
Major	77	8	3	6
First Captain	69	7	6	10
Second Captain	38	4	0	9
First Lieutenant	26	2	15	3
Second Lieutenant	22	2	6	9

All these rates were peacetime rates. In times of war pay rates changed to the following scales:

(*d*) Wartime rates for infantry officers in all provinces

Rank	Fl.	£	s.	d.
Colonel	154	16	7	3
Lieutenant-Colonel	113	12	0	1
Major	91	9	13	4
First Captain	74	7	17	3
Second Captain	40	4	5	0
First Lieutenant	27	2	17	4
Second Lieutenant	23	2	8	10

2. Cavalry

(*a*) In the German and Italian provinces

Rank	Fl.	£	s.	d.
Colonel	129	13	14	1
Lieutenant-Colonel	93	9	17	7
Major	68	7	4	6
First Captain	60	6	7	6
Second Captain	37	3	18	7
First Lieutenant	25	2	13	1
Second Lieutenant	20	2	2	6

(b) In the Hungarian provinces

Rank	Fl.	£	s.	d.
Colonel	118	12	10	9
Lieutenant-Colonel	85	9	0	7
Major	61	6	9	8
First Captain	54	5	14	9
Second Captain	35	3	14	4
First Lieutenant	25	2	13	1
Second Lieutenant	20	2	2	6

(c) In Galicia

Rank	Fl.	£	s.	d.
Colonel	125	13	5	7
Lieutenant-Colonel	90	9	11	3
Major	65	6	18	1
First Captain	58	6	4	3
Second Captain	37	3	18	7
First Lieutenant	25	2	13	1
Second Lieutenant	20	2	2	6

(d) In wartime in all provinces

Rank	Fl.	£	s.	d.
Colonel	170	18	3	9
Lieutenant-Colonel	129	13	14	1
Major	104	11	1	0
First Captain	84	8	18	6
Second Captain	53	5	13	5
First Lieutenant	37	3	18	7
Second Lieutenant	31	3	5	10

The pay (per annum) of:

a Field Marshal was	12,000 fl. or	£1,272
a General was	8,000	£848
a Lieutenant-general was	6,000	£636
a Major-General was	4,000	£424

An imperial cadet, according to von Fenneberg received only 7 fl. per month;[97] what a regimental cadet received for his duties is not discussed in the sources, but presumably he received the pay of his rank or none at all. In both these cases he would have had to live from private means.

From the tables given above it will be seen that the pay of an Austrian officer varied according to three circumstances:[98] one was the state of peace or war; the second was the particular province in which his regiment was stationed; and the third was the branch of the service in which he served.[99] At the outbreak of war every officer in the army received an extra month's pay to equip himself for the field, with rations and horses according to rank. Differences in pay on account of 'territorial dislocation'[100] were abolished for the duration. Infantry and artillery field-officers, in time of war, were also given a certain number of rations extra, namely eight for a colonel, three for lieutenant-colonels and majors. Officers of a lower rank were allowed two rations of bread and two for forage, rations being worth about 3 fl. or 6s. 4d. per month. Peacetime rations were more restricted: colonels and lieutenant-colonels in the infantry and artillery received three apiece and majors got two. That was all. The cavalry were allowed the following (R equals ration):[101]

Rank	Time of peace		Time of war	
	Bread	Forage	Bread	Forage
Colonel	8R	12R	9R	12R
Lieutenant-Colonel	6R	8R	6R	10R
Major	6R	6R	6R	10R
First Captain	4R	5R	3R	6R
Second Captain	4R	4R	3R	5R
First Lieutenant	2R	3R	2R	3R
Second Lieutenant	2R	3R	2R	3R

Officers received their pay late – on the 20th of each current pay month[102] – along with various allowances. In areas where prices were particularly high or at times when high prices prevailed a *Theuerungsbeitrag* or price allowance was given.[103] Officers from captain up received an allowance for quarters, as did subalterns, but subalterns also received an allowance for fuel which consisted of $\frac{3}{4}$ cord of softwood or $\frac{1}{2}$ cord of hard-burning wood for six months of the year in the German provinces and five months in the Italian ones. The subaltern quartering allowance was supposed to provide for two rooms, a servant's chamber and a kitchen. These items made up 99 per cent of an officer's pay. There were other trifling allowances, but they are not important enough to merit listing.

Officers from captain to colonel received a *Fourierschützen* or a batman whom they could chose from civilian life and have declared fit for military service and they received each year a separate sum of money to pay him. Subalterns were not quite so well off, but were given one of the semi-invalided men of the regiment as a private manservant.

The choice of servant took place in a curious way.[104] The subaltern concerned would search the regiment, with his commander's approval, for a good man with a good record and ask him if he would be willing to serve as his manservant a 'request' which was only rarely refused. Once the man had agreed, the regimental doctor would invent a suitable history of illness which in turn would be repeated to the corps authorities and usually to no one else. There would be no reaction. The man would be classified as semi-invalid for some or other reason, it being taken for granted that he had survived several unsuccessful attempts at cure. In this fashion the officer would acquire his manservant. Very often, though, such men paid dearly for their silence, for although officers were usually decent to their servants and did not like to see other officers mistreating theirs, it was not rare for an officer to be a moody tyrant to his man and in such cases the men concerned had even less chance of redress than the ordinary soldier.

Officers on leave for up to six weeks were liable for no deductions in pay. On the other hand, if they stayed away for more than that they would lose half. Quarters and wood were left as they were, but officers who, for special reasons, were on leave for a year would get no pay or allowances at all and servants assigned to them would be called in by the regiment, unless, of course, the officer was willing to foot the bill himself.[105]

Two final points: officers under arrest, unless dismissed from their posts, would receive their full pay; secondly, subalterns paid nothing for medical treatment although officers from captains upwards had to give medical personnel a fitting payment.[106]

The money problems of a subaltern

Maria Theresa had decreed that she wished her soldiers 'kaveliermäsig leben und Wagon und Pferde halten können' (to live like a knight and afford to keep wagon and horses'). But these were the good old days. During the period 1815–48 the Austrian subaltern, living on 24 fl. per month as a second lieutenant, 28 fl. per month as a first lieutenant or 32 fl. per month as an *Oberleutnant*[107] had little chance of leading such a life. Moreover, because it took at least four to six years to be promoted from one of these ranks to the next, he knew it would be a long time before he could think about doing so. The great thing was to become a captain, for, before 1848, a captain's pay, 600 or 900 fl. per year, was 'a pretty good income with which to live free of cares' and subalterns just lived for the day of their promotion when they would become 'haves' after years of being 'have-nots'.[108]

The first expense upon the purse of a subaltern were his uniforms, especially the white dress uniform which wore out very quickly yet which had to be worn on numerous occasions by the majority of officers, stationed as they were in garrisons. True, one-quarter of an officer's pay was deducted to pay for dress, but that did not include such necessary items as cap, gloves, underwear or shoes for which he had to pay himself. Moreover, in those days no official control of any kind was exercised over shops selling these items, and facings and buttons, decorations and insignia, golden sword handles and all sorts of extras were also *de rigueur*. To be 'perfectly turned out' during the Vormärz era, was, therefore, much more difficult than it was to be later on.

The white uniform which represented 'unblemished virtue' was practically impossible to keep clean. On the parade ground, nevertheless, a man who wore a uniform which had just been cleaned and could be recognised as having just been cleaned was looked down on and despised by his fellow officers; the same attitude paradoxically being displayed towards anyone whose uniform had thinned on the back from use. Such a man risked reading in the same day's orders 'the costly summons which was feared by all'[109] namely, 'The Herr Leutnant X must appear before me within three days in a new uniform accompanied by his company commander.'

Uniform, in this way, was manipulated by regimental commanders to set the whole regimental tone.[110] There were expensive and inexpensive regiments and the criterion was usually the colonel's views on dress. If wealthy men were wanted, a frequent change of dress would be required – undress uniform in the morning, plain civilian clothes for the middle of the day, full dress uniform for the afternoon and plain civilian full dress for the evening – and the aim would be fulfilled.

If officers did not come up to this standard, if they complained or refused to bear the expenses, their colonel would condemn them as slovenly and disobedient subordinates. Their conduct reports would be filled in appropriately and they would find themselves marked down or on the pension list for life. Subalterns, therefore, made the best of their situation and waited patiently for future promotion in the hope of better things. Meanwhile there was also a sort of social defence mechanism at work:[111] 'In spite of everything', wrote von Angeli,

we set great store by our white coat. We loved it and were proud of it, because it was a valuable and unique mark of difference, which in the whole world belonged only to the

Austrian army. And not only the officers but soldiers of all ranks thought so: they took a delight in wearing their white coats and looked forward to the awe of civilians who, dressed in their dark clothing, could not conceive how one could move about all day in a white uniform without getting it dirty or at least being excessively embarrassed by it. Certainly the uniform required a certain prudence in everyday use, but this was quickly acquired and gave the wearer a certain refined, distinguished air, for it is undeniable that even the most ordinary, dirtiest fellow behaves completely differently, if he is in nice, fastidious dress, from one who is less sensitive on account of less respect.

For newly promoted officers the financial situation was rendered even more frustrating thanks to a fiscal device known as the *Gagekarens,* a sort of army imitation of the transfer tax.[112] Under this system, for one full year after promotion, the increase in an officer's pay would be taken from him,[113] allegedly as a contribution to the pension fund. This was not so bad for a subaltern – the difference was only 4 fl. per month – but a second-class captain, previously an *Oberleutnant* had to give up 32 fl. per month for a whole year, a sum which constituted more than the whole of his last year's pay. The financial misery of captains promoted staff officers was perhaps worst of all in this respect, since the expense entailed was very great indeed – the need to buy a horse, without any help from the state, contributing not a little by itself.[114] The phrase commonly used in Austria, 'in debt like a staff officer', therefore, had a very sound basis in reality.[115]

There were many more causes of financial difficulties among subalterns. Some of these were relatively bearable – the 45 kreuzer fine they were liable for if put under *Profoss* arrest,[116] the occasional claims of the regimental *Ehrenrath*[117] or even the 3 fl. which were kept from their pay to build up a regimental library, for example – but others were unsupportable.

To begin with, there was the housing situation.[118] Every subaltern had an 'accommodation allowance'. But that did not help very much thanks to the solicitude with which the army ensured that none of this money passed out of official hands. Almost all the accommodation used by army officers was owned or rented by the army itself. Where this was not possible a sort of cartel was arranged with the municipal authorities whereby a certain number of houses were set aside for soldiers. In this way, therefore, there was never any need to pay out the allowances.

Officially the system existed to protect officers from civilian landlords who charged outrageous rents or refused to let to the military. In practice the army saved money by exploiting its own men. The source of the trouble was one pay regulation. This stated that in cases where there was not enough money available to provide officers with decent accommodation they would just have to put up with less. It was meant to be an exception to accommodation rules, but became in time the keystone to the accommodation system as a whole. Living quarters as provided by the army were restricted to the bare necessities: four walls, a roof and a floor. An officer could expect no furniture at all, except a bed perhaps if his company commander had a warm heart and a long memory, and if his predecessor had left him so much as a nail in the wall he had cause for rejoicing as it meant that his uniform would not have to lie on the floor.

The manservant, in spite of the fact that he would most likely have to share his room with the servant of some other subaltern, was distinctly better off than his master, at least as far as quarters were concerned. He belonged to the 'estate of the company' and for that reason had to be supplied with a bed, wardrobe, table, two chairs and a place to keep his bread. It may all have been plain unpainted wood, but he still knew where to find his clothes and belongings and where he would sleep for the night. His master, on the other hand, had to buy all these items, or rather, since he was poorly paid, borrow the money in order to buy them. This meant a trip to the 'furniture-lender' and 'as always and everywhere, not merely in Galicia, "brother Jew" was at hand'.[119]

The 'furniture Jew', who, of course, might not be Jewish at all, supplied the necessary items at a heavy rental. Such a state of affairs had been going on for years, but inexperienced subalterns were always being swindled and going off with badly made and totally unnecessary furniture. The bill usually amounted to another 4–6 fl. monthly.

A third source of financial difficulty was caused by travel.[120] Journeys which were made voluntarily or had to be undertaken on account of private circumstances were not, of course, underwritten by the treasury. With respect to official duties, however, the treasury seemed quite content to adopt the same attitude. Eventually the point was reached when officers themselves, not the service, were paying for army communications because even the smallest expenses, which nine times out of ten bore no relation to the actual costs incurred, were being refused by army officialdom. In most cases the army administration would claim that no expenses were due since the man concerned was in possession of a 'preparation allowance' – a claim which was by no means always true, and which, even if it were true, was a meaningless one in any case in view of the sum involved. Even if a subaltern refused to carry out a mission unless he were given something 'on account', to use the army term, another government department would merely deduct the sum involved from his monthly pay. Help could only be expected when the officer was in charge of a wagon and horses with a transport column. In that case he could claim expenses for the wagon and the horses and his own expenses *en route*. Yet even there the army administration knew how to economise and more often than not a lengthy and undignified process of negotiations had to be entered into before any claims were made good. As a result most subalterns resorted to cheating. Expenses incurred *en route* during these journeys were paid for both by the government and the local authorities. The government paid out 45 kreuzer per horse per mile and the local authorities were supposed to contribute an equal amount. The local authorities were also responsible for certifying those men who were unfit to march and they paid for the wagons. A deal was made, therefore, between the officer concerned and the local officials. The latter certified as unfit to march many more men than was actually the case and claimed that more wagons were needed than were actually used. The wagons always required four horses. In Hungary officials would even invent men to certify and claimed that this was a 'national custom'. The local officials would then pocket the extra money raised in their area and the subaltern concerned would receive the extra government contribution. This was one area of life where 'decorum' – a word much used by officers in Austria – was ignored. Subalterns had too great a need for money.

The fourth great claim on an officer's wage was marriage. Perhaps any man who contemplates marriage can expect to encounter difficulties, but an Austrian subaltern would have to face more than most. For a start army regulations laid down that only one-sixth of the officer corps could marry[121] and only then with their colonel's consent. Securing this could often represent a formidable task in itself. Once consent had been gained, another problem arose. For before any marriage could take place a 'marriage settlement' had to be arranged which involved a fairly large amount of money[122] known as a 'caution'. This was deposited in cash with the government and was supposed to provide for the officer's widow and children in the event of his death. While the married couple were living they enjoyed the interest on the money, but the principal itself could not be touched. The system, however, was not as benevolent as it seemed for if an officer's dependants were, on the one hand, guaranteed a modest income in the case of his death the need to arrange a marriage settlement, on the other, significantly reduced the standard of living of nearly all army married couples: 'Anyone who has not seen these conditions', wrote von Fenneberg, 'is incapable of conceiving what sort of really sad existence these people lead.'

The official view must, therefore, have been that only those who could afford to get married would do so. This was a very strange viewpoint for the romantic age. Yet it was a viewpoint which every couple had to accommodate and one which turned army marriages into business propositions. For the caution-money required before a marriage could be entered into would be raised by the relatives and friends of the couple concerned who would invest in their happiness in return for a secure annual interest of 5 per cent. Such investments were protected by the fact that the caution-money could not be mortgaged in any way, as well as by private agreements with the bridegroom. The end result was that despite official army policy, officers who were scarcely able to support themselves on a net pay of about 10 fl. per month would get married and find it impossible to support a wife and family. The majority of subalterns in fact, soon found themselves in debt. With 6 fl. deducted for uniform expenses, 4 fl. for furniture, 3 fl. for the library, they had only as much real pay as a corporal on which to live. Unlike a corporal, however, they still had to buy their food and carry on their social life, so that merely existing was no easy matter and without private means of support it became impossible to survive without making various sacrifices.[123]

There was, for instance, as good as no breakfast. Coffee was drunk, at the most, for a couple of days after the 20th of each month. Usually a subaltern had to make do with a glass of schnapps and a piece of bread from the canteen or travelling shop. Lunches were equally frugal. There was no proper 'mess' – that only came in the 1880s when officers could afford to be patrons – so that subalterns would group together to eat something cooked by a servant. In quantity the food was less than the men's and considerably less than the sergeants'. As for quality, it was usually bad. Supper was spent in similar circumstances. A group of officers would get together in one of their rooms and share a communal meal in order to spare the money for a glass of beer in company later on. When they did go out they presented a fine face to the world, dressed up in their 'Virginia'[124] and acting the part of dandies. But beneath the 'splendid' spirit noticed by Goethe and others was a heavy sense of irony which came out often in their soldiers' songs:

'Den letzter kreuzer, den er nun noch hat,
Bekommt ein armer, lahmgeschossener Soldat.'

A 4 fl. increase was granted to subalterns in 1840, but all that really happened was that the 'subsistence allowance' already received by officers was henceforth calculated as part of their pay. This meant that the so-called pay increase took place on paper alone.[125] The official attitude to the question was still the one made famous by Grünne: 'If you cannot live on your pay, go. For twenty-four florins I can get lieutenants enough.'

Pensions

There was no retiring age for Austrian officers. If an officer was fit enough to do his job, his age did not matter.[126] He became eligible for a pension only once a body known as the 'Arbitrirungs-und Superarbitrirungs-Commission' had categorised him as a 'temporary', 'semi' or 'real' invalid. Likewise, his length of service in the army affected neither his eligibility for a pension nor indeed the amount of his pension. Only his rank determined how much he was due; and he was allowed to retire on the pension of one rank above his own.[127]

The following was the pension-scale for officers:[128]

Rank	Per annum		
	Fl.	£	s.
Subalterns	200	21	5
Second captains	400	42	10
First captain infantry; captain cavalry	600	63	15
Major	800	85	0
Lieutenant-colonel	1,000	106	5
Colonel	1,200	127	10
Brigadier-general*	1,500	159	7
Lieutenant-general	3,000	318	15
General of the cavalry	4,000	425	0
Field marshal (full pay)	12,000	1,275	0

*A brigadier-general of long service received from 2,000 to 2,500 fl. or £212–£265.

There was never any question of a systematic procedure concerning pensions in the Austrian army because as von Fenneberg[129] put it, 'unlimited arbitrariness here exercise[d] her moody rights'. As will have been noticed already, the Austrian pension system operated on the basis that 'not the letter but the spirit gives life'.

According to regulations,[130] the question of retiring an officer arose when an officer had been sick for at least nine months. During this time he should have been repeatedly reported as too ill to serve, and if he had not himself brought up the question of retirement, it was the duty of his corps commander to do so. A request would be made to the doctor treating him to compose a history of his illness, and in this report the doctor was obliged to state into which of the three categories of illness or invalidism the officer should be assigned. This was the chief ground on which the commission would reach a decision.

The doctor's report would then go through official channels which in the first instance meant brigade headquarters. There the regimental doctor and the respective *Feldkriegskommissar* decided whether it merited the attention of the Commission at all. If possible they would see the officer concerned and if the case was accepted as genuine the relative documents were passed on to the General Command which alone had the right to decide on questions of invalidism. The Commission, put together by the General Command, consisted of the commanding general, the general command adjutant, the *Oberfeldkriegskommissar,* the ration administrator and the directing staff doctor. Its decision would be sent to the Hofkriegsrath which in turn informed the officer by *Reskript.*

In the case of an officer declared a 'temporary invalid' – which meant that there was still some hope of future recovery – he was pensioned off for one year only, after which time he had to reappear before the Commission. Then a second decision was taken as to whether he re-entered the service or was reclassified with regard to his health. If he were reclassified as a 'semi-invalid', re-entry into the service was no longer possible. Nonetheless, as a semi-invalid he might be transferred to a garrison battalion or to the Uniform Commission in which case he was not regarded as a pensioner but drew full pay. 'Real invalidism' signified a total unfitness for any kind of military service and excluded any future obligations save minor ones like sitting on hearings and court martials. Generals and staff officers underwent no such procedure and were either transferred to the pension list at their own request or summarily placed on it by the Hofkriegsrath if the Emperor agreed.

These forms and procedures were always followed to the letter; the spirit of the regulations, the idea that only officers really unfit for service should be pensioned off, was never strictly adhered to at all. When an officer really was unfit to serve, the proceedings described above were carried out. But exactly the same proceedings were also used as a convenient social device for many other purposes: it enabled conventions to be made; it provided a means for escape in case of debt; it also provided a ready-made exit for men who were personally or politically unpopular.

Take for example the case of the Jäger Lieutenant Frankowitz. According to von Fenneberg,[131] he had already been guilty of several offences, the worst of which was only drunkenness, when he was accused in Trieste of committing some or other crime and was eagerly arrested by a bitter enemy. Frankowitz was an able soldier, multilingual, well educated, but had a very sharp tongue and was disliked by his superiors. For four weeks he was kept under arrest without a hearing or a trial of any sort – against army law – and then was suddenly handed a letter from his corps commander who offered the friendly advice that he should seek to be retired. The letter ended: 'Since you hail from a house not without fortune, you can live comfortably in Carniola on an annual pension of 200 fls.'

The real point of the letter was, of course, that a trial could be avoided and Frankowitz took up the suggestion. He had fought a similar attempt to retire him on a previous occasion only to spend fourteen months in prison 'pending investigation' of his case. This time he requested a medical examination although he had never reported sick. He did not, in fact, have to wait the usual nine months. He knew too much about too many people and was retired after a couple of months. In 1840 a number of officers were pensioned off on the spot on political grounds. Their noses had been so far above the ground that they failed to smell a democratic fuse which had been burning underneath them.

Finally, there were cases of what von Fenneberg described as 'retirement from laziness', explaining that,[132] '. . . since it happens not rarely that officers, having attained the height of their earthly ambitions, namely the rank of captain, are threatened for some reason or another with a transfer away from a comfortable garrison, or, indeed with a long spell of duty in Italy, they seek to be pensioned off, something which people are only too willing to do for them, since the regiment can, after the retirement of one real captain, immediately fill six vacant places'. This was the real advantage of the pension system: by getting rid of more than its share of officers, it speeded up promotions and made everybody happy. As a social regulator, therefore, it was very important. However, from the rank of captain it also provided for a man's security in his twilight years which fact alone cemented loyalties.

Widows' pensions provided more cement. True, most widows were expected to be provided for from their marriage settlement, but if for one reason or another this was not the case, widows' pensions did exist. They were usually given only to those who really needed them, but in special circumstances the Emperor could approve a pension called a *Gnadengehalt*. Most women who were eligible for widows' pensions were, therefore, special cases. But not all. The following ladies could apply:

(*a*) Those whose husbands died in battle or from wounds received in battle.
(*b*) Those whose husbands died of a disease contracted in a military hospital during service.
(*c*) Widows of generals whose husbands were married as N.C.Os or privates.
(*d*) Those whose husbands entered the army before 29 January 1819 already married.
(*e*) Those whose husbands were former members of the Italian army.
(*f*) Those whose husbands resigned their commissions to become tobacco dealers or councillors.

In the case of orphans, the army also made special provision. Boys up the age of twenty and girls up to eighteen years old received education allowances. If, for any reason they were ill or infirm, they could each draw these allowances beyond the prescribed age, the benefits, like widows' pensions being paid without regard to their father's rank in the army. The boys were usually brought up in the regimental schools, but if they wished to learn a trade they were given the necessary opportunities. Girls were trained as servants or governesses.

Finally, there were the extra benefits for which a variety of people were eligible: every year, for example, the Hofkriegsrath would give out 'support money' to the really needy; people suffering from mental ailments were assigned to first-class places in civilian asylums; others might be given a place at Wiener Neustadt; daughters might get places in ladies' training schools; and deaf and blind children were cared for in appropriate civilian institutions. For these reasons alone the Austrian army had a strong call on the loyalty of its officers.

The cohesion of the officer corps

The life of an Austrian officer could often be rough and uninteresting. Gerard[133] called the army 'a school which gave few holidays', while von Fenneberg pointed to the growing suicide rate.[134] Life was especially unrewarding when garrison duty meant years of service in the wilds and wildernesses of northern Hungary, Galicia or Croatia, something which cavalry officers experienced all too often. Quartering arrangements made existence in these outposts fairly miserable. Officers were forced to live in peasant huts with thatched roofs, clay floors and mud walls. Their horses were stalled with the peasant's cows. Worst of all there might not be another officer to talk to within 20–100 miles as the detachment would be spread over villages scores of miles apart. Nine times out of ten the village priest was just as boorish as the peasants, who were totally uneducated and spoke a foreign language. Even the simple pleasure of an intelligent conversation became, in these circumstances, something of a luxury especially as there were no books about to read.

Many things were tried to beat the resulting boredom which was felt as much in the small garrison outposts as in the villages. Greyhound racing proved popular on the Hungarian plains. Hunting, drinking[135] and love-making were popular everywhere, and in Galicia there was the occasional Jew-baiting.[136] Even an inspection was popular since it brought larger numbers of men together. True release, however, came only when an officer went on leave or for some reason got the chance to enter anything which resembled a town. This usually entailed borrowing money with the result that nearly every subaltern got into debt. In fact, when regiments assembled for manœuvres, debts became a serious problem since gambling on these occasions was rife.[137]

Subalterns became the objects of general discussion when their debts ran over 100 fl. A debt of between 200 and 300 fl. exposed them to the danger of being called 'frivolous debtors' and once that happened the storm would break. The subaltern concerned had the choice of making a free confession to his regimental commander or being made the subject of an official complaint. If he wanted to keep his commission he needed good mitigating circumstances, because so-called 'dirty-debts' – owing money for drink or owing money to a common soldier for example – were held to compromise the honour and respect of other officers and could in no way be condoned.

However, the regulation of debt was controlled, not by the official regulations but by the rigour with which the Austrian officer corps preserved its decorum. The system worked as follows: either the debtors' friends would raise the money to keep him in the regiment or an *a conto* arrangement would be made. In extreme cases a peculiar social mechanism would be activated – the regimental court of honour.[138] An *a conto* arrangement meant that the man in trouble would write a humiliating letter to the company commander and receive an advance from his next month's salary. However, unless the man was well placed and had powerful friends no advance above 5 fl. could be expected. More often than not, therefore, the council of honour, or *Ehrenrath* was invoked.

The *Ehrenrath* was an institution which reflected the cohesion of the officer corps rather well. It promoted regimental self-consciousness and its rules if unwritten, were adhered to scrupulously, even by army officialdom. Regimental commanders were never known to oppose its decisions and very often invoked it themselves if they wished to avoid protracted legal proceedings. A form of *Ehrenrath*, in fact, was legalised after 1866.

The *Ehrenrath*, however, was not a regimental institution; each officers' rank in every regiment had one of its own and each was strictly separated from the next. The two oldest members of each rank were supposed to supervise them but any member of the relevant officer group had the authority to summon a council. When it met, the man responsible for calling it had to justify his decision and abide scrupulously by its resolution, which would be taken after a free discussion.

Only in particularly serious cases were verdicts given of unconditional guilt. In cases of debt which did not damage the officers' decorum, officers were almost obliged to prevent an official complaint going through and to help their comrade out. The debtor himself was obliged to confess everything as frankly as possible, and honour permitting the *Ehrenrath* would take over the debt. If he lied to his comrades or did not tell the whole story, he would ultimately be expelled by them. Honour was all. If a decision was given against a man, he had no appeal. There was no question of an official complaint being made. The man concerned would have to sign a *Quittierrungs-Revers*[139] and deposit it within twenty-four hours with the regimental command. After he signed that document he was free from any further military duties. Nor was there any point in refusing to sign. No officer of his own or any other regiment would serve with a man who had been condemned by a court of honour. However, the man would not leave without means. Military comradeship did stretch that far. Officers of his own rank – often others too – would make sure that he was well provided for with clothes and travelling money. His debt would be taken over[140] and the man would promise in return never to show his face again in the garrison district.

The *Ehrenrath* was one aspect of cohesion. Another was the custom that officers addressed each other with the word '*du*', the familiar form of the German 'you'.[141] This was a practice found only in Austria and there was supposed to be something romantic about two subalterns of different social class, of different ages, from different parts of the Empire, addressing each other in this way when they met for the first time. Yet there was little practical advantage to be derived from the custom. Rank still pulled its weight and much depended on the tone of voice.[142] The '*du*' form, moreover, could not be used in front of the men. Many officers, in fact, regarded the custom as a distasteful one and restricted their '*du*' to officers of equal rank, a situation which formed the substance of many army jokes. Stories abounded about the two officers who called each other '*du*' when they were of the same rank, reverted to '*Sie*' when one was promoted and changed again to '*du*' when the other caught up. Eventually, one of them would lose track, insult the other and a duel would be fought between them.

Duelling itself was hardly an aspect of army cohesion, but it did form part of the military code of honour which certainly was. It survived until the end of the Habsburg army,[143] and when in 1901 the War Ministry issued a new decree on the subject, the order was to restrict duelling, not to abolish it. In 1905 there were sixty duels among officers, fifteen in 1910. During the Vormärz period officers were more or less free to issue and accept challenges as they liked. There was, it is true, a growing opposition to the practice,[144] but an officer who refused to duel would be forced to resign his commission. In fact there was little that could be done about duelling for the simple reason that the Emperor Francis I was known to favour it. When a lieutenant was tried and sentenced for repeatedly challenging his *Oberleutnant* to a duel, his relatives petitioned the Emperor to investigate the matter. Francis concluded:[145] 'The *Oberleutnant* has done his duty in that he denounced the officer, but he is still a *S-Kerl*.' Later on the lieutenant was reprieved and his superior was placed on the pension list.

Cohesion did not stretch as far as cadets. The latter led unhappy lives, existing somewhere between the officers and men but being despised by both. They were addressed by officers with '*Sie*' and treated by them almost like servants. A cadet would serve as captain's valet at a regimental dinner, would not dare mix in conversation unless he was spoken to and would not lay aside his sword until permitted to do so. Generally speaking he was tolerated only on sufferance. Any officer seen in the company of cadets would be frowned upon by his fellows. Only a cavalry officer stuck in the wilds somewhere would welcome one for company.[146]

Among subalterns themselves, strains also existed between junior and senior officers.[147] Contributing were all the usual tensions of the 'generation gap', but *Konkretualstatus* played its part as well. The army had too many subalterns and differences in age were sometimes treated like differences of rank. *Oberleutnants* tended to keep to themselves and treated younger second lieutenants like parvenu cadets. The strain was worse when the old insisted on being helpful and offered unwanted advice. Still, according to von Fenneberg,[148] such problems were steadily diminishing and off-duty relations among officers were becoming better in all respects: 'There was a freer, lighter, less formal tone in evidence, even much common feeling amongst Austrian officers.'

How socially cohesive then was the officer corps? The question is not an easy one to answer because there is a lack of material on which to form a judgement. Still, what evidence there is appears to suggest that it was a fairly cohesive body. The remarks of von Fenneberg and Mollinary to the effect that there was a growing hereditary caste within the army have already been noted. Probably most officers had near relatives if not fathers who had also been officers. Turnball gives the following picture:[149]

The Austrian army is open to all: but its genius is, in the same sense in which the observation may be made of the British army as compared with the French, decidedly aristocratical. Both the crown and the proprietary colonels are inclined to give a preference to the members of those families which with us would be understood to constitute the gentry; and it is the policy of the state not only to engage in its service members of its own highest native nobility, but many princes likewise of the smaller reigning houses of Germany.

A pamphlet entitled, 'Austria and Italy, by an Anglo-Italian, late a Captain in the Venetian Army', published in London by Richard Bentley in 1851 included the following instructive story: 'After having bombarded Vienna, an old officer represented to his Excellency the hardship of seeing so many promotions of very young men of high rank but little merit to the detriment of veterans. "Are you a nobleman?" enquired Prince Windischgraetz. "I am not." "Then consider yourself very lucky that you are a captain – and begone."' The same pamphlet described the Prince as 'the antiquated Windischgraetz (who maintains that the animal creation only terminates with the baron, where the human species takes its commencement). . . .' Which was not a wildly inaccurate remark.

There was, however, a growing number of bourgeois in the army whom von Preradovich has traced to the generalcy.[150] Here are his figures:

Year	HN*	AN†	NNB‡	NNB as per cent of total
1804	14	20	3	8
1816	17	9	6	19
1829	13	8	3	12.5
1847	13	17	2	7
1859	9	8	2	10
1878	7	3	11	52

*HN signifies 'high nobility'.   †AN signifies 'old nobility'.
‡NNB signifies 'new nobility and bourgeoisie'.

These figures, however, ought to be treated with caution. Because the total number of people involved varies only between nineteen and thirty-seven, percentage changes are very large. More important, the categories used by von Preradovich are genealogical ones, not social ones, a point which is emphasised by the way in which he lumps the figures for new nobility and bourgeoisie together. It may be that such categories coincided with Austrian social attitudes during the Vormärz period. But, if so, he produces no evidence to support such an assumption. He merely assumes.[151]

The figures do show that the influence of the nobility in the army declined after 1866. As far as they show anything about the Vormärz period, it is that the rising bourgeoisie, assuming that it was large enough inside the army to make a mark, had still to make it. Certainly neither von Fenneberg nor von Angeli, both of whom served in the Vormärz Austrian army, were aware of a class struggle inside the officer corps.[152] Von Angeli was more impressed by the intellectual than the differences to be encountered there and wrote that 'if the variety of institutions from which the imperial officer corps recruited itself made not the slightest difference to its spirit, the intellectual differences . . . appeared more sharp . . .' Like the Archduke Maximilian, therefore, both he and von Fenneberg underlined the variety of professional competence within the officer corps rather than any variety of social background. The fact was, as Turnball pointed out, that the vast majority of officers were recruited from the nobility and gentry. The number of officers with lower social origins was probably quite small. It had to be, considering the level of pay and the demands made upon that pay by army life. Only men with private means could afford to stay the course. Again, those with a more professional background probably joined the artillery. The pay was higher there and although connexions still played a part, it was, according to von Fenneberg,[153] the only branch of the Austrian army to retain 'a gem of the Napoleonic Idea':

anyone, be he count, prince or peasant's son, serves from private upwards having to undertake all the duties of every rank without exception by himself, whether they consist of cleaning a room or solving a mathematical problem. . . . The full equality of all, among which only talent and superior knowledge, but not birth or connection can make a difference and lead to earlier promotion, has brought this branch of the service a serious respect in the army as a whole, a respect based on the same foundation of superior training and insight.

Artillery officers, however, formed a class of their own, kept to themselves and had little influence on the rest of the army. They were a distinct minority, and the bourgeois professionals may well have been a minority within that minority as a large proportion of technical officers were sons of officers who had come up through the cadet schools and the Engineering Academy. These others might not have been nobles, but they were not bourgeois either in the usual meaning of the word. Promotions occasionally were made from the ranks. But these were exercises in propaganda,[154] and the men promoted in this way were never accepted by their fellow officers. They had fifteen to twenty years' service behind them and were often junior to boys of eighteen. As a result they were only too happy to apply for a transfer to a garrison battalion or to the pension list. One final factor which contributed to social cohesion was the device of 'systematic nobility'.[155] After thirty years' service officers who had seen action in face of the enemy could apply for ennoblement; an officer who had not seen action could do so after forty years. This was a splendid regulation from the army's point of view because, as von Fenneberg describes them, it had such wonderful effects:[156]

When the bourgeois officer approaches that point in time, he eschews his liberalism, becomes an aristocrat, speaks of his long service, counts his earnings, looks aristocratically down on young officers beginning their careers, gives himself the courage to take them by the hand with good or bad advice, and takes it very badly when a younger colleague takes little notice of him, does not ask for his advice in his affairs or does not follow advice which has been offered or requested. Above all he builds up in young officer circles a respectable and fatherly authority.

Such officers, once ennobled often took titles which made them seem ridiculous: Ahsbahs von der Lanze; Donner von Blitzbergen; Schemel von Kühntritt; Froschmayer von Scheibenhof; and Teutschenbach von Ehrenruhe for example.[157]

On a different level there was perhaps a community of ignorance among the officers, which also enhanced cohesion, a dearth of enquiring minds, an anti-intellectualism of the 'their's not to reason why, their's but to do and die' type, even if losses of Austrian officers in war were notoriously low.[158] There were people of high ability in the regiments, but their numbers were smaller than they should have been;[159] moreover, they were all too often lost to the army in overstaffed and uncoordinated administrative departments or in general staff, map-drawing duties if they were summoned to Vienna.

Littérateurs were unpopular. Von Fenneberg wrote that:[160] 'Nowhere are poets and authors generally more unloved as in the military, but this is particularly so in Austria, and woe to them if they do not attend to their duties much more strictly than all the others.' Thus Hilscher, for example, the poet who was responsible for one of the best translations of Byron, died still a corporal on a straw bed in Milan despite all attempts of patrons to secure a commission for him.[161] The result was that authors of a liberal colour soon threw off their fetters if fate had led them into a military life. Very often they turned their backs on class and country and settled down elsewhere. Consequently, there were[162] 'many literary figures living in Germany and abroad who once upon a time had a place in the Austrian army'.

So much was only natural. All soldiers secretly suspect that the pen is mightier than the sword. But in Austria Metternich operated a very efficient censorship system and this affected the army too. Works of a political nature were considered taboo and could not be read – despite the existence of Rotteck's *Weltgeschichte* in most regimental libraries. Thus if Maria Theresa had pronounced the famous dictum,[163] 'Meine Soldaten sollen lesen was sie wollen, wenn sie nur tapfer a rein schlagen', nobody paid any attention to it, least of all her grandsons. The people who really complained about the Austrian army at this time, therefore, were not frustrated bourgeois cadets suffering from class prejudice – there was, after all, an attitude of mind involved in a decision to join the army. The people who really felt oppressed were those who had entered the army because their fathers were soldiers, and had subsequently developed intellectual tastes for which the army could not cater. Von Fenneberg himself was an excellent example of the type. So too was Messenhauser, chief of the Viennese rebels of October 1848. Life for these people was made even more intolerable by the presence of the political police inside the regiments. The latter were not brutal; in fact, they were supposed to be intelligent enough not to give themselves away and were not allowed to mistreat soldiers. Very often their presence was far from notorious in the corps in which they operated and this was due to the fact that, for the most part, they were merely officers who agreed to tell tales. It was not really cloak and dagger stuff;[164] just sycophants scribbling notes.

However, if von Fenneberg is to be believed, there was little need for a secret police.[165] The 'liberalism' of the Austrian officer might include a deep dislike of policemen, pen-pushers and customs officials, but it had very little to do with politics. An Austrian officer cared about his army, his wife, his dog and his horse, but not political theory. His knowledge of history was limited and prejudiced: his knowledge of foreign constitutions was nil; most likely he had never heard of the Carlsbad and Vienna Conferences; and if he did read a paper, it would probably be the *Wiener Zeitung* or the *Beobachter*. In short, he was not a natural rebel.

Probably the strongest force for cohesion in the officer corps was the legacy of the Holy Roman Empire. Deep down in the bottom of his heart, the Austrian soldier felt himself to be a personal bodyguard of his Catholic Emperor whose duty it was to defend and extend Christian civilisation in eastern-central Europe. If other soldiers fought for king and country, the Austrian fought for king and cross. The Italian and Croat alike, was a historic ingredient of the culture of the Habsburg army. The victory in 1620 'on the White Mountain' had been attributed to the fact that Ferdinand II had placed his army under the patronage of the Madonna whose image ever afterwards decked the Austrian banners. The names of many martial priests, names immortally engraven in Austrian history, served as living impersonifications of just this religious element[166] – Johann von Capistran, for example, whose fiery words raised an army and who stood by the side of Hunyadi upon the walls of Belgrade, inspiring the defenders until the Turks were repulsed. There were other manifestations of this religious bond – the great open-air mass read by the chief chaplain of the army and attended by the troops of the Vienna garrison on the Emperor's birthday, as well as the solemn blessing of the banners and all the rest of the military pomp on the day of the Corpus Christi procession which formed itself as a sort of general parade of the House of Habsburg.

The Church also had a more practical hold over the army.[167] There were 159 regimental and garrison chaplains in the army who were responsible to the Field Bishop in Vienna who was assisted by eight field superiors. Beneath them were thousands of field chaplains. At regimental level at least, they were richly paid – 600 fl. per annum plus surplice taxes and other dues along with wood and quartering allowances. These *Stolataxen* were not inconsiderable – burials could bring in 12 gulden for a captain, marriages 2 ducats.[168] Priests got along notoriously well with officers, but if some of them lacked true religious zeal the Church was well worth supporting. A conference of bishops held in Vienna in 1849 addressed the following message to the troops:[169]

Brave warriors of the army who defend the iron righteousness of law and order with a strong arm, let no one do you harm or injustice and be content with your pay. Be seduced by nobody, remain true to your oath of allegiance which you have sworn before Almighty God. Because death stands near you constantly, think of Eternity and God and His Reich. Have a conscience as clean as your weapons so that when the enemy bullet strikes your brave heart, it will immediately release a hero's pure soul to Heaven.

The Church in Austria, it appears, was more efficient than the army.

The Emperor, almost necessarily, became an object of religious loyalty to his officers. Doubtless the slightly lunatic Ferdinand had slightly less appeal, but what he lacked in intelligence he allegedly made up for in *Gemütlichkeit*. In any case the rationale of military honour was the opportunity to serve the Emperor (Christ too, indirectly). To be honoured by him was the greatest reward of all and decorations, even systematic ones, really meant something.[170] The Austrian officer boasted of his *Kaisertreue* with pride and would even seek to defend the army's military record. Was it not true that during the French and Revolutionary Wars the Austrians had won 168 out of the 264 engagements with the French?[171] Had not Napoleon told his troops that he who had not seen the Austrians as Aspern 'had seen nothing great'? The view of the average officer during the Vormärz period was that this great tradition would continue.

Chapter 2

The common soldier, 1815–1848

Recruitment

There was no uniform system for recruiting men into the Austrian army until 1845. Before then recruits from the German provinces served for 14 years, those from Lombardy, Venetia and the Tyrol for 8 years and those from Hungary for life. In 1840, however, enlistment in Hungary was reduced to 10 years' service and in 1845 a uniform 8 years' period was introduced.[1]* The Empire was divided into regimental districts, each of which according to its population was obliged to supply the army with a given number of men.[2] If one district was particularly small, a regiment would have two or more to draw on. In the German provinces the men in each district were divided into two classes, namely those aged between 19 and 28 inclusive and those from 29 to 38 inclusive. Those of the first class had to serve, if called upon, either for 20 years or until they were 40 years of age, of which period 14 years had (generally) to be passed in the line, before they entered the militia.[3] Thus a recruit of nineteen would serve 14 years in the line and 6 in the militia; a recruit of twenty-two, 14 years in the line and only 4 in the militia; whereas a recruit of twenty-eight would serve only 12 years in the line, that is, until he reached the age of 40. The second class of recruits, those between 29 and 38 years of age, served only in the militia and did so until they reached the age of 45. Not everyone, however, was liable to serve. Exemptions included nobles, clergy, graduates, government employees, students, peasants owning 5 acres of cultivated land, and sons on whom parents were dependent for their livelihood, although only one son in each family could be viewed as a breadwinner in this context.[4] As a result, the burden of conscription fell, when the local authorities could not palm off their malcontents and gaolbirds on the army,[5] on the sons of the poorest peasantry. It was only rarely, on the other hand, that any systematic enlistment took place (the government was consistently trying to reduce the army's size) and about one-third of the Austrian army appears to have been semi-permanently on leave.[6]

Nonetheless, the army had to be rejuvenated from time to time and the source of this rejuvenation was the peasantry. Occasionally, therefore, the countryside would echo to the cry that 'the commissioners' were coming, a cry which, by all accounts induced a horrified reaction. Enlistment was regarded as a 'disaster'[7] by the peasants, and from the following account it is not difficult to understand why:[8] 'The soldier had to bear arms for eight long years – eight years of the most monotonous service, of the roughest treatment and then to return home, if not a cripple, at least brutalised and as an unwanted stranger,

---

* Notes to this chapter are on pp. 252–5.

alienated from his previous way of life and from his previous form of work.'

Yet it was the very manner in which the commissioners set about their work that induced such panic among the peasants:[9]

The district commissioner would arrive in a village and ask the village officials where the lads on the village conscription lists were to be found in order to conscript them. These officials having been threatened or bribed in secret, would then tell him who was young and strong and so the game would begin. First to be visited would be a rich, lease-holding peasant who would have a drink of wine with the commissioner and who might even be his good friend or relative. He would take the commissioner aside, press a bank-note into his hand and whisper 'my neighbour has four [fine sons]'. The commissioner would then pocket the money , pronounce the sons of the rich man free, then visit the man's neighbour and despite all entreaties and tears remove all his four sons forcibly without more ado. . . . This procedure would then continue throughout the village . . . and since it was known throughout the countryside in what a disgraceful manner soldiers were procured, a cry of panic would seize each district whenever the news was heard that the commissioner of recruits was approaching. Indeed in mountain areas, it was not rare for all the young men of a village to flee, to the highest peaks in the woods. When this happened the commissioner would order 'a sharp hunt'. Peasants would be forcibly assembled from places farther afield and given arms. Then with the help of a few companies of soldiers the [man] hunt would begin. . . . In the Alpine lands it would often result in a frenzied struggle of despair on the part of the victims who would be encircled and driven together; it would end in their mistreatment at the hands of Hungarian soldiers.

Once they had been rounded up, the conscripts would be chained and taken to the *Kreisamt*. There they were allowed neither to take leave of their parents nor even to communicate with them, but were quickly transported to a regimental garrison which might be situated in any part of the Empire.

Conscription, therefore, was hardly a popular procedure in the German provinces and it enjoyed no more popularity in Hungary, Lombardy-Venetia or the Tyrol. In these last-mentioned lands, it was supposed to be carried out by ballot – although in practice the procedure was much the same as in the German provinces. The local authorities turned over the dregs of society and the poorest peasants to the army. There was, indeed, one difference in that the law allowed for no exemptions. But this was in fact only a difference in form since the rich could if necessary procure 'substitutes'. These had, it is true, to be people who had served their term of enlistment and were still in full health, or persons over the age of twenty-five who had no previous experience of the army and who as a result were none too easy to come by (a fact reflected in the considerable prices which had to be paid out to procure them, to wit c. 1,500 fl. in Italy and between 500 and 600 fl. elsewhere).[10] Yet if some middle-class families felt rightly aggrieved at having to pay such money for such services, it must be supposed that they were exceptional cases for the balloting was normally carried out with the same deference to their interests as were the enlistment procedures in the other provinces.

Material needs

If it is fairly easy to assess the financial problems of the officer corps, the financial situation of the common soldier in the Austrian army cannot be so easily adduced. Certainly a statement like the following – taken from a recent

German monograph – has to be taken with a pinch of salt.[11] It runs: 'In contradistinction to the officer corps, the men suffered no material hardships and it is noteworthy of Maria Theresa's and Joseph II's paternalism that whereas in comparison with foreign states, the Austrian officer was in a worse position, the troops were substantially better off. The material needs of the soldiers were directly provided by the state. . . . They were for the most part recruited from the poorest and most primitive classes of the population and had very modest needs.[12] In fact, any assumption that the troops were 'well off' far less 'substantially better off' than troops elsewhere should be examined very critically. For if Austria spent 140 fl. per man on uniforms and quarters compared with Prussia's 110 and Russia's 120, these figures hardly serve as a meaningful index by which to compare living standards, and, even if they did, one has to note that the figures for France, Great Britain and the United States were 200, 300 and 325 respectively.[13] It is necessary, therefore, to examine in more detail just what the common soldier was provided with.

According to von Angeli,[14] 'if his livelihood was not a splendid one, it nevertheless met his modest needs'.[15] 'Yet soup in the morning, a warm meal at night and tinned food were admittedly entirely unknown and there was no "mess money".' The soldier, instead, paid 3 kr. out of his daily 5 kr. to the mess and met his remaining needs from the 2 kr. left over and half a loaf of bread.[16] Moreover,[17] his pay was not a fixed one, serving rather as the basis for several allowances, which were calculated monthly from the 'market price certificates'[18] supplied by local authorities. He could never be exactly sure, therefore, exactly how much money he would have to spend. In any case, it would never be much – a truth reflected in the fact that his allowances were calculated to 1/64 kr.[19]

Despite being clothed and housed by the army and receiving one hot meal per day, the common Austrian soldier with his 2 or 3 kr. per day was therefore very badly paid indeed. It is difficult, of course, to make comparisons, yet if one takes into account what others earned in Austria at this time, as well as the contemporary price of meat, one acquires, despite the limitations, a reasonable sense of perspective. Thus, among the better-paid workers a spinner in a Bohemian textile mill received 40–50 kr. for a 14–16-hour day; workers in a sugar factory earned 30–40 kr. per day; in a chemical factory they could earn 35 kr. per day; and in a match-making factory 20–40 kr. per day. Among those who would receive board and lodgings as well as pay, a shoemaker would earn 18 kr. per day – a weaver 20 kr. per day; a brush-maker 20 kr. per day; and a miller's lad 8 kr. per day.[20] Tailors, hat-makers and glove-makers, who would be housed but not fed, received between 20 and 50 kr. daily. Finally, as far as the countryside was concerned, a lowly peasant, after paying all his taxes and feudal dues, might be left with 57 fl. per year or *c*. 9 kr. per day.[21] Thus, at a time when meat cost 8 kr. per pound at least,[22] the common soldier must have been economically the equivalent of a landless labourer, except of course, that, unlike the landless labourer, he had a guarantee of full employment. Indeed, there is evidence to suggest that troops could only earn a living wage if they were able to find part-time jobs, a reflection not only on their needs but on how run-down economically the army was. According to one observer:[23]

The infantry, although with the least pay, are generally the best provided; as they are usually stationed in towns, and are allowed to perform labour for individuals by which they gain not infrequently twenty to twenty-five kreuzers daily, whereof however a certain portion is paid to the captain, in regard of the extra wear and tear of the clothes, occasioned by this private labour. The cavalry are more generally quartered, for the convenience of forage, in country villages, where labour is less in demand; and whether it be so or not, the time required in the care of his horse leaves none for the trooper to apply to private emolument.

All in all, therefore, only troops from the very poorest background could really have been content with their lot. For if the army provided them with the barest necessities of life it provided them with little more.

Education; marriages; pensions

Attempts were made to educate the common soldiers.[24] They spent, in fact, some three hours per day in school where N.C.Os explained service regulations, the Articles of War and related matters to them and where they learned to read and write. Ideally they should have been taught by officers but since most officers were incapable of communication with ordinary soldiers – either through linguistic difficulties or from a general distaste for the job – the burden was carried by their non-commissioned colleagues. Captains were supposed to hold school daily for the N.C.Os, but these corresponded by and large to the schools for the men, and even von Fenneberg could declare that, 'it was a most tedious business to have to teach individuals who very often had neither the interest nor the natural capacity to learn and to see how often even the best efforts and hardest work was in vain'. Most captains therefore paid little attention to these schools and suffered little reproach as a result. Yet given the conditions under which the men were serving there is little need to explain their apathy.

'N.C.O. training schools' were organised each winter, however, and apparently achieved greater success. These were attended not only by the most promising N.C.Os but also by cadets. Among the subjects taught were 'arithmetic in its widest sense but exclusive of algebra, the preparation of all service documents used in company business, exercise and service regulations insofar as they affected N.C.Os, and spelling and grammar to enable a service report or simple letter to be written . . .'. The officers who organised these schools did so voluntarily and were not paid for doing so. Only the very dedicated took an interest, therefore, which is the most likely reason that they produced better results.

It is very difficult, on the other hand, to decide exactly how much was achieved by military educational establishments. Certainly matters had improved since the eighteenth century, and if von Fenneberg is to be believed a basic literacy was established, at least among the German regiments. For in these 'there [were] scarcely two out of every hundred [men] who [could] not read or write and answer questions correctly concerning the service regulations as they affected them personally . . .'.[25] Yet what literacy there was[26] 'extended this far and no farther since as far as the common soldier was concerned any further enlightenment would not exactly have promoted the strictest principles of subordination'. Consequently, one must conclude that soldiers were taught only enough to allow them to obey orders properly.

The lot of a common soldier was not a happy one. The pay was poor; the education primitive; the life was hard. Over and above this only four men in each company (about 200 men when complete) were allowed to marry, and those men who were married before entering the service had to leave their wives at home.[27] As a result many soldiers entered into relations with local women whom they had to desert when their regiment moved on.[28] This often led to great heartbreak and not infrequently, desertion. Finally the pension regulations in so far as they applied to common soldiers were applied without humanity. For if these were the same for the men as they were for officers, they were, on the other hand,[29] 'as strictly and scientifically applied in the case of the men as they were loosely and arbitrarily applied in the case of their superiors'. This was partly due to an important difference between the officers and the men. The latter were not supposed to serve until they died or became too ill to soldier on; rather, in the case of troops from the German provinces they were supposed to enter the militia and, in the case of the Italian, Tyrolese and Hungarian soldiers, to leave the army altogether. Those who did so were given a small gratuity on being discharged – namely 2 fl. per year for every year they had served over six.[30]

There were, however, both 'real invalids' and 'semi-invalids' to be provided for, as well as those who chose to re-enlist, a practice resorted to occasionally by cavalry and artillery soldiers who did not wish to enter the Landwehr where their skills were not needed – this, despite the fact that, by all accounts, they were little better off as a result. For as a British observer, writing in 1835 explained:[31]

Those who choose to re-enter gain little or no advantage, except escaping from the militia, a foot service which they cannot bear. The huge tin medal which is given them to wear on their breasts, in token of their being veterans they seem invariably to hold in scorn, as assimilating them to the licensed mendicants of the great towns. They often, therefore, get leave to go home and when there, they endeavour to obtain some civil employment, which may exempt them from the hated infantry service. Failing in this, they become dispirited and either die or become totally useless.

Soldiers who were ill were rigorously examined by army doctors who decided whether they were 'real invalids' or 'semi-invalids', but who mostly judged them to be the latter. In this category they could be employed as servants, porters or other lowly functionaries in military schools, institutes, offices, gaols, border posts, etc. 'Real invalids' were assigned places – if available – in military hospitals or homes in their own provinces.[32] If no places were available they were divided into two classes:[33] those who had to survive outside the army on their 'invalid pay' of a few kreuzer per day (between 4 and 20 depending on rank) but who might apply for a place if one came up in a house or hospital; and those who, if they could not manage on their own had a right to a place that came up.

Widows of ordinary soldiers received sums of money calculated on a scale of years served by their late husbands (2–6 gulden for the first six years 3–10 gulden therafter depending on their husbands' rank).[34] They might also be given places in homes kept by the army or by charities for army widows. The sons of soldiers were either sent to a regimental training house for boys and brought up in the army or else, if they desired, might be allowed to learn a trade at the army's expense.[35] Girls were usually trained as maids.[36] All in all, however, the army felt only a minimal obligation towards the welfare of its troops and of their families. It retained their loyalty by discipline, not kindness.

Discipline and superiors

'In Austria', wrote von Fenneberg,[37] 'the common soldier stands in the same relation to an officer as in Sparta a Helot did to a Spartan.' Officers avoided their men off duty and on duty adopted the view that they had no rights. 'There were few officers', to quote von Fenneberg again,

who enjoyed any popularity amongst their subordinates . . .[38] the majority of them lack the capacity to adjust themselves to the way of thought of the common man; they can never put aside the strict service point of view as if this alone determined their respect and worth. The subaltern as well as the captain is in constant contact with the common man. The officer supervises and conducts the exercises, the drilling of recruits; he holds school for the men; in short, while on duty he spends most of his day with them. Yet he never takes the trouble to study the character of the men, to speak with them in their mode of speech or to teach them their duties by example.

There were, of course, some exceptions to be found – most often, apparently among those officers of an aristocratic or academy background – and these were men who won the respect and affection of their subordinates. Particularly remarkable in this context were those officers who took an interest in the education of the common soldier. Yet they were few and far between and could rarely suffer for long the contempt in which they were held by their fellow officers, most of whom treated their men very roughly and addressed them as 'Er', the insulting third person singular.[39] On manœuvres or on exercises, such officers neglected their troops and according to von Fenneberg large numbers were left out in the wilds for days with the result that many had to be hospitalised – a horrific experience in itself.[40] It is little wonder, therefore, that relations between officers and men were governed not by mutual respect but by discipline of the harshest type.

The basis of military discipline was constituted by the imperial Articles of War,[41] most of which recommended that transgressors should be corporally or capitally punished. Especially indicative of how the army was run, however, were Articles I, II and IV. By Article I violence to superiors was at all times made punishable by death both in peace and war and whether the superior was injured or not. Article II laid down that anyone found guilty of disobedience was to be 'severely punished' or put to death. It also included the widest possible definition of disobedience and enjoined respect for superiors 'on *all* occasions'. It continued: 'Only when the commands of a superior are manifestly against the rules of service, and in opposition to the allegiance sworn to the monarch or clearly have for their object some bad end, is it permitted to an inferior (and then does it become his positive duty) to remonstrate against or even not obey the said commands. But likewise in this case, the remonstrance must invariably be made with moderation and respect.' By Article IV, mutiny was again to be 'severely punished' or made punishable by death and was likewise given the widest possible definition:

The crime of mutiny is said to be committed when a man at a meeting of few or many holds language concerning his superiors disadvantageous to the Service, the State or

Monarch; and animadverts upon them, so as to leave a bad impression on the minds of those listening. Also by endeavouring to set prisoners at liberty or to hinder executions. Also, by more than two men designedly going to their superior to demand relief from hardship or by one or more men complaining when in the ranks or even in the presence of others, of their superior in so impetuous a manner to make it likely that they might be seduced into participation.

The Austrian army, in short, expected blind obedience from its soldiers and was prepared to do everything possible to secure it. Thus to be 'severely punished' – and a cursory glance at the Articles of War reveals that this was the lightest punishment – meant exactly that. For punishment in the imperial service ranged from being flogged to running the gauntlet. As one British army officer of the time remarked,[42] 'I confess I was rather surprised when I learned that the punishments in the Austrian army are almost entirely corporal and very severe, and almost entirely without even nominal, and certainly without efficient control.'

In Austria, N.C.Os had the power to place soldiers under arrest (in which case they had to report the matter immediately), but officers alone had the authority to inflict corporal punishment on the men.[43] Thus a colonel or staff-officer in command of a battalion could, without a court martial, order fifty blows to be given while a major could order forty. A captain in charge of a company could at all times and on his own authority order twenty-five blows to be inflicted. This could be done on the spot and the instrument employed was a hazel stick carried by corporals, which just fitted the bore of a musket. The man who was punished was laid over a drum or stretched along a bench and the blows were given on the breeches by two corporals, one on either side.

In all matters of discipline the chief authority over each company was the captain who was held responsible for its good order. However, since no delay was necessary between offence and punishment and since until 1838 there was no obligation on the captain's part to report upon the punishments he ordered, there was a tendency for officers to abuse their authority. Thus, although they might order a number of punishments from extra drill or double guard duty to what was called 'long' or 'short' ironing – that is, shackling wrists and ankles together with chains for up to forty-eight hours, albeit with periodic relief – according to the British officer quoted above, it was[44] 'right to state that . . . the corporal punishments [were] intensively employed in every branch of the army and in many corps were almost the only method of discipline ever thought of'.

The most infamous form of corporal punishment and in the Austrian army one which was very frequently employed was that of running the gauntlet. This consisted in making an offender, who would be stripped to the waist, walk up and down a street formed of two rows of men, each of whom was given a switch of birch. The pace was left to the choice of the sufferer, but most preferred the ordinary marching time. The street of men was about 100 yards long and consisted of two rows of 150 men in each, facing one another, who inflicted their blows on the man's naked back. The crimes for which this punishment was ordered were usually theft and desertion, although courts martial could order it for other offences. For the first offence, the offender was usually made to pass four times up and down the street; for the second offence, ten times which was the greatest number ever ordered. This involved, of course, being struck 6,000 times and was considered the equivalent of 100 blows with the corporals' sticks.

(The 25 blows which a captain could order was, therefore, no mean punishment.) The offender was usually treated more leniently by men of his own regiment, more severely by those of another. A military doctor attended the proceedings to report to the commanding officer in case a man should be unable to endure the full measure of his punishment. In such an eventuality, the punishment might be deemed to have been fully carried out or it might be resumed at a later date. If a fit man, on the other hand, refused to run the gauntlet he would be held over a bench while the troops would file past and strike him in turn, a procedure known as a *Contremarsch*. Only the colonel of a regiment was empowered to order the gauntlet without a court martial, but he could not order the offender to run more than three times up and three times down a street formed of 100 instead of 150 men on each side.

The result of punishments such as these – and according to one account published in 1847 no less than 5,508 men were forced to run the gauntlet in one year[45] – was naturally to degrade, humiliate and brutalise the men and, not surprisingly, to encourage violence and disobedience. According to the account just quoted,[46] 'if blood is spilled from time to time by common soldiers seeking revenge on their superiors – as has happened frequently recently – one would be justified in ascribing this to the extensive and strict powers of discipline exercised by officers against the common troops'. Indeed, according to von Fenneberg there were numerous cases both of troops murdering their superiors and of troops committing suicide on account of their miserable conditions.[47] Often they murdered N.C.Os or subalterns and then committed suicide. Such behaviour, according to von Fenneberg, was the direct result of their conditions of service. Thus, having described how he had seen a private soldier shoot a corporal, he wrote:[48] 'I come back to those wild outbursts of revenge and ask what must have happened to provoke an individual of this class, otherwise so sunk in dull and sluggish apathy finally to perpetrate such a clearly long-premeditated act of violence?' His answer was:[49] 'such a deed is the result of a long-nourished, deeply-concealed resentment created by prejudiced, hard-hearted, inhuman treatment'. Yet such deeds had 'occurred repeatedly recently' and were 'a sign of the times'. In fact 'threats to murder harsh, unpopular superiors had become almost a daily occurrence'. And even punishments such as seventy strokes of the rod did nothing to improve matters, just as twenty-five strokes for an attempted suicide did nothing to deter others from trying. The life of the common soldier must, therefore, have been an extremely wretched one.[50]

Politics and the common soldier

There is very little evidence indeed of any political interest whatsoever having been displayed by common soldiers of the Austrian army in the period 1815–48. Nor is this surprising. Austria had no political system as such and even officers who looked forward to the development of constitutionalism within the Empire were ostracised by their comrades and reproved by their superiors. The President of the Hofkriegsrath declared that it was[51] 'Thoroughly reprehensible and improper for men who still belong[ed] to the army to sport political colours' and laid it down that officers might[52] 'not in principle support *any* political party whatsoever'. When some were seen supporting opposition candidates at county meetings outside Pest in 1847, he therefore advised General Lederer, the commanding officer in Buda,[53] 'to have the officers concerned warned in an appropriate manner – albeit without attracting unnecessary publicity –. . . that they [would] no longer be allowed to retain the commission of an imperial and royal officer, it they again presume[d] despite this warning, to take part in political affairs in support of the opposition'. It was not until after the revolutions of 1848 had erupted therefore that imperial officers were actively to engage in political affairs.

Even before March 1848, however, the Austrian officer had been in an altogether different position from the common soldier politically. The latter was poor, uneducated and often illiterate. He could not be expected to influence a county meeting or have a relative speak up in a local Diet. He could not afford to buy books or belong to a reading club. If he were therefore to engage in political activity he could do so only through revolutionary conspiracy – indeed there were no political programmes from which he could benefit which were not in themselves revolutionary. Prince Metternich was aware of this, with the result that the Austrian secret police was active within the army. The common soldier, however, did not expect salvation to come through revolution and the vast majority of them appear to have been politically apathetic. Thus, although a few arrests took place from time to time within the ranks,[54] in Italy, for example, in the period between 1818 and 1848 Metternich's agents in Milan reported only a single case of soldiers being successfully won over by the sects.[55] And even that was a small-scale affair which was entirely cleared up to the satisfaction of the authorities.[56]

The case first attracted attention when a cadet of the Geppert Grenadier Division was accused of circulating propaganda.[57] In fact, the only literature found to be in his possession was a copy of a famous revolutionary poem, but investigations revealed that he had been given it by a veterinary student who himself was in possession of a great deal of propaganda and who met regularly with the cadet and three others 'to discuss political matters'. Further investigations revealed that they were all members of the sect 'Young Italy', and that they, as well as two sergeants from the Geppert Grenadiers, had met in the house of an unknown revolutionary to swear eternal hatred against the Austrians. In the end, the identity of this man was also uncovered as was a list of names of those who subscribed to Young Italy's publications.

When Metternich received the news of this from Milan he passed on the reports of his agent there to the former Governor of Lombardy, Count Hartig, now a member of the Council of State, for comment. Hartig read them and in a report to Metternich made the following observations about the army.[58] 'It is perfectly true,' he wrote,

that, as far as the military is concerned, the conduct of the Lombard troops up till now can in no way be reproached. With regard to both discipline and loyalty to their oaths, no blame whatsoever can be attached to them. However the facts, as described by Torresani [the Director of Police in Milan] in the extract from his report which I have submitted to Your Excellency give adequate proof that the Lombard soldier is exposed to a greater danger in Italy than elsewhere because the propagandists do not hesitate to try to subvert the soldier and the N.C.O. and the latter do not always know how to resist these subversions. For this reason it would be desirable to be able to remove them from the area of danger or, if this were not possible, due to prevailing circumstances, care should be taken to reduce the element of danger by having the Italian garrisons changed as often as possible and assigning them only to towns where there are troops from other provinces in numbers greater than them.

However (as will be seen) the army developed no systematic procedures in this regard. Instead, it is almost certain that it was at this time that Hardegg, the President of the Hofkriegsrath reminded the army in Italy of the dangers posed by the sects. In a circular which read as follows he made the official position crystal clear:[59]

When twelve years ago the sect called the Carbonari threatened civil order in the Italian states with its complete overthrow, His Majesty warned you, his subjects, of the harmful and seditious teachings of this sect and of their criminal and treasonous aims in order 324 of March 1821. This was made known to everybody in order to ensure that even the most inexperienced and careless men, from whom the leaders of this sect took care to conceal their aims, would know of them and hence would abstain from joining the Carbonari.

The monarch's same fatherly care now compels him, in view of recent events to issue the same order with regard to a no less dangerous sect, indeed one which represents a higher form of Carbonari, called 'Young Italy'. The aim of this society is the overthrow of existing governments and of the complete social order; the means which it employs are subversion and outright murder through secret agents.

It goes without saying, therefore, that anyone who knows of these aims, but who nonetheless joins 'Young Italy' is guilty of high treason. He is also guilty even if, given that he knows its aims, he merely fails to prevent its progress or to point out its members and, as guilty, is liable to punishment under Article 5 of the Articles of War. Likewise from the date of publication of this order, no one will be able to excuse himself by saying that he was a member of 'Young Italy' and yet was ignorant of its objectives. On the other hand, anyone who, out of remorse, reveals the members of the same, its statutes, the aims and undertakings of its leaders, if these are still secret or if their work can still be prevented, is assured complete immunity from punishment and his actions will remain secret.

Such a proclamation may have had some effect on the Italian troops, but it is highly unlikely that many had any dealings with Young Italy in any case. More important seemed to be the need to ensure that the troops were not subverted by revolutionary propaganda. Thus Frimont (Radetzky's predecessor as commander of the Austrian army in Italy) laid down that[60] 'should unrest break out in a neighbouring state the borders should be protected immediately by a chain of outposts in order to close communication between our own and insurgent territory and to do the utmost possible to prevent the spread of rebellion and proclamations'.[61] Radetzky could, therefore, write in 1847:[62] 'We have erected a so-called military cordon around the Canton Ticino' – although he doubted whether it would 'protect us from the propaganda directed against us by all sorts of incendiary pamphlets and emissaries'.

Propaganda, indeed, still managed to get through. Radetzky reported at the beginning of 1848 that troops of the infantry regiment Franz Ferdinand d'Este were being given printed and written slips of paper in the streets of Reggio designed to subvert his Hungarian troops. These slips read:[63] 'Hungarians! You passionately support the cause of your nationality; we Italians support ours. In this we are agreed and ought, therefore, to unite. But we ought to hate and to dispose of all obstacles in the way of our triumph.' According to the Field Marshal:[64] 'this exhortation as expected, made no impression on the troops'. Still, the revolutionaries had taken heart and in the period before 1848 were preparing lots of propaganda aimed at Austrian soldiers. One piece, for example, thousands of copies of which were distributed in Cracow in April 1848, was printed in Mainz on Christmas Day 1847. Entitled *The German Soldiers' Catechism*, it was designed to promote the cause of republicanism in Germany.[65] It took the form of a discussion between an N.C.O. and a private and ended on the following note:

N.C.O.: How do you describe a task, a fulfilment of duty, an act of goodness a glorious deed whereby a people liberates itself?

Soldier: It is called a revolution. Long live the German revolution!

N.C.O.: What do you call a free state such as we will establish once we have made our revolution, that is to say when the princes, along with their ministers diplomats, generals, bureaucrats, myrmidons and hangmen are chased out of the country?

Soldier: Such a state, without princes, courtiers, and torturers, is called a *Republic*. Will there be a German Republic?

The officer standing near by listening to the soldier says to him: 'Comrade, give me your hand. You will be reinstated with distinction into the first class and when the day of revolution and revenge arrives, we will fight together.'

By the beginning of 1848, therefore, the pot was clearly on the boil. Revolutionary propaganda aimed at German, Italian and Hungarian troops had already been printed and it was designed not merely to promote the cause of republicanism but to do so by exploiting the nationality problem as it existed within the ranks.

The nationality problem in the Austrian army, 1815-1848[66]

The Habsburg Empire for the purpose of recruiting was divided into 79 districts from which the 58 infantry regiments, 18 border regiments and 1 (Tyrol) Jäger regiment drew their manpower. The remaining troops – cavalry, artillery and other corps – drew their recruits from the infantry recruiting districts to which they were assigned. An average recruiting district comprised 370,000–400,000 people in the German provinces and 450,000–580,000 people in the Italian ones. During the wars with the French, the Monarchy had raised as many as 750,000 men in a single fighting year (630,000 in 1809, despite loss of territory) but in 1847 its prescribed peacetime force (never fully reached, however) stood at around 400,000 men, made up of: 315,000 infantry; 49,000 cavalry; 24,000 artillery; 5,400 technical corps; 4,000 supply troops. Theoretically, at least, it was possible to raise the overall total in times of war by another 400,000 men by conscripting the 70 Landwehr battalions and the Hungarian *Insurrectio*. Thus in 1847, Metternich could boast of a paper army of 800,000 men, although one French authority writing in 1846 had put the Austrian potential total at only 622,408. In fact, for most of the period 1815–48 Metternich could count on only 270,000–330,000 troops and he preferred not to rely on them at all.

For administrative purposes the army was divided into 12 general commands (each reporting to the Hofkriegsrath) and centred on Agram (Croatia) Brünn, (Moravia/Silesia), Graz (Styria, Illyria and Tyrol), Hermannstadt (Transylvania), Lemberg (Galicia), Ofen (Hungary), Peterwardein (Slavonia and its military borders), Prag (Bohemia), Temesvar (the Banat), Verona (Lombardy-Venetia), Vienna (Upper and Lower Austria) and Zara (Dalmatia). In all there were (in 1847) 294 battalions, 268 squadrons, 56 batteries (spread out) and 121 companies of artillery plus technical troops to administer. For operational and tactical leadership, the troops were divided into 40 divisions or 91 brigades of suitably varying strengths and composition. There were only two corps – both part of the army in northern Italy. Taken by branch the army consisted of:

Infantry

58	Infantry regiments of the line (numbered 1–63)
20	Grenadier battalions
18	Grenzer or Border regiments
1	Tyrolese Jäger regiment
12	Jäger battalions
6	Garrison battalions

Cavalry

8	Cuirassier regiments
6	Dragoon regiments
7	Chevaux-légers regiments
12	Hussar regiments
4	Uhlan regiments

Artillery

5	Field artillery regiments and garrison artillery and others

In addition to these branches there were 'technical' corps (miners, sappers, pioneers), 'extra' corps (frontier guards, invalid corps) and guards (life guards, crown-watch).

The recruiting system makes it possible, of course, to break down most of the army in terms of nationality. Thus of the 58 infantry regiments of the line, there were:

2	regts (nos. 4 and 49) from Lower Austria
2	regts (nos. 14 and 59) from Upper Austria
5	regts (nos. 27, 47, 17, 7 and 22) from Inner Austria and Illyria
8	regts (nos. 11, 18, 21, 25, 28, 35, 36, 42) from Bohemia
5	regts (nos. 1, 3, 8, 29, 54) from Moravia/Silesia
13	regts (nos. 9, 10, 12, 15, 20, 24, 30, 40, 41, 56, 57, 58, 63) from Galicia
4	regts (nos. 13, 16, 26, 45) from Venetia
4	regts (nos. 23, 38, 43, 44) from Lombardy
12	regts (nos. 2, 19, 32, 33, 34, 37, 39, 48, 52, 53, 60, 61) from Hungary
3	regts (nos. 31, 51, 62) from Transylvania

Of the 18 grenadier battalions, 13 were 'German' (i.e. from provinces other than Hungary, Transylvania or Illyria) and 5 were Hungarian.

Among the cavalry, the curassiers consisted of:

4	regts from Bohemia (nos. 1, 2, 7 and 8)
1	regt from Moravia (no. 6)
2	regts from Upper Austria (nos. 3 and 4)
1	regt from Inner Austria (no. 5)

The dragoons consisted of:

1	regt from Bohemia (no. 5)
1	regt from Moravia (no. 6)
1	regt from Upper and Lower Austria (no. 2)
1	regt from Inner Austria (no. 2)
2	regts from Galicia (nos. 1 and 3)

The chevaux-léger consisted of:

1	regt from Upper and Lower Austria (no. 1)
3	regts from Bohemia (nos. 2, 4 and 5)
2	regts from Galicia (nos. 3 and 7)
1	regt from Lombardy-Venetia (no. 6)

The 12 hussar regiments were recruited in Hungary
The 4 Uhlan regiments were recruited in Galicia

Of the 5 field artillery regiments:

2	regts came from Bohemia (nos. 1 and 5)
1	regt came from Lower Austria (no. 2)
1	regt came from Moravia (no. 3)
1	regt came from Inner Austria (no. 4)

The Borderers (or Grenzer) consisted of troops of South Slav, Szekler and Romanian stock whose families inhabited the Military Borders around Hungary. Their institutions and problems will be discussed briefly in Chapter 3. For the present it is only necessary to record that they were administered by the Karlstadt, Banal, Warasdin, Banat and Transylvanian general commands which were responsible for the following regiments:

The Karlstadt General Command supervised the:

(1)	Liccan Regiment	
(2)	Ottochan Regiment	South Slavs
(3)	Ogulin Regiment and	
(4)	Szluin Regiment	

The Banal General Command supervised the:

(5)	1st Banal Regiment and the	South Slavs
(6)	2nd Banal Regiment	

The Warasdin General Command supervised the:

(7)	St George Regiment	
(8)	Kreuz Regiment	
(9)	Gradiskan Regiment	South Slavs
(10)	Brod Regiment	
(11)	Peterwardein Regiment	

The Banat General Command supervised the:

(12)	German-Banat Regiment – Germans/South Slavs
(13)	Wallachian-Illyrian Regiment – Romanians/South Slavs
(14)	Illyrian-Banat Regiment – South Slavs

The Transylvanian Command supervised the:

(15)	1st Szekler Regiment – Hungarians
(16)	2nd Szekler Regiment – Hungarians
(17)	1st Wallachian Regiment – Romanians
(18)	2nd Wallachian Regiment – Romanians

Of the 70 Landwehr battalions:

16	were provided by Bohemia
10	were provided by Moravia and Silesia
8	were provided by Upper and Lower Austria (including Salzburg)
10	were provided by Illyria and the Küstenland
26	were provided by Galicia

Neither the Hungarians nor the Italians had a Landwehr.

Of the 12 Jäger battalions:

3	(nos. 1, 2 and 6) came from Bohemia
2	(nos. 4 and 5) came from Moravia
1	(no. 12) came from Galicia
2	(nos. 8 and 11) came from Lombardy-Venetia
4	(nos. 3, 7, 9 and 10) came from Austria

These figures, when taken together, show that the following regiments were provided:

Bohemia	8 Infantry	8 cavalry	2 artillery
Moravia/Silesia	5 Infantry	2 cavalry	1 artillery
Galicia	13 Infantry	8 cavalry	0 artillery
Lombardy-Venetia	8 Infantry	1 cavalry	0 artillery
Hungary	12 Infantry	12 cavalry	0 artillery
Transylvania	3 Infantry	0 cavalry	0 artillery
Austria	9 Infantry	7 cavalry	2 artillery

Taking the Jäger and Grenzer regiments into account it can be established that in 1847 out of a peacetime army of 339,574 (i.e. not including the grenadiers, technical and extra corps) the following men were provided:

Bohemia	47,544	14.1	total %*
Moravia/Silesia	24,930	7.4	total %*
Galicia	55,540	16.5	total %*
Lombardy-Venetia	30,100	8.7	total %*
Hungary	76,179	22.6	total %*
Transylvania	18,507	5.4	total %*
Austria (Upper, Lower and Inner)	55,546	16.1	total %*
South Slavs	31,228	9.2	total %*

*To nearest one-tenth per cent.

If it is remembered that by no means all recruits in the Hungarian regiments were Hungarian and that many other recruiting areas gave less than a pure national or racial quota, it can be calculated from these figures that Austria's peacetime army consisted (very approximately) of:

21.5%	Czechs (although this figure must' include many Germans)
16.5%	Poles
8.7%	Italians
22.6%	Hungarians (although this figure must include many Slavs)
5.4%	Romanians (the Szeklers have been included in the Hungarian figure)
16.1%	Austrian Germans
9.2%	South Slavs (mainly Croats)

The Slavs as a whole must have constituted more than 50 per cent of the army in peacetime. In times of war, given that the Italians provided no Landwehr and that the size of the *Insurrectio* (however unpredictable) was less than the extra contribution provided by the Slavs, it can once again be taken that the majority of troops were Slavs.

All these figures have a special significance for they allow us to decide whether the Habsburgs had any systematic policy of 'divide and rule'. In other words, they can be used to cast light on the famous remarks attributed to Francis I, namely:[67] 'My peoples are strange to each other and that is all right. They do not get the same sickness at the same time. I send the Hungarians into Italy, the Italians into Hungary. Every people watches its neighbour. The one does not understand the other and one hates the other. . . . From their antipathy will be born order and from the mutual hatred general peace. . . .'

How ruthlessly in fact was a policy of divide and rule employed to deal with manifestations of nationalism before 1848? To what extent did it have to be resorted to in military matters anyway? In what respect did nationalism during this period pose any kind of threat to the military establishment? Professor Rothenberg has written in this regard:[68]

Especially in Hungary there was continual agitation for a national army. As early as 1790 the Hungarian Diet demanded the establishment of a national force commanded by Magyar officers and such ideas also played a role in the program of the Hungarian Jacobins. In 1808 the Diet repeated its demands and requested that Hungarian recruits serve only in national units and under Hungarian officers. Similar claims were made during the sessions of 1832–36 and again in 1840. While the national aspirations of the Magyars were the most articulate, national problems also appeared in other army contingents. In the regiments raised in Bohemia there was friction between the Germans and the Czechs. The high command was aware that the Italian formations were disaffected and had doubts about the allegiance of the Poles. Even the traditionally loyal South Slav *Grenzer* of the Military Border were restive, though the Hofkriegsrath was convinced that, especially in the case of trouble in Hungary they would not hesitate to do their duty.

According to Professor Rothenberg,[69]

to counteract national influences, the government in Vienna adopted the policy of stationing troops in areas where they would not be affected by local grievances. Thus late in 1847, of the thirty-five so called 'German' infantry regiments in Cisleithania six were stationed in Italy and four in Hungary; while of the fifteen Hungarian regiments, six were located in Italy, four in Hungary and the remainder in Inner Austria, Upper Austria and Bohemia. As for the twenty-five Cisleithanian cavalry regiments, thirteen were garrisoned in Hungary; while of the twelve exclusively Hungarian hussar regiments, only six remained in the country.

Professor Rothenberg's figures, however, should be treated cautiously, in the first place because although he claims to have compiled them from the *Militär-Schematismus des österreichischen Kaiserthums* for 1847 it seems, in fact, that he has taken them from a couple of articles written by the Austrian military historian Rudolf Kiszling;[70] secondly, and unfortunately, it would appear that Kiszling has got his figures wrong. This, at any rate is the only conclusion which can be drawn from an article published by Dr Aladar Urban on 'The Austrian military organisation in Hungary and the troops stationed in our country in April 1848'.[71] Dr Urban clearly shares Professor Rothenberg's belief that the Habsburgs had a system of divide and rule, but gives a different set of figures. Thus he writes:

The Hungarian cavalry and infantry regiments, in the spirit of the above-mentioned practice, were dislocated, naturally mainly in foreign provinces, far from their homeland. Thus at the beginning of 1848 out of 45 battalions of the 15 Hungarian and Transylvanian infantry regiments only 24 were garrisoned inside the country; of the five Grenadier Battalions, however, only two were stationed at home. The position of the Hussar regiments were similar: of the 12 regiments only four were in Hungary and annexed lands or were garrisoned in Transylvanian territory. On the other hand, 16 battalions of seven foreign infantry regiments, besides 12 cavalry regiments were stationed in Hungary and Croatia and Transylvania. That is, nearly half of the foreign cavalry regiments were stationed in our homeland and the number of foreign infantry was comparatively large.

Unlike Professor Rothenberg, Dr Urban has consulted the Hungarian archives to arrive at his conclusions; however, his figures should also be treated with caution, their value being seriously undermined by Dr Urban's working definition of 'our country'. Since this seems to be Greater Hungary (i.e. Hungary plus Transylvania plus Croatia-Slavonia plus perhaps the Military Border) it is difficult to know which troops are 'foreign' and which are not. Thus the historian has to go back to his sources and ask first how many troops in Italy in 1848 were Italian and how many troops in Hungary were Hungarian. The answers are surprising.

Radetzky in January 1848 commanded an army of between 70,000 and 75,000 men, made up of 61 infantry battalions, 36 cavalry squadrons and 108 batteries.[72] Since there were no Italian cavalry or artillerymen his Italian troops were all infantrymen. In fact, they comprised the largest contingent of infantry he had. Thus of his 61 infantry battalions, 9 were Hungarian, 6 were Czech, 24 were Italian, 10 were South Slavs and 12 were Austrian. Or in other words, the Italians were by far the largest nationality included in the Austrian army in Italy. They represented 39 per cent of Radetzky's infantry and about 33 per cent of his army as a whole. Since the Italians generally provided only 8.6 per cent of the troops in the imperial army, it could almost be argued, therefore, that there was a deliberate policy of giving national homelands a much larger than proportionate share of their native troops – hardly a policy of divide and rule.

What then was the situation in Hungary? From a letter to the Commanding General in Hungary in 1848 we discover that the Austrian War Minister, Count Latour, estimated the troop strength of the imperial army in Hungary in April 1848 at 24 battalions of infantry, 62 squadrons of cavalry and 11 companies of artillery.[73] Of the 24 battalions of infantry no less than 16 were Hungarian, 4 were Italian and 4 were Polish. Thus the Hungarians themselves supplied 68 per cent of the infantry stationed in Hungary. The cavalry, on the other hand, was primarily non-Hungarian – only 8 out of 62 squadrons were Magyars. Overall, however, the Hungarians represented some 14,000 out of the 31,673 troops in their country – that is to say, 43 per cent. Thus, given that Hungary generally provided only 22.6 per cent of the imperial troops, it could once again be argued that there was evidence of a deliberate policy to station greater than proportionate numbers of troops in their homelands. Was there, therefore, a deliberate policy of divide and rule or not? The whole question is made even more complex by von Fenneberg's assertion that:[74] 'the majority of Hungarian regiments [consisted] of Slavs and Germans and since Hungary itself [contained] only two and a half million Magyars the number of genuinely Hungarian soldiers [was] very limited'. He adds, however, that in those regiments where there were Slav, German and Hungarian troops 'all these various nationalities [got] on very well together and there [was] more unity there than one would [have expected]'.

It should be remembered in the context of divide and rule that there were other ways in which the Habsburgs could have operated such a policy. For example only the Germans and Czechs (Bohemia–Moravia–Silesia) had the necessary mixture of forces to create complete armies of their own – The Poles, Hungarians and Italians had no artillery, the Italians had practically no cavalry and the Grenzer had no cavalry either. However, there are a number of reasons to suspect that no cunning was involved here. For a start the Poles and Hungarians could very easily have acquired artillery, and the Italians could also have acquired more cavalry. Moreover, the real reasons why certain areas provided mainly particular kinds of troops were historical and geographical. The Grenzer had survived the Turkish Wars as military colonists defending the border against the Turks. Hungary and Galicia provided so much cavalry because of the geographical factor of the Hungarian and Galician plains – for it would have been futile to attempt to recruit or train cavalry regiments in the Tyrol.

It might also be suggested that the real way to divide and rule would have been to station huge numbers of troops in the least reliable provinces. Dr Urban in his article hints at something like this when he writes:[75]

According to the report of 16 February (1848) there were . . . in the country 12 companies of grenadiers, 130 companies of infantry and 72 squadrons of cavalry as well as five garrison companies and 11 artillery companies along with four transport companies. Numerically that is about 20,000 infantry, 12,500 cavalry, about 2,000 artillery and artillery transports. That is to say, *altogether* this force may have amounted to about 35,000 men. Moreover (not counting the border regiments) there were about 4,000 men under the Banat general command as well as about 5,000 regular troops in the area under the Slavonian general command. The strength of imperial troops stationed at home and in the annexed territories (not including the border regiments) was 44-45,000 men – not counting, of course, the troops then stationed in the, at that time, foreign land of Transylvania. Thus about one-tenth of the military strength of the Austrian Empire was stationed in the territory of Hungary (the area being reckoned from an *administrative* viewpoint).

Once again, however, these figures should be put into perspective and the following table does this. Taken from a book published in 1846[76] it shows the numbers of troops dislocated in various parts of the Monarchy 'in peacetime'. The ratio of civilians to military has been added in the last column.

From these figures it will very readily be seen that Hungary and Transylvania had proportionately very few troops stationed on them and that Lombardy-Venetia was in no way badly off – in fact, in view of its strategic importance it was relatively well off. Both Hungary and Lombardy-Venetia were also well off in another sense: per million inhabitants the former provided 6,333 troops and the latter 5,367. The figures for Austria, Galicia and Bohemia–Moravia–Silesia were 11,715, 11,458 and 16,744 respectively. Thus the question must again be posed: did the Habsburgs really have any deliberately worked-out policy of divide and rule as far as their armed forces were concerned?

Province	(a) Population minus military	(b) Military	Ratio (a)/(b)
Lower Austria	1,375,400	34,226	40.19
Upper Austria	844,914	12,652	66.78
Steiermark	966,863	18,466	54.72
Carinthia and Carniola	757,395	2,146	352.93
Küstenland	477,702	3,487	137.00
Tyrol	830,948	8,807	94.36
Bohemia	4,112,085	62,083	66.24
Moravia and Silesia	2,162,086	4,552	474.97
Galicia	4,718,991	78,252	60.31
Dalmatia	384,572	9,456	40.67
Lombardy	2,516,420	31,556	79.74
Venetia	2,137,608	30,945	69.08
Hungary	12,039,400	56,802	211.96
Transylvania	2,069,600	9,400	220.17
Military Border	1,147,283	56,322	20.37

One aspect of their policy is indisputable, namely the tradition of moving all regiments around the Monarchy. This may have been a deliberate or Machiavellian policy, but more likely it was a historic practice designed to keep the army an integrated whole. It cannot be denied, however, that the practice stemmed from the viewpoint that the troops were imperial and not national ones. But how systematically employed was this device? Here, for example, is the 'dislocation' record of one Italian infantry regiment (the 38th) between 1830 and 1848:[77]

1830 – Brescia	1838 – Cremona
1831 – Ancona–Cremona	1839 – Ragusa
1832 – Brescia	1841 – Fiume
1833 – Cremona	1843 – Udine
1834 – Mantua	1846 – Vicenza–Padua
1837 – Verona	1847 – Mantua–Legnano

Clearly, therefore, it did not travel far.
Here is the record of another (the 45th):

1830 – Fiume	1843 – Padua
1835 – Zara	1846 – Treviso
1839 – Udine–Mantua	1847 – Verona
1840 – Verona	1848 – Bergamo
1842 – Vicenza	

The 2nd Infantry Regiment (which was Hungarian), spent the entire period 1830–48 at Pressburg. The 37th Infantry Regiment (again Hungarian) spent the entire period at Lemberg. Of the cavalry regiments, the 1st Cuirassiers spent the entire period 1819–48 at Brandeis, the 2nd Cuirassiers spent the period 1832–48 at Lancut, while the 3rd Hussars spent the years 1832–48 as follows: 1832 – Kecskemet; 1836 – Gyöngös; 1842-8 – Saros-Patok. Thus, although most regiments moved around a variety of Habsburg possessions every few years, it is difficult to conclude that the Hofkriegsrath had worked out any highly sophisticated or diabolical system. Those who believe otherwise would have to show why so many troops were at the wrong place at the wrong time and why many of them had been there so long. One has to conclude rather that the Habsburgs had no nationality policy regarding their army other than moving most of it about from time to time and having German as the language of command for an officer corps which was predominantly German-speaking anyway.

Was there, therefore, any real 'nationality problem' inside the Austrian army in the Vormärz period? The military authorities clearly did not think so, for even in 1847/8 – before the revolutions broke out – Radetzky showed little concern about the loyalty of his Italian troops (he regularly lauded them) and did not even seem worried about the Italian sailors in Venice. In like fashion, despite political agitation in Hungary, there was no concern about the loyalty of the Hungarian troops. Indeed the archives are conspicuously empty of material on the problem – either in the form of requests to tighten up the movements of national troops or in the form of references of any kind to the mechanics of any 'system' of dislocation. Hartig's comments to Metternich regarding a possible threat to the loyalty of the Italian troops (see pp. 42–3) are significant because they are exceptional.

There were, however, two problems regarding nationality apparent within the ranks. First, the troops did not like moving around from place to place since this meant that they often had to break recently-formed personal ties and learn to live in foreign societies. This, in turn, could often lead to desertions as von Fenneberg recorded:[78] 'Most often it occurred in the Italian and Hungarian regiments where frequent desertions took place if a regiment which had been stationed in some or other garrison for 10–12 years was suddenly ordered to some far removed station.' Desertions took place, for example, in 1840 when the 48th Infantry Regiment was transferred from Bregenz to Agram. One factor motivating the deserters was that they would have had to leave their illegitimate children and common-law wives behind if they had chosen to obey orders – and apparently they had fathered no less than 300–400 children! The troops also resented having officers who could not speak other languages. Von Fenneberg described how even German-speaking soldiers could often not understand the 'posh' speech of their officers, but the situation was worse in the non-German regiments: 'One of the greatest obstacles to the speedy training of Slav soldiers [was] the noteworthy circumstance that most company officers [did] not understand any of the languages of the men.' In fact, in the non-German regiments, the N.C.Os had to act as interpreters.

The percentage of German officers in the Austrian army is difficult to calculate. Kiszling puts it at about 68 per cent. Von Fenneberg reckoned that among the Slav regiments eleven-twelfths of the officer corps were Germans or foreigners and only one-eleventh of these could understand the speech of their troops. He put the fraction of Hungarian officers in the Hungarian regiments at 'scarcely one-tenth' and wrote that they alone could understand Hungarian. Many regiments in fact had officers of a variety of nationalities. Von Fenneberg himself served in one in which 'England, France, Sweden, Denmark, Russia and the Papal State were all represented'. It was the Italian regiments, however, which supposedly had the smallest number of native officers: 'the Italian noble does not like to serve under German leadership and the few individuals of this class who serve in the Austrian army are not looked on favourably by their compatriots'. Even the Italian troops did not like them since they had the reputation of favouring non-Italian soldiers to prove their loyalty. In fact, it was commonly held that German-speaking soldiers were always promoted more quickly since these were the only troops the officers could depend on to communicate orders. For the officer himself had no incentive to learn languages other than German: it was not required of them to know the regimental tongue; many of those who took the trouble to do so discovered that their men spoke such peculiar dialects that there was still a communications gap between them; while it was often the case that commanding officers resented those with linguistic qualifications better than their own and, therefore, refused to promote them. The language problem, as a result, was a very serious one.

There is evidence to suggest, however, that although bad, it was better than von Fenneberg maintained. It is impossible to tell from the *Militär-Schematismus* of any particular year to which nationality any given officer belonged; nonetheless, by looking at names one can guess quite a lot. Thus it would appear that in some regiments the situation was not as bad as von Fenneberg implies. Among the Grenzer, for example, about 90 per cent of the officers were South Slav, but even if they were exceptions, the following figures demonstrate that in Italian and Hungarian regiments the situation varied. Thus, among the officers of the 45th infantry regiment in 1847

of	14 captains	5 had Italian names
of	5 lieutenant-captains	1 had an Italian name
of	20 first lieutenants	6 had Italian names
of	39 second lieutenants	12 had Italian names
of	37 cadets	18 had Italian names

i.e. of 115 officers and cadets, 42, or 36.5 per cent, had Italian names.

Similar analyses of other Italian regiments indicate that:

of the	23rd	Infantry Regiment	30%	had Italian names
of the	38th	Infantry Regiment	42%	had Italian names
of the	44th	Infantry Regiment	24%	had Italian names
of the	16th	Infantry Regiment	32%	had Italian names
of the	26th	Infantry Regiment	17%	had Italian names

It may be reckoned, therefore, that although Italian officers were usually in a minority in Italian regiments – and often in a distinct minority – they sometimes, on the other hand, formed one-quarter or one-third or even more, of the officer corps of these regiments.

What of the Hungarians? The equivalent figures for a number of infantry and cavalry regiments are as follows:

of the	53rd	Infantry Regiment	12.00%	had Hungarian names
of the	62nd	Infantry Regiment	21.00%	had Hungarian names
of the	52nd	Infantry Regiment	15.00%	had Hungarian names
of the	48th	Infantry Regiment	12.50%	had Hungarian names
of the	3rd	Hussars	57.00%	had Hungarian names
of the	12th	Hussars	56.00%	had Hungarian names
of the	9th	Hussars	41.00%	had Hungarian names
of the	7th	Hussars	33.34%	had Hungarian names

It would seem, therefore, that in the Hungarian infantry regiments only one-eighth to one-fifth of the officers were Hungarian, whereas in the cavalry regiments between one-third and one-half of the officers were Hungarian. Von Fenneberg was, of course, describing the infantry regiments in his description of the nationality problem. But although his figures concerning native officers as a percentage of the officer corps of different regiments seem rather on the pessimistic side, it should be remembered that on any assessment the number of native officers in infantry regiments was very low indeed. Three-quarters or two-thirds of the officers in Italian regiments were foreigners; four-fifths or seven-eighths in the Hungarian regiments. Thus, von Fenneberg's main point – that there was little understanding between officers and men – still holds.

What of the men themselves? Von Fenneberg has already been quoted to the effect that within the Hungarian regiments a surprising degree of harmony existed among the regimental nationalities. On the other hand, he maintains that this was not the case in the Bohemian regiments. There the differences between the troops were mainly differences between Czechs and Germans and the former resented what was held to be the relatively quicker promotion of the latter. This in turn led to 'bloody fights' between them which did 'not bear thinking about'.[79] In fact,[80] 'in Vienna such bloody incidents occurred so often in the years 1838–39 that the city command assigned the regiments concerned to certain districts so that they would not meet while off duty'. The nationality problem, therefore, was at heart a German one. The nationalities resented being officered by German-speaking foreigners and seeing German troops promoted more quickly than anyone else.

Chapter 3

Revolution, propaganda and desertion: Radetzky's army during 1848–1849 and the problem of cohesion

The Italian troops

It has already been pointed out that on the eve of revolution one-third of Radetzky's army consisted of Italian troops; they represented, in fact, the largest single national group within his forces. 'But almost up to the very commencement of the revolution', Hartig recorded,[1]*

their loyalty had not only not been doubted, but every allusion to such doubts – which are said not to have been wanting in the cabinet[2] – was looked upon as a violation of military honour. This prejudice was so extensively prevalent that even in the month of February when martial law against high treason and rebellion was proclaimed in the Lombardo-Venetian kingdom and the military was made subject to it, this latter circumstance was even in the highest circles of Vienna looked upon with displeasure as an attack upon the honour of the soldier, although the Field Marshal himself had consented to the measure.

Radetzky himself regularly praised the morale of his Italian soldiers, and at the height of the Tobacco Riots in January 1848 (see Part III) reported to Count Hardegg at the Hofkriegsrath,[3] 'Your Excellency can imagine the bitterness among the troops but I am satisfied with their spirit, particularly the Italians.' The nearest he ever came to doubting their loyalty was in a report – again to Hardegg – of December 1847, in which he wrote:[4]

I ask you also to consider that a great part of my troops consist of Italian regiments; I do not mistrust these troops in the least; they will do their duty; but we must not expect more of them than is reasonable, particularly when they are being led into battle against their own compatriots. There can be no doubt that these troops will be subject to all kinds of influences and will be enticed to desert; if the luck of war goes against us in the first battle, then I shall not answer for their loyalty; such an experience would not even be surprising; it is as old as history itself.

As every schoolboy knows, of course, Radetzky lost his first battle and after five days of fighting (18–22 March) the Austrians were forced to retreat from Milan and take refuge in the Quadrilateral. While they waited there for reinforcements the Field Marshal received the news that his Italian troops had been disloyal. A report from the Lombardo-Venetian general command in Verona dated 27 March ran:[5] 'The Italian troops are deserting the colours of His Majesty. The 3rd Battalion Wimpffen, the Grenadier Battalion

---

* Notes to this chapter are on pp. 255–7.

Angelmayer, the 3rd Battalion Zanini and 4 companies of the 8th Jäger Battalion have already deserted. One cannot speak of the Italian troops in Lombardy because all communication is cut.' However, FML. Welden, the commander of the Austrian forces in the Tyrol, received word from Vienna only a few days later that[6] 'the Italian regiments and battalions [had] *all* supported the revolution and save for a few isolated groups [had] deserted.' He himself replied that this[7] 'was no longer a secret'. That very day, in fact, he had already written to Count Lichnowsky, the Governor of Vorarlberg informing him[8] of 'the effects which the defection of all the Italian regiments in the army must have even on the troops located here'. His position in the Tyrol, as will be seen, was by no means an enviable one.

Is it possible to estimate how many Italian troops had really deserted? Radetzky sent in a report on 5 April[9] according to which he had lost 17 battalions, 2 squadrons and 1 battery of soldiers. Not all had been disloyal – some had simply been cut off, while others had been shipped to Trieste under the terms of the capitulation of Venice. In fact he still had 10,000 Italian troops under his command. On 27 April he wrote to his daughter that[10] he had 'lost 10,860 men through desertion as well as 13,000 who [had been] cut off from the army'. Apart from that, his losses consisted of 306 dead and 700 wounded troops, 6 dead and 18 wounded officers, and '2 officers who have been shown to have deserted'. These figures also show, that about 10,000 Italian troops and most Italian officers had remained 'loyal'. On the other hand, the Italian troops could no longer be trusted and the Field Marshal described them to his daughter[11] as 'a great nuisance and embarrassment', having already explained what he meant by this in a report to the War Minister dated 4 April.[12] 'The greatest drawback under the present circumstances', he had written,

are the remaining Italian troops. They consist of 10 Battalions. But where are they to be deployed? In the first line? There they could cross over, use their weapons against us and form a gap in the line of battle which would have to be dangerous. In reserve they threaten my rear; to keep them in the fortresses would be even more dangerous since they could then deliver them to the enemy. The only thing left is to divide them up in such a way that only partial and gradual defections can result; in the worst circumstances I would disarm and dissolve them.

Whether the Field Marshal divided up his Italian troops in the manner he described or not, we cannot say; but the 'partial and gradual defections' certainly took place. In a despatch of 12 May he ended with the words,[13] 'Finally I must report that a not insignificant desertion has taken place amongst the Italian troops. There is also a very ambiguous attitude apparent amongst the Italian Grenadier Battalion d'Anthon.' It would seem, therefore, that many, although not all of the Italian troops who got the chance, deserted.

The official history of the campaign sheds no more light on the numbers involved than do the Field Marshal's reports. On the other hand, von Wrede's *Geschichte der k.u.k. Wehrmacht* is much more illuminating and it would seem from the compressed regimental histories it contains that, of the eight Italian infantry regiments, the three which remained loyal in Italy were the 38th, the 43rd and the 45th. The 38th in fact was 'repeatedly praised' for its loyalty by Radetzky and D'Aspre and took part in much of the fighting, distinguishing itself at St Lucia and Vincenza. It participated in the recapture of Milan and the Siege of Venice and fought against Garibaldi. The 43rd and 45th regiments also fought with loyalty. Interestingly, and probably significantly, all of these regiments had spent most of the period 1830–48 in Italy.

Why then did so many Italian troops desert? To try to answer this question it is instructive to examine Welden's position in the Tyrol. He was the man who had to guard Radetzky's lines of communication with Vienna, but he was in the unfortunate position of having to rely mainly on an infantry regiment, the Archduke Ferdinand d'Este, which was not only an Italian one but one which suffered from lack of discipline. A report to General Nugent dated 13 February 1848 makes it clear that the regiment was causing problems even before the revolution broke out.[14] Welden had been asked to submit the report on the 'present state of order, morality and discipline prevailing in [the] regiment' in light of its previous involvement in a 'break-down of public security in Innsbruck' and had replied by revealing how out of hand had become the Austrian practice of recruiting the army from the gaols. In 1846, apparently, the army had ordered that the regiment should no longer accept 'the delivery of criminals directly from the penitentiary' since investigations had shown that its 12 companies already contained 284 'partly very dangerous criminals' who exercised a bad influence on their comrades. This had been done, but although in the period since then about 100 of the trouble-makers had completed their enlistment, 25 more 'real criminals' and '40 "released *ab in stantia*" ', that is to say 65 more criminals in all had been recruited before the order had been received. Consequently, there were in 1848 still 269 'depraved people' in the regiment, '20–25 of them in each company'. Moreover, their 'evil influence' was still being manifested in that since 1 January 1848 the regimental court had dealt with '18 cases of theft by forcible entry, 3 cases of robbery with attempted murder, as well as 3 cases of theft and 2 of robbery which could not be proven'.

Welden, on the other hand, did not seem particularly disturbed by these problems. In the first place it was a 'fact that among such a large number of the most hardened criminals, the company, battalion and regimental punishments were almost two-thirds less than in the Tyrolese Jäger regiment which [was] supposed to be composed only of selected troops and which could hand over its worst criminals to other regiments'. In the second place, despite the fact that there were 'detachments stationed on the Bavarian and Swiss borders' not a 'single man' in these detachments had deserted and, in fact, the 'number of desertions' in the regiment as a whole was 'very small', something which Welden attributed to the men being stationed in the countryside. There they were divided into small units – singly detached companies – and locked up in barracks at night 'on account of their dangerousness'; they were also spared the temptations of the large cities, and so did not get into trouble. Welden, in fact, believed that it was 'always good to keep these troops . . . in not too large bodies and mixed with others' and along with his report submitted proposals for the further distribution of the troops in the Tyrol. Thus, before March 1848, he did not worry much about his men. They might not be angels but at least they were 'loyal'.

With the outbreak of revolution, however, his situation became a desperate one. Indeed, by 4 April he was writing of 'the total helplessness of [his] position'.[15] The problem was that his main military force still consisted of two battalions of the Este Regiment, but since they[16] 'could not under any circumstances be used against Italy' they were, now,[17] 'totally unreliable'. Yet there were no alternative resources available and Welden could see no possible way of remedying his situation. He, therefore, lapsed into a mood of dark despair:[18] 'I cannot tolerate 2,400 men in my midst whom I cannot trust, and if nothing else helps, to save weapons and clothes, I will send them home – I cannot have them decimated, which I would prefer to do, since I have only 400 Hungarian troops here.' Once again, the dislocation 'system' seems to have worked very badly.

Welden was particularly bitter since his memoranda advocating a militia for the area (the Tyrol) had been consistently ignored by Vienna:[19] 'Thirty-three years have elapsed and there is still no military organisation in the province which, in places is completely unarmed.' Nor was the spirit of the population encouraging:[20] 'The inhabitants of the southern part being Italian, share the revolutionary spirit of the Italians; the rest have no good will for a government which they say has done nothing for them.' Welden told Radetzky:[21]

When they [the German-speaking Tyrolese] were asked recently to form defence committees for the province of Tyrol, their first question was 'How much per man per day?' and their first declaration was that they would only fight if the enemy was on their doorstep, since otherwise it was none of their business. No one will suffer military leadership and yet it is this province on which Your Excellency's army depends and through which runs like a thread the only road which connects yourself with the Monarchy.

The Archduke John, who for years had lived in the Tyrol, was instructed by the Emperor at the beginning of April to set up a provincial militia. While doing so he visited the area itself and personally issued proclamations supporting the imperial cause. But this still left the problem of the Este infantry. The Archduke[22] advised the government to withdraw them into 'inner Austria' and told the War Minister: 'Given the hostile attitude towards this regiment in the whole of the Tyrol there can be no place for it in my opinion either here in Innsbruck or in the countryside.' The best thing to do therefore was to redeploy it in the German provinces; meanwhile Este troops could 'not be left in any one garrison without other reliable troops'. But since Welden had hardly any other troops at his disposal, such a solution was hardly possible. His 400 Hungarians had only two bullets each (the real reason why he could not decimate the Italians). As commander he was, therefore, reduced to taking[23] 'bullets away from the Este infantry with the excuse of supplying the Schwarzenberg infantry' and replacing some troops of the Este infantry with troops from the Innsbruck barracks. After that, as he put it, he 'ran out of expedients'. The situation remained extremely precarious until Radetzky himself was forced to send Welden troops to secure his lines of communication.[24]

Desertions, meanwhile, had taken place among the Este troops and had done so on a significant scale. Fortunately, from the historian's point of view, it is possible from official reports, to know both how and why this occurred. In fact, the desertion reports illuminate how Radetzky lost so much of his army so quickly in 1848, particularly the report of a captain, Baron Aichelberg,[25] whose task it has been to lead a reserve transport of Este infantry from Udine to Innsbruck 'just two days after the Constitution had been proclaimed with all possible sensation'. He suggested that 'had the transport left Udine on the 16th of the month [March] as planned, instead of on the 18th perhaps the greatest part of the troops would have remained with the regiment'. But as it was they had to pass through northern Italy at a time when the flames of revolution 'were spreading like wildfire' reflecting the 'transformation which [had taken] place in the hearts and minds of the Italians'. Aichelberg describes the effect of this on his troops:

Daily, hourly almost, the Revolution won ground in all provinces which were denuded of troops and administered by weak or treasonous officials. In all the places through which the transport passed, the royal officials had been dismissed and had been replaced for the most part by the most enthusiastic supporters of the overthrow of the existing order. The priests displayed the worst attitude of all and placed themselves with incredible insolence at the head of the revolutionary movement. It was they who were most responsible for inciting and influencing the lowest classes, in particular the peasants. All symbols of imperial authority were destroyed and in their place was planted the tricolour Italian flag. In all places the men of the transport were received with shouts of 'Eviva gli italiani, Eviva l'Italia, l'indipendenza, Eviva Pio IX, etc.'. The richest people as well as the meanest monks were all wearing the Italian cockade. The men, as native sons, were everywhere given bread and wine and there were even inns where the men were given food and drink free. False, totally unfounded rumours calculated to upset people or to strike up enthusiasm in others, circulated from mouth to mouth – secret emissaries doggedly followed the transport and sought by all sorts of misrepresentation and even with money to undermine the spirit of the troops. In such circumstances the undersigned had to make his way with native sons through the provinces of Friaul, Treviso and Vicenza with only 1 officer and with N.C.Os all of whom were unknown to him.

It must have been extremely difficult for Italian soldiers to resist such pressures from their fellow countrymen. Most of them appeared to be united in a single cause; moreover, instead of discipline, they offered hospitality – free bread, free wine – and even money. The Austrians had lost all authority – there were no officials around and only two officers – and those other symbols of authority, the priests, were clearly committed to the revolution. The men were also influenced by emissaries. It is possible that they were inspired by nationalist propaganda, but on the whole it was their fears which seem to have exercised them: 'attempts were made to frighten them by telling them that they would be sent to Germany as hostages, that the time they served would be forfeited, that they would be killed in revenge for the German troops who had fallen in Italy'. These fears became more compelling the more closely they approached the Tyrol. Finally, when desertions took place (224 men out of 380) some troops may well have been forced by their comrades to follow suit.

At the beginning of June the regiment again suffered desertions – sixty-two men in all. This time the fear of being sent abroad was perhaps the key factor. An official report read:[26]

Subverted by emissaries, they had been given to believe that the battalion was being led to Hungary to die in unhealthy fortresses, etc. The soldiers believed that Judenburg was the destination appointed for them just as little as they believed that Görz had been their destination when they had set out from Bregenz – just as little, in fact, as they believed that they were heading for Innsbruck as they had been told when they left Arlberg. Similarly they did not believe they were being led to Salzburg once they had left Innsbruck.

Another factor on the side of the deserters was the force of numbers – about twenty troops, allegedly, were 'swept along' by their comrades. Finally, one officer, a Captain Bertini, had urged the troops to desert. The captain, however, did not waste his time on preaching nationalism. Aware no doubt of how the Este Regiment recruited its troops, he asked one soldier, 'Why will you not desert? Lack of money? There's always a way to get some. We'll rob the first post office we come across.'

Some of the deserters, it is true, were eventually captured. But the Austrian army had little idea of what to do about its Italian troops in the summer of 1848. Auditors (military legal officials) were brought in to deal with those who had been caught, but as for the rest of the men, the authorities were reduced to a mixture of exhortation, reassurance and threats.[27] They were exhorted to 'follow the example of the other Italian regiments (!) and not besmirch the honour of the regiment'; they were reassured that 'there was no question of them being sent to an unhealthy area in Hungary or some other fortress'; finally, they were told that if desertions continued the battalion would be 'placed under siege and if need be disarmed'.

One trouble was that the deserters were as well, if not better, informed than their officers as to what was happening in northern Italy. The example of the other regiments was only too well known to them. Thus Aichelberg, for example, had reported that his transport had entered Bassano 'at the very moment [when] the news arrived of the capitulation of Venice, of the proclamation of the Republic, of the retreat of the Second Army Corps, of the fall of Treviso and Padua, of the Piedmontese invasion of Lombardy, of the crossing-over of most of the Italian troops and of the crossing-over of the third battalion of the regiment itself'. Welden, meanwhile, who had heard that only twenty-two men had deserted, was prematurely boasting that this had[28] 'given proof that there were also Italians who knew how to uphold their oath and loyalty to their monarch'. The real truth only arrived with Aichelberg.

However, once Aichelberg arrived and the truth was known there was little that Welden could do. He requested the Hofkriegsrath to subtract one year from the 'capitulation' period of each loyal soldier in the regiment (i.e. he wanted them to serve seven instead of eight statutory years); he also put some money aside for hospitality for the loyal troops.[29] But all he could really do was to address the men personally and appeal for good behaviour. He did so with words which once again were a mixture of exhortation, reassurance and threats. He said:[30]

I give you my word of honour, never to lead you against your fellow countrymen. Therefore, resist every temptation put in your way by the many evil individuals in your midst and without. Seize these traitors and turn them over for speedy justice. Refrain from deserting your colours. This will be severely punished and in order that no misapprehension should remain, allow me to explain clearly to you that martial law is being declared throughout the land.

It was a relief, no doubt, to know that the officer corps had remained loyal – Captain Bertini had not yet made his move – and so Welden suggested to the Hofkriegsrath that the two oldest regimental captains be promoted staff-officers in other regiments. It is not known whether this suggestion was taken up, but certainly Radetzky would have looked upon it favourably. He, too, was pleased with the loyalty of the Italian officer corps – only two officers, he was to claim, had deserted – and on 16 April he had reassured the War Ministry that[31] 'the number of officers in relation to the troops [was] sufficient'. It was the N.C.Os who had deserted.

In the Este Regiment itself meanwhile, morale in the officer corps was sinking. Thus, when it became known in June that many of the deserters who had fled the regiment at the beginning of the month (including Captain Bertini and some N.C.Os) had been captured, the officers of the battalion petitioned their General Command[32] 'to bring the full force of the law to bear against' these people and to make 'a terrifying example' of them. Only in this way according to the officers did it 'still seem possible to restore regimental discipline' which had 'suffered so much on account of the mildness' which was being exercised, and only in this way too could 'respect for superiors be restored'. Indeed the morale of the officers had sunk so far that they 'officially and formally declared that after everything that [had] happened, it would seem impossible for them to remain' at their posts unless their demands were adopted. They wanted criminals dealt with speedily and a 'radical change in all ranks' made in order to 'restore spirits'. Finally, they requested 'that the troops be given the assurance from high quarters that there [was] no intention to march them to Hungary'. This belief, they said, had 'become a form of mental illness among the soldiers which had to be combated with every means since it was so [embedded in their minds]'. However, how soon and how far these demands were met one cannot say. As will be seen in Part III of this book, Radetzky's policy towards deserters was extremely mild. But it was presumably this protest by the officer corps of the battalion which *inter alia*, forced the Field Marshal to send otherwise badly needed troops to protect the Tyrol.

In the case of the Este Regiment, the evidence appears to suggest that fears of being sent abroad played a large part in causing soldiers to desert; but it is also clear that the general revolutionary atmosphere created a crisis of discipline. In other words, the restraints which normally prevented the Italian troops from abandoning their colours no longer applied. This revolutionary atmosphere in turn was the product of many influences: the cumulative force of events; the role of the priests; the rhetoric of the demagogues; the propaganda of the emissaries and the revolutionary party in general. To what extent these influences separately produced desertion, it is, of course, impossible to say, but it would be extremely remiss to ignore that part of the propaganda which was aimed directly at the armed forces. If one cannot assess its direct effect, one can at least explore the route by which it hoped to reach its objectives.[33]

A common form of anti-Austrian propaganda was the revolutionary catechism – a sequence of questions with answers, modelled on the teaching technique at that time most commonly used in churches and schools. Thus, early in 1848 the Hofkriegsrath was sent a copy of a catechism circulating among the troops directed at 'soldiers and citizens'.[34] It was designed to show Italian troops that they were Italian citizens and as such were expected to take up arms against the Austrians to achieve Italian unity. It also, curiously enough, insisted that this unity must be achieved by Italians alone – in other words it reflected the belief that *Italia farà da sè*. Thus, when in the usual pseudo-religious fashion it came to describe 'the articles of the creed' it asserted that there were five:

First, I believe firmly in the imminent, irrepressible regeneration of Italy. Second, I believe that Italy has in it all the elements necessary to raise itself to a lasting and powerful level of nationality. Third, I believe that unification and nationality must be a fount of riches, power and happiness for her children and that it is a condition *sine qua non* of the European equilibrium. Fourth, I believe in the apotheosis of all those who encounter suffering and death for the redemption of Italy. Fifth, lastly I believe that the Italians must, can and wish to do everything for themselves.

The question was then asked, 'Must we not trust in Italo-foreign intervention?' to which the answer was 'No! No! No!'

The catechism was very much a document of hate. The 'Germans' (Austrians) were to drown 'in their own blood'; Italians who fought with the Austrians were 'Cains'; those who betrayed Italians were 'Judases'; and both 'Cains' and 'Judases' would forfeit their lives and suffer 'eternal damnation'. Even those who simply did not 'believe in and profess the catechism' would suffer the fate to which 'Christ had condemned the unfruitful tree': they would be 'rooted up and thrown on the fire'. The final question was, 'And when shall we be able to call ourselves blessed in our nationality?' To which the answer ran, 'When we shall have drunk the blood of the Germans in the skulls of Metternich and Radetzky.' There were many 'national catechisms' of this kind.[35]

As a sort of mirror image to these were catechisms purportedly composed for use by Austrian troops.[36] These were written in a different fashion and were designed to remind Italian soldiers fighting for the Austrians that if they were fighting for pay, they did not receive very much of it. Thus the *Infamous Catechism of the Austrian Soldiers* dwelled at length on the hunger which Radetzky's troops were supposed to be experiencing. To the question, 'Where is your homeland?' therefore, the response was, 'Where we can eat.' And to the question, 'And if you are taken prisoner?' the reply was, 'If we become prisoners Carl Albert will give us bread.' Even the prospect of 'slaughter' was put in this perspective. The Austrian troops' reply to such a prospect was, 'If we are slaughtered we shall no longer be hungry.' However, the catechism also explained the Italian case – 'the kingdom of Lombardy-Venetia no longer wants the yoke' – and emphasised that there was no moral need for the troops to continue to obey their superiors: Radetzky was a 'rogue', Metternich was 'infamous'; while the Emperor, predictably, did not pay his troops and made them die of hunger.

Some of the propaganda circulating at the time was extremely funny. Satirical broadsheets with caricatures of Radetzky, Metternich and the Emperor were extremely common and often very ribald. One of these[37] gave an account of a *Dialogue between Radetzky and Satan* at the gates of hell whither the Field Marshal had gone to seek the Devil's advice. But even Satan had abandoned the Austrians and all he could offer Radetzky were 'the weapons of desperation'. When the latter asked what these were the Devil explained in a rather matter-of-fact sort of way, 'The weapons of desperation are to take to flight as quickly as one can, to jump down a well head-downwards, to blow one's brains out, etc., etc.' Another broadsheet described[38] 'Metternich's aid for Radetzky'. This was a particularly ribald piece which had Metternich arriving at the gates of Verona bringing aid for the besieged Field Marshal. When asked by the sentry what form of aid he had brought, the Prince replied that he had not brought bread but only the Field Marshal's chamber-pot. Radetzky, however, was overjoyed. 'Oh good, good, dear Metternich,' he was made to say, 'Your are my loyal friend. Now thanks to you I shall lack nothing but bread. A sword which is sheathed is no good. But having received this blessed chamber-pot from you, I can at least die content since I can get rid of the shit I have taken from these Italian pigs!' Finally, the Emperor himself was made the object of derision.[39] In a broadsheet entitled 'The Triumph of Charles Albert over Radetzky', for example, he was depicted as a fool who was deceived by Metternich and dominated by his wife. He tells Charles Albert who has him pinned beneath his feet: 'The infamous Metternich who ruined me has now been kicked out and my wife who used to boss me was not aware of his trickery. For pity's sake, forgive me, I will get a new minister and put things right.' Finally, the concessions he is forced to make are announced for him by Radetzky, who has failed in an attempt to disarm Charles Albert: 'I recognise your strength, Austria cannot resist it. My emperor shall concede your demands.'

Another form of propaganda was the type which was modelled more exactly on the teachings of the Church. This was particularly appropriate, no doubt, in so Catholic a country as Italy and may have been reckoned particularly effective. One of these was entitled the *Litany of the Lombard Pilgrims*[40] and had the chorus:

'Kyrie eleison
Christe eleison
Christe audi nos
Christe exaudi nos'

Each verse was prefaced with passionate appeals to Christ, the Virgin Mary, St Ambrosius, St Mark or Pope Pius IX. The final one began:

'We pray thee Lord of Armies, listen to us;
Lord of Glory, triumph with us;
God of Vengeance, help us grind our tyrants in the dust.'

It ended:

'In the name of the Father, the Son and the Holy Ghost,
Let it be.'

A similar piece was the *Pater Noster of the Lombards*[41] which after each line of the Lord's Prayer inserted an appropriate nationalist appeal. Thus it began:

'*Our Father who art in Heaven*
Have pity on our sorrows, Lord, so long
and fierce and save us from the
cruel nails of the foreigner.'

and ended:

'*But Deliver Us From Evil*
And from the Germans.
Nay! Save unhappy Lombardy
from the Aulic Council and Radetzky
Let it be.'

The author was a certain M. Maggioni.

One cannot tell exactly how effective such propaganda was; on the other hand, there can be little doubt that it did have some effect, if only by heightening the general revolutionary atmosphere.

The Grenzer (South Slavs)[42]

The Grenzer were the troops which Austria drew from the so-called 'Military Border' in Croatia the origins of which 'dated back to the Austrian frontier defences established early in the sixteenth century between the Adriatic Sea and the Drava River where Serb and Croat refugee families were granted land and freedom from the usual manorial obligations in return for military service. In time this system was expanded until it covered the entire frontier of Hungary-Croatia.' The area was administered by the Hofkriegsrath – not by the civil authorities of the Hungarian-Croatian Crown – and organised 'into regiments instead of counties, so that it [was] one vast camp, every soldier being a peasant and every peasant a soldier'. These peasant soldiers, however, were not irregulars; the 'Grenzer' as they were called were 'drilled as an important part of the regular imperial army and not merely as a militia for the defence of the frontier against the Turks'.

The Military Border, as has already been explained, was divided into several general commands, but as far as the South Slavs were concerned the most important were the Croatian-Slavonian commands (the Karlstadt, Banal and Warasdin general commands). There each regiment raised four battalions, the first two of which were on active service and in rotation furnished the frontier guards and troops for other duties.

Every man served about five months each year. When necessary, the third and fourth battalions could be mobilised and in case of dire emergency every man who could carry a musket, regardless of age, was called out to form the fifth battalion or *Landesaufgebot.* In addition, the Croatian command had a number of special units, about 1,000 picked men in all, the so-called *Seressaner,* who dressed in national costume, were used for special police and scout duties. In all, the total strength of the Croatian and Slavonian regiments was estimated at 60,000 – a very considerable force and a major factor in political and military considerations.

According to Professor Rothenberg, the leading expert on the Military Border, the reliability of the Grenzer after 1815 'was undermined by a number of economic, administrative and political factors'. For a start, the region had an almost exclusively agricultural economy dominated by large joint family communes called *zadruga.* These discouraged private initiative, kept productivity low and aggravated an economy already under pressure from growing birth rates, but the system was favoured by the military since it more easily responded to their demands for manpower than single family holdings could have done. The consequence was that there was considerable deprivation and poverty to be found, particularly in West Croatia where the soil was worst. A second source of grievance was the misconduct and abuse of power by various officers who were alleged to mistreat their men (they used them for labour services for example) and to dishonour their womenfolk. Commanding officers had virtually absolute powers over the lives of peasant-soldiers and their families and the situation was much resented by the Grenzer. By 1830, indeed, the Hofkriegsrath had to acknowledge 'the almost universal disaffection and lamentable condition of the Border population'.

However, what really worried the military authorities was the growth of Illyrianism or South Slav nationalism among the people. Until the 1840s the Grenzer families had resisted attempts by the Croatian Sabor (Diet) to limit the powers of the military regime, out of gratitude for a system, which despite its manifest defects, had nonetheless raised them to a level higher than that of the serfs of civil Croatia. But with the growth of Illyrianism the differences between the populations of civil Croatia and the Military Border seemed less and less important.

In the spring of 1848 these differences all but disappeared – the serfs of civil Croatia, hearing that the Hungarian Diet had abolished serfdom, refused to perform labour services or pay tithes and forced a Croatian National Assembly to meet at Zagreb to legalise their actions retrospectively. Moreover, it seemed that the Sabor would have to take more radical steps to satisfy the spirit of the times.

The Croatian National Assembly was dominated by South Slav nationalists or Illyrians who demanded not only the unification of Croatia, Slavonia and Dalmatia but also the incorporation of the Croatian and Slavonian Grenzer regiments within the Triune kingdom. They also demanded the recall of all Grenzer units from Italy – an issue to which we shall have to return shortly. But this was not all. As agitation spread throughout the Military Border there were requests for every manner of reform – requests which in the Szluin regiments did not stop short of demands to dismantle the entire Grenzer defence system. The military authorities, consequently, were forced to react.

The main step taken by the imperial authorities was the nomination and proclamation as Ban of Croatia of Colonel Joseph Baron von Jellačić de Buzim, commander of the 1st Banat Regiment, on 23 March. Within two weeks he had also been promoted *Feldmarschalleutnant* and military commander of Croatia and the Military Border. Jellacić was known to be an Illyrian patriot and enjoyed great personal popularity; more important, he was also known to be fiercely anti-Magyar and was reckoned by Baron Kulmer in Vienna – Croatia's representative at the imperial court – to be the man and Emperor could count on best to defeat the liberal Hungarians. 'Austria will have to reconquer Hungary,' Kulmer wrote to Jellacić, 'and for this purpose you must at all costs retain the loyalty of the Military Border.' Jellacić did all that was needed. He refused to recognise the authority of the new Hungarian government, ceased to have communication with it, instructed all Croatian officials to do likewise, placed the third battalions of the Grenzer on a war footing and declared martial law throughout Croatia. He himself toured the area to raise morale.

There was little need, however, to raise the animosity of most South Slavs against the Magyars, for if there was a widespread desire for reform in Croatia-Slavonia in 1848 there was no desire to be governed by the Hungarians. The latter had made themselves unpopular by forcing the Croats in the 1840s to accept Magyar as the language of state and by attempting to Magyarise Croatian education. They became even more unpopular in the course of 1848 when they forced the Emperor to agree in April that the Military Border should be administered from Pest and when in June they persuaded the Emperor to dismiss Jellačić from the post of Ban.

The latter step, however, not only aroused a wave of Croat indignation but also prompted further demands for the immediate incorporation of the Military Border into civil Croatia, a step which the Grenzer themselves now supported since serfdom by this time had come to an end. The Sabor, therefore, passed laws removing control of the Border from Vienna; provided for Grenzer participation in the political affairs of the kingdom; and asserted

Croatian control of the Slavonian regiments. It also abolished all economic restrictions in land tenure, although it was only later in the summer that Jellačić issued an order which conceded the right to abolish the *zadruga* and which eased occupational restrictions in the Grenzer regiments. Having done its job, the Sabor was finally dissolved at the beginning of July, by which time Croatia was more or less at war with Hungary and had massed troops on her side of the Drava in numbers greater than those camped opposite.

The final break with the Magyars, however, was precipitated by events in Slavonia. By the middle of May the Serbs of southern Hungary (Slavonia was mainly Serb; Croatia, mainly Croat) had declared their independence from Pest and had proclaimed the establishment of an autonomous Voivodina. They held a national congress at Karlowitz and there elected Stefan Suplikač, a Grenzer colonel serving in Italy, as Voivod and Josip Rajačić, the old Orthodox Metropolitan as Serb Patriarch. The result was that the Serbs now had to chose between three authorities – the new Glavin Odbor (the National Assembly of the Serbs in Hungary) at Karlowitz, the imperial military command at Peterwardein and Jellačić in Croatia who was trying to extend his control over the Slavonian frontier. Some regiments supported the Ban, some the Odbor; the civilians in civil Slavonia tended to support the latter. However, divisions were put aside when Hrabowsky, the imperial commander at Peterwardein, attacked Karlowitz on 12 June. Thereafter general fighting broke out in southern Hungary and the Croatian Sabor passed a resolution in favour of giving armed aid to the Serbs before it was prorogued at the beginning of July. One Grenzer deputy said: 'The bullets are cast, the rifles cleaned, the packs are ready and the blades sharpened. We are prepared to march whenever the Ban commands.'

Jellačić, however, did not invade Hungary immediately. He spent most of the summer frustrating Hungarian attempts to reach a compromise, while at the same time building up his army. By early September he had nearly 50,000 men under his command – 22 infantry battalions, 33 cavalry squadrons and 81 light batteries. On 4 September the Emperor reinstated him as Ban and one week later his forces crossed the Drava. What had been expected for months – open war between the South Slavs and the Magyars – had now begun. It did not end until August 1849 when Hungary was eventually overwhelmed by a combination of imperial and Russian forces, the Emperor having openly taken the side of the South Slavs at the beginning of October 1848 when he appointed Jellačić commander-in-chief in Hungary and dissolved the Hungarian Parliament.

Radetzky's difficulties in Italy can only be understood against this background, for it was to be expected that both his South Slav and Hungarian troops would feel a duty to defend their homelands and that the Italians would try their best to exploit these feelings to their own advantage.

'The Italian press followed events in the Slav lands, particularly Croatia, with great attention [and] Venice was well placed, on account of her ancient ties with Dalmatia, to act as an "observatory" in this respect.'[43] Therefore, when Croatia was in confusion during the spring of 1848 Italian leaders were quick to appeal to liberal and revolutionary sentiment among the South Slavs in order to direct events, if possible, in their favour. Thus the Venetian leader Tommaseo in a 'Proclamation to the Croats' published at the beginning of May, declared that the struggle for liberty being waged in Europe was an indivisible one. The

Italians and Croats were fighting for the same cause. He added: 'Your government is sending you Croats to enslave us Italians; but don't you understand that if it succeeds it will employ the Italians to perfect the slavery of the Croats, the Bohemians, the Slavs? Either everyone is free or everyone is a slave!' Mamiani, the Roman Minister also wanted to make contact with the Croats. But it was not easy to do this officially. Contact at first was left to students and intellectuals and to Italians who had links with Slav representatives at the Slav Congress at Prague. One of these, Vegezzi-Ruscalla, in a letter to the Congress wrote: 'Like us you want to get rid of the unjust hegemony of the Germans. You want Poland for the Poles, the Czech lands for the Czechs, Illyria for the Illyrians just as we want Italy for the Italians.' Mazzini also saw a need for links between the Slavs and the Italians. He said that 'the Italians should direct their revolutionary diplomatic activity much more towards the Slavs than towards Frankfurt. The fate of Austria will be decided one day – not far off perhaps – in Lemberg, Prague and Agram much more than in Frankfurt'. But he himself did nothing to develop such a policy; like Italy's new official leaders he was more interested at this stage in forging links with Hungary. The initiative was left with students and individual intellectuals, with the result that until the summer of 1848 the Italians had to play a fairly passive role, hoping that Slav nationalism or Pan-Slavism would achieve their aims for them, something which in the spring seemed possible.

The outbreak of the revolutions in the Habsburg Empire had filled many Slav idealists with hopes of a Slav renaissance. One Croat student for example, writing from Vienna on 13 March declared that the Austrian Empire was finished and that out of its ruins a Slav Empire would arise. But in Croatia itself, more serious steps were being taken to give Slav ideals reality. The convocation of the Zagreb National Assembly was almost a declaration of independence, and the passage of the resolution demanding the expulsion of foreign troops and the recall of the Grenzer to Croatia went very far indeed to establish local sovereignty. Not surprisingly it was this measure which above all others frightened the imperial authorities and sustained the hopes of the Italians. And for some time afterwards it was not at all clear whose fears or hopes it was which would be justified.

The passage of the motion demanding the recall of the Grenzer from Italy was followed by an avalanche of petitions requesting the same, as well as by numerous newspaper articles calling for action. The Sabor also repeated its demand when it reconvened in June. Meanwhile, students had taken to subversive action to prevent troops leaving for Italy – (the 1st and 2nd Grenzer battalions had been sent to aid Radetzky) – by infiltrating regiments and telling the soldiers 'to return home and not to go to their deaths to fight in such an unjust war'. These efforts had some effect. Ljudovit Vukotinović, one of the leaders of the Croat liberals, recorded in his memoirs that when a battalion of Grenzer entered Zagreb on their way to Italy, the crowd greeted them with cries of 'No! Not to Italy!'. He continued: 'Some ardent patriots infiltrated the troops and undermined their discipline to such a point that even some of their commanders said openly: "We want to go home".' The imperial authorities clearly, therefore, had genuine cause for concern.

The establishment of the Serb Voivodina complicated matters further. Serb students who hoped to unify all the southern Slavs and to resurrect the Serb Empire of Dušan campaigned to keep the Grenzer at home and did so all the more passionately when Kossuth refused to recognise Serb autonomy in Hungary. One of them, Svetozar Miletić, told a Serb imperial officer: 'Tell your superiors that there is no need for the Emperor to wage war, since nobody is attacking him; indeed, it is he who is attacking the Italians. And if you are assailed and forced to go to Italy, say that you would prefer to die at home than in Italy. Here at least you will die for liberty, there you will die for nothing!' This sort of propaganda was not without results. The French Consul at Belgrade wrote to Paris on 4 May saying: 'Austria's position becomes more critical every day: I am assured that a great demoralisation prevails amongst the troops who are heading from the Military Border towards Italy.'

The Grenzer troops in Italy also provided an argument for the Serb Patriarch Rajačić when he visited Innsbruck on 19 June to inform the Emperor of the decisions of the National Congress. He pointedly reminded Ferdinand that 30,000 South Slav soldiers were defending the imperial cause on the battlefield. A proclamation issued by the Congress adopted a similar line. It ran: 'Our sons, brothers and fathers are dying for the imperial throne in Italy, and while we at home are peacefully and legally claiming our rights, which we have gained with blood, the cruel Hungarians drive us to perdition and attack us like wild animals: this is the reward of loyalty!' The Serbs, in some eyes, therefore, were guilty of treason. Hrabowsky wrote: 'They have written to their brothers in Croatia and in the army in Italy describing the fantastic oppression to which the Hungarians subject them and it is to be feared that they will incite the Grenzer abroad to desert and lead them from the path of duty.' However, Jellačić, as will be seen, had reassured the troops in Italy.

Nonetheless, there were still occasions when it looked as if the Grenzer might be recalled. The deposition of Jellačić as Ban, for example, gave rise to heated debate in the Croatian Sabor where a document was introduced demanding 'the overthrow of the traitor at Innsbruck' and the 'sending of emissaries to Italy to recall the battalions of the Military Border'. These points were later eliminated, although Vokutinovič had intervened in the debate to ask: 'Must our loyalty be limitless to the point of infinity in confrontations with the Austrian sovereign?' And he ended his speech, which had attacked both Austrians and Hungarians for treating the Grenzer as 'cannon-fodder', with a request to recall the troops from Italy so that they could 'live or die . . . defending their homeland'.

The disillusionment with Austria which was felt by many Slavs increased considerably after Windischgraetz's bombardment of Prague, and a good example of how profound it became is provided by a letter written by Rajačić on 1 August to the commander of the imperial troops in southern Hungary whom he accused of launching unrestrained attacks on the Serbian population at a time when 'its sons [were] fighting like lions on the fields of Italy in support of the Emperor and in order to uphold the Empire as a whole'. This letter concluded with an open threat:

If the Serbian nation is not protected by the imperial throne or by the imperial government or by the imperial and royal army, it will be forced to seek help where it can find it quickest. It will be no wonder then, if it embraces the Russians or the Turks. Before this happens, however, it will do everything possible to help itself. Its first step will be to recall all its sons from the Italian army; the second will be to call on the help of all Slav nations; the third, that it will enter into an alliance with Charles Albert and the

Italians; the fourth that it will appeal to England, France and the whole of Europe. A drowning man clutches at a straw or at a red-hot iron.

The threat was taken seriously.

Perhaps the authorities were already aware of a plan drafted by one of Rajačić's aides towards the end of June which outlined a vast scheme of 'military and diplomatic activity against Austria and Hungary' in Russia, Turkey and the Balkans. This foresaw 'sending Hikalovič to Paris along with Medakovič to explain our position there and to win the sympathy of the French government. Once he has succeeded in this mission he should go on to Charles Albert's headquarters in Piedmont with a letter of recommendation and from there call upon the Grenzer to revolt. And having formed an alliance with the Italians he should then land in Dalmatia to attack Hungary.' The plan did not remain a dead letter. Hikalovič indeed visited Paris – but events in Italy meant that Charles Albert, who had been defeated by Radetzky, was no longer a useful ally.

One final attempt was made to recall the Grenzer. The Serb writer Miletić in August 1849 published a small book entitled *A Voice from Slavia* in which he developed his old arguments for a South Slav state which should include all the Habsburg and Turkish territories inhabited by southern Slavs. The book also included an appeal to the Grenzer troops to refrain from fighting the Italians. It ran: 'O brothers in arms fighting against the brave Italians, resolve to do this: either return en masse . . . to the Serb and Illyrian nation in order to defend your rights against the enemy; or, if this should prove impossible, cross over in battalions and regiments as quickly as you can to the Italians, on condition that they help you to return quickly to your homeland to establish the legal autonomy, liberty and solidarity of the South Slavs.' However, in Croatia itself, nothing concrete occurred to undermine Habsburg control. Tommaseo wrote in a letter to Manin: 'The Croats say that it is impossible for them to cut themselves off from Austria in the war in Italy. We are poor [they say], we need someone to give us bread. The Italians show that they support our enemies the Hungarians. What has Italy done for us? How can we attain our rights if we endanger them by futilely risking their rejection by all sides?'

There was, nonetheless, undoubtedly more sympathy among the South Slavs for the Italians than Tommaseo suspected. Brlić, Jellačić's envoy in Paris, whose job it was to counter pro-Hungarian sentiments among the Poles, always claimed that the Ban himself wished to transform the Habsburg Monarchy into a Slav Empire and in the process renounce all claims on Italian territory. The professor of theology, Topalović, also saw a convergence of interests between the two peoples and looked to the Holy See to bring about a reconciliation of the two Catholic nations which might serve to combat Russian Pan-Slavism. He even affected to believe that the South Slav troops in Italy would benefit from witnessing the Italian liberation struggle: 'God offers them the opportunity of seeing the courage of a neighbouring people and of understanding how much more wise it would be to reach an agreement and to fraternise with them against the common enemy. . . . Italy and Illyria must become two neighbours, two friends, two sisters who love each other tenderly.' There were, finally, South Slavs who were prepared to consider Italian schemes for a federation in Dalmatia over which there was dissension after Jellačić was appointed Governor there. But despite their goodwill and despite the efforts of South

Slavs, Italians and Hungarians to sink their differences after the *oktroyierte* Constitution of Schwarzenberg of 4 March 1849, nothing came of their opposition to the Habsburgs. The Grenzer remained in Italy and so did the Hungarian troops and all the goodwill in the world could not reverse the hard facts of Radetzky's victories over Charles Albert in July and August 1848 and March 1849. Realistic observers among the nationalities recognised this, although Pulszky (the Hungarian Secretary of State) recorded in his memoirs how persistent were the hopes and ambitions of the exiles and the envoys. Describing a meeting in Paris to celebrate the appearance of a new journal entitled *The Tribune of the People,* he wrote:

. . . the Polish poet Mickiewicz, the two Russians Herzen and Golovin, the French red republicans, many Poles, Rumanians, Italians and even Abbe Brlics and Herkalovics were present and by accident, I was their neighbour. The wine, but even more the enthusiastic red toasts, enflamed people's spirits. . . . Herkalovics toasted me with a full glass and drank to the union of the Serbs and the Hungarians: I was almost speechless with astonishment. Szalay sat opposite me and I asked him whether the glass I had in my hand held water or wine and whether I was drunk or the company was mad. You are drinking water as always he replied and are not drunk. But the company is indeed mad.

For much of the period 1848–49, however, Radetzky did not know and could not know whether madness would prevail. It was perfectly possible, given everything that was happening at the time, that matters would deteriorate, not improve.

Radetzky was first informed by the War Ministry of official concern about the Grenzer when Zanini, the first constitutional War Minister, wrote to him towards the end of March with the warning that[44] 'it could well be the case that Grenzer at present stationed in Italy [were] receiving all sorts of accounts from home of recent events in Hungary'. The War Minister predicated that 'many of these [would] be inaccurate', but 'they could nonetheless have an unfortunate effect on the spirit of the troops', if the latter 'felt themselves less favoured than their provincial neighbours [i.e. the Hungarians]'. The Field Marshal was advised, therefore, 'to do everything possible to avoid anything that might lead to refractoriness' on the part of these troops. Zanini suggested:[45] 'Perhaps you would find it appropriate to inform all Grenzer battalions which have already reached Italy or which will arrive from now on that the entire Military Border will receive the same concessions which have been granted to the Hungarian provinces.' He hoped that as a result of Radetzky's assurances the Grenzer troops would remember everything that the army had done for them in the past (they had, he claimed, been 'far better placed than the subjects of the Hungarian provincial authorities') and that 'a new impulse [would] be given to [their] accustomed loyalty and bravery'. Zanini's letter ended with a warning against Pan-Slav agents:[46]

There is, by the way, plenty of evidence that emissaries of a Pan-Slav tendency are inciting the people of the Military Border and endeavouring by all sorts of devilish tricks to detach them from their military calling. Since these emissaries could well be present amongst the battalions which have already left it would be as well perhaps to arrange as far as possible to protect the troops from such evil intentions and to let them know that, since such incitement can only bring them trouble, they should pay no attention to it.

However, despite official concern and reassurances the situation grew worse, not better. In a memorandum to the Emperor of 26 May 1848, the new War

Minister, Latour, explained that the very great anxiety being manifested both by Grenzer troops in Italy and by those who were still *en route* there could no longer be denied.[47] The border soldiers were most concerned about what was happening to their wives and children and 'every conceivable means' was required to combat their alarm if Radetzky's army was to be kept battleworthy. He suggested that the Emperor should issue a special proclamation praising the services of the Grenzer in the past and trusting in their loyalty in future. Such a proclamation, felt Latour, would 'enflame' the Borderers for the rest of the war. As a result, a letter was sent to Radetzky[48] in which 'regret' was expressed about the rumours circulating among his Grenzer troops, rumours which 'might give rise to exaggerated fears which could lead individuals to take inadvisable steps'. The Field Marshal was ordered to take all steps possible to end such rumours and to have his higher and staff officers reassure their men. Finally, he was to give the troops a guarantee in the Emperor's name that everything that was being done in the Military Border was being done in their best interests. The Emperor, he was to tell them, trusted in their future as in their past loyalty and promised them that as soon as victory was achieved they would be sent home to their families.

But this was not enough. In June it was discovered that the Ogulin Grenzer Battalion had suffered desertions and that one corporal and twelve men had already returned home.[49] Investigations subsequently revealed that these men 'had received letters'.[50] The worrying thing, however, was that on their return home the men had not been handed over to the military authorities but had been allotted to the 3rd Battalion of their regiment with Jellačić's approval.[51] Clearly, more radical counter-measures by the authorities were called for.

Radetzky himself came to the conclusion that only a proclamation from the Ban could be expected to make any impact and he believed that he could secure one. Jellačić had once served in the army in Italy and he held him to be a 'brave man who [was] devoted to the Emperor'[52] Radetzky, therefore, had Schwarzenberg, who was in Innsbruck at this time, arrange to meet the Ban who had just arrived at Court there proclaiming:[53] 'Arrest me if you please, but if you do, the Croatians will recall all their soldiers from Italy and I shall not be able to prevent it.' Since the Field Marshal was hoping to raise the number of Grenzer at his disposal from the 6,000 or so he had been left with after his initial reverses in Italy (about 4,000 had been cut off or had had to withdraw to non-Italian territory) to over 30,000 (the figure that was reached in December) Schwarzenberg's task was an important one. He fulfilled it ably and persuaded Jellačić to issue a proclamation.

Jellačić's proclamation[54] informed the Grenzer that he had been received by the Emperor, who had appointed him to mediate between the Hungarians and the South Slavs. He also stated that although disorders had broken out at Karlowitz he had 'taken the necessary steps to prevent any further acts of violence'. Finally the proclamation, dated 20 June, included the advice which Radetzky had asked for: 'Do not allow yourselves to be diverted by reports and fears for the safety of your country from the arduous but honourable duty imposed upon you of defending the Throne and the State in Italy. Already the praise of your heroism and your perseverance under difficulties resounds through-out Europe. Do not soil your renown by any act which would be incompatible with your oath of allegiance or unworthy of yourselves or your brave fathers.' The climax of the proclamation was, 'And be assured that we still feel strong enough at home to protect our houses and to defend our nationality without assistance from you.' It was exactly what Radetzky required.

The Field Marshal, meanwhile, was informing the War Minister of the way in which his mind was working. He told Latour:[55]

I do not wish at present to examine the question whether the over-confidence of the Magyars in their treatment of the nationalities existing beside them has given rise to the misfortunes which now threaten us from this side. It is enough that this misfortune has arisen. Yet I cannot help but admit that Baron Jellačić is a man who can render great service to the state and that he, as well as the nationality he represents, should be treated with respect and not unconditionally spurned. A rebellion, even the withdrawal of the Grenzer, would have a terrible effect on my position. What would be left for me to do if I had to fight a numerically strong army in front of me while an insurgency was going on in my rear?

He ended:[56]

I shall give no room to those thoughts. I hope it will not come to that. But let nobody in Vienna think of taking any steps which could give rise to such a situation. These events in the Banat and the news I receive of them justify my fears.

Latour replied[57] that, although he shared the Field Marshal's fears, there was nothing he could do about them, since 'unfortunately [he was] in no position to exercise any influence whatever on the Hungarian situation'. Radetzky would have to deal with events as they arose. Both men, as a result, must have been enormously relieved to hear of Jellačić's proclamation.

The situation with the Grenzer, however, was always touch and go, and as an invasion of Hungary appeared more and more likely the tension between Hungarian and South Slav troops grew daily. Radetzky, as a result, was forced to respond very circumspectly when at the beginning of September 1848 he was approached by Jellačić and Rajačić who appealed firstly for the release of General Suplikač (who had been refused permission to lead the Serbs of southern Hungary on the grounds that the Emperor had not recognised his appointment as Voivod), and secondly for political support in securing financial aid from Latour.[58] The Field Marshal responded[59] to the latter request by saying that although he was happy to act as middleman he would have to leave any decision to Latour. He added that his own supply of money was needed to administer the army in Italy and he could not provide any aid himself. With regard to Suplikac he once again referred the case to Vienna and on 8 September Latour replied[60] instructing him that, since the actions of the Serbs were held to be unconstitutional, the General could not officially be released from duty. On the other hand, he suggested that Radetzky might use a lull in the fighting to send Suplikac to Karlowitz 'on some or other errand'. The War Minister also took the opportunity to clarify the situation with regard to funds for Jellacić. He wrote:[61] I will do all I can as far as the Ministry is concerned to get them to send the money needed by Jellacić to provide for his troops. I know it will not be enough and I am sorry that I cannot do more for him. I am sorry, too, that Your Excellency is in no real position to support him.' But that, fortunately or unfortunately, was that.

It is not possible to decide with any degree of accuracy whether, had funds been available, Radetzky would have used them to aid the Croats. He had to be extremely careful to be seen to be impartial in Hungarian affairs, and in any case regretted that the imperial forces should be on the verge of civil war. Thus, in his reply to Rajacič who had also appealed to him for the release of Suplikač, he wrote:[62]

It has made my heart bleed to read the description of the position of the Serbs which you included in your letter of 18 August. Civil unrest is the greatest misfortune that can befall a country and those who have caused it will answer before God and posterity. It is only too true that our Monarchy – the once so mighty Austrian Monarchy – can no longer contain violence, with the result that people everywhere are shouting for help. People have divested the throne of its power and used the most shameful means to lower and discourage respect for the King. Now they complain that he has no power. I do not intend to set myself in judgement over both parties which now threaten Hungary and her neighbouring territories with unforeseeable misfortunes. But their leaders, whoever they are, will be harshly judged by world history. It cannot – it must not come to a split in the Austrian army. The army is still loyal and imbued with the noblest spirit. If it is forced to, it will take up its arms to save the integrity of the Monarchy in the same way that it has triumphed over her external enemies.

He ended his letter to the Archbishop with an eloquent plea:

I beg Your Excellency again to mediate between the parties; employ the respect of your holy office to prevent the shedding of blood – is there no other way to reconcile the two parties apart from the most unfortunate way of all – civil war?

There were, nonetheless, apparently several instances of desertion among Croat troops in October 1848. The British Consul in Milan reported to Lord Palmerston that 'desertions, to a great extent of the Hungarian and Croatian troops [were] continually taking place' and added:[63] 'On the 12th instant, 60 Croatian soldiers, deserters from their regiments, passed through a village called Tegnone in the Brianza.' This, he wrote, he had 'on the best authority'. But by November 1848, Radetzky appeared to have things under control and was satisfied that his policy of impartiality had proved successful. He told the War Ministry:[64] 'If, so far, I have had the great luck to see unity maintained among all the nationalities in the army under my command, the greatest part of which consists of Hungarian and Croat regiments, it has been thanks only to the circumstance that the appearance of the government favouring one nationality at the cost of any other has been avoided.' And as an example of his policy of impartiality he cited his refusal to agree to a proposal from General Nugent to send selected Grenzer home from Italy to form the cadres for new battalions. He wrote:

The Hungarians in the Italian army would have perceived an open party spirit in the government in sending these men back in this way, a party spirit which favoured the Croats against the Hungarians. They would have become imbued with a lack of trust in the judgement of their officers – something which the army has so far escaped – and desertions in the Hungarian regiments would have been the sure result. There would even have been unrest among the Croat regiments insofar as some would be favoured by being allowed to go home and others not.

Radetzky, one feels, had demonstrated excellent judgement, a conclusion which the British Vice-Consul would have endorsed. Writing to Palmerston on 22 October he had expressed his admiration for the old soldier's wisdom:[65] 'With respect to the differences that existed between the Hungarians and the

Croats, I understand that Field Marshal Radetzky, with his usual tact and talent, has managed to put an end to them.' If so, it was a considerable achievement.

The Hungarian troops[66]

The political and military situation in Croatia–Slavonia had repercussions, of course, not merely among the Grenzer troops in Radetzky's army but also among the Magyar troops. Indeed, it was obvious from the start that there would be difficulties with the Hungarians if only on account of the great ideological sympathy which existed between them and the Italians. In Hungary itself there was an enormous pro-Italian agitation, and in Italy it became evident that Hungarian soldiers were not really regarded as 'the enemy'. This was another reason why the South Slav troops and (often also) intellectuals were cautious in sympathising with the Italians.

The sympathy for Italy felt in Hungary was manifested from the very outset of the revolution.[67] Newspapers, pamphlets, petitions, county meetings and proclamations all expressed the view that the use of Magyar troops in Italy was a stain on Hungary's newly-won freedom and honour. Thus the *Marcius Tizenötödike* declared on 27 March that the Cabinet in Vienna could not expect to use Hungarians 'to oppress that good people' [the Italians]' or 'to subjugate them under the yoke of absolutism while [the Hungarians themselves were] fighting it at home'. It was a view which was echoed everywhere. The Hungarian press was unanimous in this opinion and was absolutely determined to stop any more troops being sent to Italy. Metternich and Radetzky's despotism was seen as the true cause of events in Italy, and Hungarians as a result felt no need whatsoever to defend it.

One other factor was important in reinforcing this determination. The idea was by this time already in the air of restructuring the Habsburg Monarchy by transferring the imperial capital to Buda.[68] The Hungarian element in the new Empire would be strengthened if Italy were no longer part of the Monarchy. To create an independent Italy was, therefore, in Hungary's own interests. Yet it was popular pressure more than anything else which forced the Hungarian government's hand – pressure which came to a head at a huge assembly gathered in Pest on 11 April.

The Italians had been distributing proclamations (written in Latin) among the Magyar troops in Italy.[69] These had argued that both nations were fighting for the same objectives and had won the approval of the sympathetic Magyar press. The meeting on 11 April, therefore, assured the Italians that the troops would be recalled and would no longer serve in Italy as the 'blind instrument' of their oppression. The proclamation it issued continued:[70] 'Do not doubt the friendship of the Hungarians – In their fight for freedom our soldiers cannot nurture any true feeling of hatred against you. . . .' And it offered the reassurance:[71] 'God cannot permit tyranny to triumph over eternal right. This is our faith, our hope! Therefore, be assured that our most ardent wishes are that your freedom shall shine like a splendid star in the firmament and that Italy . . . shall become free. . . . Long live Italy! Long Live Liberty! Long Live Equality, Long Live Fraternity!' The proclamation was issued in the name of the 'county of Pest' and reached Italy a couple of weeks later. There it was published with the following preface:[72]

To noble and generous Hungary we offered in the first day of our liberation the sincere salute of men who know the cost of conquering national independence.

And we sent back to the Heroic Magyar people some of the prisoners from their native land . . . in the hope that they would return safe and sound to their firesides where they could tell you of the cruelty of our common oppressors, of our valour in battle and of our humanity in victory.

This great people replied to our address immediately under the impetus of true fraternity and today we are proud to publish to all Italy their most noble reply.

It was what we yearned for and as a testimonial we can do no better than to publish it in the same form in which it reached us.

The fraternal greetings of the Hungarians are like the announcement of a victory for us!

The Italians were right. The fraternal greetings of the Hungarians were indeed the equivalent of a victory. Radetzky had 10,000–12,000 Hungarian troops in Italy and their recall would signify his defeat. Moreover, it was only with the greatest difficulty that such a recall was prevented. The assembly which had taken place in Pest had not only called for the repatriation of the Magyar troops but the suggestion had been made in the *Nemzeti Ujság* on the same day that the National Guard should block the local barracks if it were proposed to send more Hungarian troops to Lombardy-Venetia. Such was the mood of public opinion in the Hungarian capital.

The question of Hungarian troops in Italy, therefore, became a very tricky one for the country's first responsible government. Nor was it one which could be avoided since it was raised as early as 31 March in the Diet by the radical deputy László Madarász. The latter maintained that under the terms of the Pragmatic Sanction (the document which gave the Habsburgs the right to use Hungarian troops) their employment could not be justified either to oppress constitutional movements or against states which had not threatened the frontiers of Hungary itself. Batthyány and Kossuth (the Hungarian Prime Minister and Finance Minister respectively) replied to these points evasively. Without pronouncing explicitly on the continuation of the war, they argued that the troops were being employed constitutionally to protect the Sovereign. On 11 April, however, the government at last confronted the problem of recalling its forces. It stated that although it would be difficult to recall contingents immediately, a way would be discovered by which to satisfy the nation's wishes. And on 26 April the Minister at Court, Prince Esterházy was told to inform Vienna that the government could not restrain public opinion for long if a solution to this question was delayed. Meanwhile, the Ministry attempted to assuage the nation by successfully recalling from Italy the newly appointed Minister of War, Colonel Lázár Mészáros. However, the issue of the Hungarian troops remained a critical one, for at the end of April 1848 the imperial government in Vienna demanded further contingents for Radetzky.

The policy now followed by the Hungarian government has been treated extremely controversially in the history books.[73] Kossuth has been accused of frustrating both Italian and Hungarian independence by his subsequent manœuvres, although as will be seen, he was in an extremely difficult position. In the background to the question lay the 'Great Magyar' ambitions of the Hungarian government. Being advised that Vienna was on the point of surrendering Italy (or Lombardy at least) and having secured from the Sovereign in Innsbruck both the deposition of Jellacič and the promise that the

Court would come to Pest, the new Hungarian ministry believed that it was bound to become the centre of a Habsburg Magyar Empire. Italy would become both independent and an ally, as would Germany, which would include the German Austrian lands. The Ministry, therefore, wanted to do nothing to upset the Monarch before the foundations of this scheme were laid. Therefore, despite the financial gains that would accrue from recalling the troops in Italy, the government's military priorities were concentrated on raising an entirely new army for Hungary's defence. This was the Honvéd army which was meant to thwart any threat from Jellačič in the south. For the government was aware that if and when a peace was signed with the Italians, not only would the Hungarian troops be repatriated but the Grenzer would be so also. Thus it was in the national interest of the Hungarians to ensure that no steps were taken regarding Italy immediately.

Public opinion, on the other hand, did not understand this and was determined that steps should be taken and taken in a direction exactly the opposite of that in which the Monarch intended to go. Kossuth was aware of this and so proceeded with caution. Thus when the Council of Ministers met on 4 July to consider Parliament's reply to the king, he opposed Batthyány's suggestion of a straightforward acceptance of the royal proposals and, having sounded out some leading parliamentarians, proposed that no mention at all of the war in Italy should be made in the official reply. In the end a compromise was agreed: it would be noted that it was not yet possible to end the war in Italy, but, at the same time, it would also be made clear that there was no intention to oppress the Italians; in fact it was to be hoped that a peace could be concluded which would preserve the dignity of the Monarch while protecting the rights and liberties of the Italians. It only remained to be seen whether Parliament would accept this formula.

The signs were not propitious. On 7 July the *Reform* declared that the government should either refuse the King's request or resign. But on 11 July Kossuth persuaded the Chamber to vote 42 million fl. towards raising an army of 200,000 men without being trapped on Italian affairs. And in the sittings of 13 and 15 July, by means of a somewhat general denial, the government survived critical parliamentary questioning on the rumoured recruitment of volunteers for Italy. However, the nettle was finally grasped when the Cabinet put up Kossuth to defend its policy on 20 July in the hope that his well-known rhetorical powers would mesmerise the deputies. But the result was rather different; the Finance Minister, aware of the general scepticism in the Chamber, felt forced to modify the previously agreed on government line. He, therefore, declared his support for the Italians saying that he hoped that they would secure a 'free and national government' in the interest of civilisation. He also told the Assembly that although the Ministry could not recall the troops in Italy – it would face the Monarch's veto if it pressed the issue and would therefore have to resign – he and his colleagues had always advised the King to bring the Italian war to an end. Finally, he promised that further troops would only be sent to Italy if and when the Italians refused to sign an honourable peace – which later in the debate, on his own initiative, he defined as Austria surrendering Lombardy. His colleagues were naturally furious, with the result that on 21 July Kossuth had to declare that his statement of the previous day had been an entirely personal one. However, the Cabinet by now had accepted a new compromise formula: Hungarian troops, it was maintained, had only been sent to Italy to fight for peace – a peace in fact, which would guarantee 'free, constitutional institutions compatible with monarchical government'. Moreover, if this could only be secured by ceding territory to the Italians (in fact by giving up Lombardy) the government accepted that this should happen before more troops were sent to Italy. The compromise satisfied the Right, but not the Left and many speakers still rose up to condemn the government's policy. One of them even managed to extract the information that the government on three occasions had instructed Esterházy to discuss the repatriation of the Hungarian troops with the King. The result of the debate, however, was that the government's policy was adopted by 233 votes to 79. In its final form it expressed the hope that a peace would be found that would reconcile the dignity of the throne and constitutional liberties. Hungarian aid would be sent to secure this once internal peace and order had been achieved in Hungary itself and once the latter's integrity was assured. In fact, this meant that in contrast with the Croats, the Hungarians would not be sending more troops to Italy at all – even if they did not intend to withdraw the troops already there. The real result of Kossuth's manœuvrings, therefore, was to frustrate the wishes of the King. The King, in turn remembered this and Batthyány, the Hungarian Premier later paid for the policy with his life.

However, the policy once established was established very firmly. When on 16 August a new law was passed to organise the newly-created Honvéd army, the second article laid down that it could only be employed against an enemy which had attacked Hungary itself. On 18 August, after Perczel, a radical deputy, had pointed out that Radetzky's victory statements in Italy included no mention of an honourable peace, Kossuth made known to the House that Esterházy had again been instructed by the Cabinet to remind the King of Hungarian policy. However, when Jellacič crossed the Drava the government's policy underwent a radical change. By 10 October, the House had called for the return of all Hungarian troops from abroad and the government was actively seeking an alliance with Charles Albert. Count Teleki was sent to Paris to organise this, and as part of his plans appointed Lajos Splenyi, a former officer of the imperial army in Italy, to represent Hungary at the Court of Turin. One of the latter's tasks was to organise Hungarian deserters in Italy, who were to be equipped by the Sardinians, for a diversionary attack on Fiume. Splenyi, however, had little success: 'Radetzky', according to one account, 'had been careful to place his Hungarian troops far from the frontiers and had employed severe measures against anyone found in possession of proclamations advocating repatriation. Besides, given that postal and other communications between Hungary and the troops in Lombardy were blocked, the soldiers only had a vague idea of what was happening at home and the Austrian high command was careful to present them with a tendentious account.' All this may well have been true. But in spite of these and other measures, Radetzky in fact had had great difficulties in restraining his Hungarian troops from deserting. And even Splenyi had some success for in December 1848 100 Hungarian troops entered Piedmont under the leadership of a Second Lieutenant Türr. These troops became the nucleus of the future Hungarian Legion which was to fight against the Austrians in northern Italy. Still, it was much too late for Italian–Hungarian cooperation to accomplish anything significant. The fate of the Sardinian envoy to Hungary, Alessandro Monti, was perhaps symbolic in this regard. He only succeeded in reaching Kossuth in March 1849 after Charles Albert had been defeated at Novara.

In Italy itself, on the other hand, it seemed at the beginning of the revolution that there might well be a chance of detaching the Hungarians from the rest of Radetzky's army.[74] The news of the new Hungarian constitution and of the Pest Assembly's proclamation, according to Italian newspapers, 'produced an indescribable effect' among Hungarian troops. Hungarian prisoners in the citadel of Milan were reported to have thrown 'themselves on the ground thanking God for the friendship that it had pleased Him to develop between the two peoples'.

There were in fact all sorts of reactions on the part of Hungarian troops as recorded in the Italian press. In some places Hungarian soldiers deserted in order to return home to defend their country; some decided to support the Italians; and in various encounters there were reports of individuals displaying sympathy for the enemy. Thus, one newspaper reported on 28 June that a Hungarian officer who had just disarmed a Tuscan, ordered his Croat troops to leave the scene and then, with the words, 'flee in safety, brave Italian', allowed the Tuscan to escape. The revolution in Venice, it would seem, was likewise aided when Lajos Winkler – the Hungarian officer who later became leader of the Hungarian Legion in Venice – placed himself between Austrian troops and Venetians crying, 'If you want to fire, shoot me first before you shoot these unarmed people.' Hungarian troops elsewhere had also played a decisive part in events that March. On 23rd of that month the Rome newspaper *L'Epoca* declared: 'The Hungarian regiments which refused to fight against the people have contributed towards its victory.'

Not surprisingly perhaps in the light of reports like these, the Italians did not really consider the Hungarians as their enemy; indeed they often took it for granted that Radetzky's Magyar troops were fighting against their will. Thus, in his order of the day of 10 April, General Durando referred to a company of captured Hungarian soldiers as follows: 'They are brave Hungarians: the generous nation to which they belong is not the enemy of Italy. . . .' And there were, of course, persistent rumours that the Hungarian government would stop sending troops to Italy and might even recall the ones already there. The German press was also full of these rumours and the *Augsburger Allgemeine Zeitung* declared on 26 April: 'The facts speak for themselves and make one very much doubt the sympathy of the Hungarians for the House of Austria. Northern Italy is trying to separate itself from us and the whole Hungarian press is encouraging it. Hungary not only wishes not to give money or men but wants to recall its troops from Italy.' Meanwhile reports of desertions continued. Nine hundred Hungarian troops were supposed to have deserted under cover of night and to have joined the Neapolitan and Tuscan Corps when the imperial army left Verona for Mantua. At the siege of Peschiera the greater part of the deserters were Hungarian and even at Brescia the Hungarians, it was reported, did not want to fight the Italians. At Montanara on 18 May, fifty Hungarians were reported to have changed sides when a corps of Tuscans were attacked, causing the Austrians to shoot three others as a warning to the rest. But when the Austrians returned to Mantua they reportedly found its gates closed by the Hungarian soldiers they had left behind. This last report is very difficult to believe, but it shows the atmosphere which was being created in

Italy around the Hungarian troops. The Italians had thoroughly convinced themselves of Hungarian sympathy. One newspaper wrote 'It is a consolation to know that most prisoners have been set free by the Hungarians', and the *Gazetta di Milano* reported on 5 June: 'It is true. The Hungarians do not want to fight against the sacred cause of Italy and when the cavalry is ordered to charge it only advances at walking pace.'

Curiously, the news of the debate in the Hungarian Chamber on 20 July was misreported in Italy. The *Concordia* of Turin reported on 7 August that the Assembly had 'voted to send a Hungarian army to Italy' and on 14 August that Kossuth had 'lost much of his popularity on account of his declaration on Italy'. Other newspapers reported the same with the result that it was believed for many years by many leading Italians that Kossuth had 'betrayed the Italian cause'. Some newspapers, it is true, did give an accurate account of events in Pest, but the damage was done. Thereafter, although the Hungarians themselves were always believed to by sympathetic, their leader was never trusted to the same degree.

Inside the Austrian army itself, Radetzky and his colleagues were well aware of the pressures on the Hungarian troops. In February 1849 when he was writing to the Emperor on the matter of a pardon for Italians who had joined the enemy he made it clear that they had not been the only ones to cross over:[75] ' . . . there are not only thousands of deserters from Italian regiments in the enemy's army, but unfortunately the intrigue of the revolutionary party has been so unrelenting that it has often succeeded in winning over soldiers from other, that is to say Hungarian, regiments as well'. Thus measures had indeed been taken to ensure that Hungarians would not desert and the British Vice-Consul reported to Lord Palmerston that the atmosphere created as a result was a very unpleasant one:[76]

. . . no one is safe; any soldier may speak to a civilian and then say he attempted to make him desert and be in consequence condemned to death. . . . The Hungarians shew every wish to be on good terms with the inhabitants. The officers speak to the Milanese gentlemen in the cafés, the soldiers with the working classes in the wine houses. The government, fearing that this intercourse might lead to the Hungarians taking part with the Milanese, determined to put an end to anything like intimacy between them. For which purpose several of the former abominable policemen were disguised as Hungarian soldiers and sent into the different places of public resort in order to entrap people to commit themselves. It is said that the soldier referred to [in a previous report] was a disguised policeman and that on this wretch's evidence the three tradesmen were sentenced to death. The Hungarians are now shunned lest they should be policemen in disguise. So far the government has effected its objects of keeping the Hungarians and Milanese apart from each other.

The situation, not unnaturally, became most critical in October 1848 after Jellacič had invaded Hungary and the King suspended the Hungarian Parliament and constitution. The Vice-Consul reported:[77] 'It is said that the Hungarians have applied to Field Marshal Radetzky for permission to return to their native country to defend it against the Croats but that the Marshal, instead of complying with their request has placed two of their superior officers under arrest and threatened to decimate the Hungarian regiments in case he found any symptoms of insubordination among the men as to their wish of returning to Hungary.' Radetzky might well have felt it necessary to resort to such threats since clearly he could not give way to a demand which would undermine his own position. Desertions, however, still took place – twenty-five Hungarians under one officer were reported to have passed through the village of Casate Nuovo in the Brianza on 19 October[78] – although, it seems that the Field Marshal quite quickly asserted his authority. So long as his policy of 'impartiality' was seen to be adhered to, most Hungarian and Croat troops resisted the temptation to desert. On the other hand there was clearly[79] 'no cordiality between the officers and men belonging to these two races, as they [were] never seen to associate in public'. Radetzky did not care about that; the main thing was that they were there.

The other troops

There is very little data of any kind about the loyalty or attitudes of Radetzky's other troops. A little exists on the Poles, but virtually nothing on the Czechs or German–Austrians. The latter, however, can be presumed to have been utterly loyal – the Germans resented Italian claims to the South Tyrol – and there were, of course, thousands of Vienna volunteers in Radetzky's army. On the other hand, there is much evidence to suggest that most of these 'volunteers' were sent from Vienna by the authorities there to solve the unemployment problem.[80] The attitude of the Czech troops would be interesting to discover – did Austro-Slavism influence them or not? – but so far, no work has been done on this question.[81] There is one book which claims that a conspiracy was discovered in a Transylvanian regiment in Venice in 1844 aimed at turning the Empire into a Slav one[82] but since this seems inherently improbable and since the article is in Serbo-Croat and not easily accessible, the author cannot comment on the state of satisfaction or dissatisfaction with the Empire felt by Transylvanian troops of (in this case) Rumanian nationality. One is left, therefore, with the Polish troops in Radetzky's army and here, fortunately, some considerable work has been done on attempts to win them over to the democratic cause.[83] These attempts were spearheaded by the great Polish poet Adam Mickiewicz, who refounded, as it were, the Polish Legion of General Dombrowski, which during the Napoleonic Wars had supported Napoleon and which eventually attracted over 20,000 Polish deserters from the Austrian, Russian and Prussian armies.

Mickiewicz was the greatest of the Slav romantic poets. Cavour placed him alongside Dante, Homer and Shakespeare, and Mazzini described him as the greatest literary phenomenon of the early nineteenth century. Born in Zaosie in 1798, the Russians imprisoned him in 1823 for a year in Vilna before deporting him in 1824. He then began a long period of exile in Germany, Switzerland and Italy until in 1840 he was awarded the Chair of Slavonic Literature at the Collège de France, where together with Michelet and Quinet he formed a famous literary trio. The year 1848 found him in Italy. He had forsaken the France of Louis Philippe for the Rome of Pius IX and had convinced himself that 'the reign of Christ on earth' was really about to begin there.

Mickiewicz, however, soon discovered that the majority of Poles in Rome were either aristocratic priests or conservatives. They were supporters of the exiled Prince Czartorisky and had little time for his revolutionary views. The result was that when the revolutions of 1848 broke out the poet headed north towards the Austrian possessions to organise a Polish Legion of deserters from the Austrian army.

The formal establishment of the Legion had taken place in Rome in fact on 29 March. About fourteen volunteers signed up – most of them were Polish artists – and they formed the nucleus of what they hoped would become a significant fighting force in the cause of freedom. Their spirits rose when at the beginning of April they heard that both the Lombards and Venetians had made direct appeals for their assistance. The Milanese summons referred to them as 'brothers in adversity and hope' and encouraged them to 'fight the common foe'; the Venetian proclamation of 5 April, although addressed in fact to 'Croats and other Slavs', had exactly the same objective. The Legion obtained passports on 8 April and left Rome on the 10th of the month. On 27 April it was given an enthusiastic welcome by the Milanese. Mickiewicz responded by telling them: 'You Milanese have demonstrated that liberty cannot be granted but must be taken by force. . . . We have a common interest, common duties and a common enemy; the Austrian Empire.' His aim, Mickiewicz maintained, was to liberate all Slavs from the Habsburg yoke, but clearly his first objective was to detach the Polish troops in Radetzky's army: 'There are three Polish regiments in this army. There must be a number of Poles in the infantry. The artillery is practically all Polish. Finally most of the troops sent to Italy up till the end of February were Slav. To make an impression on them what is needed is a flag, soldiers and fighting.'

Still, there were obstacles to overcome before the Legion could join in any battles. Neither Charles Albert nor the provisional government of Lombardy had any sympathy for radicalism, and Mickiewicz was known to be a radical and socialist. His volunteers as a result were shunned by the Italian authorities who accorded the Legion access only to those Slav prisoners of war who had expressly desired to be enrolled in it – so great was the fear on the part of the authorities that radicalised Polish troops would undermine the discipline of Sardinian regulars alongside whom they would be fighting. Other factors also served to underline the reluctance of the Italians to cooperate. Mazzini's vocal support of Mickiewicz was one; the reservations of the Paris Polish Committee which warned that Polish troops would have to be ready to return to battlefields in Poland (where revolutionary developments were expected daily) was yet another. Thus people like Vegezzi-Ruscalla[84] – a former official of the Sardinian Internal Ministry who encouraged his government to exploit Slav nationalism – were all but isolated and it sometimes seemed as if the Polish Legion would never get the opportunity to take up arms against the Austrians. Two developments, however, ensured that battle would be engaged. First, Mickiewicz visited Charles Albert in person and secured permission to recruit Slav prisoners of war, albeit by conceding that recruitment would be limited to those who had indicated a positive desire to join. Secondly, a demonstration by legionnaires in the streets of Milan – during which the 'Marseillaise' was sung with fervour bordering on the revolutionary – so frightened the authorities that they took seriously the explanation of Colonel Kamienski, the commanding officer of the legionnaires, who attributed this radical outburst to the demoralising effects produced by having to wait so long to be sent to the battlefield. Permission to leave was accorded quickly and Mickiewicz returned to Paris to interest the French in the Legion's exploits. The Legion itself meanwhile, had grown to a strength of some 200 men. The majority of them probably consisted of volunteers and prisoners of war since there is no evidence of Polish troops deserting. They fought until the bitter end in Italy, participating not only in the campaigns in the north but also in the defence of the Roman Republic.

Inside the army, on the other hand, there was very little indication of any Polish unrest. One plot was discovered, it is true, among Polish troops in Lower Austria in June 1848[85] – the evidence connected it with another conspiracy in Cracow – but among the troops who were serving under Field Marshal Radetzky, there is no evidence at all of Mickiewicz's Legion succeeding in winning loyalties. If the Field Marshal had to take care with his Magyar and Grenzer troops – to say nothing of the Italians – he did not have to worry about his Czechs or Poles to anything like the same degree.

The conclusion which must surely be arrived at, therefore, if one reflects on the nationality problems of Radetzky's army during the revolution of 1848, is that the problems which afflicted the Monarchy as a whole were reflected in its armed forces. No doubt the wretched conditions which every soldier experienced played an important part in dissolving what cement of loyalty remained, but it is a striking fact that the troops most vitally concerned with what was happening in 1848 were those whose concern was stimulated by the general course of events in their homelands. The Italian troops, as a result, either deserted immediately or when they thought they would be sent abroad; the Grenzer and the Magyars when they despaired of returning home. Thus, in 1848, the army proved to be an extension of society as a whole. It did not collapse altogether, but at times came close to dissolution. The Monarchy, on the other hand, reflected events within the army. Radetzky was able to keep it together by holding his army together in Italy.

Part II

Radetzky and the civil power in Lombardy-Venetia

Chapter 4

The army before the Revolution

The entry of Austrian troops into Lombardy in the summer of 1813 had been the occasion for widespread satisfaction and even rejoicing among the local population.[1]* French rule during the latter period of the Napoleonic Kingdom of Italy had been particularly onerous and the bitterness and resentment which had thereby been generated had only been exacerbated by the exigencies of the French retreat. The Austrians, however, succeeded in squandering the asset of their initial popularity:[2] they retained the services of many of Napoleon's administrators; and instead of repealing much of his fiscal legislation they added fiscal burdens of their own; finally, when it came down to human behaviour, the soldiers of Austria were just as rough and raped just as well as had those of France. The Italian welcome for the Austrians therefore, was very short-lived. The Austrians themselves soon realised this and the imperial Chief of Police, alarmed by the reports that he was getting from Milan, was warning as early as 1817, against a quietness that was only 'apparent'.[3]

The Austrian army, on the other hand, which also observed the changing mood of Italian public opinion, harboured fewer fears concerning potential unrest. In the summer of 1816, the Commander-in-Chief of the Austrian forces in Italy, Count Bubna, wrote to Field Marshal Schwarzenberg, informing him that there was 'nothing to fear'.[4] Troop strength was being reduced and the garrison in Milan alone had already lost 1,000 men. While agreeing that 'the material for revolution' existed in Lombardy, he drew a distinction of the kind that Metternich, for example, could never make, between the 'sects' and the 'dissatisfied'. The sects he regarded as a potential rather than an actual threat. He wrote:[5] . . . Their power has to some extent diminished. Those who are still active in sects are that part of the nation who have nothing to lose and can only profit from any change – reduced officers, lawyers, ruined businessmen, a few scholars and so many fools.' On the other hand, nearly everybody was dissatisfied: some had lost a lot; others had gained less than they had expected; Milan was no longer an independent capital; and every class could find some kind of grievance – even the poor and reliable peasants whose self-sufficiency was being undermined by inflation. Opposition to Austrian rule, he believed, was therefore more likely to materialise in the guise of 'partial revolts' occasioned by hunger or religious fanaticism rather than in subversive political movements.

Right up until 1830 this view prevailed. It suffered a temporary setback in 1820–1 with the military revolts in Naples and Piedmont and the fiasco of the

Confalonieri conspiracy in Milan; yet the Neapolitan revolt proved easy to suppress – perhaps too easy[6] – and the conspiracy in Milan received less support then than it has done since.[7] Austria quickly recovered her confidence and during the 1820s her reliance on the military for internal security diminished steadily. 'Italy in 1829 was denuded of troops.'[8] The same was true for other parts of the Empire for in 1840 the Austrian statistician, Johann Springer, could write that:[9] 'in peaceful times it is usual for a third or even a greater part of the men to be on leave and to keep only those who are indispensable for duty. In particular, the peaceful years 1816–29 allowed so greatly extended a use of this system, which is occasioned by economy and industrial considerations, that in each of the years, 1825, 1826, 1828, almost one half of the men were on leave.' When the revolutions of 1830 broke out, the Commander-in-Chief of the Austrian forces in Italy was himself missing, heading what another general was later to refer to as a 'so-called Court Commission' in Vienna.[10] He was, however, quickly sent back to Italy with a hastily improvised army corps and no revolution took place in Austrian territory. Piedmont worked hand in hand with Austria and the revolution in the Papal States was quickly suppressed.[11]

The events of 1830 did, however, cause great consternation in Vienna. Metternich expected the King of the French to turn into a second Robespierre and was decidedly worried by the danger that now seemed to threaten Austrian possession of the Kingdom of Lombardy-Venetia. His right-hand man, General Clam-Martinitz, was therefore despatched to Italy to review the situation. This he did and submitted a report.[12]

Clam's report is full of interest. General Frimont, the Austrian commander, according to this document, was doing a good job and the military position was 'very satisfactory'. Metternich was warned, however, that he could not rely on the support of the Italian people; the Austrian position relied instead on his 'disposing of an impressive military force' and on that alone. Clam even suggested that no recruiting should take place in Italy in 1831 and that the army should make up its strength by calling in those on leave; true, those on leave would represent an unstable element in the population, but chances were that recruiting procedures would provoke even more unrest. In order to underline his message, Clam specifically warned Metternich against 'harbouring any illusions'; in the event of war, he prophesied, 'everybody will desert us'. He obviously despaired of winning hearts and minds; perhaps he even despaired of winning battles; in any case his final recommendation appeared to originate in his diplomatic rather than in his military training: 'Here it is not a matter of numbers but of appearances . . . to prove to them that we are not asleep as they allow themselves to hope and say.' Appearance and reality; unity and diversity. Clam had stumbled once again upon the old dilemmas of the Austrian condition. His answer was the traditional one, perhaps the only solution: Metternich was to govern by mirrors. The report was taken very much to heart in Vienna and very soon after it was submitted, Radetzky was appointed Commander-in-Chief of the Austrian army in Italy.

Radetzky, one of the Empire's most distinguished soldiers, has received very little attention from historians outside Austria, perhaps not enough of the right kind from inside Austria itself.[13] On the seventieth anniversary of his death a Hamburg newspaper printed a picture of him with the caption underneath:[14] 'The Austrian Field Marshal Count Radetzky, made famous by the Radetzky

March, composed by Johann Strauss.' The man of whom Grillparzer was to write, 'in thy camp is Austria', was thus presented as the extraneous object of musical curiosity. Yet why had Strauss composed the march? After the loss of the Italian provinces, nobody wanted to know.

The future Field Marshal of the Austrian Empire was born on All Saints' Day 1766 at Trebnitz in Bohemia. Historians occasionally refer to him as Czech, but he always used the term *wir Deutsch* and often spoke in *wienerisch*. Schooled at the Theresianum in Vienna, he joined the army as a cuirassier cadet in 1784. He served as an ordnance officer to both Lacy and Laudon during the Turkish Wars of Joseph II, but he reached what must have seemed the height of his career in the wars against the French, distinguishing himself in the battles of Novi, Marengo, Hohenlinden, Wels and Wagram. His talents were noted and at the age of forty-three he was promoted Chief of the Austrian General Staff under Field Marshal Prince Liechtenstein; in 1813 he was appointed Chief of Staff to the Allied commander, Schwarzenberg. Little wonder then that when the wars were finally over, he was restless, bored and embittered; encumbered with financial worries and neglected by the army, he saw nothing much to look forward to.[15]

In 1816 he went to Odenburg to command a cavalry division; in 1818 he moved to Ofen (Buda) as *Adlatus* to the Royal Commissioner to Hungary; and shortly afterwards he was sent to command the fortress of Olmütz. He thought it would be his last post and was still there at the age of sixty-four. Then came the revolutions of 1830 and Radetzky was summoned to the Emperor.[16] 'I want you to do me a favour', said Francis, who then requested him to get the army in Italy into a state of battle-readiness. Before he left Vienna, however, the new commander was instructed to see Prince Metternich to receive some final advice. At the end of the meeting, Radetzky once again met the Emperor, who asked him how he had got on. 'Please excuse me,' he replied, 'the Prince spoke for three hours and I know nothing.'

The Emperor's choice was not everywhere welcomed.[17] Kübeck, for example, noted in his diary:[18]

The Archduke Charles was consulted confidentially about the choice of Radetzky as commanding general in Italy. The Archduke welcomed it but only because he thought that Baron Frimont would retain the supreme command.[19] Otherwise he would have recommended Bianchi. Now Radetzky stands alone, and just for that reason, not in his [proper] place, for he is still as garrulous and changeable in his views. Every other hour he has a new plan without ever being able to bring any order into any (single) one.

The scene was set therefore, for what was to follow – a relationship of mutual miscomprehension between Vienna and Milan, between the central government of the Empire and the army in Italy.

Nevertheless, on so much they could agree. Clam had spoken up about the need to maintain appearances and Radetzky, therefore, was empowered to organise manœuvres in northern Italy on a scale which Europe had rarely, if ever, witnessed before. Indeed, it was really much more than mere show. Here, repeated every year for the moral benefit of Italy and Europe, was a massive exercise in propaganda.[20] During the winters the troops were thoroughly instructed in the theoretical background to the manœuvres, using sand models and other devices; in spring or at the beginning of summer at the latest, Radetzky led them away from the monotony of the parade ground into prepared camps in different parts of the country; in the autumn, after camp exercises, they at last were brought together in order to take part in one great manœuvre involving everybody.

Austrian historians have always agreed in crediting the army's success in 1848–9 to just these tactics and training. No doubt they did help to some extent – the army became intimately familiar with the terrain of northern Italy and the new methods of instruction introduced by Radetzky were indeed valuable improvements – but there is reason to believe that the value of Radetzky's work in pre-March Lombardy-Venetia has been somewhat overrated.[21] The Archduke Maximilian d'Este, for example, the brother of the Duke of Modena, and a leading Austrian military innovator, had very little respect for Radetzky's staff officers, the supposed pride of the Field Marshal's army. He wrote:[22]

The general staff and aides de camp should consist of the most outstanding and choicest individuals and nobody should be accepted into this branch who does not possess in addition to a complete theory of the art of war, the ability to put this into practice. However, it appears that just this branch, in Italy at least, is so designed to enable the promotion of certain favourites to respectable jobs with no risk to their lives. Only a small part of this branch can be used to any effect, and this part carries the burden of the whole; the rest idle around pursuing their pleasures. The entire headquarters is full of officers of the general staff; during hostilities very few are to be seen. It is the common voice of our army: our general staff is fit for nothing; and this truth is everywhere confirmed.

Another trenchant critic was Fenner von Fenneberg who himself had served in Radetzky's officer corps and who in October 1848 was to become chief military adviser to the Viennese rebels under Messenhauser.[23] A disciple of the French thinker Saint-Simon, he regarded the manœuvres as socially and economically wasteful; their general popularity he attributed to the excuse they provided for large numbers of officers to get together and indulge their tastes in drinking, gambling and general camaraderie. The military aspect did not impress him; while the officers pursued their pleasures the men themselves were so neglected that they fell victim to a demoralisation which lasted long afterwards. Many became very ill and ended up in barbaric field hospitals where sick men were subjected to hunger cures and fit ones suffered relapses. At the height of the manœuvres the sick rate rose to one man in three so that given that many men were also lost for days, battalions were often reduced to something like 30 per cent of full strength before the manœuvres were over. Apparently there was also a fire risk; fires would break out that proved impossible to contain, the results of which could debilitate the army for months. Altogether, therefore, he considered the manœuvres as a downright waste of money: '[They] cost the country . . . untold sums of money, half of which would do to regulate the flow of the Etsch which every year makes thousands destitute. It could at least provide permanent and public work.' Whatever advantages they brought – and he included among these 'a political demonstration [designed to] reveal an impressive, well-trained mass of troops to the unreasonable' – he nevertheless concluded that these were 'far outweighed by a superior number of connected disadvantages'.

However, it was FML. Baron D'Aspre, commander of Radetzky's Second Army Corps, who delivered what perhaps can be considered the most damning indictment of Radetzky's pre-March record. A memorandum, dated 3 December 1849, which can be found among his papers in the Kriegsarchiv in Vienna, begins with the words:[24] 'It should not be necessary to investigate the reasons which have been responsible for the great losses suffered in Italy during the revolution. In my opinion these can be traced to the way in which the army was run.' The memorandum then goes on to point to the glaring deficiencies which had existed in the Austrian command system, deficiencies which Radetzky had never tried to reform but ones which cost him the lives of many men and almost the campaign itself. However impressive he had been as a propagandist the old Field Marshal had been remiss in tackling other problems. That Austrian historians have never seen fit to say so is yet more proof of how effective the propaganda was. In many ways the Austrians themselves have always been the greatest victims of it.

Clam-Martinitz's advice had been that the Austrians should frighten a people which would always regard them as strangers. The army's presence in Italy, therefore, was never meant to be a reassuring one and its propaganda produced the inevitable result: Italians hated it – and particularly when it appeared in the guise of officers. General von Stratimirovic recorded in his memoirs:[25]

In the Austrian Italian provinces the position of an imperial and royal officer was in no way envious. The population hated us and despite precautions we were involved in numerous clashes with the Italians. Many incidents took place. As a result of these we were advised to wear our civilian clothes off duty. In spite of this it happened that single officers who were returning to the suburbs from the city were set upon by vagabonds hiding behind trees, completely stripped of their clothing and tied to the trees to await being freed by a passing patrol.

The chance to reconcile Italian and Austrian had already been missed – perhaps deliberately. According to Schönhals:[26]

Soon after the coronation [1838] a greater division was noticeable between the two nationalities; the weak social links which had existed up till then became more and more tenuous; one noticed a disquiet in the temper of the people and it could not escape the careful observer that the political drift would take a different direction from the one up till then, that this state of affairs had spread and extended itself over an area it had never before held. The middle classes, the lower classes of the people had remained free of this feeling so far, but now the giddiness seized them too. That this situation could not last, that it must lead to a break, was so clear that no one could doubt it for a minute; how far, however, the poison had already contaminated the social organism, was naturally a secret and those contaminated could not themselves yet know.

Despite its manifest unpopularity, however, the Austrian army was determined to maintain its dominant position. 'Your Excellency may rest completely assured', wrote Radetzky to the President of the Hofkriegsrath, Count Hardegg, 'I am and will remain master of Italy.'[27] The extent and earnestness of this commitment he revealed in a letter to the Viceroy of 9 February 1848:[28] 'I have sworn to the Emperor, my lord, to fight his enemies and defend his throne and rights; I will remain true to this oath till my last breath. I will weep over the blood that must flow, but I will spill it and let the Hereafter judge me.

'Your Royal Highness will excuse the warmth of my words but the most holy interests of our most illustrious *Kaiserhaus* are at stake and to the service of this House has my whole life been devoted.' Naturally he did not spare much thought for the Italians:[29] 'Their naïveté is truly laughable', he wrote. 'In all seriousness, they ask, why, if they do not want us here, we do not go away?' But why did they not go away?

Army men always pride themselves in having a thoroughly practical outlook on life. No doubt, therefore, an Austrian officer, presented with such a question would have based his answers on practical grounds. Practical grounds, to be sure, often beg moral questions, but, as will be seen, the Austrian army believed that it could provide the moral answers also. At any rate, any Austrian officer justifying his right to be in Italy would probably have prefaced his remarks with considerations of strategy. The Archduke Maximilian certainly did so when he began to analyse the problem[30] and the argument ran as follows.

Suppose France were to collect an army at Dijon as she had done in 1800. If she wished to attack South Germany she could then advance 'at a minute's notice' along either the left bank of the Po or the right bank of the Danube. In both ways a French army had succeeded in reaching Vienna. *Que faire donc l'Autriche*?

Austria could, of course, split her armies. One part could protect northern Italy, while the other – allied with German states like Bavaria – could withstand a French attack from Strasbourg. Yet Austrian strategists of the time saw no solution in this, because the French were always given certain built-in advantages. For a start, the terrain in northern Italy was held to favour an attack from the west; it was also reckoned that the French could secure their own rear by stationing 50,000 men at either Lyons or Strasbourg, thus enabling them to concentrate a large force for the attack on either river basin; finally, it was calculated that should the French in fact choose to invade the north of Italy, a strong observation corps would be enough to lock up most of the Austrian garrisons within their fortresses and cut them off from the rest of the Austrian troops. The importance of the Quadrilateral was almost discounted in a confrontation with the French.

The position of the Austrian army in Italy was, therefore, in a sense rather like Metternich's. It, too, worked with mirrors. Or rather it itself was a mirror, a mirror of events in France. Perhaps this is what Radetzky meant when he referred to the year 1834 as 'the fifth year of the July Revolution'. In any case, his forces went up in numbers as confidence in France went down. Soon after 1830 they reached the 120,000 mark, but as Louis Philippe grew more and more conservative, the Austrian army was reduced to less than half that size.[31]

Yet there was another danger. Implicit in the concept that Austrian strategy could only be a reflection of the French, was the idea that Austrian strategy was only a reaction to the French, i.e. that France would have the initiative of selecting the theatre of war. Partly this was because, territorially speaking, Austria, in the words of the Archduke Maximilian, was 'as satisfied as any European Hausmutter'. Probably, however, the Austrians did not expect to win in a straight fight with France in any case.[32] Radetzky saw that the best chance of maintaining Austria's hold on Italy was, therefore, to be secured by simply retaining as large an army in the area as possible. 'We must dispose of a superiority', he wrote, and demanded 130,000 men with which to provide it. At the same time, Radetzky argued, this would provide proof of Austria's willingness to defend the established order of things in Europe and make her a European necessity.[33] It also meant that the Empire was more than just a collection of Slavs and Magyars.

This sort of strategical analysis explains, however, not only the presence of a large Austrian army in Italy but much more besides. Because the Austrians saw Italy as so important, the main burden of the defence of the Rhine was willy-nilly given over to the Prussians who were encouraged in this way, even in the Austrian mind, to become the future leaders of Germany, a rather ironic development when one remembers that Metternich was a Rhinelander. An explanation is also afforded for the alliance system which Metternich built up. The Chancellor of Austria was merely relying on the Prussians and Russians to do his fighting for him.[34] This, after all was the tradition of Austrian foreign policy.[35] The Austrian forces, then in the Clam-Martinitz tradition, were really stationed in Italy to fool the French, the Italians and, if possible, the whole of Europe. By winning in 1848–9, they even fooled the Austrians as well.

A second practical reason for keeping so many troops in Austrian Italy was, not unnaturally, the threat of internal revolt. If Radetzky lacked sufficient troops for his army to make strategical sense in the eyes of his strategists, then he had men enough to guarantee the rule of law and order. Maximilian, who did not share Radetzky's views about superior numbers (he had other ideas which will be discussed later) believed that this aspect of the army's position positively hindered its strategical usefulness:[36]

There are three main causes why such great striking forces are required in Italy.

The first is that there are so many forts which swallow up enormous garrisons which are, in the event of war, totally lost to the active army, since these garrisons dare not move outwith a cannonshot's range of their fortresses. They can, therefore, render no other service than the highly indifferent one of depriving the enemy of possession of a fortress.

The second cause is that what remains of active troops, once deductions have been made for garrison duty, if attacked by an enemy who is superior in numbers, no longer has a secure haven in which to remain unattacked, or from which, by means of great unexpected sallies, to cover the entire countryside and wait until, by retaining communications with the rest of the Empire, it can once more resume the offensive.

The third cause is that due to circumstances, into whose origins we do not want here to enquire, the government of these lands has been reduced to the state where no delegate or district commissioner believes himself able to rule his allotted district or districts, or trusts himself to rule over them, without the permanent presence of the military.

By the beginning of 1848 the Archduke had changed his opinion slightly, or rather, sharpened it. The two causes which he now listed were:[37] 'Firstly, because we can no longer trust the king of Sardinia. Secondly, because people now fear the spirit which is held to rule Italy; no city of this country now believes it can govern without a strong military occupation.' And he added this extremely significant comment:

'Both causes are of such a nature that they will never end, and yet we cannot, either with regard to financial or to military considerations, keep such an army in Italy and have the other provinces denuded of troops.' Perhaps the practical grounds for keeping the army there were not practical after all?

This was a conclusion which might well have forced itself on von Fenneberg. His, after all, was the point that the army could only maintain a strategical position if the political, social and moral contexts were adjusted. Most officers of his day would have quarrelled with him. Strange as it may seem to modern minds, they saw the army almost as a democratising force in Italy. What moral scruples they had were easily satisfied.

It cannot be denied that Austria had economic motives for retaining her Italian provinces. Radetzky himself can be cited in support of such a view.[38] However, in an age when certain types of economic historians can see imperialism in any adverse trade balance the name given to the economic relationship does not matter very much. The point is that the Austrian army was very proud of what Austria had done for Italy and not a little surprised at what it took to be Italian ingratitude. Perhaps this is the view of all imperial rulers. Perhaps the Austrians were just that. In any case, the view was one which had to be reckoned with and historiography has tended to support it. Even Bolton King, no friend of Austria in Italy, could write:[39]

Though the emancipation of Lombardy and Venetia was the dream of every Italian patriot, Neapolitan and Roman and Piedmontese might well envy the institutions under which their inhabitants lived. The Austrian Empire was too strong, too much in evidence, to condescend to the indecent corruption of a petty tyranny . . . there was a regularity and robustness of administration, an equality before the law, a social freedom, which, except in Tuscany and Parma, was without its parallel in Italy.

He also calculated that, 'it is probable that on a basis of wealth she (i.e. Lombardy) paid no more than her quotum'.

Austrians historians have, of course, never disagreed.[40] To them it has always been clear that Lombardy-Venetia had benefited from the reforms, not only of Joseph II and Maria Theresa, but also of Napoleon, whose reforms the Austrians had never reversed. Moreover, when changes had been made they had been for the better. The civil code of 1814 was in some respects an improvement on the *Code Napoléon* and the peasants welcomed the protection it gave to them against their landlords. If there was censorship it was probably the lightest in Italy and the political police was no more of a burden that the equivalent in Piedmont or Rome. This was appreciated at the time. After the revolts in the Papal Legations in 1845, there was even a pro-Austrian backlash. It was described in a report by the American representative at Turin, R. Wickliffe Jun. in a report to the American Secretary of State, Buchanan, on 3 October 1845: 'It is not for liberty but for bread they rise and much as Austria is detested by all Italy, the Legations are reduced to such dreadful extremities that they would gladly seek refuge from priestly extortion in the more orderly and better regulated despotism of an Austrian Prince.' The American representative held political views which made him a hostile observer of Austrian Italy. Yet even he was forced into a grudging recognition of the Austrian achievement.[41] Subsequent history writing has obscured these facts, but the Austrian army knew who 'made the trains run on time' and kept living standards higher than in the rest of Italy.[42]

How politically democratic was the Austrian army in Italy? Radetzky's views were not always consistent with regard to political questions, but he was without doubt the most 'liberal' of all the great men in the counter-revolutionary armies. As early as 1827 he had written in a memorandum[43] that, 'It is better to join with intellectual progress than to fight it. Progress can indeed be made difficult and delayed by a government; it can never, however, be completely checked.' In 1828 he went further and expressed the view that if statesmen were to be 'wise and intelligent', they 'would give all states appropriate constitutions'. His prediction was that, 'within a short time', all the states of Europe would receive them anyway; adding 'in this way the end after which all peoples have for so long been striving in vain will be fulfilled'. Once in Italy, however, his views began to change and he talked more and more frequently about the 'predominance of liberalism' in a tone which no longer indicated full support. The events of 1830 had strongly influenced his outlook.[44]

In Italy, on the face of things, the Austrian army was insensitive to Italian demands and to *la vie italienne*. Schönhals claimed that the Italians were not 'gemütlich' and were 'distinguished by a gift for phantasy'.[45] Maximilian parodied their ambition 'to appear on the stage of the World Theatre' or as 'members of the Great Nation or of their own Italian mock-nation' and ridiculed the sight of Italians in embroidered uniforms, officers of the Great Army, as he put it, shining in the light of their own victories. But this, he wrote, would be 'at their own astonishment' and he dismissed it all as 'nothing but soap bubbles'. Perhaps he was only 90 per cent wrong.[46]

Still, it would be totally wrong to believe that the army failed to see the nationality problem at work in Italy or ignored the striving after unity. It merely saw these things in a different light. There was in fact a great paradox here. Precisely because the army was so used to seeing the rivalries of the different Italian cities and states,[47] it believed that only it itself could impose any unity on the peninsula. Otherwise Italy would be just a 'geographical expression'. Nor was it wrong. By providing a focus for Italian hatred, the Austrian army did indeed unite Italy.[48] Yet another paradox. It was all, in fact, rather like the British Raj in India. It might contain Punjabis, Bengalis, Sikhs, etc. but take away the British and what was left? Certainly not a united India. Similarly, if the Austrian army were to get out of Italy, it would leave no Italy behind it. In a sense the same was true for the Empire as a whole: without the Austrian army, it could not exist. Hence Italy was regarded by the army as the thin end of the wedge of Habsburg fortunes, a question of life and death for the *Kaiserreich*.

Consequently, the natural ambitions of the Italians were supposed to find an outlet inside the Habsburg Empire:[49]

Austria . . . can be called the common haven of all the surrounding nations for she is their common refuge in every need, their protecting wall against every attack. Men of all these nations find in Austria not only friendly hospitality but are employed in the army, in all branches of administration, even in the Ministries and *Hofstellen*. No difference is made between those of native or foreign birth, much less does anyone stop to think to which nation anyone belongs. In this way it is just absurd and laughable to want to create a national conceit against Austria.

Most absurd of all is it for the Italians who would do well to consider how many of their countrymen have reached the highest military, civilian and *Hofstellen* posts in Austria and have thus acquired a European reputation with which even the dream of a united Italy cannot deceive them.

Those accepted into the Austrian Confederation of Nations should be much prouder to belong to this Central National Confederation of Europe, to belong to the Central Power which keeps the whole of Europe in balance, which is protected, loved and feared; they should be proud and hold their heads up high, instead of making themselves the laughing stock of Europe through dreams and silly pronouncements.

That, at least, was the theory of the Austrian Empire. Feelings of nationalism were to be subordinated to the obvious virtues of *Kaisertreue*. Almost inevitably, therefore, the army's view of the political situation was coloured by complacency. Schönhals[50] concluded that the Kingdom of Lombardy-Venetia enjoyed 'national and administrative independence as far as this was compatible with a centralised monarchy', a judgement which begged all the important questions. He even blamed the Congregations for neglecting their constitutional duties,[51] although he implied that the Italians were just as well off anyway since elected representatives made little difference. 'The country', he wrote,

was administered bureaucratically but well and justly. There is no doubt that this state of affairs can often be somewhat boring, but is it any better or for that matter any different under a so-called constitutional administration? Does the cry of the tribunes expedite administration in constitutional states, or is the rule of Ministers the more moderate in its use of power, in the employment of nepotism, because it is supposed to be, as people say, responsible? We do not wish to speak here about bureaucracy; we know that it can degenerate into a scourge; but at least it has the advantage over *Ministerialismus* of stability. We doubt whether the welfare of French subjects gains in any way by the change of prefects.

Yet he did condemn the activities of the police and censorship.[52] 'It is more difficult', he wrote,

for us to combat the charges levied against the Austrian secret police and censorship. We will not even try, because we are not disposed to protect an abuse. We know quite well that in times like our own, no state can exist without a police; but it is the duty of every state to make this necessary evil as little vexatious as possible, for nothing is so hateful than this constant interference in people's personal freedom, this tutelage over even their most innocent affairs. Never yet has a police force prevented a revolution. How easily, on the other hand, does it degenerate into tale-bearing and defamation.

The army's outlook, therefore, was complacent but not totally uncritical. Its view of the political situation, if anything, was more enlightened than that of the imperial government. This did not really matter, of course, so long as it played no active part in politics, but by 1848, its views were beginning to count.

Chapter 5

Civil-military relations before the Tobacco Riots

The role of the army

'The first step in the downfall of a state is the participation of the armed forces in the internal political struggles of the state.' So wrote Radetzky in one of his many *Denkschriften*.[1]* The fact remained, however, that in Lombardy-Venetia the army was indeed involved in the political struggle, although to its many officers its role was confined to maintaining law and order. Be that as it may, it was required to deal with political subversion, with opponents of the Austrian regime who wore no uniforms and carried no arms. Its conduct, therefore, was subject to regulation. On minor matters such regulation was weighted in favour of the civilian authorities and here, for example, are Hardegg's instructions regarding the conscription of political suspects:[2]

The forced enlistment into the army of individuals suspected on account of their political activities is an exceptional measure which is only rarely to be resorted to in individual cases.

In accordance with the Sovereign Resolution of the 8th of this month, it has pleased His Majesty to decree that political suspects consigned to the military are to be informed of the reasons behind such suspicion and that the army is to conduct itself in accordance with this regulation.

In cases where such individuals are consigned to the army by the appropriate political authorities, they are to be conscripted immediately for the full period of enlistment into the appropriate regiment attached to their recruiting area. If necessary the matter should be raised immediately with the Hofkriegsrath which shall issue appropriate instructions, especially when such individuals are to be consigned to a military corps of a different nationality which is stationed far away.

The military corps to which such a suspect is consigned must watch him very carefully and cannot issue him with a pass before he has, over a number of years, given proof of good conduct and principles.

The commanding general will furnish appropriate instructions to subordinate commanders, conscription authorities and the military bodies which receive these recruits from these authorities.

All very straightforward.

Less straightforward, however, were the instructions regarding the army's behaviour in clashes with the civilian population. These perhaps were designed to ensure that some control was exercised, but it was not at all clear just how

---

* Notes to this chapter are on pp. 260–2.

this was to be done, for in spite of their apparent clarity, the instructions concerned could be easily manipulated and in the final analysis depended for their effectiveness on the cooperation of the military with their civilian overseers. If that cooperation was non-existent the army had the right to some considerable initiative. That this was so is abundantly clear from the relevant instructions of 8 October 1844:[3]

In the rules of conduct which apply to commanders called in by the political authorities to render assistance during civil disturbances and to restore the order that has been threatened, one of the most important points is constituted by the question at what time and under what circumstances is the actual use of weapons finally and inevitably necessary.

Experience has shown that up till now it has not always been possible to adhere to one guiding principle in solving this question.

In order to remove any room for uncertainty in a matter of this importance and in order to establish a generally uniform and appropriate procedure it has pleased His Majesty the Emperor to lay down the following principle, the simplicity and clarity of which can leave no room for ambiguity.

The actual use of weaponry – and then in all earnest – can be resorted to in two cases.

The first case that can be taken as a guideline occurs when the political commissioner to whom the military assistance is offered and who is primarily responsible for the use of force, declares that any further efforts as dissuasion on his part would not succeed in restoring order and, therefore, demands the actual employment of weaponry. The second case – in which the use of weapons has been immediately resorted to without this demand on the part of the political commissioner – occurs when the troops have themselves been attacked or have really been so insulted by the demonstrators that under the circumstances they have reached such a degree of insensitivity that they have had to resort to force to defend their honour.

Your Etc. shall take note of this principle, which has received imperial sanction, in order to raise it in the instruction given to troop commanders regarding such military assistance, as well as to inform the political authorities of the nature of the decree.

Since, however, there are cases which arise of various types for which no generally appropriate rules can have individual application, it must be left to the good judgement of the commander involved in such military assistance, whether in any given case to call for a bayonet attack by the infantry in closed order and in deadly earnest – and always, as goes without saying under the protection of a detachment brought up from reserve since in the meantime a more delicate situation could arise – or whether to resort immediately to rifle fire, which must always be discharged in volleys and never in single shots.

Finally, the need, which is in any case emphasised in the existing instructions' for the greatest possible care both in estimating the strength of force required and in the choice of leaders, is once more recommended to commanders called upon to render military assistance.

The whole assumption behind these instructions was the close cooperation of the civil and military authorities. However, a situation were to arise in which the army decided to make a bid for the upper hand, it clearly had the legal means which it could exploit to further its aims. This is exactly what the Austrian army was to be accused of after the Tobacco Riots in January 1848; yet the great explosion of temper which then occurred had been threatening to take place for some time and the fuse that finally ignited it can be traced back to 1846.

Metternich and the 'occupation' of Ferrara

The revolutions of 1848 in Italy were preceded, as revolutions usually are, by a relatively short period of ever-rising tension. In Italy, undoubtedly, this period began with the election in June 1846 of Pius IX to the Papal See. Pio Nono was known to have somewhat liberal inclinations and the news of his papcy – and more especially of the reforms which he quickly enacted – electrified the whole political atmosphere in Italy. Metternich was completely taken aback:[4] 'We were prepared for everything but a liberal Pope,' he said 'and now that we have one, who can tell what will happen?' Radetzky's reaction was somewhat similar:[5] 'Things are quiet here but the fire is burning beneath the ashes. God alone knows how it will end. The Pope is flirting with the liberals and believes that he is converting them.' The election of Pius, however, was only the beginning of an accumulation of circumstances, all of which seemed to conspire against Austria. The same year that saw the new Pope established in Rome, witnessed the republication of Gioberti's *Primato*; on 5 December 1846 the centenary celebrations of the expulsion of the Germans from Genoa took place; and on 30 December the body of Confalonieri was brought to Milan amidst scenes of wildly anti-Austrian sentiment. Fate also decreed that the following year would sustain this rise in tension: the death of the German Archbishop of Milan before the end of 1846 brought Austria under inevitable pressure to appoint an Italian successor. This was done, but when the Bishop of Cremona, a member of the Romilli family of Milan, was appointed to the see, the imperial choice was everywhere greeted as not much short of a surrender. The entry of the new Archbishop into Milan in September 1847 provided yet another occasion, therefore, for anti-Austrian demonstrations. Even before then, however, the political temperature had risen to almost fever level on account of the 'occupation' by Austrian troops to the papal town of Ferrara.

Austria, according to the Treaty of Vienna, had every right to maintain a garrison in the citadel of Ferrara; but on 16 July 1847 Radetzky reinforced that garrison and had his troops patrol the town itself. Such a move had been rumoured in Italy since at least the beginning of 1847; the secret police had even suggested that it would meet with popular approval;[6] yet, given that it was bound to be seen as an Austrian attack on the Papacy, it was a move that was fraught with diplomatic dangers. Radetzky, on the other hand, was prepared to ignore these:[7] 'I do not understand diplomats,' he once said, 'May I have nothing to do with them.' Frustrated and furious with the course of events in Rome, he ordered his troops to patrol Ferrara.

Inevitably and immediately he became the butt of international protests: Britain delivered a strongly worded diplomatic note:[8] even Guizot was forced to rap Metternich gently over the knuckles;[9] but worst of all, the Papacy was stung into delivering a strong rebuke which found an echo in Turin. Indeed, Charles Albert was able to score an easy diplomatic point by proclaiming his support for the Pope in the *Gazetta Piemontese*:[10] 'To see the city in the hands of the Austrians', it read, 'and to be able to do nothing to liberate it, is a torment that every Italian heart will understand.' He even offered to put a warship at the disposal of the Pope to bring the latter to Turin – a very effective, if somewhat extravagant gesture.

Radetzky had committed a first-class blunder:[11]

The strengthening of the Austrian garrison at Ferrara, undertaken in the year 1847 with military ostentation . . . was quite lawful for Austria and was only the repetition of what had taken place under the previous Pope, Gregory XVI, and had been acknowledged by him with thanks.

But the commander in Lombardy committed the anachronism of forgetting that in 1847 a different head wore the tiara and that this head was influenced by different opinions. . . . For the movement party, the protestation of the Papal government was a powerful weapon against Austria, since it afforded an ostensible ground to preach a crusade against the alleged enemies of the Church, in which course they were zealously assisted by the Italian priesthood, who are for the most part an ignorant body, and who do not esteem the Germans to be genuine Catholics.

So wrote Hartig and not merely with hindsight. He was careful to add:[12] ' . . . But the Cabinet in Vienna cannot be blamed for this anachronism, for it first became acquainted with the fact when it was accomplished, and it was obliged, therefore, to assert its own legal rights.'

The occupation, in fact, had been the direct result of a military order given by Radetzky. Metternich knew nothing about it beforehand, but was forced to back it up.[13] The excuse he found was that an officer of the Austrian garrison had been attacked by an Italian mob. He was not altogether unsympathetic and by no means perturbed by Radetzky's move;[14] nonetheless this unilateral action on the part of the Field Marshal certainly contributed to Ficquelmont, Metternich's right-hand man and possible successor, being sent to Italy to advise the Viceroy there (the Archduke Rainer), for in a letter accompanying his instructions Metternich wrote:[15] 'Marshal Radetzky meanwhile has stretched his authority to the limit and has adopted a very pronounced position. . . . There can be no question of military measures at the moment; these measures will have to be taken within the context of a sane policy. The Marshal will be ordered by the Hofkriegsrath to reach an understanding with you about these, should they become necessary.' And almost a year after Metternich had given him these instructions, Ficquelmont himself wrote that the mission which he undertook in Italy in 1847 'had the object of centralising observations and bringing more unity into the reports of the government and the military commander'.[16]

Radetzky himself must have guessed as much, but he suffered no rebuke. Conservative opinion in Vienna had welcomed his stand, which was compared favourably with what was regarded as Metternich's pusillanimity over the Sonderbund War in Switzerland.[17] The Chancellor, therefore, was at pains not to upset the Field Marshal and, indeed, when he wrote to inform him of Ficquelmont's impending arrival he found it necessary to indulge in some gushy sentimentality. For example,[18] ' . . . Politics and warfare', he wrote, 'are indivisible strengths . . . we, you and I, my dear Field Marshal, have lived through difficult times. . . . May Heaven preserve you for a long time yet for the Emperor and the State.' Ficquelmont managed to go one step further, stating,[19] ' . . . Your Excellency has given the first proof of strength and decision in Ferrara. It is already sure that it will bear good fruit. With regard to Roman Italy, Ferrara is the Citadel of our Rights.' They nevertheless succeeded in arranging with the Papacy a convention that the army regarded with disdain.[20]

Ficquelmont, at first, was a puzzle to the soldiers. 'I do not trust myself to give any judgement about the activity of the latest *expositus* Count Ficquelmont', wrote one army captain to another, 'Up till now people do not see much change since he did not trust himself to give definite replies to some significant questions.'[21] Radetzky, on the other hand, displayed a downright hostility from the very start. So openly, indeed, did he voice his criticisms that the man whom he thought was 'ready to reduce (Ferrara) to ashes', the new commander of the garrison there, Count Auersperg, was almost driven to resign. He confided to his wife:[22]

I intend to make my position about R. [Radetzky] very clear to you. He sees everything with a soldier's eyes and heart in the usual old way and cannot submit at all to the views of the Cabinet if they differ from his own. He persists in and holds fast to his own opinion, hopes for intervention in Rome and Tuscany and wilfully ignores everything that the diplomats say or assure him with to the contrary. Ficquelmont very clearly expresses the view that we shall in no case become involved in external affairs, that up till now our experience has been that intervention in Naples and Rome has only cost everybody money and that after our departure affairs have only returned to their former situation. This is *the view of our Cabinet* and it is almost childish of R. to go around everywhere saying that he is not satisfied with Ficquelmont sharing these views. My God what can he expect from an emissary of the same Cabinet than that he be directed in this sense and had Radetzky known of this sooner and not acted so quickly against Ferrara, the outcry against us might not have arisen in the whole of Europe and the catastrophe might not have reached the stage where we are threatened with losing the rights we have exercised here for 33 years.

Metternich's policy in Italy at this time – as he made clear to Ficquelmont before the latter left Vienna – was essentially pacific.[23] The 'basis' of it was 'not to intervene in either the Kingdom of Naples or in the Papal States . . . but to erect the strongest barrier to disorder and to defend [Austrian] rights tenaciously wherever they [were] attacked'. He also regarded it as 'essential' to save Piedmont 'from herself' and to win her back into the conservative camp. The question naturally arose of what would happen should disorder force Austria to hit back across her boundaries, but Metternich was prepared to leave that question aside. All in all, he was envisaging a defensive strategy.

Probably, however, he had adopted this view reluctantly. Although Radetzky had acted unilaterally over Ferrara, Metternich at almost the same time had been toying with the notion of a mobile task force which Radetzky could use to strike at external threats. Ironically enough, it was almost certainly Radetzky's own impatience that put paid to this idea.

In a memorandum he submitted to the Emperor on 17 July 1847 Metternich described the situation in Italy as one on which would ultimately depend 'not merely the possession of the Kingdom of Lombardy-Venetia, but the moral indeed the internal calm of the Empire as a whole'.[24] The threat to imperial peace, however – certainly as far as Italy was concerned – was an external rather than an internal one: Metternich apparently had no misgivings about the internal security of the imperial possessions there.[25] The real problem, as he saw it, was the need to be able to 'effect the greatest possible repressive influence on any revolution that [might] break out in Central Italy', an ability which would necessitate 'a special mobile force . . . whose strength and disposal [would] depend on the task it [was] required to do at the time'. The ideas behind this proposal were clearly far from worked out: any operation that might be undertaken by such a force could never be of a *preventive* character – that would entail a full-scale holding operation in Lombardy-Venetia itself; 'it could only [therefore] be a question of *repression*'; finally, the troops involved that were operating in foreign territory would have to 'live off the land'.

Probably in order to give form to these proposals he requested permission to take up the matter with both the treasury and the army.

Only three days later, on 20 July 1847, he discussed the subject, but in outline rather than in detail, with Kübeck, head of the treasury, and Hardegg, the President of the War Council.[26] He had no idea, he said, of how many troops were at the disposal of either Piedmont or Naples to resist a revolution; in Central Italy, certainly, there were far too few; and those that there were in Tuscany and in the Papal States he expected would desert to the enemy. Therefore, any action that would be required as a result of a revolution would mean that Austria must bear the burden. He was primarily thinking about the Papal States and an intervention there, he reckoned, would require a force of at least 25,000 men with reserves of another 10,000. Hardegg said that Radetzky at that time had about 50,000 men, which number he could easily raise to 64,000 by calling in those on leave and putting some batteries on a war footing. These figures, apparently, were very reassuring since Metternich emphasised that any intervention 'would be more of a police measure than an extended military operation' and since Hardegg was of the opinion that 64,000 men 'would be more than enough to maintain order in the Kingdom of Lombardy-Venetia'; the latter could even add that 'the 25,000 man strong operation corps mentioned by the Prince Chancellor with regard to Central Italy along with the necessary reserves could be taken from this force'. It would then be a simple matter of filling in the gaps inside Lombardy-Venetia itself.

It was Kübeck, predictably, who struck a note of caution. Such steps might well be necessary for the security of the Empire, but he was at pains to make it clear that they would have to be taken in secret. Otherwise public credit would immediately be adversely affected and his own position would be made more difficult. He also made the inevitable condition that as little money should be spent as possible and finally, perhaps to ensure that the whole idea was feasible, he got the other two to agree to a meeting of all officials involved in order to examine the proposals in more detail. Hardegg, however, had to be realistic about secrecy and felt compelled to tell Kübeck that there was no chance of that in Italy where troop movements of any kind were bound to come to light. He implied, on the other hand, that this need not matter: Kübeck could plead 'security precautions' and, in any case, 'any reference to the possibility of an intervention would be carefully avoided'.

What would have emerged from these discussions, it is impossible to say. In any case there is no evidence to prove that they were ever continued. Ferrara was not mentioned in the course of them so it is likely that the news of Radetzky's actions was received in Vienna only after – probably immediately after – they took place. The reaction of the treasury can easily be imagined; and a likely conclusion would be that the international response to the Field Marshal's blunder would effectively have tied the hands that were about to help him. Moreover, by finding the extra troops to garrison Ferrara he clearly ran the risk of giving the impression that he had sufficient troops already.

Growing tensions

The demonstrations which occurred in Milan during the second week of September inevitably revived the question of the security of northern Italy.

They did so also from a somewhat different standpoint since the crux of the problem no longer centred around the external, but around the internal, threat. This of course represented a deterioration rather than an improvement in the Austrian position, but it should also have afforded for that very reason an opportunity for closer civil–military relations. For a number of reasons, however, the opportunity was allowed to pass. The question of Ferrara was always in the background; Radetzky's motives were always suspect; finally, there was the fact that Ficquelmont's own commitment to a political solution implied a subordinate role for the military. The issues of substance on which they clashed were two: whether there was a need for martial law, and whether the army required more men. The real clash came over the first of these matters, but even with regard to the second it was manifestly clear by the end of the year that each side mistrusted the other.

Ficquelmont first heard of Metternich's reactions to the demonstrations in a letter from the Chancellor dated 23 September 1847.[27] In his anxiety to avoid a repetition of such events, Metternich had proposed to the Emperor that he should be ready to introduce into Italy the decree of 6 October 1846 which had established martial law in Galicia. Ficquelmont replied expressing his approval of this news, an approval which came also from the Viceroy.[28] Both men had assumed, however, that the decision had already been taken. They were quite wrong in this: the decree empowering the Viceroy to declare martial law was not put into his hands until 24 November, a whole month later, by which time Ficquelmont had changed his mind about it and was concentrating his attention on a plan to reform the provincial government instead.[29] In his report of 3 December, therefore, he had written with reference to this issue that since 'there [was] no threat for the moment of an open rebellion which [would] lead to acts of violence', the situation was one that could be dealt with 'by the intelligent use of the ordinary means available to the government and the police'. Lots of the malcontents were not 'decidedly hostile' to the government; he believed there was a chance to win them back; the introduction of such a sweeping measure would not solve things at a stroke.[30] One of the Viceroy's advisers, Pilgram, agreed with him in a report of 20 December: it was useful for Radetzky to have these powers to rely on, but the time had not yet come to implement them. He wrote:[31]

The power of martial law which Count Radetzky has at his disposal at present might serve to prevent an armed clash by the moral impression its existence would make upon people; but it will not dispose of all the excitement . . . [although] when Count Ficquelmont writes in his report of 17 December . . . that there is at present no reason that would justify the publication of regulations of martial law for political crimes and activities . . . such a reason 'could appear at any time and it would then be advisable to have the means at hand in Milan.'[32]

Ficquelmont was also able to persuade the Viceroy to agree with his views on martial law, although in order to secure the necessary agreement he had to expound his arguments at considerable length in a memorandum of 10 December.[33] His conclusion was:[34] 'that the publication of martial law should only take place should the attempts at opposition to the government assume a serious and active character or should the threat of an attack from outside already have reached the stage where its repercussions on those who are already its abetters would give cause for concern'.

He had reached this conclusion for a number of reasons. The people who were committing acts of high treason were characterised, he suspected, by attributes other than numbers; indeed, there were not enough of them to justify martial law. A lot of the trouble was of the kind to which it would be dangerous to over-react – the daubing of nationalist slogans on walls, the singing of nationalist songs. In any case, should there by any attempts to stir up opinion directly or to make the government look foolish, the police had all the necessary means at hand to take care of the situation. There was a case for sharper punishments, heavier fines, prompter justice, but, 'This division [between German and Italian] has gradually assumed such a size that it will not quickly disappear since a reconciliation can only be voluntary.'[35] Ficquelmont clearly was placing all his hopes on organic reform from Vienna.

The Viceroy, as well as the Governors of both Lombardy and Venetia, accepted this view and Rainer decided not to publish the imperial regulations, a decision which he took, as he put it, 'Field Marshal Count Radetzky notwithstanding'.[36] Ficquelmont's memorandum had, in fact, been requested by the Archduke on 1 December, the day on which he had informed Radetzky of the Emperor's decision for the very first time. Radetzky, not surprisingly, had strongly urged the immediate publication of the relevant regulations, arguing:[37] 'The whole social order is about to collapse . . . the Revolution will only be kept in check by fear . . . we have no time to lose . . . [otherwise] streams of blood will flow . . .' His views, however powerfully presented, were totally disregarded.

If there seemed little prospect that the two sides could agree over the issue of martial law, there was, on the other hand, considerable ground for optimism with regard to reinforcements. Radetzky did not, it is true, expect to receive much help in this respect. He told his daughter: 'My position is all the less enviable as our finances have no money for the army.'[38] Yet Metternich and everybody else agreed that the case for more troops was a strong one. For this reason, during the two months that led up to the Tobacco Riots, the necessary steps were taken to reinforce Radetzky's army. However, they were taken in such a way that despite the increase in numbers the respect and confidence that should have resulted between the civil and military authorities was never produced.

Despite his lack of optimism, Radetzky had submitted a demand for more troops after the September riots and Charles Albert's reforms of October in Piedmont. Vienna took some time to review the matter, but the total complacency which Hardegg had displayed as recently as July was no longer prevalent. Discussions came to a head on 18 November and Metternich, without waiting for the Emperor to return from Pressburg, sent both Ficquelmont and Radetzky a memorandum which he was about to submit and which recommended an increase in troops.[39] This he had done with the approval of the Archduke Ludwig, who had already agreed to an increase, but before the decision could be finalised, there were some questions which had to be answered. If Radetzky could answer these soundly, 'Vienna and Milan', wrote Metternich, '[would] then be in agreement.'[40] Ficquelmont received his letter on 21 November and agreed that Radetzky should submit a report immediately.[41] Rainer wrote to Metternich on 22 November actually enclosing a copy of the report and offering his support. He stated:[42]

The description of the political condition of the Kingdom of Lombardy-Venetia made by the Field Marshal is so absolutely correct that I can neither add to it nor detract from it in any way. The military reinforcements which he claims are necessary are in my opinion all the more urgently required since his view of the future, in my opinion, is also well founded. If we are going to face up to the events which he describes, then the demands which Count Radetzky makes must be conceded and conceded quickly. Should his demands be refused or delayed, the possession of Lombardy may become a problem for us. I find myself obliged therefore, to beseech you most urgently, to work from your side to expedite the approval of the Field Marshal's demands.

Ficquelmont, too, wrote to Metternich in support of the Field Marshal:[43] 'His exposition is convincing; the facts speak for themselves and cannot be refuted . . . I entirely agree with his view, particularly his calculations, all the more so since I am convinced that an increase in the numbers of our troops in Lombardy is the only warning that might be effective against the indecisiveness of the King of Sardinia. We have no other attack to fear but one from the direction of Sardinia.'

The final decision on the reinforcements was taken at a meeting of the Vienna State Conference on 5 or 6 December. Metternich sent Ficquelmont a report of his contribution to the debate that preceded it, although Hardegg, he wrote, would pass on the official resolution. However, from his letter to Ficquelmont, it is clear that the Chancellor had failed to give Radetzky's report his uncritical approval. On the contrary, he wrote:[44]

If I am not mistaken, the Field Marshal is taking into consideration the possibility of an *offensive* operation in Italy from our side. I felt myself obliged to object to this presupposition on the following grounds: Firstly because an offensive against either Sardinia or the central Italian states is not our intention – yet also, having been confronted with [the possibility of] an offensive, I had to view the increases proposed for the forces under the Field Marshal's command as insufficient for an offensive operation; all the more so since, as could be gathered from the order of battle enclosed with his report, the number of troops left over to guarantee the internal security of our provinces would be greatly inadequate.

Metternich believed that if an offensive operation were to be contemplated an army of 110,000–120,000 men with reserves of 30,000 would be needed. There could, however, be no question of that at the moment. He agreed with the figure of 80,000 troops regarding internal security, but added the reservation that 'for economic reasons' these troops might only be sent 'as time and circumstances' demanded. On the other hand, he was prepared to listen to Radetzky's views about the demands of time and circumstances. Fundamentally, however, he did not share Radetzky's sense of urgency – partly because he was negotiating a defence arrangement with the Duchies of Parma and Modena, more importantly, because he did not want a repetition of Ferrara. Therefore, in a second letter to Ficquelmont on December 6 he wrote:[45]

I leave it up to you to decide what it will be useful to say to the Marshal by way of caution. I am sure you will share my views about rejecting any notion of an offensive, for the reasons I developed briefly in my exposition. The Marshal has all the qualities of a good soldier; he loves battles. As head of the diplomatic service I love battles when they are necessary but I recoil from them when they are not. Now, the position today requires a material offensive neither against the Pope nor the King of Sardinia. If the situation should change sometime in the future, then active operations might be called for; but there is no question of that for the moment. *Today* we have no intention of taking the offensive in Italy and if we judged the situation differently we would be making a great mistake.

The final decision of the State Conference, therefore, was to give Radetzky his extra troops but to supply them in dribs and drabs, a decision that upset even Ficquelmont who supported the Field Marshal to the hilt in his view that there was no time to lose. The Italians, he told Metternich, were 'willing instruments in the hands of foreign leaders' and a show of strength was needed to frighten these leaders.[46] Radetzky heard of the decision from Hardegg on 8 December and reacted to the news quite violently. A few days later, in a report to the Hofkreigsrath, he wrote:[47]

It still appears that the situation in Italy is regarded in Vienna as not sufficiently urgent to justify more than the usual security precautions. People forget, however, that we are dealing not with cabinets or the fickleness of princes or their ministers, but with a people that hate us and believe that the moment has come when it can finally throw off our yoke and can once again enter the ranks of great nations. . . . People forget that this nation has not yet sunk so low that it is incapable of a sudden resurgence. Great intellectual forces slumber in it. Napoleon was also an Italian . . . Italy may have declined but she also possesses the strength to rise again and never was the feeling of her insignificance and her striving after a national unity stronger and more universal in her than it is today. No statesman, no politician can foresee when and how the crisis which we face today will end. . . .

Not that he in any way meant to indulge Italian nationalism, for he exhorted Hardegg in the following terms:

Your Excellency! The loss of Italy would be a fatal blow for our Monarchy. I will not live to see it. I will remain [here] to the end. Can destiny prepare a more enviable fate for me than to triumph or die on this soil which has been so bloodily contested? Both of us, Your Excellency and I, have lived through a great past. God spare both of us to fight until the end of our days against whatever calamities may befall the Monarchy. Your Excellency as head of the supreme military administration, I as commanding general of the Italian army. I count on the helping hand of an old comrade-in-arms who has shared so many dangerous but also so many famous days.

The Field Marshal, on the other hand, was not merely a man of passion and sentiment. He could not afford to be. If he was to get his own way he had to base his case – and what he wanted was immediate reinforcements that would bring his strength up to the 80,000 mark – on strategical necessities. This, he had done – or so he believed – when he had written to Hardegg on 21 or 22 November, but he had failed to be understood. At the root of the trouble was the fact that the River Ticino formed a political but not a strategic boundary between Lombardy and Piedmont. Indeed, both these lands were really a geographical whole. Given that this was so, Radetzky found himself attracted to an essentially defensive strategy which depended, however, on the launching of a quick offensive; but when he came to explain this plan to others he very easily sounded aggressive.

The fate of Milan and indeed of Lombardy, according to Radetzky, would be decided in any war with Piedmont according to whichever side won the decisive battle which, he reckoned, would have to be fought within the first four days of hostilities breaking out. To ensure that Austria would win such a battle, Radetzky believed that Austria required (*a*) sufficient troops, and (*b*) the military initiative. 'Any other defence apart from a quick offensive is just not possible', he wrote on 12 December, and a few days later,[48] 'We must advance with the first cannon-shots of the enemy.' Piedmont, he calculated, could rely on 120,000 men with good artillery, and even if she mobilised only half of them she could also rely on help from other Italian states and from inside Lombardy itself. Austria, therefore, could not 'temporize' or 'flinch' – 'attack I will meet with attack'; 'forward lies our chance of victory; in retreat lies weakness and destruction'.[49] The Field Marshal wanted 50,000 men with which to beat Piedmont, 20,000 to guard the Po and 10,000 for garrison duties. If necessary, he counted on reinforcements from his rear.

Metternich, however, had only been alarmed by these arguments and when Radetzky heard that he was considered something of a warmonger, he sent the Chancellor, through Ficquelmont, a rather stiff and condescending letter:[50]

It is with great regret that I perceive that I have been entirely misunderstood. It appears that the misunderstanding has arisen above all on account of the vague conception people have of the meaning of 'offensive' and 'defensive' in military science. I would like to clear up this misunderstanding. . . .

I spoke of the necessity to take the offensive and Your Excellency appears to fear that on this account I intended a political solution of the question. That was not at all my intention. But in strategical terms it is impossible to separate the concepts of 'offensive' and 'defensive'. A war can be defensive in form and yet envisage a great offensive and vice-versa. When Russia drew Napoleon into her wilderness, she acted defensively, yet her final objective was offensive. So long as the Italian revolution does not attack us, we shall let it live on in peace; but given the direction it has taken up till now, we must be prepared for an attack from it. . . .

That I intend no invasions is manifest from the modest proposals which I submitted; it was indeed my intention to act with courage and decision but not with foolhardiness. I am not versed in the politics of Europe and the policies of cabinets, but I do understand from them that we shall not take the initiative in the conflict which threatens us. I will not fire the first shot, but if I am attacked – and my whole case rests on this assumption – then it seems to me that questions of politics must obviously give way to those of strategy.

Radetzky was absolutely certain that he would be attacked:

We have had nothing to do with the internal organic changes of these states. We have not interfered with their reforms; we threaten them with no invasions; we leave their development entirely to themselves; and yet only one cry is heard in the whole of Italy from the Alps to the sea coast of Messina – 'Hatred and Death to the Austrians.'

Curiously enough, therefore, Radetzky and Metternich were really in agreement about both strategy and numbers – at least on an abstract level. Indeed, Ficquelmont, writing to Metternich on 18 December, thought that the differences between them had been entirely cleared up. Referring to Radetzky's letter of 16 December, he wrote:[51] ' . . . this will serve to assure Your Excellency, since from the passion of its contents it is clear that Count Radetzky will all the more adhere to the view of Your Excellency, since he already intended the same thing anyway, and the misinterpretation of his views arose merely from his insufficiently clear use of the expression "offensive" '.

In fact, the situation was slightly more complex than that. True, Radetzky was reluctantly prepared to accept Metternich's strategy, but they differed widely in their interpretations of the seriousness of the threat that confronted Austria. Radetzky was convinced that Charles Albert was preparing an attack, arguing that[52] 'The King of Piedmont has removed the mask and is at the head of the Revolution; I see myself compelled, therefore, to place myself in a state of war in order to fight before the gates of Milan at the beginning of next spring' – a remarkably accurate forecast. Vienna, on the other hand, had an altogether more sanguine future in mind. According to Hartig, a former Governor of Lombardy who was now advising Metternich on Italy in Vienna, even in January 1848 'an attack by the King of Sardinia was hardly credible' and in March the whole thing came as a surprise. He wrote:[53] 'An attack from King Charles Albert, without a previous declaration of war, and in direct opposition to his assurances of friendly alliance, could not but appear to men of justice and honour, such as were then in the Austrian cabinet, to be a moral and political impossibility, more particularly after the explanations given to the treaties of 1815 by the European powers with a view of acknowledging the bearings of these treaties upon their relations with Italy.'

By the end of 1847, therefore, relations between the civil and military authorities were very strained indeed. The army wished to adopt a policy of 'backs to the wall' – a combination of martial law and immediate troop increases in preparation for an attack which it expected from Piedmont. The local civil authorities, on the other hand, were pinning their hopes on a political solution while backing the increase of troops. The imperial authorities, meanwhile, were clearly under the impression that the seriousness of the situation was being exaggerated. 'In Vienna', wrote Hübner at the start of 1848, 'people seem to have forgotten that Lombardy-Venetia exists.'[54] According to the Archduke Maximilian d'Este, the opinion prevailed there that the land beyond the Alps was inhabited by barbarians who were not really worth ruling.[55]

Chapter 6

The Tobacco Riots and their aftermath

Ficquelmont, despite all his differences with Radetzky, saw grounds for optimism regarding the military situation as the year 1847 drew to a close. Metternich had concluded a defence agreement with the Duchies of Parma and Modena which allowed Austrian troops to station themselves along a further part of the Piedmontese frontier and the troops took advantage of this arrangement at the very end of December. On 29 December, therefore, Ficquelmont wrote to Metternich:[1*] 'I believe it is possible to designate this moment as the one which will mark a change of direction in the way people think.'

He was, of course, utterly mistaken. People in Lombardy were thinking now more of a tobacco boycott than anything else. Tobacco in the Kingdom of Lombardy-Venetia – as in the Empire as a whole – was a state monopoly and one which netted 4,386,000 lire per annum at that.[2] It was not surprising, therefore, that the 'nationalist' opposition should have planned a protest move against it; indeed much less so since tobacco boycotts had taken place before in Milan in 1751 and 1766 and were, therefore, part of the Milanese political tradition.[3]

The tobacco boycott of 1848 was meant to have begun on 1 January, but was postponed until 2 January since it had rained the day before. As a political protest it was obviously popular and Italians of all classes duly resisted the urge to smoke or take snuff. The Austrians, on the other hand, could hardly have been expected to abandon the habits of a lifetime on the Italians' say-so, especially the troops. They instead were allowed to go about in groups of no less than three and to smoke if they wished to, an opportunity of which they took full advantage. Whether the trouble started when an Austrian blew smoke in the face of an Italian or when an Italian knocked a cigar from out the mouth of an Austrian is one of those mysteries of history which will never be solved; in any case, riots ensued on 2 and 3 January which cost the lives of half a dozen Milanese and wounded many more. Italians and Austrians were now utterly divided, two separate communities on the verge of war. Each side naturally blamed the other – 'nowhere were our troops the attackers but were involved only through necessity and self-defence', Radetzky wrote to Hardegg on 5 January[4] – and it took the British Consul-General to put the blame on both parties.[5] Their reactions, however, were different in one way: while the Italians closed ranks, the Austrians split asunder.

On 3 January Ficquelmont dined with Radetzky and Prince Felix zu

Schwarzenberg while reports were still arriving about the riots outside. He left early but returned later accompanied by Casati, Spaur and Prince Belgiojoso who wanted to know what the Marshal would do about his troops.[6] Radetzky, meanwhile, had denounced Ficquelmont at the dinner table with the result that when the latter heard about it he wrote to Metternich demanding that the Marshal should be sacked: He even suggested that he might do the job of commanding the troops himself.[7] 'Although out of active service in the army for many years, my rank, my experience and the present difficulties could make me think of taking up military service again. I do not want to believe it, but it could come to that eventually.' Radetzky's remarks, whatever they were, must, therefore, have stung to the quick. Ficquelmont, was, after all, seventy-one years old, suffered from lumbago and could no longer ride a horse. His offer to resume a military career was, under these circumstances, a distinctly generous one. Still, a final breach was averted. General Wallmoden had succeeded in calming Radetzky's temper on the night in question, and far from picking a quarrel with Ficquelmont on his return, the Marshal had simply informed him that the troops had been consigned to their barracks and that the streets were being patrolled.[8] However, the Governor of Lombardy, Count Spaur, who already had a bad reputation among the troops on account of his conciliatory behaviour during the September riots, was silly enough to pass on to the Field Marshal a note which included the following passage:[9]

I have just received the evidence that a great number of military men are going about the streets with cigars in their mouths. In view of the great excitement which already exists among the public, this manœuvre can only have bad results.

As I have only to suppose that Your Excellency is not acquainted with this temporary state of affairs, I hasten to bring the matter to your attention in the conviction that Your Excellency will not hesitate to take the necessary steps to remedy it.

Radetzky's reaction was predictable. The very next day the Governor was sent a stern rebuke:[10]

Dear Count,

In a letter which Your Excellency was kind enough to pass to me yesterday evening, you expressed the view that our soldiers had provoked the unrest which has been taking place these last two days by smoking cigars in the street. I am herewith most solemnly obliged to reject this interpretation which people are putting on the present situation. Your Excellency knows just as well as do the people of Milan who the authors of such high treason are, yet they still go around free, with the Podestà at their head, giving the impression that they are the representatives of the people of Milan. Against whom are these attacks directed? – against the state revenue, against an article of commerce which the state alone produces and sells! and under these circumstances am I supposed to forbid our soldiers from smoking openly because the Jockey Club has so decided? Your Excellency cannot possibly believe that I would be capable of such a cowardly step. Our soldiers have not torn down the government's orders from walls and trampled them underfoot; they have done nothing but exercise their right of self-defence; I have been cited only a single case where they were the attackers. Judge for yourself, Your Excellency, the insults which you and your family experience every day and you will have a measure of the disgusting treatment and shameful insults to which the soldier is daily exposed.

So long as His Majesty has faith in me and leaves me at the head of the army in Italy, neither the Podestà of Milan nor the Jockey Club will usurp the legal authorities.

I am informing your Excellency only by the way that the same scenes are taking place in the provinces; I have already received proof of this from Como.

In order to keep the troops under control, I have consigned them to their barracks.

I take this opportunity to pay Your Excellency my highest respects.

Radetzky, F.M.

Ficquelmont commented:[11] 'It is General Schönhals who usually conducts his [i.e. Radetzky's] correspondence but what I am submitting to you was not thought up by him. All the correspondence of the Marshal in the Ferrara affair will prove to you in what spirit his affairs are conducted.'

Ficquelmont was clearly on Spaur's side, certainly as far as this question was concerned, and in one letter to Metternich he even referred to the riots 'in which our soldiers played so troublesome a part'.[12] His advice to the Viceroy, therefore, was 'that at all times the use of force should be measured against the capability to resist of the people involved',[13] but he did admit that the relevant regulations were not 'easy to put into effect', especially when 'the tactics of the leaders of the movement [had] not yet extended to arming the people'.[14] However, in order to avoid the possibility of further riots he asked the Marshal to do much more than Spaur had ever requested – in fact 'to reimpose the old decree whereby all soldiers are forbidden to smoke in the streets; to consign the troops to their barracks on Sundays and on public holidays; to reduce the number of those going out on other days; and to order them always to keep far away from large population centres such as the Cathedral Square and the large Corso and the Street de la Scala'.[15] Indeed, he probably now saw the army as the main obstacle to all his reforms and a viceregal proclamation was published with this in mind. For as Ficquelmont explained to Metternich:[16]

The great anxiety which was troubling the whole population was the product of the idea that the commanding general was absolutely independent of the Viceroy and the civil authority. People were afraid that the bloody scenes they had witnessed would take place again. Fear does not reason; people did not take any account of the unforeseeable, fortuitous circumstances which led to these events. It was necessary to tell the public that the Viceroy had concentrated all authority in his hands. . . .

The army soon gathered that it had become a scapegoat. One unknown soldier wrote:[17]

Does Austria exist only to be duped from every side? To surrender, to take half-measures, sometimes none at all? If our government persists in this delusion, it will regret it bitterly and our future generations will and must curse the men who now and for such a long time have so feebly directed our affairs. We only have to look through the latest journals to see what is to be done at the start of such revolutionary movements. Ah! Why do we not have a Nicholas at our head – how tamely, how meekly these Milanese would then kiss the cane that thrashed them!

General Mengewein wanted to resurrect the spirit of the old Austrian motto:[18] 'Osterreich über Alles, wenn es nur will.' Sympathy for the Field Marshal also encouraged such feelings.

Radetzky – the old man 'with snow on his head and fire in his heart', as he was often described – had a particular *rapport* with his troops. A few words from him to one of his soldiers was capable of reducing even the strongest among them to tears.[19] 'His talent for getting on with soldiers', wrote one of his biographers, bordered on the incredible.[20] He spoke daily with more than a hundred soldiers. Always he would suddenly join a group of grenadiers or Jäger and ask each one of them about their personal circumstances. Before they marched off too, he often mixed among the ranks, greeting an N.C.O., putting his hand over the shoulder of an officer, speaking cheerfully with the hot-blooded Vienna volunteers. What he learned from his soldiers on these occasions, his marvellous memory retained for years afterwards. When he saw them again, he immediately called them all by name and asked them what had happened to them in the meantime. The esteem and love with which the soldier, from the lowest to the highest, regarded this treatment, was immeasurable.

The army, therefore, closed its ranks around its commander:[21] 'Our poor Field Marshal is to be pitied most of all' wrote one high-ranking officer.

This man, so given to his duty and to his Emperor, is, so to speak, proscribed. The popularity which he enjoyed among the people has now turned into the blackest hatred. . . . But on this account, he has the solitary consolation that the army, which has always held him in the highest esteem and respect, is enthusiastically behind him. I am firmly convinced that should the slightest harm come to him from the side of the people, it would require every effort to restrain the soldiers from excesses. Woe to anyone who laid a finger on him. Then there really would be a bloodbath.

Radetzky, like everybody else, was aware that he was supposed to head an assassination list – ' . . . A few days ago, I was still a popular man; now I stand in the way.'[22] His political enemies, however, were not merely the Italians; by the second week in January 1848 the division between the Austrian civil and military authorities appeared almost as unbridgeable as that between the nationalities.

In Vienna, naturally, Metternich came under pressure from both sides. Radetzky wrote to Hardegg criticising the régime of our 'sleepy Viceroy' suggesting that it was 'high time' that the government provided 'prudent leadership and strong action'.[23] His soldiers were 'embittered to the highest degree possible' on account of the 'usual tactic of the factions', which was 'to keep them under perpetual strain and to exhaust them'.[24] He warned that under these circumstances, unless the government acted, a situation would arise in which 'military defiance and excitement' would confront popular 'frenzy and hatred' and he did not care to contemplate the results.[25] The real object of his venom, of course, was the local gubernium, which he characterised as in a state of total 'paralysis':[26] 'The whole city knows who is behind these troubles. People point them out and yet nothing happens. No proclamations forbid unlawful assemblies. The policeman-soldier can often just contain his rage at seeing himself exposed to the derision of the paid mob. The patrols go on their way but no one tells the people to disperse and hundreds of people follow these police patrols mocking and whistling.'

Metternich for his part was inclined to agree with Radetzky. Firmness on the spot rather than an organic change in the constitution was the Chancellor's answer to the *Buberei*. He told Ficquelmont:[27]

Instead of *acting,* the authorities have been addressing *demands* to Vienna. Even today, Milan is awaiting instructions which there is no need to wait for according to existing regulations. Do the Lombard authorities need imperial orders to close the clubs? Are orders required to stop some club disturbing the public peace by a ban on smoking? Who gave the club the permission? Who has done nothing to oppose the avowedly revolutionary efforts that have been made? Is the central imperial government to undertake to run the police force in a town across the Alps? Is the central government to stoop to the level of town magistrates in charge of the public peace? People want a stronger law for the Italian provinces and I share the view that our law is too soft. But does that mean that it is necessary to prevent the existing law being implemented? . . . The whole position is a tissue of faults, the greatest of which are to be found in the local administration.

Metternich, therefore, decided to back up the army because, without civilian backing, he claimed that 'military force [would become] brutal and force of this kind [would] use itself up very quickly'.

In fact, there was a real danger that the army might become not merely brutal, but disaffected. On 9 January the emperor wrote Hardegg a letter in which he claimed that it had come to his attention 'in a confidential way' that several highly placed officers in Lombardy had permitted themselves to express opinions concerning 'the untenability of our position itself and the need, should any untoward event take place, of withdrawing to the Mincio line'.[28] This was language which, as the Emperor pointed out, could only injure military pride, nay worse, have a pernicious effect on public administration. Hardegg, therefore, was to ensure that 'under no circumstances' would such language ever be heard again; the high military was to conduct itself in a proper manner. Such language, of course, had been the result of the army's general frustration so that it was abundantly clear in Vienna that the imperial army in Italy was in need of some moral support. The Emperor, therefore, in another *Handschreiben* to Hardegg, did his best to supply it. This document, which, he was later told, was received with 'real jubilation' and which 'left a profound impression', read as follows:[29]

Dear Count Hardegg!
Remarkable efforts have been made for a number of years to maintain my Kingdom of Lombardy-Venetia. As a result of these, a battle-ready army stands at its head.

You know what reinforcements have recently been placed at its disposal by me.

In these arrangements which I have already made is manifest my firm determination to protect my Lombardy-Venetian Kingdom with all my power, like any other part of my state and to defend it uprightly and in accordance with duty against any enemy attack whether from without or within. This, my decision, will find its most effective support in the loyal devotion of my army. You must make my unswerving confidence known to my troops in Italy through Field Marshal Count Radetzky.

The Emperor's wishes were indeed made known to the troops through a proclamation of a general army order issued by Radetzky on 15 January. The Field Marshal, however, added a rallying cry of his own:[30]

Soldiers! You have heard the words of your Emperor. I am proud to proclaim them to you. The machinery of fanaticism will break upon your loyalty and valour like glass upon a rock. The sword which I have wielded with honour through many a battlefield for sixty-five years rests firmly in my hands. I will use it to protect the peace of a still recently happy land which a lunatic party now threatens to plunge into most inconceivable misery.

Soldiers! Our Emperor counts on us. Your grey-haired leader trusts you. This is enough. May no man force us to unfurl the banner of the two-headed eagle. The power of its wings is not yet lamed. Our motto is: peace and protection for the peaceful, loyal citizen; destruction to the enemy who dares wantonly to impugn the peace and happiness of the people.

Hardegg congratulated Radetzky on his eloquence.[31] It had to be the 'greatest comfort to our Emperor and master' that his army in Italy was commanded by this man. 'All that you have told me till now concerning the spirit of your troops could not surprise me. The spirit of troops whom you command could not be other than excellent.' He underlined the 'you' in blue pencil.

Other reactions to Radetzky's proclamation were very different. The Marshal was commonly supposed among the diplomatic corps of Europe to be an advocate of war in Italy and the British, especially, therefore, were very worried about the tone of the general order.[32] Lord Minto, a Cabinet member who was then *en mission* in Rome wrote to the British Ambassador in Vienna:[33] 'You will not be surprised when I tell you that Radetzky's general order of the 18th. [*sic*] has raised a prodigious storm throughout Italy. . . . What I dislike most is the too plain evidence of the ascendency of a new influence at Vienna and the abandonment of the pacific Metternich policy.'

The British Ambassador replied to Minto telling him that there had been no change in policy.[34] Nevertheless, as Ficquelmont foresaw the riots were bound to signal the beginning of a reaction. Thus although there could be no doubt that both he and Rainer had already achieved some considerable success in keeping the military under control – the imperial proclamation had been required after all because the demoralised troops were only too aware that despite Radetzky's bluster, he had cooperated fully in confining them indoors – they now determined to consolidate their success and let the army know that its role was a strictly subordinate one. On 14 January, therefore, Rainer wrote to the Governors of Lombardy and Venetia reminding them of their duties should they be called upon, as seemed very likely, to summon military aid to control civilian demonstrators:[35]

It is absolutely necessary that the intervention of the military in such circumstances should be limited only to extreme cases, and if it must occur, it should do so with the strictest possible observance of those formalities which are appropriate when the use of force is justified; moreover, the force employed should always be calculated according to the resisting powers of the conspirators. Although the various existing decrees all make provision in this respect for the above objective, I nevertheless remind you of your duty to bring it to the attention of your subordinates. They should observe these regulations as accurately as possible and make it their duty to adhere to them strictly. Moreover, it is a decision for the political authorities whether to call in the army and how to supervise it.

Ficquelmont transmitted these to Metternich, commenting:[36] 'I feel obliged on this occasion to remark that it appears absolutely necessary in my opinion that similar instructions should be sent to the army command here from the Hofkriegsrath – all the more so since in Padua recently the case has arisen – which will also be examined – of a dragoon pursuing a civilian and instead of seizing him, making use of his weapon to wound him seriously. The man, it is true, was throwing stones, but otherwise he was unarmed.'

Metternich dutifully passed the buck to Hardegg who was asked to advise the Emperor on the possibility of issuing special instructions to the army. This, however, was a course of action that Hardegg wished to avoid:[37]

From my own humble position I must declare every further instruction relating to the very delicate relationship [between the civil and military powers] as decidedly disadvantageous both on account of the very difficult circumstances of the present time as well as the very regrettable position of our Italian provinces where it can no longer be a question of isolated fortuitous clashes, but one of open premeditated revolution.

I would be assuming a very serious responsibility if I now agreed to detailed instructions being issued.

Of the many regrettable results which must – according to my innermost convictions – inevitably ensue from this, the most dangerous in my opinion, would be that the troops would be placed in an uncertain position regarding their conduct in the first place; that they would show themselves to be too weak and unsure in such scenes as are to be feared every day; and that robbed of their moral strength, their effectiveness at their time of greatest need would be paralysed. For it remains an uncomfortable truth that in such affairs the moral superiority of the soldiers and their absolute decisiveness are elements of the highest importance when – as is mostly the case – they have to operate with little in the way of material support.

. . . Where would it lead us if the military – in whose hands alone almost lies the maintenance of order in the Kingdom of Lombardy-Venetia under the present circumstances – were to be undermined in its dominant position regarding the troublemakers and were hereby to lose the respect it has gained by its generally correct behaviour, nay if this respect were finally destroyed, as could not for a moment be doubted?[38]

Metternich agreed with Hardegg rather than with Ficquelmont. If the civil authorities had done their job in the first place, the trouble would never have arisen. On 23 January, he wrote to his second-in-command:[39] 'Why has not the government in Milan seized upon the ban on cigar smoking as an opportunity to deal severely with those who have seen fit to make such a manifest assault on the liberty of their fellow citizens?' He added: 'If I had been in charge of the public services in Milan I would not have hesitated in handing over the authors of the ban to the police immediately, irrespective of class, either after a confession or the disgrace of legal proceedings.'

That was Radetzky's position, and between the end of January and the middle of March events appeared to be going his way. Certainly, no further instructions were issued.

* * * * * * * * * *

As a result of the December agreement, Radetzky's army was to be raised from 55,000 to a maximum of 80,000 men. The Field Marshal managed to arrange for 9,800 men to be sent right away with the promise of an extra 13,000 in case of an emergency. An agreement was also reached to divide the army in Italy into two corps – one in Lombardy and one in Venetia – and during the course of January Vienna conceded the need for another 9,000 men – the result of which was that on paper, at least, Radetzky had a potential 85,000 men under his command. At the beginning of February, he made it clear that he believed that another 30,000–40,000 men would be needed if his position was to be really secure, but had to content himself with a further two battalions of infantry, six squadrons of cavalry and two batteries. The cost of all this to the Austrian treasury for 1848 was 5 million fl. These are the figures given by Hartig;[40] but if there is no reason at all to suppose that he invented them – the archives confirm his figures with regard to the number of troops involved[41] and common sense would respect his figure with regard to their cost – they are figures which have to be put into perspective.

The troops, in the first place, were committed on paper only; secondly, they were sent by the cheapest possible means of transport – on foot. Despite reports, therefore, that Lombardy-Venetia was being saturated with troops, Radetzky had only 75,000 men under his command when war broke out.[42] Metternich, almost until the very outbreak of hostilities did not finally convince himself that Charles Albert was intent on war – Hartig has already been quoted to this effect – but this is also to be concluded from Metternich's own previous commitment to 120,000 men with reserves of 30,000, the figures which he had quoted to the State Conference when discussing the eventuality of an attack from without. As it was, Ficquelmont was more worried than Metternich with respect to the military establishment. As early as 11 January he was writing to Metternich:[43] 'We have reached the stage which you designated, my Prince, as the one at which not the 80,000 men demanded by the Marshal would suffice, but at which there would be a need for 120,000 men.' He then added: 'A few days ago the Marshal asked the Hofkriegsrath to raise the army in Italy to 100,000 men. As for me, I adopt the figure of Your Excellency. It will be impossible for Austria not to become involved in the affairs of central Italy sword in hand. I have only fully realized that this must be so since the recent events in Milan. It is a grave subject which requires thought and proof.'

Metternich himself was not quite as excited about all these events, which he thought of as a *Buberei*; in any case there was still the problem of finance. Solomon Rothschild had not come up with funds which he had promised in November and treasury resistance was always strong in matters of military expenditure. On one level, Metternich took the simple step of reproving Rothschild towards the end of January:[44] '*Politically things are all right (politisch stehen wir gut)*; the exchange is not. I do my duty but you do not.' The Chancellor went on to suggest that if the funds for the army were not immediately forthcoming then 'Hell' would stare them both 'in the face' – an effective threat in the event. However, despite another promise of support from Rothschild, Radetzky was beaten by the treasury men when the ultimate battle for funds for reinforcements was fought. The Field Marshal submitted request on 1 February 1848 to have his army raised by another 30,000–40,000 men, although his immediate need was for three Jäger battalions, two more infantry battalions, six squadrons of light cavalry and four rocket batteries.[45] His request was right away passed on to the treasury, and from the protocols of the meeting that took place between the treasury and the army representatives at the end of the first week in February it is possible to form some impression of the state of mind in Vienna.[46] The treasury men were, in fact, reasonably impressed by Radetzky's arguments, especially those relating to developments in Piedmont and to the fact that discontent inside the Kingdom of Lombardy-Venetia had now spread 'even to the lowest classes of the population'. Accordingly, they raised the previous limit of 80,000 men to 90,000, a figure which, they claimed, represented the 'outermost limits' of Viennese help. Regarding the Field Marshal's immediate needs, they also went so far and no further – he was promised reinforcements which would bring his potential strength up to only 86,000 men, a figure which represented something short of his demand. Otherwise, they laid down a firm treasury line: 'disadvantageous consequences' would ensue from 'ever-continuing' troop reinforcements, which were already having a bad effect on 'public credit and the financial position of the Monarchy'; in future, therefore, no reinforcements would be granted until 'a close look' had been taken at the whole Italian position; Radetzky had based his claims on the 'evil mood' and 'spirit of discontent' of Lombardy and Venetia in particular, but 'this appeared to the representatives of the treasury as no sufficient motive for sending further troops to Italy'. Finally, a different view might be taken only when 'the position of things' was 'really' changed by 'events' which 'really' necessitated an increase. And they defined 'events' as follows:[47] 'Such an event might well only be recognised in the outbreak of a significant rebellion inside the Kingdom of Lombardy-Venetia or in a malicious, hostile attack from any one of the neighbouring states, whereas mere worries and fears, admittedly arising from full cause, but from causes which already are accounted for in the forces already standing at Count Radetzky's disposal, might not offer proper cause for further reinforcements.'

To paraphrase the Archduke Charles, Austria had all the elements of a policy but no policy.[48] Radetzky would have to be attacked before he could expect reinforcements, despite the fact that his whole strategy was built around the need to fight the decisive battle after only a few days of hostilities, before, in fact, Vienna might even hear that a war had been declared. Little wonder then that he wrote:[49] 'What makes our isolated position so difficult is the impossibility of reacting to the danger which threatens us, the sad necessity of having to sit back peacefully until we are attacked from within or without.' He lamented: 'This enforced and unnatural defensive position – unnatural, because, as the first power of Italy, we are robbed of any influence on our fate, unnatural because it impugns the honour of a great and powerful monarchy, forces us to think at least about the means with which we can play this enforced role without injury to honour.'

Metternich, as will be seen, had been giving much thought to how he could reconcile Radetzky and his army to their essentially defensive posture, but soon after the meeting of the treasury and army men, he himself was thrown on the defensive. Indeed, by the end of February martial law had been declared in both Lombardy and Venetia after the outbreak of disturbances in Pavia and Padua.

In Padua, as it turned out, the urge to impose martial law was at first resisted by the Governor of Venetia, Count Palffy, who rejected Rainer's offer to declare it there during the middle of the month. The citizens of the town, the Govenor declared, had taken 'no part at all' in the disturbances, which were all the results of 'sheer terrorism' on the part of the university students; and since the latter had been quelled by a few patrols under N.C.Os, there appeared to be no need for further measures. The Viceroy accepted this view and withdrew his offer to impose martial law.[50]

In Pavia, on the other hand, where Colonel Benedek was commander of the garrison, events were destined to take an altogether different turn. There, too, students had been harassing the troops. The latter had been smoking and the local delegate, Lugani, had asked Benedek to follow Spaur's advice to Radetzky. The garrison commander was loath to accede to such a demand and told the delegate bluntly:[51] 'His Excellency, the provincial commander, F.M. Count Radetzky, has empowered me through orders, dated Milan 9 February, to inform you that His Excellency does not recognise the authority of the street committee formed to forbid smoking on the streets and that if the civil authorities cannot contain these attacks on public order, the provincial commander will himself assume responsibility for maintaining law and order.'

Lugani, in turn, astonished by the strength of Benedek's language informed Count Spaur that if Radetzky were to persist in this attitude, he personally would no longer be responsible for the running of the city.[52] Spaur's response was to instruct the delegate that the Marshal's stance was an illegal one; but he was also careful to refer the matter to the Viceroy. Radetzky, he complained, 'had issued the order without any previous understanding with the provincial civil authorities'.[53]

The Field Marshal, in any case, had been to a large extent bluffing, a conclusion that can be drawn from a letter he wrote on 12 February to the Viceroy.[54] Benedek, he declared, had been instructed to avoid clashes with the students but, although he stressed that he 'would not recognise nor tolerate any secret tribunal which attacked and insulted peaceful smokers on the streets and dared to exercise an illegal power', he conceded that the troops had been forbidden to smoke. He did so even though, 'such a ban under present circumstances constitutes an unjustified subservience and subordination to the will of the revolutionary faction'. His letter, however, revealed more than just a bluff; there, too, was the plea that 'given the continuing treacherous attacks on isolated soldiers, I see no other means of avoiding further bloody scenes but the publication of martial law – in Pavia too – just as Your Royal Highness has agreed to order this in Padua'. The Viceroy, predictably, relied on Ficquelmont to tell him what to do.

Ficquelmont's advice was almost as predictable as the Viceroy's action. It ran:[55] 'Since the reports coming in from the military authorities are composed from a totally different standpoint from those of the civil authorities and since they differ so much from each other that it has become absolutely impossible to discern the truth about what happened from the interpretations presented . . .' a committee should be appointed consisting of both Benedek and Lugani along with a couple of others to get at the truth, to advise on possible remedial measures and to restore public confidence. The Viceroy could then use their report to enable him to decide whether to declare martial law or not. According to Ficquelmont this was only the common-sense solution, 'the best means not only of bringing about some agreement between the two sides once again [and of] determining what steps should be taken to prevent a repetition of such regrettable scenes, without having recourse to the most extreme measures'.[56]

Radetzky, meanwhile, appeared to have reconciled himself to all the indignities of civilian rule, for in an order to his troops published at this time he advised them as follows:[57]

Patience and resignation, forbearance and decisiveness are virtues which the warrior always requires, but most of all at a time when called upon to defend the throne and the law in times of civil dissension and against internal enemies – we find ourselves in this position; therefore, Soldiers! I ask you to keep these virtues in mind today! Go about your usual tasks in peace as if in times of the most profound tranquillity; insult nobody; give no cause for trouble; provoke nobody by unusual treatment; but never forget the demands that are made on you by honour and duty. Behave in such a way and the peaceful citizen will respect you, while the lawbreaker and the disturber of the peace will fear you; the arrows of calumny shall be powerless against your reputation and shall rebound against your honour. This is what I expect of you and you have never let me down.

In fact, the Field Marshal had already won, for on 19 February Rainer received instructions telling him to publish a decree of martial law throughout the kingdom.[58] This he did and the relevant notices went up in Milan on 22 February and in Venice on the 25th. There is, however, some doubt about how the decision was finally taken.

By the beginning of the second week in February Metternich had regained his confidence.[59] He convinced himself that the representative systems which were growing up in Italy would be more likely to resist the financial demands of a war – a conclusion that reinforced his complacent judgement of the situation inside Lombardy. Thus, having just written to Ficquelmont to inform him that representative governments were less likely to go to war, he despatched another note to Milan to tell him how this affected the Austrian position in the north:[60] 'I say in my note of today that with respect to military measures, *they have all been taken*. I foresee that the Marshal will be perturbed by this remark on my part. If you should get this impression then make him understand that I draw a distinction between measures of internal and external security. Now it is not the latter that I am referring to.' In the context of the Austrian position in northern Italy Metternich's distinction was not a very meaningful one. More important, he was not really very serious about it, since his letter continued:

The Marshal dreams of political war and there is no question of that. The wind may change but when it does so also will our intentions. At the moment the Italian provinces have all the military forces they require. What they lack is strong civil government and I am the first to despair that that might ever be provided by the Viceroy. . . . Let us try . . . to remain the masters in our own Italian provinces. That is the Marshal's true task today. Let him leave the political details of the situation to us.

These letters, however, had been written before the Chancellor had been informed of the trouble that was brewing in both Paudua and Pavia, that is, at a time when he might just have thought that the tension was about to relax. The news of further disturbances must, therefore, have been exceedingly exasperating for him. Yet despite his own frustration and the impatience he undoubtedly felt with regard to practically everything that touched on Lombardy, the evidence suggests that, no more than Ficquelmont did he wish to commit himself to the final step of martial law, even although he was under pressure from a number of sources to do so. As late as 17 February, therefore, he was writing to Ficquelmont in a tone of resistance as well as despair:[61]

If you find yourself in the middle of complaints about governmental inaction, be assured that the position of the supreme authority is no different from your own.

. . . The people want examples to be made, their national pride is wounded, they want the government to take some action and the weakness of the governments in Venice and Milan exasperates them. The great public does not say against whom action must be taken; it merely wants the government to act.

I am not part of this public; I ask myself against whom the action must be taken and since I find a total population seduced, living, crying, shouting under the influence of some fascination, a population which has sunk to the depths, I cannot understand the demands of the public. . . .

The public cries, 'Put the Kingdom of Lombardy-Venetia in a state of siege!' I confess that I cannot understand how this can be done to 5 million people who have the natural support of another 15 million! People cry *'if only there were military rule'*; to govern is to govern; it does not matter what colour the uniforms are, whether the costumes are military or civil. By getting rid of the civil government, you make a vanguard out of your reserve; where then is your reserve?

In Metternich's mind the answer was the old one, the necessity 'for the civil government to have the courage to do its duty and to rely on the army, but *not to hide behind it*'. On the other hand, 'the army must maintain itself as a force that can provide discipline; it must never take the initiative, but should hit hard. The time to do so should be indicated by the civil authorities.'

How then was the decision taken? One of the sources of pressure on Metternich was certainly constituted by a reactionary group around Prince Windischgraetz who on 23 February himself wrote to the Chancellor telling him that Radetzky should have supreme powers in Lombardy and even declaring that if Radetzky were too old for this task he was willing to take it on himself.[62] Yet by the time Windischgraetz had written this letter the decision on martial law had already been taken; and in any case the fact that Metternich could soon appoint Ficquelmont to be head of the Hofkriegsrath over Windischgraetz's claims is an indication that he was by no means reliant on support from that camp.[63] The final pressure came most likely from Radetzky himself, although it is difficult to believe, as one authority has stated, that this pressure took the form of a resignation threat not only from the Field Marshal but from forty of his highest-ranking officers.[64] It is probable that the decision was taken *faute de mieux*. Hübner, who was soon to replace Ficquelmont, noted before he left Vienna that 'the military and civil authorities are mutually convinced that ruling Upper Italy has been made more difficult because of each other and there are ceaseless complaints of mutual disrespect'.[65] In order to stem the flood of these complaints, Metternich must just have decided to yield to popular pressure. Some time between 17 and 19 February, his breaking point was reached.[66] A letter from Prince Hohenlohe, Hardegg's deputy, to the Field Marshal, dated 27 February, would seem to add at least some substance to this interpretation, for in it he gave expression to the desire that 'the necessary harmony and cooperation which is doubly needed in so troublesome times between the civil and military authorities [should] not be disturbed by mutual accusations about the causes of the present situation' – a fairly broad hint that both sides should make up their differences and get on with the job.[67]

One factor which may have influenced Metternich was a letter from Palffy, the Governor of Venetia, dated 12 February which informed the Chancellor of the growing desperation of the Austrian position there.[68] According to Palffy, 'the outbreak of general revolution' was 'inevitable' if the government took no 'decisive step' . . . 'right away', and in order that Metternich might have no illusions on this score he sent Count Marzani to Vienna to describe the situation '*as it [really was]*'. However, Metternich treated Marzani as some kind of fool, describing him to Ficquelmont as bereft of ideas[69] and a travelling companion of the Count's was subjected to a very bizarre interrogation:[70]

'Venice,' I asked him – 'can Venice support herself separated from Austria?' He answered me with a categorical 'No'. 'Well then tell this to the town and to the country. Since when has Venice ever agreed with Milan and Genoa and Ancona?' 'You are right,' he replied. 'The Venetians have to be told this.' I invited him to write it down in his notebook. What always astonishes me in circumstances like the present is the number of good things to do and say but which are never done and never said.

This does not seem to indicate that it was merely the Venetian situation which made Metternich agree to martial law.

Martial law having been declared, at first all seemed well: the upper classes were irritated; the middle ones were content; the country as a whole quite stunned and quiescent.[71] When Ficquelmont's successor, Count Hübner, arrived in Milan on 5 March, he wrote that he had noticed 'nothing extraordinary'; indeed an officer that he had met at Treviso informed him that since the law had been introduced, the situation in the kingdom had entirely changed and that the troops were no longer insulted.[72] In one respect, however, nothing had changed, for the military and civil leaders were still attacking one another: Ficquelmont, who left Milan convinced that peace would prevail,[73] informed Count Hartig, on reaching Vienna, that Radetzky was 'only a name';[74] and inside the army, meanwhile, the voices of despair, which should now have been silenced, were heard again instead. On 7 March, Prince Hohenlohe received an imperial *Handschreiben* which read curiously like the previous one received by Hardegg on 9 January.[75] It warned the revolutionaries were working tirelessly and with great ingenuity to bring about the downfall of the European order and stressed that in order to counteract these efforts the confidence of all subjects would be absolutely necessary. The Emperor, however, seemed less than 100 per cent certain that he was being given this confidence since the point of the *Handschreiben* was that nothing did more to undermine it than 'servants of the monarch' (i.e. soldiers in this case, since the documents had been addressed to Hohenlohe) who took it upon themselves, even from the best of motives, to criticise the government. Such behaviour, according to the monarch, was 'incompatible with duty', although he added that it was not a question of anyone being forced to accept views which did not accord with their convictions – merely that people should be 'mindful of their duty' in 'their own interest and in the interest of the common good'. In Lombardy-Venetia itself, therefore, dissension was rife until the outbreak of revolution.

Given that this was so, the army tended to give any credit it felt was due to Metternich. Schönhals wrote later that if 'Prince Metternich [had] often been reproached and accused of being the cause of this lack of energy' (commonly held to have been displayed in Vienna before the revolutionary outbreaks)'. . . [he was] not of this opinion';[76] and when the Chancellor eventually returned from exile to Vienna, Radetzky himself assured him that his name enjoyed 'the finest reputation in the army'.[77] Absence indeed makes the heart grow fonder.

Chapter 7

Divided we fall

Radetzky had had two problems to contend with regarding the civil authorities before the end of February 1848. One had been the dispute over the introduction of martial law. The other had been his struggle to raise the number of his fighting forces. These problems had, of course, been qualitatively different ones: the first, essentially, was a dispute over principle; the second, really a difference over means. At the end of the month, therefore, the Marshal did have grounds for satisfaction. He had won the decision in principle and had gained some ground in the battle for troops. His position, in fact, was even stronger than would at first appear to be the case, because Metternich, in an early attempt to appease the Field Marshal, had agreed to support the latter's plans for the fortification of Milan. At the time, no doubt, this did not seem to be a very great concession; yet it was a decision that was important for at least two reasons. When war broke out his personal commitment to the Lombard capital was to be an important element in Radetzky's thinking; more immediately, like a projected invasion of part of Switzerland, it showed that Metternich was concerned to boost the army's morale by paying a lesser price than the introduction of martial law.

The projected invasion of the Canton Ticino

The part of Switzerland which Metternich had planned to invade was the Canton Ticino which, according to Schönhals, played a role that was 'worse than open hostility'.[1]* Cutting deep into Austrian territory in Lombardy-Venetia – it extended to within forty miles of Milan – it posed a serious problem for the imperial authorities since, on account of various geographical factors, the boundary between it and the Austrian provinces was exceedingly difficult to police. Moreover, the frontier guard was almost wholly disaffected so·that the cross-border traffic in guns and ammunition, which was what was really worrying the Austrians, was very seldom interrupted.[2] The smell of revolution was already in the Lombard air[3] and the imperial army was desperately concerned lest the Swiss authorities in this strategic area should attempt to spread the ideological war that was then being fought in Switzerland to the territory of their ideologically hostile neighbour, Austria.

Gun-running was one thing, but on 16 January Radetzky reported that the Swiss were preparing for war or had taken measures that indicated that they

---

* Notes to this chapter are on pp. 265–8.

were shortly expecting hostilities.[4] Passports were being refused to males between the ages of eighteen and forty; orders had gone out that, before the end of January, 2,000 men in every canton should be exercising with carbines at specially selected assembly points (Lugano and Bellinzona in the case of the Canton Ticino); military uniforms were being worked on day and night in Lugano; and rifles were being imported into Switzerland from France only to be re-exported in large numbers into Lombardy. These weapons, according to Radetzky's information, were being transported from Lake Maggiore down the Ticino or by canal in wooden boats to Pavia and Milan. On February 19, the Field Marshal reported that 20,000 men were being made ready to defend the Canton Ticino and that an understanding had been reached between Piedmont and Switzerland to invade the Austrian provinces, 'in the secure hope of an uprising there'.[5] In fact, by this time, it was the Swiss rather than the Austrians who should have been worrying about an invasion, for on 1 February 1848, Hardegg had received from Metternich copies of a correspondence between the Chancellor and Ficquelmont relating to plans, approved by the Emperor, for a military occupation of the Canton Ticino.[6]

Among these documents was an analysis which Metternich had made of the position of the canton from the political, moral and military viewpoint. As a piece of thinking, however, it was hardly profound. From a moral standpoint, all he could find to say was:[7] 'That the insolent rabble would not dare to deliver a hard blow against us in revenge, would be moral.' His political analysis, too, was rather superficial. Despite the fact that under the heading 'military aspects', he had concluded that an invasion 'could bring advantages', he confined himself in his political analysis to noting that it was 'always useful' that nothing could be done to stop him 'punishing' these 'grotesque political goings-on'. The point of this part of the document seemed to be that the 'most common political considerations' turned what was, after all, just an expedient into 'our sternest duty'. He never actually got around to defining the advantages which he had earlier postulated. Evidently, the whole plan was based on the assumption that a show of force against a weak opponent could do the Austrians no harm.

The Canton Ticino was cut off from the rest of Switzerland by the Grundbündlen Canton and the St Gotthard Pass. Since the latter was 'easy to obstruct' and since from 'all reasonable calculations', there 'could be no fear of an attack against Austrian occupation' from the Grundbündlen Canton, Metternich planned 'to push forward our line of defence' by 'clearing up' the 'radical rabble' there in order to stop them 'suppressing peaceful people', and thereby establish military security. The canton, he noted, had twice surrendered to radicalism that had been expressly directed against Lombardy.

The Chancellor, apparently, was in no doubt that what he was planning was the only solution to this particular problem. 'I do not recognise any other possibility', he told Ficquelmont.[8] At the right time, therefore, the canton was to be invaded and the guerrilla fighters who were behind the gun-running were to be expelled. Once occupied, it was to be given a 'military administration' headed by 'an appropriate general' who was to be assisted by a board composed of reliable local residents. All radicals 'of whatever nationality' were 'to be cleared out of the canton' and the sequestration of their property was to pay for part of the operation costs. Until they had been expelled, the army was to rule alone, something which was to be spelled out in a proclamation which would be issued before any invasion by the Commander-in-Chief in Italy. However, until a decision had been reached concerning the timing of an invasion, Metternich warned Hardegg that the plan was to be kept top secret. He wrote:[9] 'That a profound silence must be observed regarding this matter is so apparent from its very nature, that no special mention of it is required.' Hardegg communicated the plan to Radetzky 'in closest confidence' stressing that it was 'of a purely defensive nature'. The Marshal was put in charge of the 'purely military steps', but, as far as political considerations 'were concerned', Ficquelmont was the man responsible. Radetzky, however, had not been taken completely into confidence, because the following week Ficquelmont could write to Metternich:[10] ' . . . as soon as the circumstances which have been foreseen actually arise or even appear imminent, I shall not fail to communicate to him [i.e. Radetzky] Your Excellency's full and official instructions on this matter'. The 'appropriate general' apparently was General-Major Strassoldo who was to have been given a task force of eight battalions, three squadrons and one battery to do the job. What 'circumstances' had been selected as opportune, one cannot say. In any case, it hardly matters, since for one reason or another, they can never have presented themselves.[11] The invasion never took place.

The plan can perhaps be regarded as a throwback to Metternich's earlier ideas about a mobile task force to operate under Radetzky, ideas about which he had held discussions as early as July 1847. The aim behind this task force seems always to have been to boost military morale and achieve limited political objectives at the very minimum cost. In July, Metternich had argued that the troops involved would have to live off the land that they invaded; similarly, he now argued that should an invasion of Switzerland take place the cost should be kept to a minimum, partly by charging the Swiss themselves and partly by refusing to make up the number of troops in Italy.[12] The key to the argument, however, was that the operation would be a quick one since the Swiss had nothing to fight back with. Quick, cheap and easy, it was something he could offer the military, and Metternich no doubt hoped that he could keep them happy this way. The plan to fortify Milan presented a similar opportunity.

The defence of Milan

By the beginning of 1848, Radetzky had become more and more obsessed with the position of Lombardy's capital. He saw it as the key to the defence of the whole of Italy. 'A victory in the streets of Milan', he told Hardegg,[13] 'is a victory over the whole of Italy.' In another letter, he told the President of the Hofkriegsrath that if Austria wished to remain 'master of Lombardy' – a favourite phrase of his, which was often rendered 'master of Italy' – she would have to keep control of Milan.[14] He had been genuinely shocked when the Emperor had informed him of the defeatist rumblings within the army. Retreat behind the Mincio? That meant abandoning Milan. How could the 'master of Italy' retreat from her foremost city? On 15 January, therefore, he had given the Emperor an absolute commitment to the city's defence:[15] 'Everybody knows that such a retreat could take place only over my dead body.' These were portentous words. They go far to explain his conduct during the months of war and revolution.

The imperial *Handschreiben* of 9 January had been passed to Radetzky with more than just the proclamation to keep him happy. Hardegg had also commissioned him to find out quickly how best the borders of the North Italian kingdom could be defended. Treasury influence was, nonetheless, apparent, for he was told to come up with something that involved 'no considerable expenditure of time or energy', words which were really meant to read merely 'no considerable expenditure'.

Radetzky replied on 24 January.[16] He had worked very hard on the project and hoped that the Hofkriegsrath would waste no time in coming to a decision. His report and that of his General Staff show just how important Milan had become in Austrian military thinking. His own report in particular was an essay on the political importance of the city and how this had to be reflected in military terms. Nonetheless, he did use conventional military arguments also.

The western border of Lombardy was formed by the River Ticino, from Lake Maggiore to its junction with the Po below Pavia. According to Radetzky, the river was a 'military obstacle', but 'no position, no defensive line' – because it ran 'between flat banks in a very cultivated plain'. Of greater importance was the fact that the right bank overlooked most of the strategical points on the left bank and the right bank belonged to Sardinia. There was simply no point on the left bank which could be made defensible by Austria, no point at least which was within riding distance of the river. Pavia, to be sure, was an exception. There was a 'massive stone bridge' with its own defences across the river and this gave the town some strategic importance. From Pavia, the Austrians were capable of attacking any invading Piedmontese army in the flank almost at their own 'discretion'. Yet, in the final analysis, the town occupied too extreme a flanking position to be useful. It did not really cover Milan. An enemy army, having crossed the Ticino, would find there was nothing to stop it. According to Radetzky, therefore, the task of the Austrians was to find a point behind the Ticino which corresponded better with their defensive needs. 'Here,' he wrote, 'we immediately come up against Milan.'

Milan lay at the apex of an obtuse triangle whose almost equal sides rested on the end points of the Austrian border, Como and Pavia. It was the meeting point of all the great lines of communication 'no matter where they [came] from'.[17] Should Austria choose to take the offensive, Milan lay on the shortest line to Turin, 'her primary objective' in any war. From Milan, Pavia could be reached after one 'heavy march', Magenta after one 'ordinary march' and Como after two 'light' ones, even though Como represented the most extreme position of the Austrian right wing. All these towns made possible a vigorous defence of the Ticino line, but they depended for support on Milan. Therefore, the military case for defending it seemed very strong. Moreover, the Lombard capital also 'threatened Switzerland as much as Piedmont'.

However, the 'political and moral influence' of Lombardy's capital was 'even greater than her strategical significance'. She was 'without doubt ... the crowning point of Northern Italy', a city which, under Austrian rule, had risen to such a power and wealth that it 'set the tone' for the whole of Italy. There was still, to be sure, a *Munizipalgeist* which haunted the peninsula, but for all its divisiveness, any political movement which arose in any one part of the peninsula must needs be transmitted all round. Moreover, even that *Munizipalgeist* stood 'in contradiction to monarchical institutions'. It was 'republican by nature'.

Radetzky had also by this stage given up any hope that might have been left of reconciling the city to Austrian rule: 'No matter what we do to win the love of her inhabitants, to bind them to us with bounds of loyalty, it is useless.' Austria had only spared the blood of so many traitors in vain. Her magnanimity in letting so many traitors return had gone totally unrewarded. Saving traitors from the scaffold, refusing to 'confiscate' their possessions, had only increased the hatred felt against her. The Austrians, wrote the Field Marshal, no longer 'governed' – 'we rule now only with the sword in our hand'. He did not have the 'means with which to criticise the law', but of one thing both he and his advisers were sure: a hostile Milan had to be 'kept in check' and on no account 'could we leave it unguarded in our rear'. For all these reasons, therefore, he put forward plans for the fortification of the city.

Radetzky, of course, would have liked to have done something for Pavia as well, yet the Emperor had been only too explicit about the need to limit expenditure. All the money available, therefore, was to be committed to the defence of Milan. It had to be. Strategically, Milan might occupy in Lombardy a position similar to that of Paris in France, but no one was under the delusion that Radetzky was going to be given the '300 millions' which had just been voted by the French Chamber to Louis Philippe for the defence of his capital.

Certainly Milan was in need of fortification. Radetzky wrote of it in his report that it lay open to the enemy; Schönhals described it as 'really an open city'.[18] According to the Field Marshal, an enemy which marched on it would come 'not before its gates, but into its very centre'. It did have a strong, fortified wall – so broad in fact that people used it as a promenade – but it was not very tall and could easily be scaled with ladders. The doors in this wall were described, again by Schönhals, as 'only barricades'.[19] The city, at one time, had had a citadel which had been capable of withstanding a fairly lengthy siege, but the defences which had protected it had been destroyed by the French and only the inner part of the citadel remained – as barracks for the troops. The city, therefore, was a standing monument to Austrian military neglect, and Italians viewing the Lombard capital might well have understood the lament of Radetzky's adjutant:[20] 'We have done nothing for the defence of our western borders; we have traditionally relied on the cooperation of Piedmont.'

Everything was now to be staked on making good the neglect – even the Field Marshal's body. In order to do so, Radetzky submitted along with his report a project that he had had drawn up by a Colonel von Tayber of the Engineering Corps. It consisted of two parts: the first involved the fortification of the citadel itself by building tower-type redoubts on its five greatest bastions; the second placed its hopes in seven 'detached forts' which were to be built around the town in fixed positions, or, as Radetzky preferred, at *places du moment*.[21]

Other proposals had been suggested, but Radetzky believed that the von Tayber plan was cheaper, less time-consuming and more appropriate. The forts on the bastions, he argued, would protect not only the city but the space between the detached forts as well. Convinced the plan was a good one, he pressed Hardegg to let him have a decision as soon as possible and to use all his influence in support of the proposals. He himself, meanwhile, would regard himself as empowered to get on with the job as soon as the good weather returned: ' . . . if we are not involved in any foreign war in the spring, I shall have enough to do for one and a half years to get Milan into such a condition that we can watch unruffled the activities of the innovators who are now shaking Italy at its foundations from the extreme tip of Sicily to the Alps'.

Radetzky's plans were submitted to the Emperor on behalf of the Hofkriegsrath by Prince Hohenlohe; an imperial decision followed on 1 March.[22] Hohenlohe, however, had failed to give Radetzky his full support, so that only the first part of von Tayber's proposals were actually approved. He had advised the monarch:[23] 'As far as the second part is concerned, its execution does not appear to me to be of the highest importance.' The Emperor followed his lead to the letter and ordered only the fortification of the citadel: 9,300 gulden – hardly a princely sum – was made available for the project and there the matter rested. Should any more money be needed, the Emperor decreed that it would have to be found by cutting back on other military building projects. Radetzky's enthusiasm for the defence of Milan had hardly rubbed off in Vienna. Despite the Tobacco Riots, the February revolution in France, the recent developments in Piedmont and the revolutionary activity in Sicily and Rome, Vienna could not afford to give extra thought to the defence of its greatest Italian city. The army had succeeded in extorting martial law from a reluctant imperial government; the price it had to pay for that was imperial indifference thereafter. It had got its way; it was now on top; it could, therefore, get on with the job. Radetzky, meanwhile, had committed himself and the reputation of his army to his ability to defend Milan. He had, after all, given Vienna the lead to judge the country by the capital. He himself had told Vienna that with the fall of Milan, Austrian influence in Italy would come to an end. Vienna often forgot or ignored what he wrote, but his views on this particular subject were destined to be remembered.

The fall of Milan

The old Field Marshal had asked for one and a half years of peace to get his defences in order, yet only three weeks after the imperial decision of 1 March the revolution had broken out. The man who had been predicting it off and on for months beforehand[24] was, in fact, caught out; and the city to which he had attached such great importance, after only five days of street fighting, fell to the mob.

The evidence that Radetzky was indeed taken unawares on the day is provided by himself. He wrote:[25]

For a few days I had been receiving news from various sources of plans for an uprising which was to take place here in Milan on the 18th. On the evening of the 17th news of the events of 15 March in Vienna had arrived by telegraph. According to this His Majesty had granted great concessions. By this morning, posters had appeared on all the street corners [and] it was believed that this could only have happened had I been asked by the civil authorities to so order. About midday unsettling rumours began to reach me according to which people were gathering here and there and children were being taken away from school by their relatives. The troops were consigned to their barracks; the outbreak of a general uprising, however, did not seem probable to me. I was in my office when the storm broke loose so that it was necessary for me to flee to the Citadel in order not to be engulfed by a mob.

It is hardly necessary to describe here the details of the 'Five Days of Milan'. The important point is that after only five days he was forced to abandon the city:[26] 'It is the most frightening decision of my life, but I can no longer hold Milan. The whole country is in uprising.' On the next day he was writing to Ficquelmont from Melegnano:[27] 'My retreat is completely successful. It is one of these sad masterstrokes of the art of war.' The Austrians did not look like the masters any more. Their living quarters had been plundered and all that they owned stolen:[28] 'Taken by surprise, all we could save was what we wore on our backs.' Yet surprise or no surprise, he was in no mood to take the blame:[29] 'One consolation remains for me – Vienna, not Milan has beaten me. Until the very last moment, at all points, I was the victor. Had I only a few days' supplies enabling me to hold out, Milan would have been in my hands and with it the whole revolution would have collapsed.'

Milan, however, was not in his hands. The man who had told the Emperor that a retreat could take place only over his dead body had retreated after all.[30] The city which he had described as the 'crowning point' of the whole of Italy had gone over to the revolution and he had been unable to prevent it. He had been 'taken by surprise' – his own words – after warning for months of what was likely to happen. Vienna, to be sure, had done little to help him given the threat from Piedmont, yet at the time of the uprising he had had 48,000 of his about 75,000 men in Lombardy, and of these *c.* 14,000 had been in the city itself.[31] Given that this was so, his boasts now rang exceedingly hollow.[32] Even worse, his humiliation was made complete by the capitulation of Venice.

The capitulation of Venice

Schönhals did all he could to save Radetzky's reputation when he wrote his account of the fall of Milan.[33] His account of the fall of Venice, in fact obscures the truth.[34] He wrote:[35] 'It was remarkable that shortly before the outbreak of the revolution, no reports reached the Field Marshal from Venetia. In particular no report whatsoever was confirmed from either the General Command or the two Corps Commands concerning the position of things there. One consoled oneself with the hunch that the authorities had nothing to report [*an Stoff gegehlt*] and that order had in no way been disturbed.' Radetzky's Adjutant-General then proceeded to castigate the treason of the postal workers!

Yet, was ever a man more condemned out of his own mouth? What general who daily expects the outbreak of a revolution can afford 'to console himself with a hunch'? Schöhals, moreover, compounds his error for when he writes that no reports had reached Radetzky on the state of things in Venetia, this was simply not the case. While it is true that many reports from the Venetian Command are missing in the archives, there are reports enough from Venice to indicate that the Field Marshal had every cause to be alarmed about his position there. Radetzky, in fact, had been warned on numerous occasions between January and March 1848 that only the worst could be expected. So, too, had everyone who counted in Vienna.

The first report of impending disaster which was received from Venice was sent by the commander of the Venetian garrison, Count Zichy, to Radetzky on 18 January. There can be no doubt that Radetzky received it because he himself forwarded it to Vienna on 21 January.[36] Given that it was addressed to the supreme commander, the document was very blunt indeed. Zichy stated outright that he expected a revolution to break out in Venice if revolutions took place in Naples or Piedmont. Radetzky by then was already receiving reports of the Neapolitan revolution.[37] The garrison commander even warned that if he did not get the troops that he was writing to demand, there could be no hope of saving Venice. Yet nothing happened.

On 7 February, Radetzky again informed Hardegg of a report from Zichy, according to which the spirit in Venice was deteriorating rather than improving since the number of men 'without bread and without work' was growing larger all the time.[38] Radetzky, however, remained relatively optimistic:[39] 'So long as England does not in some way interfere . . . I have no fears for Venice.' He wrote that he was taking precautions – but these precautions, it should be noted, were being directed against an external foe. He meant, in fact, that he was arming the 'beach batteries'. The thought that the Austrian position could be endangered from within had still not struck him. Venice, he wrote, could be defended by rail 'in a few hours'. He might have added 'anyway'.

The same sort of complacency is revealed in a third report to Hardegg of 16 February.[40] Zichy had sent yet another 'gloomy picture of Venice' and had this time waxed eloquent about the probability of barricades, window-sniping, pitch and boiling water. If left the Field Marshal somewhat cold. He did not believe that, 'The impudence of the malcontents would go to extremes as is commonly said in Venice.' Still, to be on the safe side, he said that he would send a battalion of Grenzer to Venice. They did not go right away.

Attention was only really given to the problem after a detailed report by Zichy was received dated 18 February.[41] The Venetian commander was wise enough to follow this up with another, similar, report which he sent on 19 February, not to Radetzky but direct to the Hofkriegsrath.[42] If the move was an intended slight to Radetzky, he was later to pay for it.

Zichy's report of 18 February is a most revealing document. It gives a full account of the situation in Venice. Excitement in the town was growing daily. Already the trading community had heard news that the barricades were up in Paris and there were signs that the same kind of thing could be expected in Venice. The police had already clashed with crowds in the Mezeria and it was Zichy's belief that through more and more incidents like this, the people would become embittered against the Austrians. His main fear, however, was not about the small riots. These he could put down. What really troubled him was the position of the army and navy's military stores in the Venice Arsenal: 'A movement in the Arsenal would be the most dangerous.' Yet there was growing unrest among the Arsenal workers and when Zichy wrote of the 'danger in which Venice stands' he was primarily thinking about them.

The main complaint of the Arsenal workers concerned their pay, 'which not even to the slightest degree keeps pace with the rising inflation'. Zichy himself was all in favour of paying them better wages, but the Archduke Friedrich, head of the Austrian navy, had personally vetoed the idea, despite the support given to it by the navy commander in Venice. Zichy was now very much afraid that the workers would take things into their own hands and pointed out: 'Inside the Arsenal they have everything – weapons, powder, shot. They are masters of an Arsenal which contains some 20,000 rifles and which cannot be defended – or at least only with difficulty – while they are lords of the masses and [while they are] cut off from terra firma.' He therefore requested a battalion of troops (Grenzer or Jäger) with which to secure the Arsenal and other island depots.

Finally, there was the danger that the workers, to spite an Arsenal administration whose recent reforms stopped them from 'stealing unhindered' as they had done in the past, would free the 600 condemned prisoners who did forced labour inside the building. None of these men were friends of the government. 'If I were giving the orders I would send these men away for they can do no good here', wrote the garrison commander. Meanwhile he could only wait for help and watch the situation deteriorate. Government employees 'through inclination or fear' were siding with the malcontents; people were 'very lukewarm about fulfilling their duties'; most people saw duty as 'something casual'; and worst of all, the navy was being contaminated by crowds of people who followed young officers about trying to subvert their loyalties. Two days later, Zichy returned to the theme of navy disloyalty.[43] In a report to Radetzky, he wrote that sailors had to be seen as 'true Italians'. They were disaffected. Even worse, among navy officers, an agitation was now discernible against the military of the line. Zichy's mind was made up. Should Paris fall, so too would Venice. He added, however, 'I hope that this will not happen'.

These reports provoked no urgent response. According to Ficquelmont, Radetzky read out Zichy's report (presumably) of the 18th to the daily conference on 20 February (again presumably).[44] The conference in its wisdom then decided that the main danger lay with 'the high traitors in the Arsenal' and concluded that the best thing to do would be either to send them all away and give their jobs to the Venice poor, or at least to send away the most dangerous ones. In either case the city would be spared a considerable danger.

Radetzky, in his report to the Hofkriegsrath,[45] was less committed. He admitted that something would have to be done with the 600 prisoners, but he did not know what! The tone of his letter was somewhat complacent again. He relied on the naval commander to restore the morale of the sailors. He repeated his intention of sending a Grenzer battalion to the city and gave Hardegg the reassurance that should an uprising break out in Venice, Zichy had been empowered to declare a state of siege. It really was not very much in the way of help and Radetzky gave his reasons why: ' . . . Moreover, however bad the spirit of things in Venice may reveal itself to be, I harbour no fears on that account because, on the one hand, there can be no more unfavourable ground for a popular uprising, and on the other hand, it is so easy to reinforce Venice that I myself would have no difficulties in putting down any attempt at uprising.'

Nor did the Field Marshal display too much concern about the navy. Ficquelmont, in his letter to Metternich of 21 February, wrote that 'anxieties [had] for a long time been expressed' about the loyalty of the navy, anxieties which now extended to the whole naval establishment – sailors, officers, staff. Because no state could be secure 'without the loyal, active co-operation' of its navy, he warned Metternich that the situation was now of the 'highest importance' and that Austria, in the interests of her security, should keep Venice separated from the rest of her possessions and use all her powers to do so.[46] Radetzky's concern, on the other hand, was much less animated. His views on the situation were sent to the Hofkriegsrath on 22 February, in a report which was signed in his absence by General Wallmoden.[47] True, he expressed the opinion that before the navy could be trusted, a 'complete transformation' would be needed. Yet his report continued: 'The Italian troops daily give me unambiguous proof of the best and most praiseworthy spirit and so I cannot despair of this from the sailors, especially if care is taken no longer to train them exclusively from Italians.' The point was that it was already far too late to talk about 'a complete transformation' and the sailors did indeed give cause for despair.

On 26 February, Hohenlohe approved Radetzky's 'very appropriate measures', gave him a free hand in case of 'further eventualities' and instructed the army and navy commanders in Venice to take all necessary steps to secure the weapons in the Arsenal.[48]

The battalion of Grenzer promised by Radetzky did not arrive 'in a few hours'. Far from it. On 28 February Zichy was still waiting for them.[49] He expected them to enter Venice the following day and hoped that they would 'make everything safe'. His plan was to send two companies (400 men) into the Arsenal where three magazines had been cleared to provide them with barracks. Another 150 men and 6 officers were to be stationed nearby. Given these reinforcements, Zichy looked forward 'with confidence to seeing paralysed any uprising' which might take place inside the Arsenal. 'People forget that they are not dealing with Neapolitans,' he wrote.

The navy was quite another problem. Zichy had no hopes of loyalty left from them. Ever since the July revolution they had been 'trained in every respect, not as Austrian sailors but as Italian ones'. That had been all right as long as the Italians were still pro-Austrian. Now it meant that Zichy had to keep a close watch over young officers who were Venetian by birth and who lived 'with their relatives and friends' and whose 'best friends' were 'young people the majority of whom are inclined towards the enemy'. Among officers and N.C.Os there were even individuals who belonged to 'Young Italy' so that Zichy lamented: ' . . . how can people believe that the greater part of the navy is not evilly disposed towards the House of Austria and will not seize weapons to use against us at the first opportunity'.

The situation, he wrote, had been like this 'for some years'. Yet what could the navy commander do? He could not make known his suspicions by dismissing every Venetian officer. That would mean the dissolution of the entire navy officer corps. Besides, that was a step which could be ordered only at 'a higher level'. The truth was that 'the situation of the chief of this branch' had now reached the pass where all he could do was to watch 'a complete navy uprising take place', something, Zichy concluded, which was 'now happening'. However, if he expected the Hofkriegsrath to pay any attention to his warnings he must have been bitterly disappointed. The reply from Vienna which he received at the end of the first week in March[50] betrayed very little anxiety. It approved the measures which he was planning to take and expected them to keep the peace. Otherwise he was merely advised to keep in close touch with the navy command.

However, Zichy had not waited to hear from Vienna before submitting yet another ominous report.[51] The news of the success of the Paris revolution had clearly made him panic. Despite the armies of the monarchical powers, he now expected that republics would be set up in Belgium, Naples, Turin, Genoa, Florence and Rome: 'Without any doubt the military are just as untrue to their princes in all these lands as they are in France.' Quite clearly, he saw Venice following a similar path, because he expected the majority of navy officers to go over to the revolution and lead the navy against the city whose fortifications were 'in no way satisfactory'. The position of the city, according to its commander, had, therefore, 'completely' changed and a demand was made for more than 15,000 extra troops without whom Zichy saw no prospect of surviving in such an 'extremely hostile land'.

The navy commander in Venice, Admiral Martini, was no help in this situation. In his report of 25 February, Zichy complained that Martini, who had been posted to Venice only in January 1848, had no confidence in himself and no confidence in his sailors. Martini, an honest man to the last, in fact had already written to tell Vienna precisely that,[52] but the reply he received was astonishing. It read:[53] 'You certainly do not fail to recognise the difficulties of your present situation, but on the other hand, one expects complete pacification from the steps now being taken by the high command which entitle everybody to hope for the best.'

What steps?

There can be no doubt at all that Radetzky had received more than sufficient warning from Venetia of what was to lie ahead. He simply did not believe that the situation was as hopeless as the Venetian commanders said. It is clear, too, that he had no idea how bad was the system of communications inside his army – otherwise he would indeed have feared for Venice. However, his illusions must have been quickly shattered by Admiral Martini's next report.[54] 'Very sad but completely true' was how its author described it. And sad it was.

The Admiral's report was written in Venice on 21 and 22 March. The city was clearly tottering and the picture it gave of the authorities was scarcely flattering. 'The police force does not exist any more . . . the government has practically no authority.' The real leaders of Venice were the men of the municipality and of the National Guard, and only they were capable of maintaining law and order. The military commander had given out 600 rifles and 250 words to these people and did not want to think about what would happen next. There was no postal service; lies were circulating about the reliability of the troops; and nobody knew exactly what was happening elsewhere. Everyone was wearing cockades and national colours and every effort was being made to win the Italian troops for the revolution. According to Martini, the only thing that might save the situation was the possession of steamships: 'Our possession [of the city] almost depends on them.'

His report the following day, however, was clear proof that he was not likely to get any, clearer proof still of how the mighty could fall.

Everyone was gripped by nationalism – the sailors as much as anybody else. This made the situation 'dangerous' because the authorities were powerless in face of the city and the people:[55] ' . . . the two ships which are in the harbour here', he wrote,

can only move if they are taken in tow in a completely peaceful manner by many barges; they are situated amidst a throng of merchant ships which have no other anchorage and I would be in no position to move them except by firing at them. I have no more than a small steamship of 20 horsepower; the Arsenal is not capable of being defended – it lies in a quarter of the city which is controlled by the rabble and is daily visited by 800 civil workers and 350 condemned men in chains. The whole position is, therefore, priceless, full of dangerous elements. There cannot be a more forsaken one than mine, for the garrison, too, has no authority inside the city – half the troops are Italian and all connections are narrow streets and canals. . . . Added to this is my personal ignorance of navy duties and the immense details of an Arsenal administration, details which I have been unable to grasp in two months – particularly in our troubled times when so much time has had to be devoted to other things. Finally, a general hatred has arisen against Colonel Marinovich, the only man who was acquainted with all the new regulations which were introduced by my predecessor. It is so violent that he cannot be kept at his post.

Martini closed the first section of his report by saying that time was too pressing for proposals and requests to be made. He took up his pen once again, however, to describe a tour which he had made of the Arsenal.

The Admiral had decided to inspect the building to see for himself just exactly what the position was. Colonel Marinovich had volunteered to accompany his chief, but Martini, conscious of the general hatred which was felt for the man, had written to him advising him not to come. Unfortunately, the letter got lost somehow and Marinovich turned up anyway. Martini then gave orders to have the back door of the Arsenal kept open – just in case the Colonel should be forced to beat a retreat. It was an act of foresight. Yet somehow or other there was once more a failure of communication and the back door was not opened quickly enough. The unfortunate Colonel was spotted by the workers who pursued him with tools and pick-axes and hacked him to bits. 'It proved impossible to save him', wrote the Admiral, whose attempts to save his colleague had been frustrated by 'the impossible inner geography' of the Arsenal. 'In times of great excitement', he added, 'one must expect everything.'

Martini now found that his own life was being threatened. Rumours were sweeping the city that he was planning to burn it down. Rather than risk his life, he, too, gave in to the demands of the rebels and turned over the Arsenal to the National Guard. His report ended: 'I do this, partly because I cannot prevent it, partly because the Arsenal workers are already operating through a civil guard in the Arsenal.' On 27 March the army high command of Lombardy-Venetia despatched its own report to Vienna.[56] It began with the words, 'Venice has really fallen'. No doubt the Field Marshal had once again been 'taken by surprise'.

The fall of Venice robbed the Austrian army in Italy of supplies and money whose value could be measured in millions of gulden,[57] and since the rebels gained what the imperial forces had so effortlessly lost the revolution seemed to be 'so well organised' as to make 'resistance' of any kind 'practically impossible'.[58] That at any rate was the initial view of the army command, although this did not prevent it from trying all the same. On the other hand, its whole lifeline now depended on its retaining Trent and on living on the supplies which were left in Verona; its funds were down to 102,000 gulden and the troops were due to be paid at a time when banknotes were no longer accepted. Such was the condition in March 1848 of one of the 'finest' parts of the Austrian army.

Who was to blame? The Lombard-Venetian General Command stated that 'all legal government has ceased through impotence, weakness and treason'. But this satisfied no one. Schönhals put the blame exclusively on Zichy;[59] and went to great lengths to exonerate the Field Marshal, writing, 'The military importance of Venice had earlier been the subject of an extensive correspondence between the Field Marshal and the Hofkriegsrath and it was due to his unending pressure that not unimportant improvements were made to the defence system of Venice.' But even he sounded just a little apologetic:

'Admittedly one had the idea in mind more of an attack from an external than an internal enemy. . . .' Perhaps Zichy was supposed to use the beach batteries.

There can be no doubt that Zichy had a lot to answer for. (Declaring a siege, as Schönhals suggested though, would not have altered the situation.) He had formally capitulated without a fight; he had agreed to remove the Grenzer from all public buildings; and he had surrendered the Arsenal with all its supplies to the enemy. He had also failed to call upon the aid of Baron D'Aspre whose Venetian Army Corps was stationed not far off. He had one excuse – namely, that given his inadequate resources there was little point in putting up a fight – and that was what he told the army when it arrested him.

His claim was neither base nor baseless. He had warned his superiors on many occasions of the hopeless position in which he believed the city was, but they had failed to give his warnings proper attention. More seriously, they had failed to provide the troops which he required so that the story of the capitulation is really a condemnation of them all.

Radetzky's army in Italy was to win for itself a very high reputation in the history of warfare, a reputation which was based on its victories in 1848 and 1849. It was, however, far from being a model army, and had a confused and sloppy command structure. Fortunately, from its point of view, the shambles of an opposition which it had to face in the Italian army did much to obscure its many own shortcomings. In the aftermath of victory its failures were forgotten.

The lack of communication extended further than Italy. The differences in outlook between Vienna and Milan had contributed in their own way to the initial defeats and setbacks. Radetzky's question to Hardegg, 'How can a machine be maintained as a whole, if its parts are working against one another?', had been very much to the point.[60] There had been singularly little cohesion during the winter of 1847/8 between the civil and military authorities in Italy; but the same had been true regarding the civil administrations in Vienna and Milan. The Emperor himself became a victim of the communications muddle. On 10 March he had informed Prince Hohenlohe that he was following the military correspondence with respect to Italy in order to 'know what to do when the time came' ('davon eintrettenden Falls den zweckdienstlichen Gebrauch zu machen').[61] By 24 March, however, he had realised that reports were no longer coming in from either Rainer or Radetzky although he wanted to tell both of them that should difficulties be encountered in maintaining law and order, the army was to act in accordance with the Articles of War. A courier, therefore, was despatched to give them this order 'wherever [they] might be'. The Emperor meantime, to quote his own words, was 'left to suppose that [his] cities in the Kingdom of Lombardy-Venetia [were] also in revolt'.[62] The time he had been waiting for had come. Yet no one had told him.

Chapter 8

Victory from the jaws of defeat

The Hartig mission

Palmerston received the news of Metternich's fall with a mixture of relief and satisfaction. 'Happy would it have been for the Continent of Europe if this had happened some years ago' he wrote,[1]* and added, 'But better now than later.' The fate of Lombardy and Venetia he considered already decided.[2] 'Northern Italy will henceforward be Italian and the Austrian frontier will be at the Tyrol.' The King of Sardinia would pick up not merely Lombardy-Venetia but also Parma and Modena, and in this way he would become 'a sovereign of some importance in Europe'. Yet Austria, according to Palmerston, had no need to feel dejected. Northern Italy had been a 'source of weakness' to her, and if her army had been unable to hold it down there was really no point in attempting to recover it. In London, therefore, the feeling was that the best thing for Austria to do was simply to cut her losses.

It was not only in England, however, that such a feeling was growing. In Vienna, too, it had taken root and no less a person than Count Hartig[3] was attempting to persuade Count Ficquelmont, now Minister-President, to enter into negotiations with Sardinia.[4] Thus, during the first week of April 1848 he sent him a memorandum outlining a possible basis for a peace settlement.[5] Yet the imperial Cabinet did not share Hartig's views completely. They agreed that so long as there was no immediate possibility of a military solution the prospects for a negotiated settlement should be explored;[6] on the other hand, they supported Ficquelmont's contention that[7] 'His Majesty [could] only negotiate with his own subjects'. Or in other words, their primary objective in any negotiations was to try to separate the Lombards from the Sardinians. Ficquelmont, in any case, was still relying upon Radetzky to reconquer Venetia, at which point he thought he might resurrect the old Kingdom of Italy.[8] Thus when Hartig was authorised to 'pacify' the Italians, his task was limited to restoring civil government and to sounding out the Lombards on their terms for a compromise peace. He received no instructions to proceed further than that.[9] He was authorised merely to station himself with Count Nugent's army which was advancing from the Tyrol to reinforce Radetzky and to take over the civil government of northern Italy as the imperial forces moved forward.

As it turned out, Hartig reached Nugent's army at Görz at the moment when the General, advised by Count Marzani, was drawing up terms for the

---

* Notes to this chapter are on pp. 268–71.

capitulation of Udine – terms which naturally involved a host of political and administrative details. Hartig, however, was excluded from deliberations since neither Nugent nor Marzani had been informed of his mission. Thus it was with some frustration that he reported back to Ficquelmont on 27 April that he was still awaiting Nugent's permission to take up the duties assigned to him.[10] He added, however, that he himself had now acquainted the General with the purpose of his mission and hoped that Ficquelmont would do the same with regard to Field Marshal Radetzky. For as he put it,[11] 'disputes over authority and contradictory instructions would not be conducive to filling the Italians with confidence in the new order of things'.

Ficquelmont in fact, had already written to Radetzky, but had done so, perhaps predictably, in a style which was only superficially diplomatic.[12] An uprising 'as general and decisive' as the one which had taken place in Lombardy-Venetia, he explained, could 'be put down only by an equally decisive war or by way of negotiations'. But 'even if [Austria] had the means to wage such a war of repression' it was not at all clear whether she could do so in the light of world and Italian opinion. The decision had, therefore, been taken to pursue peace negotiations even while the war was in progress. He held out the prospect that 'with luck' the struggle might be 'contained in the Venetian provinces', but the main point of his message was that 'advantages in war' could 'only contribute to the restoration of peace through negotiations'. He, therefore, looked forward to 'the closest identification of the military leadership with the attempts to reach a peace' and expected Radetzky to do everything in his power to support Hartig's pacification work. However, given the tone of Ficquelmont's letter, Hartig's job would be to pacify Radetzky.

The former Governor, meanwhile, was still clarifying his position *vis-à-vis* Nugent. He gave him a copy of his instructions as they related to the military and an accompanying letter which explained that he was[13] 'authorized to assume the direction not only of the political administration in the reconquered provinces but also of finance and legislation'. His letter contained the words:[14] 'Not only is my position independent of that of the Viceroy but . . . significantly supersedes it'; he was careful to add the assurance, however, that he had no intention of interfering in military operations.

Hartig's instructions made him potentially very powerful. Article XII stated that as soon as hostilities ended 'the relationship of the Count Commissioner to the army command and to the army as a whole [would] remain the same as it [had] always been constitutionally'. In other words, he was to run the reoccupied territories as something akin to a governor-general; even in the event of partial hostilities, support for the work of pacification was, according to Hartig's instructions, 'a condition, the importance of which [was] to be absolutely respected by both sides'. Thus Nugent and Marzani were quick to come to an agreement with him which they signed at Udine on 1 May.[15] According to this document, Hartig assumed responsibility in the reoccupied provinces for administration and finance but left Nugent a free hand with regard to the provisioning and transportation of his troops. If Nugent felt compelled to issue orders encroaching on matters of political and financial administration, such orders could only be regarded as provisional. Finally the civil and military commanders of all reoccupied provinces came under Hartig's authority, although the latter's competence with regard to the troops extended only over the administration of finance and justice.

One reason why Nugent and Hartig could so easily agree was their mutual commitment to a liberal settlement with the Italians. The Convention of Udine, which had been composed without Hartig, had, in fact, been a remarkably generous document. It allowed for[16]

a complete amnesty, the recognition of all outlays of the revolutionary government, the provisional retaining at their posts, insofar as they still occupied them of all officials employed on 23 March, the abolition of martial law, the abolition of the tax on personnel, the lowering of the salt price, the reconstitution of the provincial assembly under the presidency of the civil and military commander, the assumption by the latter of the gubernatorial powers, the extension of authority with regard to their own funds of communes, the governing bodies of churches and charitable institutions, the abolition of all limiting legislation on associations under the decree of 20 March 1806 . . . and finally the important arrangement that the costs for stationing troops, costs that were usually borne by individual communes, should be divided between all the communes of the provinces.

Indeed, Hartig was so impressed by it that he informed Vienna that he would have to be careful himself[17] 'to avoid any steps which could awaken any anxiety of a return to the old regime' and described his job as 'to undertake immediately those modifications in the branches of the administration which would obviate the most notorious grievances of former times'. In a sense he felt as if he had the Convention of Udine to live up to, so that he determined not to resurrect either the secret police or the censorship. And since both he and Nugent were aware that the National Guard was locally unpopular, he conceded that an entirely new means would have to be found of maintaining law and order. He even seemed to regret that a totally free press could not be set up behind the army's front lines, so radically had his views altered from their pre-March position. On the other hand, he had to adopt a stance at least as liberal as Nugent's in order to persuade the Italians to assume a negotiating posture, and as early as 19 April – more than a week before his agreement was signed with Nugent and Marzani – he had issued a proclamation to the 'Italians of Lombardy-Venetia'. In this[18] he had promised in the Emperor's name that

in the new order of things now established in the Monarchy you will enjoy liberties and guarantees corresponding to your needs with respect to language, character and nationality, [all of] which will be protected in the widest sense. The administration will be entrusted to you under the supremacy of the state. The laws will be made under your influence, the press will be free and those taxes which press most heavily upon the less leisured and most numerous classes will be especially lightened.

The Count Commissioner, it seemed, was, therefore, off to a fine start. Indeed, he had even begun negotiations with the Lombards.

On his arrival in Trieste, Hartig had reported that, in their public notices at least, the Lombards appeared to be adopting a position less extreme than the Venetians.[19] They had not, perhaps, 'cut off all roads to a return' and thus might 'not be indisposed to come to an agreement'. This point of view, at any rate, had been put forward to him and although he himself did not 'hold out any hope' that it was true he was nevertheless prepared 'under the cloak of a mutual exchange of prisoners' to take the opportunity of sounding out Casati.[20] Not wishing to commit the imperial government too far, he contacted the head of the provisional government by private letter only.[21] In this he reminded Casati of his affection for the Italians and wrote that he wished to bring about a peace and 'satisfy the desire of all Italians with respect to guarantees of their nationality and that form of constitutional government which is most suited to them . . . '. A fortnight later he sent two merchants, Brambilla and Mondolfo to Milan to try to effect a conciliation.[22] They were to tell Casati that the imperial constitution which had just been published in Vienna had made no mention of Lombardy-Venetia because the Emperor desired to honour with a special constitution the particular needs of his North Italian subjects. As things turned out, however, Hartig's original pessimism was fully justified. By 15 May the merchants had returned with the news that the Lombards would negotiate only on the basis of complete independence and Hartig was telling Vienna:[23] 'There is no hope at all of bringing back Lombardy under the sceptre of His Majesty by means of peaceful negotiations.'

What then was to be done? Lombardy, argued Hartig,[24] should not be abandoned so long as there was 'any hope of retaining it'. But,

. . . should the means be not at hand to defeat the King of Sardinia immediately before Verona and Mantua should the effort which a longer, perhaps more general war would require be neither feasible nor forthcoming – given the present condition of the other parts of the Monarchy including Hungary and Transylvania – then my humble advice [wrote Hartig] would be to conclude an immediate armistice with King Charles Albert on the basis of the status quo and with the condition of his neutrality in the struggle against the, in any case by him unrecognised, Republic of St. Mark, and to turn all our available forces as quickly as possible against this Republic which they could quickly defeat.

In other words, if Radetzky, could not save Lombardy in the immediate future, Austria should give up that province in the hope of saving Venetia.

Two more attempts were made, however, to reach agreement with the Lombards. On 28 May, another old hand in Italian affairs, von Phillipsberg, was sent to Milan with the offer of[25] 'a constitution voted by representatives chosen by yourselves, a separate, completely national administration, which under a Prince of the Imperial House as Viceroy would guarantee the Lombardo-Venetian Kingdom such freedom of movement, such autonomy and finally such political guarantees as could be offered to it by no other arrangement to so great an extent'. In such a framework, Lombardy-Venetia would enjoy both the freest internal development and the benefits of belonging to a powerful empire. The von Phillipsberg mission, however, had an unexpected outcome: the Austrian envoy was imprisoned by the Milanese for want of satisfactory credentials. Much more important historically was the decision of the imperial government to send another experienced diplomat, Hummelauer to London to plead for British diplomatic mediation.

Hummelauer's mission appeared to be born of desperation. He was told:[26] 'We find it impossible to give you any precise instructions. It is absolutely necessary for us to bring the Italian problem to a speedy end. See what support can be got from the English government. The essential thing for us is that a part of the state debt should be taken over. We lack the means to wage a war, in a sufficiently effective manner and even a battle won would not solve the problem. Let us know how you find things.'

Hummelauer did his best.[27] First of all he asked the British to mediate on the basis of complete autonomy for Lombardy-Venetia within the Austrian

Empire. Palmerston rejected this offer on 23 May. On 24 May, therefore, he suggested mediation on the basis that Austria give up Lombardy but retain Venetia. Palmerston was willing to accept this formula, but his Cabinet colleagues rejected it formally on 3 June. Therefore, Hummelauer had to return to Vienna empty-handed.

Meanwhile, the idea that Austria should surrender Lombardy was gaining ground. Hartig had already hinted at it. Hummelauer had discussed it with Palmerston; and now Count Wessenberg, a former diplomat, who had been called out of retirement and put in charge of Austrian foreign policy, was approaching a similar conclusion. In a letter to Hartig, dated 5 June 1848 he hinted:[28] 'His Majesty, the Emperor, would be prepared to make significant sacrifices to secure a quick peace.' However, the real purpose of his letter was to seek Hartig's own views on the situation, views which, it turned out, were pessimistic ones.

Hartig replied on 9 June and pointed to the general state of the Empire in order to underline the weakness of Austria's negotiating position.[29] There had been the overthrow of the 25 April Constitution; the flight of the Court to Innsbruck, 'the barricades and the rule of the mob in Vienna', the Slav Congress in Prague, not to mention the feud between the Magyars and the Croats. More important, he claimed there had been 'the destruction of confidence in Field Marshal Radetzky'. Indeed, as he put it two days earlier,[30] 'the fall of the fortress of Peschiera, the unsuccessful attack on the bridgehead at Goito and the lack of a successful follow-up to our victory at Curtatone [had] put any possibility of . . . a [simple] ceasefire right out of the picture'. In fact, Radetzky could no longer be expected to seize victory between the Etsch and the Mincio and Lombardy could no longer be retained. His advice to Wessenberg was, therefore, that[31] 'it would be better to submit to this very painful amputation [i.e. the loss of Lombardy] immediately, than to delay until such time as the rest of the body of the State should be even further exhausted by unsuccessful efforts to retain the part that is to be cut off'. Thus, as Hartig saw matters, the army had lost its chance to retrieve its position with the result that the diplomats would have to pick up the pieces by negotiating the transfer of Lombardy to Sardinia. But would Radetzky and his army be so easily written off?

As early as 15 May, Hartig had complained to Vienna that Radetzky was 'ignoring' him.[32] He had received no word at all from the Field Marshal and had to rely for military news on private reports and the newspapers. The situation, he wrote, would be laughable, if it were not so serious. Radetzky might well have agreed with him for the Field Marshal viewed the Hartig mission as an ill-timed piece of nonsense. Thus he had informed Ficquelmont on 3 May:[33] 'There are many people who desire peace but we must back them up with force.'

His true feelings regarding Hartig's mission were to be found in his letters to Latour. The War Minister was told[34] 'not to harbour any illusions and to expect no results from all the work of pacification.' The Austrians were being deceived and the Milanese were playing for time: 'Have we been deceived so often that we always want to be deceived?' The provisional government in Milan, he wrote, were[35] 'the personification' of arrogance and falseness and could never be trusted. He had negotiated with them at Milan before his retreat and had seen his 'misplaced generosity' returned with 'the most infamous calumnies and mockery'. The work of pacification, therefore, would 'be taken for weakness and ridiculed'. Radetzky told Latour:[36] 'I confess frankly to your Excellency that I will negotiate with these people only with the sword in my hand. From that I promise good results; any other way I hold to be incompatible with Austrian honour.' Latour sympathised with the Field Marshal but pleaded with him to understand the new order of things. He explained:[37] 'I can as a soldier only share completely the feelings and views which Your Excellency expressed. . . . However, as much as I beg Your Excellency to convince yourself of this, I must also ask you to think of my position as Minister of a constitutional state. . . . ' Radetzky, however, had other things to think about.

His objections to 'pacification work' were not based simply on principles alone. The policies pursued by Hartig and Nugent simply exacerbated his difficulties in the field. Thus the Field Marshal was caustic in his comments on the Convention of Udine:[38] 'If the General loses too much time through negotiations [of this kind] the noose will tighten steadily around me and the survival of my army will become even more difficult.' The Convention had produced 'no favourable impression'[39] and in Radetzky's blunt language[40] 'no costly time should be wasted in negotiating with open and insignificant towns which do not deserve this honour and which would be more impressed with a more imperious tone'.

Likewise, the Field Marshal was unimpressed by the measures undertaken by Hartig. He described his proclamation as[41] 'this inferior piece of work . . . so hostile to Austria' and once again condemned the practical results of 'pacification'. For example he pointed out that the Italians were making a mockery of Hartig's press policy by publishing two editions of their newspapers. 'Only one edition' would be known to Count Hartig, whereas the other, although bearing his imprimatur, would contain items hostile to Austria.[42] Thus the *Spettatore Friulano* of 9 May contained reports that Verona was about to fall to the Sardinians; that Hungary had recalled her troops fighting under Radetzky; that the latter had 'abandoned themselves to enthusiastic demonstrations shouting "Long live Hungary! Long live Italy!" '; and that a general armistice had been concluded among the belligerent parties.[43] The same paper also reported[44] that in Verona 'the troops want[ed] for nothing but that the populace [was] starving'. It added that the city was suffering 'all the rigours of a state of siege', that 'all the generals [were] calling for a retreat' and that only Radetzky wanted to 'fight to the last man'. Yet Hartig had specifically asked the delegate of Verona, Hofrat Greller, to request Radetzky to have this edition of the newspaper circulated in the town so that the townspeople might read of his promises of reconciliation which it also contained.[45] Radetzky would not allow this:[46] 'I know only too well that people can now print what they like but it is one thing to print, another to propagate; all the more so in a city under a state of siege with the enemy at the gate.'

A similar dispute arose eleven days later over a complaint lodged by Hartig with the Emperor against the commander of the fortress of Mantua.[47] Radetzky professed that it was 'not so much on the ground of the complaint' he wrote to Latour, although he spoke in glowing terms of his subordinate – the man had 'done what no commandant in recent times under similar circumstances had done', namely through 'means which he alone knew how to fashion' enabled an 'untenable' town to withstand a siege – rather, Radetzky wrote to the War Minister to show how in practical terms the Hartig mission was in danger of undermining the military position. For when towns were in a state of siege he could not 'tolerate any but a purely military authority' to be exercised over them.

Yet clearly there were larger issues at stake than press reports and the spheres of authority of garrison commanders. For at stake was really the question of Radetzky's position *vis-à-vis* the Count Commissioner. The Field Marshal had not raised this matter when he had complained of press abuse.[48] He had simply begged Latour 'in confidence' to ensure that no 'seed of dissension' would be 'sown from the very start' between himself and Hartig and expressed his desire that through the War Minister 'harmony [could] be brought to the steps of two authorities to whom the confidence of the monarch [had] given such difficult tasks'. He even declared that he was 'ready to make sacrifices to go along with' the Count Commissioner. Yet after the affair of the Mantua commander the Field Marshal took the bull by the horns, and in his letter of 26 May he raised the question as he saw it:[49]

What I fear most of all is that the position of Count Hartig will confuse the present situation. . . . He has let me know that he will soon arrive here and bids me henceforth to submit to him matters which used to go to the Viceroy. However, the viceregal authority has been abolished as incompatible with the new institutions; shall we now resurrect it in a new guise? We cannot lose sight of the fact that our authority in this country only extends as far as our weapons and that we literally find ourselves in the position which the enclosed extracts from the Imperial *Handschreiben* foresaw.[50] There are still officials here only in the fortresses we control; but their authority is fully absorbed by the state of siege.

Radetzky again assured Latour that he would do 'everything to work hand in hand' with Hartig to pacify the rebel provinces. However, there was 'no other way' of doing that but 'by means of force' and that force could not and 'must not suffer any paralysis'. He closed his letter by stating that the aim of his report was 'none other than to prevent any possible misunderstanding' being put down to his account, since he was now informing Latour of 'the position of things beforehand'. Vienna, therefore, had the task of somehow avoiding a confrontation. It was running two policies at once and would have to choose which one to follow. Fortunately, Radetzky knew nothing either of the von Phillipsberg or of the Hummelauer missions, so that the situation was not as explosive as it might have been. Still, the pot was beginning to boil.

Pillersdorff, the Minister of the Interior, was asked by Latour to adjudicate on the matters raised by the Field Marshal and did so on 31 May.[51] He wrote to Hartig pointing out the significance of the *Handschreiben* to which Radetzky had referred and reminded him that the position of Viceroy had been abolished as 'incompatible' with 'military institutions'. Pillersdorff, in fact, gave his backing to Radetzky and told Hartig that the Field Marshal was in no position to comply with his requests. He added, however, that if he used good sense, there need still be no cause for disagreements. A copy of this letter was sent to Latour who was left to decide on the question of Mantua. Latour, in turn, forwarded a copy of Pillersdorff's letter to Radetzky and one can only suppose that the old Field Marshal was delighted.

Nugent's army meanwhile had joined up with Radetzky's on 25 May and Hartig decided to visit the Field Marshal in person, not only to put him in the picture with regard to his peace diplomacy but also to let him know of his intention to take over the direction of civil administration in the reoccupied areas. His aim there, as he would outline it to Wessenberg a little later, was[52] 'the immediate re-organisation of the Venetian provinces according to the principles of constitutional government and a purely national administration'. Accordingly he wrote to Radetzky on 6 June informing him of his arrival in Verona and expressing the hope that, since they would soon be in daily contact they might come to some agreement regarding their respective spheres of duty.[53] Hartig reminded the Field Marshal of how they had worked together in the past and how in the final analysis their aim was exactly the same – to bring back the kingdom under the sceptre of the Emperor. Only their methods, he suggested, were different: Radetzky wielded a sword; he an olive branch. He added in a postscript that it was his intention to retire with the former viceregal chancellery to Roveredo, since no state of siege had been declared there. But clearly, he anticipated establishing a *modus vivendi* with the Field Marshal first.

Radetzky although also in Verona, took a week to reply, ostensibly because Hartig's letter had arrived 'at a moment when [he] was almost day and night in the saddle'. He wrote:[54] 'I wish from the bottom of my heart that I could make over to Your Excellency part of my heavy duty to pacify our rebel Italian provinces; however, given the way things are at present, I believe that we must first win a decisive victory over King Charles Albert before we can hope for any results from an attempt at pacification.' As it was, the state of the country meant that he must keep the forts in a state of siege 'since otherwise [his] position would be absolutely impossible'. Moreover, the country could 'only be pacified through military rule'. Radetzky's tone, on the other hand, was not one of intransigence for he ended his letter with the hope that circumstances would soon change. Indeed 'it will be the happiest day of my life', he wrote,[55] 'when I can say to Your Excellency, "Italy is becalmed. Build on the secure basis of this condition, for the sword is no longer alone required to maintain order." '

Yet Hartig was not to be put off. He himself now raised the constitutional issue in Vienna, and this time Pillersdorff [56] complained to Latour that his position was being made 'difficult to the point in fact, of being wholly untenable'. Pillersdorff reminded his colleague that he himself had always respected the military point of view, but gave him clearly to understand that his patience was now wearing thin.[57] 'It seems suspicious to me', he wrote, 'that the directives which are being carried out to the disadvantage of the country and the army all seem to stem from the army command.' He supported Hartig's apparently well-documented complaint that popular ire was being stirred up by 'dissimilar negotiations with different towns' in Italy and expressed his fear that it would become impossible 'to win over the Italians to a peaceful settlement' even – and here he used a phrase that would wound Radetzky – 'even if the fortune of war [should] favour us more than hitherto'. Therefore, he asked Latour to give the army 'the most precise instructions', ordering them to make over the civil and financial administration in the theatre of war to Hartig so long as there was no 'categorical necessity' preventing this; in fact the military in future were to make no unilateral decisions in those areas but were to inform the Count Commissioner of their demands instead. Latour agreed to pass on these instructions, but at the same time counselled Pillersdorff not to be misled by Hartig's account and in particular by his account of the cooperation he had received from Nugent.[58] 'Count Nugent', wrote Latour, 'had the task of restoring the loyalty of an insurgent area more through a military invasion than by any real use of force. Count Radetzky finds himself in a completely different situation, given that nearly the whole countryside is in revolt and that he has a large, hostile army to fight. Thus the use of exceptional means and administration according to military considerations can and must appear necessary much more often.' Nevertheless, in the letter to Radetzky which passed on the Interior Minister's views, Latour encouraged the Field Marshal to abide by Pillersdorff's instructions and 'deeply regretted' Radetzky's failure to meet with Hartig. He wrote that[59] 'a verbal agreement on these matters' would have led 'much more easily, quickly and surely to the common aim of mutual understanding'. The Field Marshal replied in turn on 19 June saying that[60] he had just received his letter and had 'found therein the confirmation of what [he had foreseen] from the very first moment he was told of Count Hartig's nomination as Count Commissioner and Pacifier'. He claimed, however, that he was ignorant of the accusations being made against him by Pillersdorff, but that in order to defend himself he enclosed his correspondence with Hartig to date.

Hartig apparently had written to Radetzky on 16 June complaining as usual that he was being ignored.[61] The Field Marshal had recently sent him only four short letters – all of them on matters of no great substance and he suggested sarcastically that perhaps the others had gone missing. On 18 June, therefore, Radetzky wrote to him making his position perfectly plain.[62]

I cannot recall that I have interfered with Your Excellency's position or authority in any way. I have spoken of my view on conditions here in my letter of the 12th of this month, conditions which through the conquest of the entire Venetian terra firma have meanwhile improved, but which are still far from enabling a military hand to be removed.

What His Majesty decides to do in future in this respect is for me the law. Should he order the removal of the state of siege of Verona, Mantua and Legnano, I as a loyal subject can do nothing but obey. But I would then, however, be compelled to lay down my command.

Radetzky was still convinced of the justice of his approach: 'Excited spirits and liberated nations', he wrote to Latour[63] 'cannot be appeased with sweet words or pacification proposals if they are not to be lost. . . .' He favoured the stick before the carrot and repeated that if necessary he was determined to resign. If the state of siege were lifted, he would 'lay down [his] command and [his] successor [could] carry out the order'.[64] As for Hartig, he told the War Minister:[65]

Up till now I have had no proper conception of his authority although perhaps a personal conversation would have cleared matters up for me. . . . [However . . .]
I beg Your Excellency to take into consideration that I simply do not have the time to correspond with so many authorities and give chapter and verse for what I do, as Count Hartig appears to expect. As Commanding General, I remain responsible to the War Ministry and to his Majesty, should my operations and the position of my army necessitate my taking measures which are not accounted for by the usual administrative regulations, I shall be responsible for them to Your Excellency. Any other authority I cannot recognise in this respect.

Radetzky finished his letter with the rebuke, 'If the Count Commissioner can run this country without an army so much the better', and declared that 'those in Milan' regarded Hartig's mission as an 'object of derision'. He did not say this, he wrote, 'to disparage Count Hartig and his measures', but 'to show the character of the people against whom we have so often entered the field with our optimistic attempts at reconciliation'. There was little prospect, therefore, of any compromise between the Count Commissioner and the Field Marshal. This was in any case made crystal clear by a letter sent to Wessenberg by Hartig.[66] The latter had learnt of Pillersdorff's advice to Latour – that the civil and financial administration should be made over to him so long as there was no categorical necessity which prevented this – but wondered whether 'the exception might [not] become the rule on account of the evasive habits of the military'. The Field Marshal's age Hartig hinted, had become an obstacle to progress. He objected that the *Handschreiben* of 1 March was being abused. The fact that 'every oral or written understanding' was being evaded, was not, he declared, his fault. An impasse, therefore, had been reached between the civil and military authorities in northern Italy. Hartig now returned to Roveredo to issue orders rather than force the issue with the Field Marshal; Radetzky, meanwhile challenged the government to back Hartig to the hilt or let him get on with winning the war. However, the resolution of these differences was reached not over internal but over external matters of policy.

It did not take Wessenberg long to make up his mind which direction Austrian foreign policy would have to take. On 11 June he wrote to Radetzky informing him that the Emperor had agreed to negotiate over Lombardy, and therefore that a ceasefire would have to be effected.[67] He promised to let him have more details in a day or two once Vienna had decided on its negotiating chief. Meanwhile, the instructions regarding the ceasefire were drawn up. These[68] directed the Field Marshal to enter into negotiations 'immediately' since a settlement was now a matter or urgency. As for the terms he was to secure he was told that they had to be 'the most advantageous possible in a military–political sense and must at least leave [Austria] in possession of what [she held]'. The Emperor relied upon his 'proved intelligence and loyalty' to obtain them.

In a letter accompanying the instructions,[69] Wessenberg informed Radetzky that the Emperor and his Ministers had decided to end 'the costly war in Italy' and 'to give the army a well-earned rest'. Once the Field Marshal had secured a ceasefire, therefore, Vienna would negotiate on the basis of surrendering Lombardy – albeit on certain conditions. According to Wessenberg, negotiations would have been started earlier if he had not been convinced that there was still a chance of containing the rebellion by use of force; however, other factors now persuaded him that negotiations were imperative. At the basis of his thinking was still the hope of creating a diplomatic breach between the Lombards and the Sardinians. Charles Albert, it was proposed, would be invited to participate only in the negotiations respecting a ceasefire; he, after all, had intervened merely in support of the Milanese and they alone, therefore, would be asked to discuss matters of substance. In this way Wessenberg hoped to generate differences within the Italian camp and thereby secure some badly needed diplomatic points for Austria. Meanwhile, the man chosen to negotiate with the Milanese was Schnitzer-Meerau whose instructions were[70] 'to open with the government established in Milan negotiations to be based upon the separation and independence of Lombardy'. The imperial government's 'equitable conditions' for this were 'to comprise principally of the transfer of a proportionate part of the state debt of the Austrian Empire to Lombardy, plus a settlement which should secure certain advantages for Austrian commerce and certain stipulations concerning certain properties of the imperial family and losses suffered by civil and military employees as a result of recent events'.

On 16 June Wessenberg again wrote to Radetzky[71] and on 17 June to Hartig.[72] His tone was fairly optimistic for he asked the Field Marshal to get naval hostilities included within the armistice and told him to inform Charles Albert that peace negotiations had begun with Milan. He was hoping in fact, that Milan would not make peace dependent on a ceasefire. To Hartig he displayed a similar optimism: his information was that both Sardinia and Milan were in favour of a quick peace. Yet most important of all was the fact that Vienna needed one: the war was tearing the Monarchy to pieces; it was costly; and the sooner it ended the better. What Wessenberg did not yet know was that Charles Albert had already assumed the title 'King of Lombardy' thus making his diplomatic strategy redundant.[73]

Radetzky reacted to Wessenberg by sending his political and diplomatic adviser Prince Felix zu Schwarzenberg to Innsbruck. That he meant to oppose any attempts at negotiations was made clear from a letter he sent to Hartig after the latter had informed him for the very first time of the von Phillipsberg mission. He wrote:[74] 'We have sunk low, but by God, not yet so low that we should take orders from Casati.' Hartig wrote to Vienna telling Wessenberg[75] that he would see from Radetzky's tone 'that the agitated spirit in Verona which [had] so often been described by [him] continue[d] to exist'. But Wessenberg was already well aware of the tone of Radetzky's opposition.

Schwarzenberg, already in Vienna, had put forward the army's case:[76] there was nothing to fear from the Sardinians who were in no position to launch an attack, and, since the same was true of the Austrians, a *de facto* ceasefire already prevailed; moreover, with an extra 25,000 men Radetzky might well be able to deliver such a blow against the Italians that he could 'dictate' a peace in Milan. Finally, if a ceasefire were to be concluded before 'a greater, more glorious feat of arms' could be secured, the army's morale, which was then sufficiently high to see it through to the last man, would henceforth assuredly deteriorate. For all these reasons the Field Marshal hoped that negotiations could be postponed.

Wessenberg himself had given the counter-arguments:[77] the country's finances could no longer afford a war and only the prospects of peace could restore the country's credit-worthiness; granting more men 'merely to reconquer a country the possession of which might have to be relinquished' would be difficult to justify before the Reichstag; even a great victory 'might only bring new complications' since the French might then feel compelled to intervene and England would do nothing to stop them – 'in such a case we might well', Wessenberg contended, 'have to surrender all hope of saving the Venetian provinces also'; finally, there was the argument that conditions within the other provinces of the Empire were so bad that there was little hope of sparing the extra troops Radetzky needed. By 19 June, however, Wessenberg had heard unofficially of the union of Lombardy with Sardinia.[78] He therefore, wrote to Radetzky telling him that while he would have to await the results of his diplomacy, he nonetheless felt that the ceasefire would be postponed. By 25 June, Schnitzer-Meerau confirmed what Wessenberg had suspected.[79] Casati had declined to take up the offer of negotiations on the grounds that fighting was taking place not over the future of Lombardy but over that of Italy; the question of Lombardy could not be settled without reference to either Venetia or, for that matter, the South Tyrol. Charles Albert, reported Schnitzer, had meanwhile agreed to keep his troops in Lombardy, but the Italians were counting on the probability of French intervention, something which aroused greater enthusiasm in the ordinary Lombard than the prospect of being governed from Turin. Schnitzer concluded that one good victory by Radetzky would most likely destroy whatever unity there existed in northern Italy.

On 26 June the Italian question was discussed by the imperial Council of Ministers.[80] Schwarzenberg was also present and read out to the others a report which Radetzky had drafted.[81] The military position in northern Italy, it read, had changed. With the reconquest of the Venetian cities the Austrian flank and rear had been secured; but they would only really be secure if Lombardy was also once more under Austrian control. Otherwise, the example of a constitutional state next door would be a permanent cause of unrest which must eventually lead to a renewed war. It would therefore, be 'even in the best interests of the finances' to have the matter settled on a 'lasting and realistic' basis and to continue the war until a decisive peace could be assured. The Field Marshal was not unduly worried about France. 'All the interests of France and the Austrian Government', he wrote, 'respecting the Italian Question coincide with the present state of affairs.' France, he argued, could not agree to the establishment of a significant power on her eastern frontier; if Austria, therefore, were to assure her that she would not annex Sardinia, there need be no clash of national interests. Radetzky, finally appealed for more men. Charles Albert was staking everything on the present campaign; if he lost, he therefore lost everything. One good victory and there 'would be no more danger from that side'.

Given the failure of Wessenberg's diplomacy there was little the Ministers could do but adopt Radetzky's arguments. Wessenberg wrote to Hartig:[82] 'At this point, given the above-mentioned, altered position of the Provisional Government, it is neither a question of negotiations nor of establishing a ceasefire; people are now occupied with the thought of how to strengthen the army in Italy.' By 23 June in any case, the decision had already been taken to replace Hartig by Count Montecuccoli on account of his 'differences' with Radetzky.[83] The Count Commissioner had asked for some leave and the Ministry had decided to make it permanent. Latour conveyed his information to the Field Marshal, adding:[84] 'That I completely shared the views put forward by Your Excellency in the controversy between yourself and Count Hartig I was earlier in the position to be able to explain both to you and the Minister of the Interior.'

Hartig finally resigned his mission on 3 July. It had been based, he wrote,[85] on the principle 'that obedience should no longer be extorted by force . . . that obedience today, as the political world understands it, can be maintained only by a voluntary agreement to self-restraint'. The irony was, of course, that he could only have secured agreement to this principle with military backing – backing which Nugent had been willing to provide but which Radetzky was not. The latter had ignored him and had corresponded with Vienna through Latour. Once his views had prevailed, however, the Field Marshal's natural generosity at once revived. He wrote to Hartig on 30 June:[86]

I too honestly regret that there had to be differences between us in many respects concerning our views on the present state of Italy. However, I have had such bitter experiences, partly on account of the disloyalty of the Italians, partly on account of the neglect of all my warnings and forecasts about conditions here, that Your Excellency will not reproach me if I now consider that out of this general wreckage I have at least kept my military honour unblemished. I also harbour the hope that Your Excellency will retain these friendly feelings towards me which you so often displayed in earlier and better times.

Victory

Despite his political victory over Hartig, Radetzky could not feel absolutely sure of his position until he had proved his worth militarily. The trouble was that to be able to do this he needed reinforcements, for he had to take into account, as always, that a large proportion of his men were required for garrison duties. Thus, on 18 May he had reported to Latour that out of 48,561 men, no less than 21,736 were so accounted for and that, artillery apart, he had only 16,373 infantrymen and 3,818 cavalry.[87] Moreover, one-fifth of his infantrymen was still made up of Italians and these, he stressed, would have to be handled 'gingerly'. The situation had not improved dramatically, even by mid-June.[88] His army was now divided into a First and Second Corps with a reserve of 9,121 infantry and 2,341 cavalry, accounting for 25,659 infantry and 3,979 cavalry in all, but basically his position could still be summed up with the words: 'I must have reinforcements.' Nugent had brought him only 18,000 men, after seven helpless weeks; 'I march with everything I have', he wrote, but there seemed little he could do.

He prided and sustained himself with the knowledge that he had done his best and reacted sharply to Pillersdorff's comments to Latour on the fortunes of the war. To the War Minister, he wrote:[89]

After my retreat from Milan I found an army deprived of everything, fortresses which could not sustain an enemy attack for a week, no gold in the kitty, no supplies in the magazines, the whole of Italy right up to the borders of Carniola and Carinthia in the hands of the enemy.

Today the fortresses are secure against an attack, the whole of Venetia with the exception of its capital has been reconquered, the King of Sardinia, robbed of allies, has himself been forced on the defensive, and were my own forces not so limited, I would already be at the Ticino instead of the Mincio.

The forces required to do all this were not sent from Vienna, nor could be sent, as Your Excellency knows best. I had to seek them in the countryside and in a restricted area; had I not used extraordinary methods, Charles Albert would today be standing at the foot of the Carniolan and Carinthian Alps and Austria, once-mighty Austria, would have sought peace from a King of Sardinia – I never like to talk of what I have done, but when I am forced to, I must.

It was Radetzky's complaint that events elsewhere in the Monarchy had always meant that he had been weakest in Italy.[90] Thus, in March and April he had had only 20,000 mobile men against the enemy's 40,000; at the end of May, when he had taken the offensive with 40,000, the enemy, he discovered, had 60,000. Welden, the General in charge of the Tyrol, had promised him an extra 6,000, but he knew that 6,000 on paper meant only 2,000 more in reality. He calculated, therefore, that by mid-June he could dispose of about 53,000 men against 65,000 of the enemy. More men were needed for his 'battle of Italy' than that.

'How is one supposed to fight a decisive battle?' On 21 June Radetzky wrote to Latour posing a 'short question':[91]

Shall I pursue the enemy right away with 50,000 men and risk a battle on good luck – which at the moment I am prepared to do and await only your reply for I cannot do it on my own authority or; shall I, once I have received the Haller Division which has been promised to me, fight a battle, perhaps with equal forces, but supposing this should happen, without following it up or advancing on Milan; or shall I, finally, be so supported that, reinforced by 20–30,000 men from Vienna, I can hope as Victor of Lombardy, to lay down the law in a manner worthy of a state such as Austria?

He awaited the Minister's answer.

Latour replied to Radetzky's letter on 27 June informing him that he had consulted the Council of Ministers and the Archduke John.[92] The result was that 'it is possible for Your Excellency to undertake an offensive operation with 52–53,000 men'. Radetzky, it was assumed would have the advantage of collecting a superior force to fall upon an extended point of the enemy's position (between Curtatone and Rivole) and overpower it; Charles Albert, it was assumed, would not have time to concentrate his forces. Latour wrote in exactly the kind of language which Radetzky had been trying to extract.[93]

I do not hold myself entitled to decide from here in my capacity as War Minister when the right moment will arrive to give battle to King Charles Albert of Sardinia; I am much more of the opinion that this decision must be left to Your Excellency as the supreme commander who has the experience of war and the trust of the monarch, the government and the army to so high a degree. For was it not always objected to the old system that it wanted to make war from the cabinet and that generals were often given orders which were no longer appropriate on account of changed circumstances by the time that they had been received?

He told Radetzky 'You must have freedom to decide what to do with regard to the enemy' but added:[94]

I am empowered to tell you that His Imperial Highness [the Archduke John] and the Council of Ministers have such great confidence in your wise leadership of the army that they are convinced that it can be left to your proved judgement where the decisive battle must be fought, which battle must now inevitably take place sooner or later since the answer already received by the Foreign Minister from Count Casati withholds any hope of a successful attempt at pacification. . . . Under such circumstances an honourable peace can only be secured by our brave army under its fine leadership.

Vienna was now obviously singing a very different tune. Radetzky was to risk everything on military success in one decisive encounter. It had been hoped to get him the extra troops he needed – the troops which he had said would guarantee his success – from the northern commands of the Empire, particularly from Prince Windischgraetz in Prague but Windischgraetz had refused to help:[95] 'To weaken the armed forces stationed around Prague in order to send a part of them to Italy', he wrote, 'would mean surrendering advantages which have been won with great difficulty and sacrifices, as well as abandoning Bohemia. This is my incontrovertible opinion based on exact knowledge of the situation and on account of which I am obliged to declare candidly that were I formally forced to send troops, neither I, still less anyone else, would be in a position to retain Bohemia and I am, therefore, determined to go to Innsbruck to put my case before the Emperor.' Latour received Windischgraetz's answer 'with deep regret'.[96] What had been at stake had been the army's honour, the salvation of Lombardy and the restoration of calm and unity to the Empire. Without another 20,000 men it did not seem possible for Radetzky to win the 'decisive undertaking'. The Empire, it now appeared, would let down Radetzky and not vice versa. The Field Marshal had often said as much and Latour, perhaps, remembered jibes like the following:[97] 'I only wish, for my part, that the Minister [Pillersdorff] could have as much success in battle against the intelligentsia of our time, the law-giving bands of students with their bought communist allies, the workers, as I am now having, despite being in the minority, in battles and skirmishes with the King of Sardinia.'

The fortune of war, however, now favoured Radetzky. The decisive battle was fought at Custozza on 25 July and Charles Albert's main army was defeated and put to flight. Vienna received the news at five past nine on the morning of 29 July.[98] Radetzky wrote to Latour:[99] 'A decisive victory has been the result of this hot day.' The risk had paid off after all.

The re-entry into Milan

On 26 and 27 July the Austrian army again defeated the Piedmontese at Volta.[100] The result was that on the following day two Piedmontese generals and a colonel appeared at D'Aspre's headquarters requesting a ceasefire on behalf of Charles Albert and proposing the Oglio as the line of demarcation between the two armies. Radetzky reported:[101] 'I have rejected these proposals and instead have put forward the conditions contained in the enclosed letter and am determined, should these not be accepted by 5 a.m. tomorrow, to resort once more to arms in order to pursue the enemy with my combined forces.' Radetzky had demanded that the demarcation line should be the River Adda; that the fortresses of Peschiera, Pizzighettone and Rocca d'Anso should be returned to the Austrian army within two days; that both Parma and Modena should be reoccupied by the Austrian army in three days; that the suspension of hostilities should apply to both Venice and the Venetian terra firma; and that all Austrian officers held prisoner in Milan and elsewhere should be set free immediately. It was made known to the Sardinians that the Field Marshal was not in any way prepared to compromise over these terms, which were, in fact, a rather astonishing set of proposals. Radetzky, it seemed, was prepared to stop before Milan and Latour congratulated him:[102] 'While I can only express my warmest congratulations on these brilliant new successes from your glorious army, I can only completely approve that you have rejected the King's proposal for a ceasefire along the Oglio and that you have made the surrender of all fortresses as well as our prisoners a precondition for negotiations.'

Others, however, were far less happy with Radetzky's action. The army was surprised by what it took to be his timidity and Welden wrote to him in terms of reproach:[103]

In view of the rumours of a ceasefire which are going the rounds here, I feel myself duty-bound to point out to Your Excellency the altogether hostile impression that this assuredly false news is producing. The troops are driven to despair at having shed their blood for such an end. The Italians rejoice for to them it is a sign of our weakness; they are also well aware that neither Charles Albert nor any other revolutionary authority will stick to treaties since these have never meant anything to them. They know too that Venice cannot be included since Charles Albert gives no orders there. There, however, as in Milan, are the headquarters of the revolution which snatched Italy away from us and which would do so a second time even if we reconquer it; it would be perilous to give them time to unite to do the same again.

He continued:

Your Excellency could not possibly take these thoughts amiss; they stem from the deepest loyalty and enthusiasm for the best and from the most intimate knowledge of the state of Italy and its inhabitants – who are the most villainous rogues who have ever walked the earth and who will only respect authority when they are completely repressed.

However, since Welden was protesting about the terms which Radetzky himself had proposed, he also wrote to Latour:[104]

Charles Albert is to withdraw his troops across the Adda, to give up Peschiera, to remove his troops from Venice, to give back Modena and Parma – at headquarters people seem, intent on hearing propositions, above all, the advice of Prince Felix Schwarzenberg. The army has revolted at the thought of having spilled its blood for such an end – all the more so since at this time according to practically everybody the army also has a claim which by all accounts merits consideration.

Welden's complaints were important in that his disgust at Radetzky meant that he would soon take action unilaterally. Radetzky, meanwhile, crossed the Oglio on 30 July when the Sardinians rejected his proposals.[105] Latour was now very anxious as to what he would do next. He sent him his good wishes, but aware that he was under pressure from those who thought like Welden, he was careful to warn him in the following manner:[106]

In the same hope of further successes by the army commanded by Your Excellency, the question was further discussed in the Council of Ministers whether the pursuit of the Piedmontese army should take place even across the Ticino, something which, however, when viewed from a general political standpoint was seen as distinctly inadvisable lest France after the defeat of our enemy might be invited by him to intervene militarily in the affairs of Lombardy-Venetia. . . . I must, therefore, urgently request you to avoid crossing the border with Sardinia.

On 31 July Radetzky reported that Cremona had been taken;[107] on 3 August he took Lodi, again without resistance, and began his preparations to take Milan.[108] Exactly what was happening was not clear in Vienna, and Latour could only wait upon events. Wessenberg was in Frankfurt and the War Minister who felt uneasy in the Reichstag had nonetheless to try to explain to the deputies there just what was happening in Italy. He did his best. Radetzky, he told them, had been ordered to 'attempt to take Milan by agreement'; he would 'regret if force had to be employed' to take the city.[109] But he was talking in something of a vacuum. However, since the Field Marshal had already come under criticism for having reinstated the Duke of Modena, Latour wrote to point out:[110] ' . . . I must urgently request you herewith to resist all political tendencies and simply to follow only the necessary strategical steps.'

His chief worry regarding the Reichstag, however, was not so much the behaviour of Radetzky, but Welden, who had invaded the Papal States on his own initiative and was advancing on Bologna, something which even 'otherwise very moderate deputies' had viewed 'with astonishment' since it had led only to 'new complications and recriminations'. The Ministry, therefore, was obliged to instruct Radetzky 'to pull this general out of the Legations immediately and to order him simply to restrict himself to the right bank of the Po'.[111] Welden's chief transgression was the proclamation which he had issued of the severe terms exacted by him from the town of Sermide. Latour had been questioned in the Reichstag about this and so wrote to the General in rebuke:[112]

In today's session of the Reichstag I was asked to give an explanation of the proclamation issued by Your Excellency in which you give as a terrifying example your severe reconciliation with the town of Sermide. I cannot hide it from Your Excellency that this behaviour – announced by yourself – has made a bad impression on the Imperial Assembly. I limited myself to saying that I awaited a detailed report on these events from Your Excellency, one which, I hope, can be laid before the Chamber as a justification. The news of the occupation of Pavia and a glorious victory on the road to Milan has fortunately, diverted the attention of the Chamber from your proclamation and prevented further questions being asked which would have placed me in similar difficulties, difficulties which I feared I would not survive. The private reports in the newspapers tell of your advance on Bologna – the entire Ministry is very dissatisfied on this account and I have already explained to the Field Marshal the necessity to recall you immediately from the Legations. However, to save time, I will request you to get away from Bologna immediately and to restrict your operations to advancing at the same speed as the Field Marshal along the right bank of the Po. The Reichstag, England and France are pressing for the quickest possible opening of peace negotiations; nothing could have a more disruptive effect than the occupation of Bologna from no military necessity and moreover it would lead to the immediate occupation of Ancona by the French. Your Excellency will send by courier an immediate explanation of your proclamation and the motives which have caused you to advance against Bologna and will point to the beginnings made by your army corps to quit the Legations.

Welden had already written to Latour, in fact, saying that he had taken his action in order to exploit the shock produced by the recent Austrian victories; to cover the operations which Prince Liechtenstein was then conducting against Modena; and to destroy the last refuge of the revolutionaries who were operating against Venetia.[113] Latour, however, was in no mood to accept these explanations and on 11 August wrote again to Welden instructing him to quit the Legations at once.[114] The episode demonstrated that if Radetzky had to be treated gingerly, the state nonetheless regarded its generals as its obedient servants.

Attention, meanwhile, had been diverted to Milan. There had been clashes between Austrian and Sardinian troops outside the Lombard capital on 4 August, and on the following day at 2 a.m. a couple of Sardinian generals, both of them parliamentarians, had arrived at Radetzky's camp with proposals from Charles Albert,[115] to the effect that the city should be evacuated of Sardinian troops, that a day's march should be left between the opposing armies, that the Sardinians should get provisions at the expense of the Lombards, that they should leave the country within two days, that provision should be made for the sick and wounded and that those who had 'compromised' themselves should get twenty-four hours to flee Milan. Another curious proposal was that the 'past' should be 'forgotten'. Radetzky once more refused the Sardinian terms. He gave those 'compromised' only twelve hours to quit the city and refused to commit himself about forgetting the past – 'The Field Marshal thought himself unauthorised to enter into this political question; therefore expressed only his own views on this article' – but offered the counter-formula: 'Insofar as he is concerned, he promises to do all that is equitable regarding the past.' The Sardinians, in turn, rejected Radetzky's offer, which the deputy-chief of their general staff described as 'unsatisfactory', at 2 p.m. Milan, they said, would 'hold out to the end'. The real trouble was, of course, that the Milanese, suspecting that Charles Albert was about to betray them, were refusing to let him go. Radetzky meanwhile reported that Milan had succumbed to 'party in-fighting, anarchy and confusion' and began his preparations to besiege the city.

A new deputation now visited the Marshal, led by the Mayor and the Archbishop of Milan,[116] pleading for 'mild conditions' for the capital. Radetzky relented, leaving thirty-six hours for the 'compromised' to flee. The deputation accepted his terms and the occupation of Milan was set for noon on 6 August. Radetzky told Latour:[117] 'On account of the more detailed knowledge I now have of the state of the city and on account of the requests of the consuls of all nations I have deliberately agreed to modify the above conditions and to give Europe an example of our moderation. On the other hand, I have lost no time, since the preparations for encircling and enveloping the city will take a couple of days anyway.'

At noon on the prescribed day, therefore, Radetzky re-entered Milan. The Sardinians had withdrawn the previous night and had until the evening of 7 August to be out of Austrian territory. 'The city of Milan is ours', wrote the Field Marshal in triumph to Vienna,[118] 'Two weeks ago the army launched its offensive from Verona. Since then it has· won splendid battles at Sommacampagna, Custozza, Volta, Cremona, Pizzighettone, and again two days ago before Milan, until *now on the fourteenth day,* it is master of the Lombard capital. In this way, the army and its leader believe that they have loyally fulfilled their duty to their beloved Emperor and Fatherland – for no enemy remains on Lombard soil.'

At 12.55 p.m. on 9 August, a telegram informed Latour that the Field Marshal had entered Milan 'amidst general rejoicing' three days before,[119] the town itself, it added, was 'completely peaceful'. The War Minister replied that he could 'only express [his] admiration which all the world shared with [him]' and that the news had been received with 'unalloyed joy' by the Reichstag.[120]

Misunderstandings

The very capture of Milan, however, brought about yet another misunderstanding between the army and the civilians. The details of Radetzky's ceasefire did not reach Vienna until 12 August and Wessenberg, who meanwhile was still in Frankfurt, appears to have been so far behind events that before he realised what had happened he had already agreed to British and French mediation along the lines sketched out by Hummelauer on

24 May.[121] Latour also felt uneasy: not only was Welden's behaviour having an unsettling effect but the War Minister was not completely aware of the Field Marshal's intentions. Radetzky had told a British diplomat on 3 August,[122] 'that as a soldier I can and may only trouble about political considerations insofar as they affect military ones'. Latour in his letter of congratulations, therefore, had reminded the victor that[123] 'the mood of all foreign cabinets as well as the wishes of the assembled provincial deputies absolutely rule[d] out any crossing of the Ticino at the present moment'. He wanted Radetzky to gather his army on the frontier with Sardinia merely as a diplomatic exercise. Radetzky, however, had been fully aware of the considerations involved, for on 10 August he had written to Wessenberg:[124] 'I sincerely believe . . . that I have done my share in avoiding any conflict with any foreign power, in particular in having been able to prevent any interference on the part of France.' But he pointed out at the same time that he had been fighting to preserve northern Italy for the House of Habsburg:[125]

. . . the idea of an independent Lombardy must be given up as completely inadmissible. This country – by itself – would be the prey for intriguers of its own and of other lands – it would be too weak to defend itself and would, therefore, always be under foreign influence, from Piedmont and France in particular. In any case, it is too rich and too beautiful not to be desired by someone, and would, therefore, in turn become the prey in all great political developments for which-ever power was momentarily the stronger.

He continued:

Finally, in granting such a concession to the Lombards we would be sowing the seeds of great misunderstanding and mistrust between the mother state of Austria and the Venetian provinces which as independent states of old would demand equal rights; we would be failing to consider that in making Lombardy independent, she would immediately declare herself a medieval republic and would undermine Piedmont to the west and Venetia to the east as well as much of the Papal States and Tuscany as possible in the south in order to bring them under her weak rule and to contaminate them with the same pernicious principles.

Wessenberg, who at the time of Radetzky's triumph, was in Frankfurt, had a slightly different perspective on events. He wrote to congratulate Radetzky on his victory at Custozza[126] – 'the honour of the Austrian Monarchy has been saved by our valiant army' – but was worried lest the Milanese might even yet prevail upon the French to intervene. His outlook, therefore, was extremely cautious:[127] 'Should our army', he wrote, 'already have occupied such positions as would make peace negotiations easier, it would be wise to limit itself to that and to try to negotiate a ceasefire which would secure the possession of these positions and which could serve as a basis for negotiations.' When he heard that Radetzky had actually rejected Charles Albert's terms for a ceasefire on the Oglio, Wessenberg wrote to Montecuccoli to say that he could not conceal the fact that he had been 'to a certain extent shocked' by the Field Marshal's action in which he saw 'the possibility of greater embarrassment'.[128] He continued:[129] 'The aim of continuing the war was to win a secure position in which an honourable peace was possible; this we would have achieved with the Oglio and probably peace offers would have been made to us from the side of the enemy from which we would have benefited more than from the first peace offers proposed by us.' He wanted Montecuccoli to put pressure on Radetzky to conclude the quickest possible peace stressing how 'regrettable' it would be if 'advantages gained by our troops and which have covered them in glory should only serve to make our position more difficult'.[130] More ominous, however, was his following passage:[131] 'That we are no longer strictly bound to the peace proposals made in the first half of June is evident; however, reason of state demands that conditions should not be set too high, if we can in this way win our objective. . . . We cannot deceive ourselves that the continuation of the war in Italy weakens our strength and also aggravates the political position of the government at home.'

Wessenberg was almost beginning to echo Pillersdorff when the latter had told Hummelauer that even the success of a big battle might not be enough to save the Austrian position. In fact, on 8 August he wrote to Montecuccoli telling him that he did not believe that Austria could retain Lombardy. Both the British and French governments were eager to intervene and he did not believe that he was in a position to stop them. But Montecuccoli, who had never even met Wessenberg, and who was flattered at being brought into the peace negotiations, however indirectly,[132] wrote in reply that the Minister was behind events and that his judgements were based on out-of-date information.[133] A ceasefire had been established, the enemy had vacated Austrian territory and the only question that remained was that of regoverning the reoccupied territories.

The wires remained crossed, however, for a few anxious days. On 11 August Wessenberg informed Lebzeltern from Frankfurt that the British and French had agreed to mediate on the basis of the Hummelauer proposals.[134] He had, of course, let them know that the situation had somewhat changed since May, but had obviously not felt strong enough to reject their demands altogether. Lebzeltern now passed on the letter of his chief to Latour, along with complaints about Welden and some other officers and a general hope that the military would 'not go too far' in its behaviour.[135] Latour, predictably, was absolutely flabbergasted and replied to Lebzeltern in a tone of utter intransigence:[136]

I gather with pained astonishment from the enclosed copy of the despatch from the Herr Minister to Your Excellency that the former is of the view that the proposals of 24 May of this year, proposals in which the line of the Etsch is fixed as the frontier of our future territory, can be taken on the whole as the basis for forthcoming negotiations.

I can only explain the assumption on which the views of the Herr Minister are based by the presumption that he was not aware of the latest successes of our army when he drew up this note which is dated Frankfurt, 7 August.

Given the present situation, however, given the Monarchy's honour in the eyes of Europe and the Minister's responsibility towards the other provinces, I cannot consider it permissible to negotiate on the basis of the 24 May and thereby give up the whole of Lombardy and a part of the Venetian provinces after having just reconquered them both from the enemy at the cost of such terrible sacrifices in blood and treasure and having reduced the call to revolt to silence.

The situation, Latour explained, had 'completely altered' since May: 'Only the greatest moderation on the part of the Ministry with respect to the views of England and France can *diplomatically* justify our not having followed up our victory by forcing the King back into his capital and *there* having dictated a peace on our own terms: *militarily* this omission will never be justifiable.'

Negotiations on the basis of the Hummelauer proposals were therefore rejected by Latour as 'totally impossible'.

Further reports from Radetzky and Latour were sent on to Wessenberg by Lebzeltern in the following days.[137] On 16 August, he replied that nobody was more willing than he to acknowledge the army's deeds and that England had been informed that the position had changed.[138] Latour passed on this information to the Field Marshal, noting with 'great pleasure' that the Minister's views on a future peace appeared to coincide with their own.[139] On 25 August, Wessenberg wrote personally to Radetzky endorsing his views of 10 August and congratulating him.[140] 'Your Excellency has done the impossible', he wrote and added that if peace came, it would be due to Radetzky's 'perserverance and leadership of genius in operations of war'. On 25 August, too, Schwarzenberg was named as Austrian peace negotiator with instructions merely to secure a 'just indemnity'.[141] The time had at last arrived when everyone on the Austrian side appeared to be in agreement, and on 7 September Radetzky passed on to Latour a letter which he had just received from Wessenberg with the comment:[142] 'It is the first time that I have received satisfaction from the desired source.' The letter had informed the Field Marshal that within a few days a declaration would be made to the effect that Lombardy would remain Austrian. Thanks to the man whom Ficquelmont had once described to Hartig as 'no more than a name',[143] the Austrian possession of Lombardy-Venetia was no longer negotiable.

Chapter 9

Dividing the spoils

Radetzky and Wessenberg

Austrian possession of Lombardy-Venetia was now secure; it remained to be seen, however, in what way the Austrians would administer these territories. Wessenberg intended to introduce a pacification programme as soon as possible and the Field Marshal, at first, appeared to be in complete agreement with him. Indeed, it was Radetzky, who on 9 July pleaded with Latour to do all that he could to speed up the arrival of Count Montecuccoli in Italy:[1]* 'It is my duty to acquaint Your Excellency', he wrote, 'with the pressing need to send here the Government Commissioner with all the necessary authority to take command once more of the various branches of administration and to get the machinery of government moving again. . . . It is absolutely necessary to re-establish unity in the administration of the provinces.' Moreover, the Field Marshal foresaw no trouble with Hartig's successor:[2] 'We shall easily be able to reach a verbal understanding with each other on all important matters affecting the interests of the country and the state; written communications take up too much time and often lead to misunderstandings. Indeed that was the case with Count Hartig. . . .' An understanding was vital:[3] 'I for my part', wrote Radetzky, 'cannot deal with the reorganisation of the captured provinces myself; I lack the means, but most of all, the time. . . .'

The Field Marshal, on the other hand, appeared to assume that the new Commissioner would have so much paperwork to be getting on with, that he would not have time to concern himself with political decisions. Radetzky himself expected to have a determining voice in these, and as soon as he had succeeded in taking Milan, he made known his views to practically everyone. These did not, however, coincide with the views of the imperial government, and after his entry into Milan instead of issuing to the Lombards a proclamation granting them the same constitutional freedoms already enjoyed elsewhere in the Monarchy by other peoples – a course of action which had been recommended by Latour[4] – the Field Marshal submitted to the War Ministry a long report on the political situation in which he undertook 'to express himself most candidly'.[5] This was yet another objective which he achieved, for if the government had not yet learned the lesson of the Hartig Mission, Radetzky was at pains to spell it out for them:[6]

If I, in a country like this, which, as yet has scarcely been conquered and in which cities like Como, Bergamo and Brescia, cities which previously were firing on our troops, are

---

* Notes to this chapter are on pp. 271–2.

not yet even occupied . . . if, I repeat, in a country whose capital only two days ago had to be taken by force of arms and where the whole fury of unsuccessful resistance still exists to the fullest degree amongst a great part of the inhabitants of such a vengeful nation, and if, finally, the enemy with which it is allied is positioned only two hours away on the border – if *under such circumstances – in such a critical position for me* – I am supposed even now to start talking *about measures of reconciliation* – when the whole force of the law for some time to come will hardly be in a position to maintain these rebellious cities in enforced obedience – then Field Marshal Radetzky must do what any leader of the army would do – lay down his sword.

If I am to be responsible to the state then I intend to be master of the situation ('so will ich Herr sein zu handeln'); if not, then those who believe out of misguided philanthropic views which do not apply to this country, that they can govern it in some other way, will lose this land for the Emperor even more quickly than I have conquered it.

Radetzky ended this section of his report by saying that 'there [could] be no talk of reconciliation for a long time to come'.

The Field Marshal, however, clearly did not expect to have to resign for having made known his position in principle he then outlined the system of administration which he was setting up in order to run the provinces in the immediate future. It was an administration in which the principal voice was given to the army:[7]

I have – correctly, I believe, in view of our position – regarded this whole rebellious country as conquered territory and subjected it, therefore, to a military government; law and order, after all, is the first priority and among such excited people it can be secured only with the drawn sword. Should these people calm themselves a little, should the situation in the country improve a little, I shall let Your Excellency know of this with pleasure so that you can so inform the Council of Ministers. . . .

However, for the moment, with a wholly medieval *Munizipalgeist* still foaming and fuming in the towns and even in the countryside – albeit amongst only a small proportion of the population there – no army can maintain the security of the country for long, unless the military and *that alone* is allowed to put down every attempt – every source of rebellion – with all its pulverising force. My position and duty as well as my full knowledge of this country compel me, therefore, to warn against any contrary proceeding as fatal.

Where possible, I myself have already made over the civil administration in Venetia to the authorised Minister, Count Montecuccoli; regarding Lombardy, however, I must request Your Excellency to express to the Council of Ministers my deepest conviction that if, instead of by military force, instead of by a state of siege in the cities, instead of by the prohibition which I have decreed on the freedom of the press and liberal assemblies, it is already intended to introduce here and now exactly the same freedom which His Majesty granted to his other provinces or merely to re-establish normal civil government, the army which is weak enough in any case, will, within a week, once more, be on the Etsch or in the Tyrol as a result of the uprisings that can be safely expected once more inside the cities.

Radetzky's, however, was essentially a practical point of view; he was no reactionary by the standards of his age and fully expected that there would be political changes in northern Italy once the country was becalmed. In his letter to Wessenberg of 10 August, for example, he went so far as to state:[8]

In my opinion we must and ought not to give any more concession to our Italian provinces than those the Emperor has already given; both provinces ought to be treated equally and represent one united state in roughly the same relationship to Austria as Hungary was before her recent uprising. Foreign affairs, finance [and] military affairs would be administered from Vienna; internal administration, however, with some sort of gloss of independence, by an Italian Ministry here in Milan. This, in my opinion, is the only possible way of reconciling Italian independence to a link between these provinces and the Monarchy [and] finally and most important of all, of retaining for Austria as the greatest Italian state the main voice in all affairs of this country.

The Field Marshal, on the other hand, was chiefly concerned about the short-term situation and on 12 August rejected Latour's advice to promise the Italians a constitution on the first auspicious occasion.[99] In a letter which curiously echoed Metternich's pre-March warnings to Ficquelmont on the danger of concessions, he argued that to make such a promise would be tantamount to committing high treason. He simply would not listen to such advice:[10]

Do people want to ruin everything in this country that the sword has so far secured? Only then could they promise such concessions *beforehand*. To do so would only reinforce the imagination of the Italians – even the better ones – and the order which has scarcely been restored in the country, would thereafter be destroyed. The evildoers count on this for the start of new treachery – renewed discontent and ever more violent demands – until even 150,000 men would not suffice to pacify the land again by force. Can people not wait to lead this nation, which has been through all sorts of revolution, step by step? – must we let ourselves be overthrown again and sink back to where we were? I will have no part of it – it would be high treason to the Emperor and the state of a kind of which history, after the experience which we have survived, could afford no second example.

Radetzky was no doubt right to expect trouble from Vienna, but his instincts were correct with regard to Montecuccoli. The latter, who by 10 August was still in Vienna, wrote to Wessenberg that 'there [could] be no doubt' that it was promises of liberal and national institutions that had led 'directly' to the revolutions – although he also argued that in the climate which now prevailed in Europe there could be no going back to the old system.[11] Montecuccoli's attitude was really one of 'wait and see', but since he felt that to grant immediate concessions to the Italians would only lead to revolution in 'a very short time', his views fell into line with those of Radetzky. His duty, as he saw it, was to assume exclusive control of the internal administration in northern Italy but to do so only once the stipulations of the ceasefire had been met and once the external security of the country had been fully restored by the army. 'For the time being', he wrote,[12] 'the only guarantee of the security of our possession and of the possibility of executing whatever reforms and innovations our government shall see fit to grant this country, resides in the army (which will have to remain concentrated in these lands for some time to come)'.

Having arrived in Verona, Montecuccoli took up the question of the future of the Italian provinces in a letter to Wessenberg dated 17 August.[13] He may well have conferred with Radetzky by this time, but their views at this stage were in any case so similar that it is pointless to speculate as to the influence behind the letter. According to the Government Commissioner, the Foreign Ministry had last discussed the subject of the internal government of Lombardy-Venetia on 10 April, at which time it had been decided that after any reconquest the immediate thing to do would be to administer the provinces in the traditional way until 'after successful pacification' an assembly might be convened composed of representatives of the country who would then debate all administrative and financial questions and whose decisions would be adhered to by the imperial government. As Montecuccoli pointed out, however, such an arrangement was only to be considered if and when law and order had been restored and if the Italians had agreed to contribute an appropriate sum towards defence, foreign affairs and imperial administration. More important still was the fact that the execution of the plan was clearly linked to a peace settlement with Piedmont. The Emperor would only agree to changes once the war had been won and Austrian rule consolidated.

Montecuccoli, on the other hand, had little doubt that a quick peace settlement was in the offing – 'the weak', he wrote, 'cannot speak to the strong about conditions' – and believed that once this had been settled Austria should give the country 'a constitutional form of administration corresponding to the wishes of the nation'. Lombardy-Venetia had always wanted the fullest possible autonomy within the Austrian Empire and after recent events the only realistic solution was home rule. Meanwhile, until a peace and law and order were secured, change should be kept to a minimum and the army should control the government. Only once the necessary guarantees had been met should the projected assembly be announced as 'a magnanimous present from the victor'.

Wessenberg, meanwhile, was collecting his own thoughts on the subject and on 25 August presented his views to his fellow Ministers:[14] the two provinces were to be treated as one unit – like Hungary before the revolution – with Vienna retaining control of foreign affairs, defence and the imperial budget while internal affairs would be run, after an agreement between Vienna and the Congregations, by Italian 'higher administrative departments, if you like, a Ministry' which would be granted a certain degree of autonomy. Wessenberg envisaged summoning the Congregations to Verona to debate the matter there with a government plenipotentiary in the form of the Trade Minister, Bruck, but before anything was done he wanted Montecuccoli to talk the whole thing over with Radetzky.[15] Strangely enough, although he acknowledged the need for any constitution to be 'precisely formulated' he nonetheless contemplated making political promises to the Italians 'without delay' and with Radetzky's consent. Thus, although Wessenberg and Radetzky appeared to be at one on the way in which Italy should be governed, the stage was set for a clash between them over the timing of political change: Wessenberg wanted to speed things up; the Field Marshal was all for caution.

The clash itself was delayed for a few weeks. Wessenberg was fully absorbed in the negotiations which were continuing with France, Britain and Piedmont; Radetzky was tightening his grip on Lombardy and had decided to send Schwarzenberg to Vienna once again rather than involve himself in another war by correspondence.[16] Radetzky, in fact, was no longer prepared to argue. On 22 September 1848 he wrote to Latour informing him that however much he would like to surrender the 'pressing burden' of directing the Lombard civil administration, it was 'not only not possible for [him] under the present circumstances to fulfil this wish' but that he had reached the conclusion that 'on account of the present circumstances [he was] compelled to place [himself] at the head of the internal administration of Venetia as well.'[17] The Field Marshal argued that the Austrians were still, in fact, on a war footing in northern Italy, and that those parts of the provinces which were still very restless would so remain as long as Venice itself was in the hands of the insurgents. He was worried by the fact that most civil servants and priests were on the side of the rebels and that it was proving difficult to disarm the erstwhile National Guard. In short, the necessary precondition for the introduction of a constitution – the guarantee of law and order – was just not there and 'gentle treatment and conciliation' would, therefore, be viewed by the Italians as a 'sign of weakness'. It was at this point that Radetzky gave the old argument the new twist. The preconditions for the introduction of constitutional change would only become possible, he wrote, 'when I place myself at the head of the administration of the whole of Lombardy-Venetia, since I alone have the means at my disposal to give the necessary force to administrative orders and to carry these through despite all opposition.'

To establish the military and administrative unity which he so ardently desired the Field Marshal informed Latour that Montecuccoli had already been summoned by him to Milan to discuss the organisation of the new administration. Montecuccoli, apparently, had offered no resistance to the scheme and indeed, given his views, there was no real reason why he should. Radetzky was obviously well pleased with this development and reported:[18] 'The latter has declared himself to be ready from now on and for as long as the present situation lasts, to continue, at my side and under my authority, the organising work which he has already begun with such good results.' Montecuccoli was now to help look after the army's supply problems as well as to give his attention to questions of a political and financial nature. He was prepared to take his orders from the commander and so could be trusted.

If Radetzky believed, however, that he had upstaged Wessenberg by presenting the Italians not with a declaration of principles but a display of his own political strength, he was merely deluding himself, for despite an assurance from Latour on 29 September that the Council of Ministers agreed with his views,[19] Wessenberg had already, on 20 September, secured the Emperor's signature to a manifesto which promised full constitutional rights to the Italians and bound the Emperor to respect their nationality.[20] Moreover, it also fully pardoned those who had taken part in the rebellion. Radetzky's *démarche* encouraged Wessenberg further; on 29 September he wrote to Montecuccoli asking him to send two experienced men to Vienna in order to get preparations for elections under way.[21] His train of thought was following an entirely different timetable.

On 3 October, Montecuccoli confronted Radetzky with a proclamation of the Emperor's manifesto, telling him that he had been instructed to publish it right away.[22] The Field Marshal, not surprisingly, implored him not to do so and in fact suspended the orders to the publishers until a courier could be sent to Vienna. As far as Radetzky was concerned the only possible result that might be expected from the proclamation was an incoming flood of former agitators and rebels. Montecuccoli was therefore once more apprised of the army view and was as usual half-convinced by it. But this did not matter, for on the following day the manifesto was published in the imperial capital in the *Wiener Zeitung*. Radetzky had been outmanœuvred and had to publish the proclamation in Milan after all 'in order not to compromise the reputation of the imperial name which appeared on the manifesto'.[23] As things turned out, however, he need not have worried. Legation Secretary Metzburg whom

Wessenberg had recently sent down to Milan to keep an eye on both the Field Marshal and Montecuccoli reported to his chief on 10 October that the manifesto had been a very damp squib:[24] 'I truly regret to have to report to Your Excellency that yesterday's publication of the Imperial Manifesto has made no impression on the Milanese and that it was read in the entire city with great indifference.' The Italians, in fact, were still placing their hopes in the French, the British and the Sardinians. Thus, Metzburg concluded that Radetzky had been right all along:[25] 'Until that point in time when peace is concluded the great aim of preserving law and order in the land can only be attained by the maintenance of a state of siege and military law.'

However, before the Milanese reaction was altogether apparent Radetzky had written to Wessenberg with yet another hint at resignation:[26]

I cannot conceal it from Your Excellency that at a time when we are still in the throes of revolution [to grant] this form of government will be seen as a cowardly act, a concession wrung from us by foreigners, a concession demanded by the Reichstag and it will, therefore, be ridiculed as an act of weakness; on the army, however, it will make the same impression as a battle lost since the army will thereby lose every support which up till now it has been guaranteed by that military government which alone for the past two months has brought peace to the country and protection to its inhabitants.

He added, 'As for my personal position, I shall know within a few weeks what I shall have to do.'

Yet once again, the Field Marshal was not called upon to make good his threat. On 6 October Vienna had succumbed to revolution and was not rescued for the dynasty until the end of the month. The men who rescued it were hardly liberals and the climate they created was not one in which liberal home rule might be granted to Lombardy. The rise to power, which now began, of Prince Felix zu Schwarzenberg gave Radetzky the upper hand. After November 1848, he had no reason to fear the introduction of a liberal constitution in Italy.

Radetzky and politics

The October revolution in Vienna, however, altered the situation in another way: it hardened the Field Marshal's own attitude towards the prospect of reform. Radetzky, who had always accepted the need for 'progress', came to believe that the Empire was not yet ready for it. He sought the answers to the Empire's problems no longer in constitutionalism but in a radical brand of paternalism.

Radetzky's belief in the inevitability of constitutional government had not died with the outbreak of revolution. He had had no qualms, for example, in accepting the imperial constitution of April 1848 and had written to the first constitutional War Minister, Peter Zanini:[27] 'Yesterday I received the new Constitution from the Minister of the Interior. It rests on so liberal a base that I take it to be the most liberal in Europe. That the press will find something in it to blame, we must of course expect, but I hope, however, that the best part of the nation will find in it a guarantee of all the wishes and ideas with which they believe their happiness is bound.'

The elected Reichstag, however, was soon to provoke his outright contempt – after all that the army had done to save Italy for the Empire, the deputies refused to congratulate it on its success. The trouble was, as a liberal deputy was later to write,[28] that 'the Left in the Reichstag was of the opinion that this struggle was being waged only in the interest of the dynasty but not in the interest of the people and it was clear that possession of the Italian provinces could be maintained only by a colossal army, permanent martial law and permanent court martials'. It, therefore, shared Balbo's opinion that Austria's future lay in the Danubian lands and that the Italians should be left to themselves. Nor was it prepared to accept the assurance of the Archduke John that the war was directed 'not against Italian liberty', but 'was merely being conducted to maintain the honour of Austrian arms against the Italian powers'.[29] It was not impressed by the demands of military honour and so when, after Custozza, a deputy called Seelinger proposed a vote of thanks to the army, his motion was not carried.

Seelinger's motion was widely suspected by the Left of being a put-up job. In their eyes it was not so much a 'surprisingly outspoken eulogy on the army and its feats of arms' as 'a vote of confidence and approval for [the government's] policies in Italy' – policies which they were determined not to accept.[30] The Left, moreover, was already in dispute with the government over the issue of conscription – the troops fighting in Italy had never been sent there with the approval of the Reichstag. 'It is remarkable', wrote the above-quoted deputy,[31] 'that the Ministry never dared raise this question in the Chamber. They did not wish to run the risk of a defeat but [wanted rather] to keep the Chamber in ignorance of how many troops were being raised and for what purpose they were being employed.' When Seelinger proposed his motion, therefore, the liberal Left insisted on a full-scale debate on the government's Italian policy rather than pass a quick vote of thanks to the army. The government, after a short debate, managed to defeat this proposal, but only at the cost of the vote of thanks and on this account a wedge was driven between the military and the Constitution. The Right did all it could to exploit what had happened:[32]

Although nothing was said on this occasion against the army or its members the refusal to adopt the motion was immediately exploited by the reactionaries with their usual dishonesty and the democratic left was pilloried in nearly all the reactionary newspapers and Füster and Violand [two deputies] even had put into their mouths words which they had never spoken but which thundered against Radetzky and the soldiers. These newspapers were eagerly distributed amongst the soldiers and all efforts were employed to embitter them against the Reichstag and the constitution and in this way to win over the bayonet against liberty. . . . Nobody . . . had questioned the bravery of the Austrian army; objections had been raised only against Austrian policy in Italy and the use of the military for purely dynastic interests. . . . But no effort was spared on the part of the reactionaries to dream up the most incredible stuff for the army, stuff which was supposed to have originated in the Reichstag. . . .

The Left had obviously been very naïve to expect that anything else would happen, for the military reaction was just as the Right desired it should be. Nevertheless, when on 24 September Latour issued a circular reminding army commanders that obedience to orders also meant 'upholding and respecting the constitutional institutions and arrangements in the state', which arrangements 'should in no wise give cause for complaint', Radetzky could still reply in the following terms:[33]

The hostile feeling against the army in Italy which has often been voiced in the Reichstag and which has found an echo in many other parts of the Monarchy – although the best and greatest part of the population thanks God that through the victories won by its misguided support they are spared the need to enter public mourning and that the Fatherland has not been dragged through the mire – makes me suspect that the content of Your Excellency's despatch No. 5259 M.K. of the 24th of this month was primarily directed against the troops under my command.

The army has no reason to retain any predilection for the system which has fallen. This system was, if it can be called a despotism, a civil – not a military despotism. The army was neglected, slighted; it, therefore, expressed no spirit of hostility at all towards the free institutions which His Majesty conferred upon his peoples. The army of Italy was far too occupied with its great and heavy duty to pay any special attention to political goings-on; but when political leadership passed from the hands of experienced statesmen and true patriots to those of adolescents and treacherous rabble-rousers, when the Emperor had to leave his capital and seek refuge amongst a loyal race of people, then the army's resentment was aroused. It thus failed to understand liberty. The behaviour of a part of the Reichstag in the question of the Address could hardly have contributed to winning over the army's sympathy; however, the army – that part under my command at least – remained dumb. None of the addresses directed at the troops from many sides over the Hungarian-Croatian question was answered; this was known to be against my principles; I wanted no manifestos – which are always untimely – if they were not the direct products of negotiations.

If the complete freedom of the press gives everyone the right to say what he thinks, it is only natural if here and there the voice of some military man is raised against the unlimited abuse of freedom, if indignation should consume the soldier, who, although he has shed his blood in battle for the honour and rights of his Emperor and Fatherland, is called an enemy of liberty by the would-be fathers of the Fatherland. Rome did not reward her army in this way; nor did Greece; nor did the bloody French Republic; it was reserved for modern Liberty to present such an unworthy spectacle to the world.

Let us cast a painful glance over the desperate position of our army in Hungary; there, Austrian soldiers are fighting one another in the name of the same monarch, which one lot call Emperor and the other King. I am bold enough to assert that only the Austrian army is in a position to give such an example of self-abnegation and sacrifice. But from where is the army supposed to derive its love for institutions that can bring forth into the world such moral and political abortions? May this unnatural situation reach a speedy end for otherwise the splendid spirit of the army will be lost.

I feel the burden that weighs upon your shoulders and regret that you are often, no doubt, in the position of having to speak against your convictions; for this reason too, I feel the need for once to open my oppressed heart to you. I stand at the head of a great part of the army; I stand surety for this army, for its loyalty, for its devotion to the constitutional freedoms granted by His Majesty. But this army loves its Emperor; his person is holy to it. May God forbid what could happen! Should the spirit of innovation so forget itself as to encroach upon the rights of the Emperor, or indeed, to threaten the security of his person, then things could happen which by all means would jeopardise the new freedom.

Latour drafted a reply to Radetzky at the beginning of October denying that his complaints had been at all directed towards the army in Italy.[34] On the contrary, they had arisen due to the behaviour of Windischgraetz's army in Prague. The letter, however, was never despatched for on 6 October the Vienna mob invaded the War Ministry, and murdered Latour. The Vienna garrison not only proved unable to prevent this happening; it was also partly responsible for the revolution breaking out in the first place in so far as things had got out of control when part of the garrison, a company of grenadiers, objected to fighting in Hungary.

Radetzky's reaction to the tragic news was to issue a very famous proclamation in which he addressed the Vienna garrison as 'Field Marshal and the oldest soldier in the army'.[35] He was obviously dismayed at what had happened and did nothing to hide his sense of shame at the inadequacy of the garrison's performance. 'Have you done your duty?' he asked it; he implied that it had not. Nonetheless despite 'the pain which consumed him and the tears which filled his eyes,' he was discerning enough to blame the disgrace of these events on a 'small handful' of troops only. The rest he exhorted to save the Empire and he did so in language which clearly indicated his belief that only the army was now capable of this task:[36]

Soldiers! Open your eyes to the abyss that opens at your feet; everything is in flux: the mainstays of the social order have been destroyed; property, morality, religion are threatened with destruction. Everything that is holy and dear to man, everything on which the state is based and which it upholds, people are determined to destroy. That, not liberty, is the aim of every rabblerouser who wants to drag you down to your ruin and shame.

Soldiers! In your hands resides the security of the throne and with it the preservation of the Empire. May God's grace allow me to see the day when people will say, 'The army has saved Austria' – then and only then will the 6 and 7 October of this year which has been so full of calamity be atoned for and forgotten; then will the army of Italy which presently protects the boundaries of the Empire against external enemies, stretch out its hand in brotherhood.

The army in Italy now placed all its hopes in Schwarzenberg taking over from Wessenberg. General Hess, Radetzky's Chief of Staff, wrote to him on 21 November telling him how happy the army would be if only this would come about.[37] In fact, of course, it already had; but the final proof of the army's contempt for the Reichstag came when it publicly rejected Strohbach's motion calling for the election of soldier deputies.[38] Metzburg reported to Schwarzenberg that the deputy's motion had merely aroused the 'general indignation' of the troops,[39] since the Reichstag 'for good reasons', did not 'possess the confidence' of the army.[40] On 23 February the army of Italy had published in the official *Milan Gazette* a petition to the Emperor Franz Josef; it was signed by most of the leading officers and made the military's position quite clear. The army rejected with contumely the proposition that it should associate itself with a body which had previously refused to honour it. The job of the army was to protect the Emperor – nothing less, nothing more. The petition argued:[41]

In every constitutional state there are two powers, the legislative and the executive, which can never be united. The army as an integral part of the executive power, can never, therefore, take any share in the legislative.

The soldier can as an individual sit in Parliament as well as any other person, not, however, as a representative of the army as a body, since it is evident that a number of deputies, who might close their propositions by these powerful words: 'A numerous army supports our opinion', would soon put an end to the freedom of discussion.

Faithful to the laws of its country the army acknowledges only in Your Majesty its lord and leader; it cannot take, nor will it ever take part in any discussion which might place it in contradiction with its duties and undermine its honour.

Having then discussed the Seelinger affair in much the same tones as Radetzky had once used to Latour, the authors of the petition closed their appeal with the words:[42]

No, Your Majesty! the army does not seek to take part in Parliamentary debates; you would soon perceive in it a want of harmony, a want of discipline, you would perceive the ruin of the monarchy. The army seeks to encircle Your Majesty's throne, the confines of the Monarchy, with an iron bulwark; it seeks to watch over the laws of the country, to protect the monarchy against domestic enemies as well as to preserve its integrity against foreign enemies; but it seeks to remain within the limits of the position which the legislature of all nations assign to the army.

With profound respect we pray that Your Majesty will not grant the Sovereign Sanction to the said Parliamentary proposition.

When Schwarzenberg finally wound up the Kremsier Reichstag, Radetzky heartily congratulated him.[43] Ever since he had reconquered Milan, his efforts in aid of 'progress' had proceeded along economic rather than political lines. He now offered the Italians not a liberal constitution but a paternalist's version of the class war.

Part III

Radetzky as communist: The social psychology of the revolutionary crisis

Chapter 10

The background

Divide and rule

In 1848, according to Marx and Engels, a spectre was haunting Europe – the spectre of communism. Other people, too, had arrived at this conclusion, although there were different ways of defining communism. For Marx and Engels, of course, it was a complex system of social and historical ideas which could be used by a class-conscious, industrial proletariat in a scientific way to bring about the transformation of bourgeois society. For most people, however, even in 1848, the word had a much more general meaning and the adjective 'communist' might be applied to any movement which threatened to undermine the bastions of political or social privilege. Communists, therefore, could be found anywhere and indeed, if the views of one commentator, writing in 1847, are to be given credence, some of them were to be found in the strangest places, for according to him, the real communist threat to the social order of Europe came not from below but from above, not from the masses but from the Austrian ruling house and its supporters. 'Here', he wrote,[1]* 'is the great social fact to which Europe cannot pay too much attention. . . . This empire is already powerless to combat the communism professed by its bureaucracy; it appears that the system which destroys all liberty has powerful attractions for the class which governs.' The claim seems fantastic but should not be dismissed.

'Divide and rule' meant more to the Habsburgs than setting one nationality against another; it could also mean setting class against class. If – and this was the case in the 1840s – the opposition to Habsburg rule in the non-German provinces of the Empire was led by nobles and aristocrats, the ruling house was perfectly willing to forge an alliance with the more traditional enemy of the nobleman, the peasant. The Habsburgs were a callous breed; they had very few qualms about setting the peasant dog at the noble throat. Thus, in 1834, for example, the Emperor's representative in Transylvania, the Archduke Ferdinand d'Este, had toyed with the possibility of stirring up the local peasantry against their Magyar landlords.[2] The Magyar landlords, in Hungary proper as well as in Transylvania, were only too well aware of such schemes: Metternich's army of hack writers were less than subtle in their allusions and Milkós Wesselényi had referred to these warnings in his famous speech at Szátmar before his arrest and trial.[3]

Such allusions, however, came from the very top as well as from the bottom of the imperial administration. The Hungarian historian, Erzsébet Andics has

---

* Notes to this chapter are on pp. 272–3.

written recently that[4] 'we repeatedly find in the confidential correspondence of this time the reference that it might be necessary to keep the liberal Hungarian nobility in check by the spectre of a peasant uprising stirred up from above'. She provides examples. Metternich, for instance, told the Archduke-Palatine of Hungary 'that only the fear of the monarch taking such an appalling step [was] holding back the Hungarian liberal nobility from revolution'.[5] He told the Tsar:[6] 'When their passive opposition has to make way for acts of force, on that day – it can be taken for granted – the powerful majority of the people whom the Hungarian liberals regard as nothing more than a *misera plebs* will offer their support to the king. Indeed, more than this can be reckoned on since this whole class is absolutely embittered against its landlords.' Finally, Ficquelmont, when Austrian Ambassador in St Petersburg, had told the Tsar in 1837:[7] 'It would need only a word from the court to wipe out this opposition by making the peasants think of an improvement to their lot, something the nobles have no wish to grant them.'

But were the imperial authorities really so complacent about the thought of a peasant uprising? Would they really welcome one even if it would serve their interests? How far were they bluffing? By 1846 the Archduke Ferdinand d'Este had moved from Transylvania to Galicia, where in February 1846 the Austrian bluff was called by a conspiracy of *émigré* Poles that attracted the support of some Galician nobles. The conspiracy failed because it provoked a peasant jacquerie in which hundreds perhaps thousands of the local nobility lost their lives. In the circle of Tarnow especially, the peasants indulged in the most horrible butchery and seemed to be possessed by some kind of bloodlust. Almost immediately afterwards the charge was made that the jacquerie had been an Austrian plot. The Archduke Ferdinand, it was said, had refused reinforcements because he had already organised the Galician peasantry.[8] The most controversial charge, however, was that Breindl, the *Kreishauptmann* of Tarnow, as well as Benedek, the local military commander, had paid out 'blood-money' to the peasants – between 5 and 25 fl. for every noble corpse brought in. Polish nationalist historians have always accepted these claims and according to one recent survey, 'the evidence for this view is massive'.[9]

The evidence used to substantiate these claims, however, has always been circumstantial. The Archduke Ferdinand, for example, is known to have asked village leaders in December 1845 to cooperate in apprehending 'trouble-makers'. He even informed them that 'appropriate payments' could be made if such cooperation was forthcoming.[10] It is also known that in January 1846 *Urlauber* from Galician regiments were allowed to rejoin the ranks and the Archduke reported to Vienna that he had no need of reinforcements.[11] But does this really add up to 'massive' support for the charge that the local military authorities were about to engineer a jacquerie? The truth is that the nationalist historians have somewhat twisted the facts to suit their own claims, so that a few precautionary measures taken at a time when Galicia was full of all sorts of rumours have been made to assume an altogether sinister character. Ferdinand, it is claimed, was promising 'blood-money' in 1845, the *Urlauber* were 'called up' in order to 'receive Instructions' which they could secretly pass on to their relatives in the countryside. The scene was set for premeditated mass-murder.[12]

The documents tell another story.[13] Far from encouraging a peasant jacquerie in order to quell an expected uprising, neither the Archduke

Ferdinand nor Benedek believed in either possibility until after both had broken out. Breindl believed otherwise, but could not convince the authorities in Lemberg of the seriousness of his position in Tarnow. The local Brigadier supported him, but Ferdinand dismissed the Brigadier's reports as gross exaggerations and the President of the Hofkriegsrath went as far as to cast doubts on the mental stability of their author. As a result, Breindl did not receive the reinforcements he had asked for and in all probability panicked when the jacquerie took place. Even he, however, did not 'organise' a plot. He merely found himself helpless in the middle of a local civil war and it is likely that the peasants extorted some money from him.[14] He lacked the military support necessary to discipline the peasants until Benedek arrived on the evening of 23 February – five days after the jacquerie had got under way. Benedek himself was appalled by what he discovered in Tarnow and did everything possible to put an end to the peasant bloodlust. He paid out no 'blood-money'; he asked instead for huge reinforcements and in no way emulated the tendency of the Archduke Ferdinand to balance criticism of the peasants with praise of their *Kaisertreue*. Yet this was the policy which prevailed and which prevailed so strongly that the truth about Galicia was easily obscured. Austrian newspapers were so determined that the moral of the tragedy should be learned all over Europe that they often forgot to express an appropriate concern for the victims of it.[15] They sometimes managed to convey the impression that they could not have cared if there had been a plot. 'Perhaps the local officials did set a price?' was the rhetorical question in one Austrian article on the subject. Its author continued, 'Well in that case the whole complexion of the matter is completely changed – for what government, when all is said and done, is responsible for individual officials?'[16] The result was that practically everyone in Europe – and many in Austria – assumed that the Austrians had indeed been to blame. The myth arose, also, that Austria could rely upon her peasantry in all parts of her Empire to keep her alienated nobilities in check. Nobody did more to sustain this myth that the State Chancellor of Austria himself.

The other provinces most directly affected by the events of 1846, as it turned out, were Lombardy and Venetia. By 1848, Benedek who was widely if erroneously thought to have helped mastermind the Galician jacquerie, was garrison commander in Pavia, Breindl's brother, an army officer, was also stationed there. In northern Italy, too, at this time was the Archduke Maximilian d'Este, one of the foremost military minds in the Austrian army and brother of the Archduke Ferdinand whose ideas on divide and rule he fully shared. Not unnaturally, therefore, comparisons began to be drawn between the situations in Italy and Galicia and although, thanks to the bad press which Austria had received as a result of events in Galicia, not even the most ardent Habsburg supporter wished to contemplate the massacre of Italian nobles, the belief nonetheless became widespread that such a massacre *could* be arranged. Ficquelmont himself shared this opinion;[17] and, indeed, it is easy to demonstrate that for a number of reasons, a sort of social psychology was at work in Italy which fed upon the mythology of 1846 in Poland. This psychology was shared by Ficquelmont, Metternich, Radetzky and probably by most of the Austrian officer class. As the crisis intensified, it encouraged them to seek the solution to their Italian problem by employing the threat of a 'Galician programme' in Lombardy-Venetia.

Metternich was determined that the Empire as a whole should draw the appropriate lesson from the events of 1846. To Count Apponyi, the Hungarian magnate who was then Ambassador to Paris, he wrote:[18]

Apart from some noble and honourable exceptions the upper classes in Galicia were devoted to the cause of revolution; it is the people who have done justice to the conspirators. . . . One country over which the valiant and loyal resistance offered by the Galician people to the seductions of the upper classes will exercise a great influence is Hungary. According to many reports the peasants there are still in the same position from which Austrian legislation has protected the Galician people. The example of the justice meted out by the latter to its seducers could easily turn against the upper classes in Hungary; I have nothing to teach you in this respect and you know as well as I do what an effect would be produced in the country if the King appeared to be appealing to the people.

He also made sure that the good news spread to Italy by writing to Radetzky:[19]

An extraordinarily significant event has just taken place . . . the attempt by the Polish Emigration to start a second revolution in the former Polish territories has been thwarted. The attempt was smashed by the Galician peasantry. This fact in my eyes has the full worth of an unparalleled phase in world history. . . . The real people are devoted to their monarch because he protects them; the landlords rule them but they love only the moderates among them. Now the experience of all ages proves that the liberal-talking landlords who do not burden their subjects are exceptions. The revolutionary Galician landlords had no doubts that the peasants would stand by them if they ordered them to rise against their Emperor; they have made a mistake and paid for it perhaps with their lives. . . . A new era, therefore, has dawned whose influence will not be limited to our monarchy. The democrats have mistaken their base; a democracy without the people is a chimera.

The Viceroy was specifically instructed to spread the news across the Po:[20] 'It is desired that the news of the result of this revolutionary undertaking is spread in Italy across the Po as quickly as possible. I trust Your Royal Highness will take care of this and beseech Your Excellency to do so by all possible means at your command.' The Governors of Lombardy and Venetia had already received similar instructions regarding their own provinces for the latter replied that he had done 'what was necessary to spread the good news' and gave Metternich the assurance that it would reach 'the desired audience'.[21] The Viceroy added in one of his replies:[22] 'Moreover, I have confidence enough in my knowledge of the peasantry in the Kingdom of Lombardy-Venetia to be sure that any attempt to stir them up against the government would be fruitless.'

The Austrians and the class war in Italy

In a memorandum, composed in exile in 1850 and entitled 'The nobility', Metternich wrote:[23] 'To the list of symptoms of a sick, degenerate age belongs the completely false position which the nobility all too often adopts. It was they nearly everywhere who lent a hand to the confusion that was being prepared. . . .' He was certainly convinced that it had been the Lombard nobility which had been behind the trouble in Italy. In January 1848, he had written to Ficquelmont:[24]

What do the Lombard nobility want? Do they intend to renounce their moral and material existence? How can they do so? Yet their conduct must make one assume this. The driving force behind the unspeakable position of the country is coming without a shadow of a doubt from their side. Do they want to surrender their fortunes on the high altar of some incredible divinity and bring on the holocaust? Do they intend to support thɔt party which today can only triumph at the cost of their life and prosperity? . . . They cannot want that. Otherwise they do not know how to judge what they want or where they are going.

Ficquelmont, however, was only able to confirm their bad judgement. He wrote of a 'conspiracy' to give Lombardy-Venetia to Sardinia and added:[25] 'The most eminent families among the Lombard nobility are the promoters of it. The plot is already very old but it is only a year since the pact was made with Turin. It is the Italian movement which the Pope has extended to all the peninsula which has precipitated the enterprise.'

The Austrian army saw the situation in the same light. One colonel wrote to a member of Radetzky's staff:[26]

If Vienna should do anything it should start with the poor. As long as the court is open to the rich and the poor are left to starve, il Ferdinando will have no party. . . . The wanton, rich *dolce far niente* living *Sciori* (i.e. *Signori*) are the ones who should be trodden on – the highest nobility most of all. Where does one hear the greatest recalcitrance against the government these days and who gives the most trouble? The high Milanese nobility with its newly-baked *Toisonisten* at the head. These people could go to court; instead, they overwhelm the Viceroy with insults. I have been in this country too long not to know the Italian aristocracy. Every good Austrian aristocrat should express his disgust for them – they conspire in secret; in public their paid *balossi* do all their dirty work for them. A contemptible, miserable lot of aristocrats. And for 32 years Austria has actually had her representative open his court to these people and neglect as a result the hard-working citizens and tradesmen.

Metternich had already expressed his disgust. 'The most gangrenous class of the population . . . this bastard race of a fallen aristocracy' was what he called them.[27]

On the other side of the political fence, the leading role of the aristocracy was also conceded. 'It appeared our duty', wrote one republican,[28] 'to keep quiet and we beseeched Mazzini to shut up and give a free hand to Gioberti, Balbo, Azeglio, Salvagnoli, Lambruschini, Centofanti, Mamiani and the other moderates.' Another republican account also put the nobles in the lead:[29] 'The year began with the harmony of hatred rather than of ideas. The nobles and the rich took the lead more and more . . . the country had already placed its faith in the wisdom of the *patrizi*.'

Between 1846 and 1848, therefore, the Austrian authorities in Lombardy-Venetia became obsessed by what they obviously regarded as the 'class treason' of the Lombard aristocracy. This obsession, in fact, was to dominate the future conduct of the Austrians in Italy and yet it has never been examined by historians.

The forecasters

The political structure of Austrian Italy in the 1840s was commonly analysed by interested parties in terms of social class; this was not after all a way of looking at things which was invented by Karl Marx. The latter may have introduced the dialectic into socio-political analysis, but in explaining political phenomena in terms of class interest he was indulging in the intellectual commonplace of his time. Writers, both of Left and Right, adopted this perspective in the 1840s and curiously enough, when they applied it to northern Italy their researches often led them to very similar conclusions.

The author of perhaps the most impressive work on Lombardy-Venetia was Luigi Torrelli, who, in his *Pensieri sull'Italia di un Anonimo Lombardo*, published in Paris in 1846, set out, among other things to discover whether there could be any justification for an attempted revolution in that kingdom. The conclusion he arrived at was that 'a conspiracy planned in the Kingdom of Lombardy-Venetia would lack every element of success; the public mind is not educated to the point of being able to envisage it'. Attempted uprisings would be 'pernicious' and 'futile' in his opinion, since their inevitable failure would give Italy a reputation 'for indifference and apathy'. The revolution, therefore, would have to wait.

Torrelli, however, had reached these conclusions by following a careful path of social analysis, which it pays to retrace. He first of all noted the differences between the town and the countryside – in Lombardy-Venetia only *c.* 700,000 people out of a population of *c.* 4,900,000 lived in towns – and then proceeded to estimate which elements of either population might be relied upon to support a revolution. His calculations began with an analysis of the countryside.

Conditions in the countryside varied, depending on whether the inhabitants lived on the Lombard plain or in the more mountainous districts to the north. There were seven provinces in the plain; eight of plain and mountain; and two in the mountains. On the plain, almost all the land was given over to large estates and the peasants worked exceedingly hard to make enough to pay their landlords. Their life was a difficult one, but nothing could be expected of them politically since they never came into contact with government and had no conception of *patria*. Moreover, they were absolutely determined not to get involved in schemes from which they could expect no tangible rewards. Property in the mountain provinces, on the other hand, was much more subdivided: here the ratio of proprietors to non-proprietors was 1 : 20 or 1 : 10 rather than 1 : 100 on the plain. In some places such as Brescia and Bergamo or the Valtelline, it was as small as 1 : 3. Nonetheless, these proprietors were 'poor and restricted'; they might feel the weight of government, but they were uneducated, had 'something to lose' and 'no spontaneous sacrifice [could] be taken for granted even from them'. According to Torrelli's calculations there were about 84,000 proprietors in the Kingdom as a whole, one for every fifty inhabitants of the country. However, eight-tenths of them were really only *piccoli possidenti* who lacked the education necessary to understand public affairs so that only the remaining 16,800 large landowners might be expected to interest themselves in politics – and half of these lived in the towns.

The city populations amounted to 700,000 inhabitants, divided by Torrelli into four categories as follows: (*a*) the mass of citizens; (*b*) merchants and shopkeepers; (c) the rich living on rents; and (d) the professions. Class (a), which amounted to eight-tenths of the city populations gave little cause for hope. They were little better than peasants and among them was what Torrelli described as 'the scum of society'. Class (b) was equally unhelpful from the point of view of revolution: they were undoubtedly hit by the 'intolerable burden' of government financial measures, yet no 'active support' could be expected from them since, once again, only a very few – the rich merchants and bankers – were sufficiently educated to understand politics. Class (d) of course, contained the lawyers, priests, doctors and engineers who had the education to constitute the greatest potential recruiting ground for revolution, but Torrelli found that in spite of this and in spite of their cultural grievances against the administration, most of them were uninterested in revolution, depended on government jobs and were carefully watched. The most 'dangerous' category, therefore, was formed by class (c): these men had wealth, leisure, learning and grievances and not a few had been involved in the 1821 conspiracy; but then again others preferred *la dolce vita* and were pompous in their support of Austria. Torrelli concluded, therefore, that if the revolution could depend only upon a part of the landowning class plus a number of professional men, it would be better not to have one. Moreover, since any revolution would almost certainly involve a war with France, incentives were well-nigh non-existent.

Another Lombard who had arrived at the same conclusion before the outbreak of revolution was Carlo Cattaneo, author of the classic account, *L'Insurrection de Milan en 1848*, published in Paris in 1848. Cattaneo, however, is much more reliable as a military critic than as a social one – for he had an axe to grind against the royalist aristocrats who politically outmanœuvred him. Nevertheless, his account of the background to the revolution is full of interest, less because of his conviction that it should never have taken place – a conviction he held on the grounds that there had been no proper military preparations and that the Austrians in any case were on the point of conceding all – but because he sustains the case that it was the aristocrats who, from Austria's viewpoint, were the most subversive social element. He does not mean to do this; but in arguing another case, he protests so much that he gives the game away.

Europe, he wrote, was under an 'illusion' in supposing that 'the revolutionary spirit was born amidst the aristocracy and thence had to infiltrate little by little amongst the bourgeoisie'. Nothing, he argued, could be more false. 'The middle class constituted the heart of the national party.'[30] His bitterness was unlimited, therefore, when in 1848 he had to witness 'at the head of this grand enterprise . . . a backward aristocracy, an absolute king and a pope'.[31] 'Was there not a flagrant contradiction here?' he asked,[32] before going on to pose (*but not to answer*) the question:[33] 'Why had the middle classes, who were truly revolutionary, failed to assume the direction of the movement?' The contradiction one suspects, was in his own analysis; yet, despite his prejudices, he had no choice but to admit that the revolution in Milan was led by the local nobility.

Cattaneo, on the other hand, merely hinted at the reasons which had caused the aristocracy to assume such a role – their 'former accomplice' Charles Albert was now in a good position to help them, especially since the policies of Pius IX had given popularity to a previously lost cause. However, for a much deeper analysis of the role of the aristocracy, the Austrian records are far more revealing, all the more so since they are not merely the results of intellectual speculation but the background reports on which Austrian policy was based.

Before 1846, the date which both Cattaneo and Ficquelmont designated the watershed as far as aristocratic subversion is concerned, Austria's attitude towards the Kingdom of Lombardy-Venetia was marked by total complacency. A report of the Chevalier de Menz of 1833 completely set the tone.[34] A long document which examined the various levels of political activity within the kingdom and which also gave 'a review of the different classes of the social body in Lombardy' it did not anticipate any trouble at all.

Politically, according to Menz, the situation was highly satisfactory: 'The surveillance and the most active research undertaken by the police has been unable to obtain any positive data with respect to the existence of any real organization of the sects in Lombardy.' Conspirators were few in number; 'liberals' existed 'in large numbers' among the upper classes and 'even' among the middle ones, but this liberalism was 'an object of fashion and vanity' – adopted by 'elegant ladies' and 'young men determined to make an impression' – and was 'inoffensive' in character. The 'great majority of all social classes' were politically indifferent and the lower down the social scale one went, the more indifference one found.

His review of society led to similar conclusions. The peasants were 'simple' and 'resigned to their lot'; they were even 'useful' to the government in 'a negative way' since conspirators could never count on their support. The artisans in the towns were also reliable since the opulence of the cities enabled them to create 'quite considerable fortunes' so that life was 'much too convenient' for them to bother about political change. Even the lower classes, which had more to complain about, posed little of a threat since Lombard prosperity meant that they were found in relatively fewer numbers there than elsewhere.

Moving up the social scale, Menz described the merchants and the bourgeoisie – defined significantly as *propriétaires non nobles* – in a light exceedingly favourable to the regime:

The class of merchants and bourgeois, which in other countries has often shown itself the most inclined to favour political changes, is in Lombardy, in this respect, much more solid and aware of its real interests. Internal trade being so brisk on account of the abundant produce of the country; the exchange of goods so rapid in view of the sufficiency of means with which to satisfy the various needs of life and luxury; and external commerce having been given such a boost by the silk trade whose income this year has been calculated at fifty million Milanese pounds, the merchants are indeed right to be content with their situation and to fear rather than support a revolution which would destroy their ventures and their credit.

The aristocracy was likewise distinguished by its wealth and prosperity. The nobility had large fortunes and the same applied to other landowners who lived in a state of comfort much superior to landowners elsewhere. The heads of landowning families were, therefore, in no way disposed to 'support upheavals'. On the other hand the younger generation of this class was less reliable: younger nobles went abroad illegally and joined revolutionary sects while those who remained affected to have superior and enlightened minds. The same was true of the scions of the bourgeoisie 'albeit to lesser degree', but Menz's only worry appeared to be that of integrating the younger nobles into the ways of their fathers in order that they might shed their 'chimerical theories'.

By the end of the 1830s, it seemed that something like this had been accomplished. A celebrated reconciliation occurred between the nobles and the dynasty with the coronation of Ferdinand in Milan in 1838 and the amnesty which was at that time granted to those in gaol and exile. Yet by 1846 reconciliation had given way to recrimination and the younger generation of which de Menz had written had been alienated rather than accommodated. Why? Because the longstanding grievances of the Lombard nobility failed to secure redress. These were continuously brought to the attention of Vienna and regularly ignored.

The Lombard nobility under Austrian rule

At the end of January 1848, Ficquelmont reported to Metternich the views of the Count of Castelbarco, one of Austria's last supporters among the Lombard nobility. He wrote:[35]

The principal point to which monsieur de Castelbarco attributes the disaffection of the Lombard nobility is the position in which it was put by the Austrian government. It has been left without rights, without privileges of any kind. . . . My interlocutor is, therefore, of the opinion that it is absolutely necessary to regulate the position of the nobility to secure more agreement on the principles to which one wants them to submit. He strongly deplores the social rupture that has taken place and which, as far as he is concerned places him in complete isolation since he does not wish to be forced into the position of being understood to believe in something he does not.

The Austrians in many respects had only themselves to blame for this situation, since at the end of the Napoleonic Wars and with the dissolution of the Holy Roman Empire they had undertaken, but without finesse, to examine the validity of all titles of nobility in their North Italian provinces. The process began in 1814 with the setting up of heraldic commissions and continued right up until the 1840s. Most probably the decisions were fair enough – the officials appear to have been accommodating in their views – yet the whole process was necessarily unsettling and undignified for those concerned and there had to be losers.[36]

Field Marshal Bellegarde set up the first Commission in Lombardy on 26 October 1814. It confirmed the titles of the old Italian nobility and the titles bestowed by the French – in so far as such titles had been bestowed by diploma. Most titles, however, had been awarded *ad personam* and the Austrians were willing to make these hereditary only if the recipients could give proof of their service to the Monarch or the state. Both categories of titles were, it is true, placed on equal terms with German ones, but documentary evidence had to be forwarded to the Commission regarding all claims.

In 1816 a similar Commission was set up in Venetia, the main concern of which was to examine titles bestowed by the former Republic of Venice. A significant change was now exacted since the difference between the *Stadt adel* and the *Adel der terra firma*, a difference which sustained the special position of the Venetian patriciate, was abolished against the wishes of the Venetian gubernium. This change not only made these two types of noble equal, but in so doing placed the patriciate nobility behind that of Mantua and Milan and 'caused much bad blood'.

Both Commissions differentiated between titles conferred by republicans and those conferred by a sovereign. Hence titles of 'conte', bestowed by Mantua and Milan were made equal to the German 'Graf' whereas the Venetian title of 'conte' was to remain untranslated and was held to be the equivalent of Austrian simple nobility. There were still other grievances. The Italian title 'duc' also remained untranslated and was reckoned only to be equal to the German 'Graf'. Holders of such titles could no longer be addressed as 'altezza', nor could they call their daughters 'princess'. All the efforts of the Venetian gubernium to better the situation proved futile. The Viennese government even adopted the position that the right to promotion must needs be considered in the light of age, service and fortune and so adopted the French law of 1808 whereby a minimum fortune of 200,000 fl. was required for a prince, 30,000 for a Graf, 15,000 for a Freiherr and 3,000 for a Ritter. Various concessions were granted concerning so-called mis-marriages', but the gubernium misinterpreted the law, called in all titles and consequently pleased nobody. In 1820 a new law abolished the patriciate in an effort to sort things out, but not until 1825 were the regulations concerning the title 'conte' clarified.

As the Commission proceeded with their work, all sorts of anomalies arose to give rise to bad feeling. Certain groups of Italian nobles did not fit neatly into heraldic categories. Groups like the *nobili araldici* and the *nobili diplomatici* had their titles recognised but not confirmed. This was also the fate of the *cittadini nobili* of Mantua and the *ordine dei segretari* and the *cavalieri vessiliferi* of Venice. Titles such as 'eques auratus' and 'conte palatino' were confirmed; but the latter were no longer the equivalent of the German 'Graf' but merely 'bürgerlich'. Finally, there was the problem of the provincial and town nobilities. Regarding the first, only the Valtelline and Sondrino titles were confirmed and only then by the special grace of the Emperor as late as 1842; the towns presented a problem which was solved by granting recognition only to the nobilities of towns which had been recognised by the Venetian patriciate, a solution which in practice meant the end of many city nobilities.[37]

These changes, coming as they did from a regime which had accepted the abolition of privileges decreed by its French predecessor, almost inevitably left the Italian nobility with the feeling that they were regarded as second-class nobles. The attitude of the Austrian nobility and the practices of the Habsburg viceregal court did nothing to disabuse them of such suspicions.

'The author of a recently-published, interesting work on the Italian provinces of the Austrian Empire', wrote a French pamphleteer,[38] 'wanted the imperial court, in order to attract the great families of those provinces to Vienna, to seek to bind them by marriage to the families of the German provinces: "It ought", he said, "to mix the blood of the Contarini with that of the Schwarzenbergs." ' The pamphleteer continued: 'These ideas must have astonished, if not made smile, those in Austria who would have read this book. . . . Social links between Vienna and the Italian provinces are rare and even if they were common it would be difficult for ties to be established between people of differing ideas and sentiment; in Austria the aristocratic mentality prevails in all classes, whereas in northern Italy the concepts of ambition and rank are scarcely known. . . .'

Ideally, of course, the viceregal court in Milan should have served as a 'melting-pot' for the aristocratic world but, in fact, for many reasons, the opposite occurred and by 1848 the local aristocracy was actively boycotting it. The Countess Ficquelmont described the life she led in Milan in 1847 as 'in total isolation from the Milanese' – indeed, as if in 'an outpost in enemy territory'.[39]

The viceregal court, of course, was run on the cheap – the Viceroy's appanage of 100,000 fl C.M. was much too small to exude the magic that might compete with the memory of Eugene's lavish hospitality[40] – and since the German Archbishop of Milan lived with equal frugality, there one day appeared under the statue of Milan's 'man of stone' the words:[41]

'I was always alone but now we are three,
The Archbishop, the Archduke and me.'

The court, nevertheless, was run along the lines of the strictest Spanish etiquette: court summonses were sent out rather than invitations issued; worse still, not everybody who came was allowed to enter so that as Ficquelmont put it, 'to go to court and remain in one place until your name and rank is discovered is no longer a favour which it is impossible to resist'.[42] The Lombard nobility as a rule were much more interested in the fortune rather than the pedigree of their ladies they married; as a consequence, according to one witness,[43] 'it was taken badly when a number of ladies who had first been admitted were chased away. Many said, "I will not enter any house from which I have been chased".' Nobles of recent origin were also excluded – so many quarterings were absolutely essential – but even those who were eventually received were given the distinct impression that they could in no way compete with the high nobility of the former Holy Roman Empire. The court's policy was completely anachronistic. In an age of growing wealth and expanding social ambitions imperial recognition was being bestowed on ever fewer Italians. It was in vain that the pro-Austrian noble di Capitani told Metternich:[44] 'It would be no bad thing to increase the number of nobles in Lombardy. The ancient families have died out. If the wealthy are to be treated one way and the nobility another there will always be more trouble. Grants of nobility will win over the influential families. The hope is spreading among the bourgeoisie understandably enough that such concessions would be rewards for their services.'

The younger nobles and the wealthy young non-nobles who aped them, demanded more from the regime, of course, than the chance to be received at court. More specifically, they expected to be able to staff the higher bureaucracy and complained bitterly that the jobs which they believed should be reserved for them were going to Germans. 'The principal civil and ecclesiastical posts in the Kingdom of Lombardy-Venetia are reserved for foreigners', said di Capitani to Metternich:[45]

The possibility given to Italians of occupying only middling and lower posts which demand much more work, profound study and long practice and bring a minimum reward and very little influence cannot win the interest of the patrician families and the wealthy of the Kingdom. It is a short step, moreover, from being excluded from the service of the state and joining the opposition; yet by conceding modest rewards, it would be easy to attract Italians into ruling circles. The young above all might hope to follow those careers, but in view of the difficulties they have encountered and the impossibility of their adequately fulfilling their own ambitions, they feel all the more alienated from public life and instinctively submit to the attraction of an opposition whose liberal and national ideas are not in their interest.

In 1847, Gabrio Casati made exactly the same point to Pillersdorff and drew exactly the same conclusions.[46] 'The youth of the rich', he wrote, 'are naturally discouraged and in their disgust they do not stop at removing themselves from the pursuit of an honourable public career but go a step further and develop an aversion against the government.'

In a land whose political tradition was to develop into *connubio* and *trasformismo*, the opposition to Austrian rule was demanding to be bought off. The Austrians, however, refused to do this. Not only did they refuse to create sinecures; they justified this by reference to other facets of the so-called Italian 'national character'. Thus General Schönhals could write:[47]

But he who knows the disinclination, particularly of the Italian upper classes against everything which constitutes state service, he who knows how little inclination they possess for serious study, will understand that Austria could not seek her governors, supreme judges or generals among the Italian nobility. Look through the matriculations of the universities of Pavia and Padua and see if one meets with a distinguished name there. The theatre and the cafes are not the places where statesmen are produced and tiresome working up the ladder of service posts is not to the taste of rich Italians. We do not blame them for this. But at the same time they cannot accuse the state of violating nationality, of partiality and of neglect.

Chapter 11

The Austrian army and the Lombard aristocracy

Despite the patronizing attitude of Schönhals's memoirs, the Austrian army regarded the Lombard nobility in a much less detached way than the imperial government. This, to some extent, was only natural because the issues which divided the nobility from the government brought it into headlong collision with the military. Austrian officers asked themselves why, if these people really wished to serve their King, did they not join the army? Yet they did not, so that the Austrian diplomat Philippsberg could report to Metternich in 1847:[1]*

It is a sad sign that the Lombard nobility shows an increasing antipathy towards Austrian military service with every day that goes by, and it takes real moral courage for the few Lombard officers garrisoned in their homeland to bear their nation's condemnation and remain in service. An evil star, it seems rules over all Austria's attempts to mix the Italian nationality with the German and the government's arrangements to win over the young nobility through civil and military service, however well thought out, are immediately negated in practice by misconceptions so that after a few years the youngest product of this effort is already a veritable sore.

With the accession of Ferdinand a regiment had been created called the 'Noble Lombard-Venetian Guard' which was designed to bring sixty young noblemen within the orbit of the Emperor. Phillipsberg reported, however, that there was difficulty in finding candidates and that it lacked all national respect.[2] According to an Italian writer of the period, the noblemen who joined it were regarded as hostages for the 1838 amnesty.[3] The problem was still a worrying one, therefore, even when Ficquelmont arrived in Milan. He asked Casati why none of the nobility took up a military career, but was simply told that there was 'a certain repugnance' involved in joining an institution which was not a national one.[4]

There was, of course, a certain truth in this in so far as it reflected Italian discontent with the measures undertaken by Austria in 1814 when the army of Italy was dissolved and most of its officers retired.[5] The Austrians had been very thorough in their efforts to exorcise the spell of a national army: dissolved along with the army was the Italian Ministry of War, the General Staff, the Artillery and Engineering Corps, the military schools, the Topographical Institute, the arms factories, etc., etc. – in fact the whole Italian military establishment. Henceforth Lombards and Venetians had to join the Austrian army and wear the imperial colours. On the other hand, most young Italian noblemen were little inclined towards a military career in any case, and those

---

* Notes to this chapter are on pp. 273–5.

who were so inclined complained less about the uniform than about the *longueurs* of the promotion system:[6]

. . . there are not as many Italian officers in the army as there should be given that there are 30–36 thousand Italian soldiers. There should be 10 to 12 colonels but there are only 2. It is said that the number of other Italian officers below this is very small. These young people enter a regiment and return to their families after a few years without hope of advancement. His Majesty could have a table of Italian officers presented to the Hofkriegsrath. It would then show whether the complaints of the military men are justified.

The truth was that for almost everyone in the Austrian army during the pre-March period promotion was painfully slow. Those with social connexions among the higher nobility of Austria might expect to make their way more rapidly, but it was precisely these social connexions which the Italians did not have. The result was that they often withdrew from military service to join their fellows who[7] 'did not wish to submit to military discipline and [whose] education [was] rarely sufficiently advanced to permit them to take up a diplomatic career; they remained therefore, at home, living among themselves and continuing to form a caste in which each family had its allotted place; they were jealous and envious of one another, one keeping an eye on the other afraid lest one of them would become reconciled to the imperial court and be seen to grow in honour and fortune'.

The army might well have been content to maintain a rather patronising attitude towards these people if it had not been for the obvious attractions that were held out for such noblemen by Piedmont. The greatest part of the Lombard nobility after all had significant estates in that country and formed, therefore, 'a class of subjects which belonged to neither of the two states and under the title of *sudditti misti* formed a true class between'.[8] The consequence was that[9] 'the Milanese nobility became accustomed . . . to half-acknowledge the King of Sardinia as their ruler. They frequently went to Turin, where they were treated respectfully by the ·court and often returned decorated with orders.' The great landowners of Novara, on the other hand, 'had remained Lombards and all lived in Milan' despite the fact that they were Piedmontese subjects,[10] so that the aristocracy of the Lombard plain tended to form a social whole in spite of territorial divisions. The trouble was that after the accession of Pius IX and the customs war in 1847 between Piedmont and Austria, the whole of this body began to take up Balbo's argument that it should acknowledge only one sovereign. And the sovereign, clearly, who had most to offer was the Sardinian, Charles Albert.

The Lombard nobles, however, if they wished to pursue this policy, were clearly obliged to play a dangerous game. In the words of one of them, Count Vitaliano Borromeo,[11] 'one strove to be at the same time cesareo and pontifico, guelfo and ghibellino'. He might well have used the words from Goethe's *Egmont*:[12] 'We serve the king in our own way, but between ourselves we can confess that we know only too well how to balance the rights of the king against our own.'

This balance occasionally was in danger of being lost and the Austrian army, for example, regarded as treasonous the fact that Borromeo and Casati sent their sons to the Sardinian Military Academy. One of Radetzky's staff officers wrote to another:[13] 'He [Casati] has said that his sons would never wear the white uniform [of Austria] and now sends his second son into Piedmontese service, where the first is already an officer.' Count Buol, the Austrian Ambassador in Turin even accused Casati to his face of bringing up Sardinians.[14] However, if the Lombard aristocracy was involving itself in a balancing act, so too was the Austrian army. It knew only too well what was going on and with its knowledge of what had happened in Galicia, it decided to give the balancing act a twist. If the nobility could take up the cause of the King's enemy, then the servants of the King could take up the cause of the Lombard peasantry. The army, too, had examined the social dynamics of Lombard society and had concluded, just like Torrelli or Cattaneo, that an attempted revolution would certainly fail. In order to make sure, however, it was prepared to organise the peasants.

The balancing act

Radetzky himself wanted to make such preparations and a talk he had with the Viceroy has survived to prove this:[15]

'The country', said Radetzky, 'What does the "country" really mean? The peasant cultivates his field and vineyards. He pays his taxes and produces soldiers. Whom he pays and who he serves does not matter at all. He does no more for us than he would have to do for an Italian King or an Italian Republic. Why should he trouble about politics? What interest does he have in national aspirations?'

'And the bourgeois?' asked the Archduke.

'The bourgeois is dissatisfied and will remain so. The nobility too. But there are lots of peasants and only very few nobles and bourgeois. It is the noble "Signori possidenti" who exploit the peasants. It is the city-dwellers who fight against the peasants' interests. Therefore the state, the Austrian state to which he belongs gives him very little trouble. Therefore he remains loyal.'

'I have done everything that can possibly be done in Vienna for the Italian peasant', said the Archduke. 'He remains freed from the legal rate of paper money. We left him the free administration of justice of the French rule, which the French decreed during the revolution. He can, of course, speak Italian in the courts and with the administration, since he does not understand anything else. Whenever the occasion arises I appoint Italians as civil servants and judges.'

'Italian bourgeois,' replied Radetzky reflectively, 'that is just it. If we could fill these leading positions with peasants, we would be all the more secure.'

'Impossible. The peasant is uneducated. He can neither read nor write and cannot be bothered to learn.'

'So Austria gains nothing from his loyalty,' maintained Radetzky. 'Nobles and bourgeois count for little. But the nobles have power over the peasantry and the bourgeois has money. That is how it goes. Revolutionary intrigue is fed by the personal influence of the lord over the peasantry – which is the same as serfdom – and by the bourgeois's money. Austria only has the peasantry on her side but however great its numbers it remains politically insignificant. It is not enough to keep the peasants in a good mood.'

'So what can we do?' asked the Archduke.

'Austria must create more rights for the Italian peasants', said Radetzky. 'It must grant him the possibility of giving expression and influence to his loyalty in political life.'

'But, dear Radetzky, you are speaking like a revolutionary. For me that would be a too risky experiment.'

'Time marches on, Your Imperial Highness. When Kaiser Joseph II freed the German peasants he risked much more indeed.'

'Perhaps we will be forced to do that yet, if people sit around all year like the two of us here, my dear. But I could never make the court in Vienna understand that.'

'It is Austrian statecraft, Your Highness. It has always consisted of holding the balance. Here in Italy, Austria has the bourgeoisie and the nobility against her. The counterweight is the peasant. The peasant, although in the majority is too light in weight. From the standpoint of raison d'etat, what is more natural, more advisable and more reasonable, than, so to say, giving him weight through political rights?'

A memorandum setting out this point of view did indeed go to Vienna. Apparently it got lost somewhere in the bureaucracy.[16] Still the notion was deeply embedded in the army consciousness that salvation lay in the farms and fields around them. Inevitably it ignited a spark in the fertile mind of the Archduke Maximilian, who conceived a plan which was very much less bold, but infinitely more cunning than anything Radetzky had thought up. It also had the ring of practicality about it, despite, perhaps, an overlarge dose of social engineering.

The Archduke was very worried about the costs involved in financing the North Italian fortresses:[17] 'The Kingdom of Lombardy-Venetia supports, in relation of population to forces, not half as much as the other provinces of the Empire and requires in the middle of peacetime and apparently with no set limit, three times as many forces as any other province merely for the maintenance and support of its government. The state can not afford such a nuisance for long; it exhausts its finances; chains and absorbs the greatest part of its troops, which could be urgently required elsewhere.' Having given the matter some thought, and having been inspired by the example of the Modena militia,[18] he produced an almost Machiavellian military–social solution,[19] the basis of which was the peasant.

The peasant, he argued, had not yet been smitten by the fever of nationalism since in Italy this class displayed unparalleled religiosity and conscientiousness. Besides, the peasants had no idea of what had been going on in the towns and understood even less. They simply did what their priests and masters told them. They had other good qualities as well. It was well known that they had loathed French rule and had welcomed the Austrians as 'liberators'; they were also stronger in body and more reliable in mind than the townsfolk; yet, most important of all they were the overwhelming majority of the population. Maximilian quoted the census figures for 1843. The number of people living in towns with a population of over 7,000, he put at 1,190,449. The number living in the countryside amounted to 3,674,158. The latter figure, together with the intimidated and feeble supporters of the government who lived in the towns,[20] was held to constitute the government's mandate in this statistical democracy.

Maximilian wanted 50,000 peasants to form a militia in Lombardy-Venetia which could control internal dissent. But how was he to get them? He wanted only volunteers. Moreover they had to be 'real farm labourers'. No one else would fit the role – only the so-called Mezzadri. To ensure that he got these men and no one else, Maximilian proposed that all volunteers would have to be certified by their local priests and mayors.[21] They had to be reliable, because part of the Archduke's plan was to give them a uniform, armour and a rifle which they were supposed to keep at home. The uniform was to be a simple one – they lasted longer that way – and each man would only be allowed to keep three 'sharp bullets' at home,[22] yet even that was a sign of considerable confidence. The scheme, of course, was open to questions: What incentives would encourage the peasants to enlist? How would the officers be selected? How would the scheme be paid for? In answering these questions, the Archduke Maximilian proved himself almost startlingly original.

In providing incentives for his peasant volunteers, for example, the Archduke indulged in the purest irony:[23] 'To get these peasants to enlist voluntarily, it must be established that every militiaman on entering the militia is allowed to free a young man from liability to conscription before the same year's recruitment.' In other words, if a peasant volunteered for the militia he could save a fellow peasant from the army. An incentive indeed. Again, Maximilian stressed that the man to be freed would have to be a fellow peasant,[24] 'a real peasant, a farm labourer and, to wit, from the same commune'. Presumably he would also have to have been certified. The importance attached to his status was obvious. If the militiaman had the right to set anybody free, he could sell that right to the highest bidder – which, in Italy, of course would mean the nobility and the upper classes. That was the very last thing that the Archduke had in mind. His scheme purported to threaten these people, not make life easier for them, by, in effect, reducing the price of replacements. Moreover, the army would then suffer too: the replacements which the nobles were accustomed to hire were veterans and the army kept some of its best men that way. Worst of all, however, might be the effect of such transactions on the militiamen themselves: they would get rich quick – and no longer be 'real peasants'. They might also acquire bourgeois aspirations. What use could be made of them then?

On the other hand, if militiamen could free only poor fellow peasants from the horrors of the Austrian army, the situation took on an altogether different perspective. There would be an almost negligible risk of corruption for a start. The peasants had no money. Better still, the scheme had a built-in bonus: peasant wives and mothers could be expected actively to encourage their menfolk to enlist in this wonderful institution and the net result would be a surplus of peasant volunteers from among whom the authorities could pick out the best. Certain guidelines were laid down by Maximilian; the volunteers would have to pass conscription age themselves; once they had been accepted they would have to be carefully watched and any man who committed a misdemeanour or who somehow outgrew his peasant mind or status must be immediately expelled – the man he had freed from the army, would then, of course, find it suddenly interested in him once more.[25] The scheme had to be made as watertight as possible.

There was the problem that, once having secured the 50,000 stalwarts, the army would suffer from an inferior quality of recruits. Maximilian discounted it. Good recruiting material, he wrote,[26] was 'superabundant' in Lombardy-Venetia in any case. If changes in the pattern of recuitment were necessary, he reckoned that they would be seen in more veterans staying on rather than in the recruitment of inferior soldiers. After all, if the countryside could not provide for the required number of recruits, the burden would just have to fall on the towns – and the towns would pay for the veterans instead. In future years recruitment for the militia would be limited to a few replacements per year, so the problem was viewed by him as a temporary one in any case.

The problem which really troubled the Archduke was the selection of officers. They had to be completely loyal – as in Modena – because only then could he discount the possibility of 'the nonsensical siren song of the Italian nation state' misleading the people.[27] Here too, however, Maximilian displayed a resourceful imagination:[28] 'Men of all classes who are loyal to the state should be eligible for selection to officers' posts. . . . In this way an avowed pro-government party, which at present evidently does not exist, will come into being among the educated classes.'

This was a new departure in the way in which the Austrian military mind thought about officer recruitment. Maximilian knew, therefore, that he would have to make such officers socially respectable to get his schemes to work. Accordingly, he proposed that retired army officers be taken 'from here and there' and made militia officers. This, he reckoned, would have two advantages: the officer who had been retired would receive more pay; and he would bestow on the militia the esteem of the regular army.

Maximilian held that it would be a good thing if the militia officers could speak Italian. They could then win the support of the peasantry all the quicker. That did not mean, however, that all the officers should be Italian. The Archduke believed that nearly all the Austrian officers in Italy could speak the language anyway, and in any case the Italian peasants had not been seized by the 'giddiness of so-called nationality' and 'often trusted a foreigner more than a native' who was just as likely to be his oppressor.[29] He did lay down, however, that officers would have to live within the Delegations – a rather obvious measure.

It was proposed to turn the plan into reality by appointing a special organising commissioner who would have a knowledge and understanding of the people.[30] It would be he who, after consultations with the government, would appoint all officers from captain downwards. He would start organising in the north – presumably the safest area – and would only move on to another area when his work had been completed in the previous one. It was envisaged that a company of about 250 men would be set up in about 250 areas, thus producing a total of 50,000 men – that is, about one militiaman to every 100 of the population, a figure which as usual the Archduke borrowed from Modena.

It was the Archduke's suggestion that the militia could be called out at any time of the day or night on a given alarm signal. They were supposed to collect at a central place of assembly already uniformed and armed. There they would receive their extra ammunition from the N.C.O. who held the key to the company depot. The latter person would have to be a retired or invalided soldier. While on duty, the militia were to be treated exactly as ordinary soldiers. This was only natural; after all, it was the ordinary soldiers who they were supposed to be replacing. On the other hand it meant that they received soldiers' pay and lived in barracks. However, they were not allowed to carry weapons about off duty. Still, the whole idea was to get good-quality soldiers at cut prices[31] – the professionals could then go where they were needed without having to hang around doing futile and expensive garrison work.

It was an amazing piece of ingenuity on the part of an Austrian archduke and it did seem like an answer to all the problems.[32] But it arrived too late. In the fourth draft of his plan Maximilian was already trying to fit in the National

Guard.[33] Like most people who have drawn up complicated schemes based upon the class war, the Archduke was quite surprised when a revolution actually broke out.

One final point has to be made about his proposals. How did he plan to finance them? If the militia had been summoned by the army or by the Delegations, Maximilian proposed that the body which sent out the summons would be the one to pay the costs. Yet, concerning the normal expenses of the militia, he had another idea:[34]

The money for carrying out the plans outlined above should be furnished by those who are the source of such measures, namely, by all malcontents in the whole of Austrian Italy, by copying the former French expedient of levying an 'opinion tax' and by levying it in exactly the same way in which the French did, namely on those who do not know how to recognise their lawful government.

Everyone who utters an anti-government opinion must immediately have such a tax levied on them and if a register of all previous utterances were used to this effect, a fair amount of money could be amassed, particularly from rich Milan. This money would be more than enough with which to pay for the creation of a militia. . . .

Thus once again, the issue was that of the army versus the nobility.

From theory to practice: the beginnings

By the beginning of 1848, it became apparent to the Lombard aristocrats exactly how the Austrian mind was beginning to function. The realisation dawned that 'the grand strategy of Austria aimed at exciting the hatred of the people against the nobility'.[35] The army was seen to be at the heart of this strategy because incidents like the following were reported in Milan:[36]

During the afternoon of last Wednesday, the 5th of this month, an officer of the Paumgarten Regiment garrisoned in the house found at No. 2713a in the Road San Girolamo entered the dwelling place of the married couple Clemente Ziboldi and Elene Panzani [the former a worker in the small 'casa d'industria a San Marco', the latter a maid in the house below the said casa] whose door opens on to the entrance hall; there, even without somewhere to sit, he began speaking with the most unexpected affability to these poor people about that morning's riots [i.e. those of 3 January 1848] and having made an argument of the misery of their abode, he tried to persuade them that it was the government's intention to improve the lot of the poor, that it wished to make the *signori* work them less and pay them more but that the *signori* on the other hand, foreseeing how much would be demanded of them, were trying to arouse in the poor, old and silly grudges against the Germans, etc. However, he and the government were well aware that the poor people of Lombardy had too much good sense to pay attention to these perfidious insinuations of the *signori*. Moreover, they would understand that very few *signori* would profit by the government's changes and that the poor people, whether they were involved in anything or not, would always end up worse than before [if there were a change of regime]. . . .

There could be little doubt, therefore, that the class war was about to be fought out and that the sides were lining up albeit in a curious and highly unexpected fashion.

By the end of 1847, in fact, the rupture between the court and the nobility was absolutely plain. Ficquelmont described their boycott to the Viceroy as 'a formal act of rebellion against His Majesty the Emperor'; it was 'a plan of high treason' since the aim behind it was 'the separation of the country [from the Empire]'.[37] By the end of December 1847, he had proposed the following to Metternich:[38]

The Lombard nobility is rich; it loves money above everything; public opinion is opposed to the Spielberg; [but] nobody would say anything about the confiscation of property. Count Pozzo, a former conspirator, is living in his old Milan hotel with the whole of his former fortune augmented by the economies of exile. Arconate has just established himself in Florence with all his Lombard fortune. The Princess Belgiojoso travels around Italy like a high priestess of insurrection, having spent years in Paris in the newspaper she founded there, the *Ausonio*, and it is with her Lombard fortune that she is making war on us.

Metternich agreed that it was 'necessary to make some examples'[39] and in the wake of the Tobacco Riots the 'daily conference' agreed to arrest a number of Milanese aristocrats and bankers. Radetzky at last could give Ficquelmont his backing on something concerning security. 'It is certain', he wrote,[40] 'that if we arrested a dozen of the most rich and distinguished good-for-nothings and had them exiled to some far-off province for a couple of years, the rest of them would receive such a shock that peace would soon return – as well as confidence in the government, which at present is completely lacking in the pacific part of the population.'

Their lack of confidence, however, proved thoroughly warranted. When the police went to arrest the marquises proscribed, they found that most of them had already fled so that the Viceroy backed down completely and revoked these measures. He also informed a deputation from the nobles' Club de Lions that their premises had been closed not by the local authorities but by Vienna. This failure to execute even the simplest of counter-measures provoked amusement and contempt from all. 'Everybody in town', wrote Ficquelmont,[41] 'is laughing about it.'

The laughter, however, soon began to sound a trifle shrill on account of the attitude that the authorities appeared to be adopting with respect to the peasants. Even in 1847, the nobles had been suspicious that the imperial security to which they felt entitled had not been as much in evidence as they had desired. In February of that year, for example, about 4,000 peasants, hungry on account of the harvest failures and the potato blight of the time, had assembled from the valleys around Lecco and had marched with flags and drums upon the town where they sacked the house and warehouses of a rich merchant. 'The soldiers who were garrisoned in the city', however, 'offered no resistance' and 'allowed themselves to be disarmed and to be locked up in their barracks.'[42] Since the soldiers everywhere appeared slow to intervene, memories of Galicia were inevitably revived.

Indeed, by February 1848, the Austrians themselves were actively reviving them, although whether they would have welcomed a repetition is very difficult to say. Metternich's standpoint was somewhat ambivalent. On 23 January 1848 he wrote:[43] 'The government of the Kingdom of Lombardy at the beginning of 1848 resembles only too much the government of Galicia in 1846. God save the Monarchy from a similar kind of aid!' At the height of the crisis over the Tobacco Riots, however, his emphasis had been somewhat different:[44]

'If the Lombards were Poles, we would have had the same scenes across the Alps at the beginning of 1848 that we had to deplore in Galicia at the beginning of 1846.'

At any rate, so determined was he to exploit the fears aroused by a 'Galician programme' that in January 1848 the *Augsburger Allgemeine Zeitung* carried a report which ran:[45] 'People in Italy are making the same remarks as were made in Galicia. The masses in Italy, as in Galicia, are not interested . . . in [political] movements and if the Lombards are forced to pay the cost of their revolution, it will not be the farm labourers who will suffer as a class; the repayment shall be made by the landowners and the rich and since they alone are guilty, they alone should pay the price.'

Passages like this, not unnaturally, instilled great anxiety in the local aristocrats who reacted by involving themselves in large-scale acts of charity and in enterprises such as the construction of the Treviglio–Brescia railway line, which were designed to provide work for the locally improvident.[46] The noble ladies of Milan did their share too: led by the Countess Maria Borromeo, they organized a committee for the relief of poverty which collected 108,600 lire to distribute to the poor. Another conspicuous, not to say ostentatious, act of charity was the large-scale distribution of bread and other commodities from the home of the House of Litta. The Austrians, therefore, kept up the pressure and on 2 February the *Augsburger Allgemeiner Zeitung* commented acidly:[47]

Industrial activity has ground to a halt; commerce languishes; the exchange is worried; and the poor man who has no work suffers as a result. The *patrizi* and the reformers have now thought up the Machiavellian expedient, partly of fomenting hatred against the government, partly of pretending to be benefactors to the paupers in order to win their devotion so as to make use of them in their schemes. They send deputations of two *signore* dressed in mourning from house to house, to collect money in aid of poor families. The Italians do not lack an inventive mind. But what will happen should the light infiltrate the inner regions of the people and if the people should discern the reason for its dissipation? Ought the government to be blamed if, God forbid, the horrid scenes of Galicia have to be re-enacted upon the fertile fields of Lombardy?

In the early months of 1848, therefore, both sides were preparing for the class war. The Austrians were confident that if it came to the crunch, they could repeat their Galician success of 1846; the Lombard nobility on the other hand, obviously respected their confidence. Yet history rarely repeats itself exactly, if for no other reason than that there is always somebody who wants a different ending. The Lombard aristocrats did well to take precautions, for in March 1848 the people fought on their side of the barricades. That is not to say, however, that the class war went unfought. The Austrians, after all, had a tradition of entering wars with little in the way of an army.

Chapter 12

The reckoning

The provisional government

Radetzky's faith in the Lombard peasantry proved utterly unfounded when in March 1848 the Austrian army in Italy was forced to retreat inside the mighty Quadrilateral. 'The insurrection of 18 March in Milan had not remained isolated, but had been accompanied by the simultaneous revolt of the provinces and the countryside.'[1]* The poor in no way rallied to the Austrians and among the dead on the Milanese barricades were few nobles or bourgeois but 61 carpenters, 53 shoemakers, 51 porters, 43 servants, 41 peasants, 39 blacksmiths, 36 bricklayers and 30 weavers.[2] Moreover, the poor inside Milan were helped by the poor outside the city:[3] 'The people came running to the walls of Milan to aid it.' 'The city', wrote an Austrian officer,[4] 'was surrounded by armed and uproarious peasants who came running in their thousands, shooting at the soldiers standing on the bastions just as they were being shot at from the inside of the city.' It was much the same elsewhere in Lombardy: on 20 March about 2,000 armed peasants took over Lecco;[5] 'columns of armed peasants' marched on Como;[6] and Bergamo and other towns had similar experiences.[7] Charles Albert found the demonstrations of support for him in the countryside 'even more remarkable than those in the towns'.[8] More to the point, the peasantry persuaded thousands of their fellow peasants who were serving under Austrian colours to desert.[9]

Two factors were of paramount importance in determining the revolutionary role played by the peasants in 1848: their economic grievances and the priesthood. With regard to the first, of course, these differed considerably depending on which part of the country the peasants came from. Basically, however, they wanted 'free possession of land'.[10] In the mountain region they wanted restored to them most of all the *beni communali* which had been sold on the open market after 1839.[11] In the provinces of Como and Brescia they refused to pay tolls and taxes on food; and in areas of share-cropping they wanted to see the system extended.[12]

The influence of the priesthood was also strong, something which Radetzky had not failed to recognise since the priests were so clearly opposed to the army. There were, of course, some very good reasons for this. It had, for example, been the priesthood as well as the nobility which had been slaughtered in Galicia in 1846. About eighty priests had died in the Tarnow circle alone and this had led to Europe's most famous denunciation of Austrian conduct there – Montalambert's speech in the French Chamber on 2 July 1846.

---

* Notes to this chapter are on pp. 275–9.

This speech had been 'the protest of the Catholic world' and 'had stiffened the resolve of every Italian;' its religious overtones had 'separated the Catholic cause from the Austrian one in the public mind' in Italy.[13] More important, however, had been Radetzky's occupation of Ferrara – which had seemed like a declaration of war on Pius IX – and the clashes between the troops and the populace when Archbishop Romilli had entered Milan. The result was, as Radetzky put it,[14] 'the Italian clergy with few exceptions belong to our most open and dangerous enemies'. A minor official, echoing him, wrote:[15] 'Their priests are the promoters of these disorders, their priests are in touch with the first priest of Rome who is the revolutionary number one.'

Radetzky had been wise to remove his troops from the influence of the priesthood – he had ordered them to confess to army chaplains[16] only – for once the insurrection began, the 'enthusiastic participation of the clergy' served almost 'to confer the character of a holy war upon the insurrection of Milan'. At least 100 priests fought upon the barricades[17] and the poet Tasca included in his *Lettera del Croata* the lines:[18]

Petri e fratri in mezzo a balle
Sempre star con croce in mano
Pregar cielo per Taliano
E Tedesco maledir.

At first it was thought that special battalions might be formed from the priesthood to serve in the Lombard army.[19] This came to naught, but the provisional government employed priests as missionaries of patriotism with instructions to raise support, men and money for the national cause in areas of lesser enthusiasm.[20] While individual priests received letters of thanks for doing this, the Archbishop of Milan was praised for fulfilling a similar function on a national level: 'Aurum Ecclesia habet, non ut servet, sed ut eroget et subveniat in necessitatibus', he had told his priests and so got the Church to support the war effort.[21] The provisional government must also have appreciated his assurance that God would 'bless the holy work of liberation'[22] for they allowed unhindered communication between the Church in Lombardy and the Holy See.[23] Yet there was nothing cynical in this partnership between the Church and the emerging state. The latter's recognition of the 'spontaneous, generous and charitable work of the clergy in the liberation' was as patently sincere as the support it had been given.[24]

On the other hand, it had clearly never been the intention of the provisional government that the poor should inherit the earth. The priests, if necessary, had to tell the people that 'equality [did] not mean communism',[25] since the provisional government had no intention of undermining the landowning class to which it was so closely linked and in whose interest it was clearly determined to govern. Thus, although some steps were taken to alleviate the grievances of the peasantry – notably by lowering the price of salt – the excise tax remained, as did the capitation and the tithe.[26] Moreover, the 'weight of the war was made to fall principally upon the poorer sections of the people and on the bourgeoisie employed in industry and commerce, protecting the landed bourgeoisie and aristocracy as much as possible'.[27] Indeed the war finances of the Lombard government were so ordered that industry and commerce which accounted for less than one-fifth of the country's wealth was to contribute about one-third of the cost of the war; moreover, whereas some attempt was made to tax industry and commerce *progressively* there was never any question of introducing a *progressive* tax on land. The result was that the landowning aristocracy contributed in proportion to their wealth no more than the peasantry to the cost of the war.[28] The latter, exasperated meanwhile by falling prices and Piedmontese requisitioning in the countryside, were hardly drawn to the government's support so that when on 25 June the government made known its plans to call up those (between the ages of twenty-three and twenty-five) who were liable to conscription under the Austrian system as well as those between the ages of twenty-two and twenty-five who had already served under Austrian colours, the mood of the Lombard peasantry turned from one of disappointment to one of rejection.[29] From now on, the cry of 'Viva Radetzky!' could be heard around the countryside and Charles Albert – *il re dei signori* – and his generals found themselves in an increasingly hostile environment.[30] Around Monza the song could be heard:[31]

Viva Radetzky e viva Metternich
La forca ai sciori e viva i povaritt!

The Field Marshal himself was receiving *vivats* from peasants all along his route to Milan,[32] so that it is not surprising that by the time he reached the Lombard capital he believed that he could now begin a class war and win it. The circumstances of Charles Albert's departure did nothing to undermine this opinion.

Another score to settle

If the plan to arrest the leaders of the Milanese aristocracy in January 1848 had sadly misfired on account of the bungling of the local gubernium, Radetzky nevertheless retained his opinion that the original plan had been a sound one. When, therefore, at the end of April 1848, he had to take special care 'to safeguard [his] only remaining connexion with Vienna and the inner provinces of the Monarchy' from the possibility of an "insurrection" in Trent, he gave his full backing to Colonel Baron Zobel who had arrested four of the city's counts and had them transferred to Salzburg as hostages.[33] However, Count Brandis, the Governor of the South Tyrol was forced to release these counts after a deputation of their friends had taken up their case with the Ministry of the Interior, the latter body having found no grounds on which to hold them.[34] Brandis was furious. 'This principle', he wrote,[35] 'has cost us Lombardy and Venice.' Were the bureaucrats of Vienna all set to compound their error? Radetzky himself was none too pleased; he had just sent another thirteen 'dangerous men' from Verona to Innsbruck and told Zanini,[36] 'I hope that they shall not be sent back to Verona.' He had meanwhile taken up the case of the four counts with the Archduke John, who had been sent down to the South Tyrol to rally imperial support there. He wrote:[37] 'I know what I owe to the abandonment of this measure in Milan; this untimely forbearance led to the insurrection in Milan and the loss of Lombardy as well as to the unfortunate results in Venice. Shall we sit back quietly and watch these events repeat themselves in the South Tyrol?' He admitted quite frankly that he was not interested in any trial of the people who had been arrested – 'Whether there is written evidence against these individuals to warrant a trial for state or high treason I know not.'[38] In fact he thought that probably there was not. The evidence did not really matter as far as he was concerned:[39] 'It might be difficult to prove their guilt, but there can be no doubt that they are guilty.' What really worried the Field Marshal was the impression that would be created when the news was spread that the counts had been released. 'I shall be compromised', he wrote and the whole imperial position, he implied, would be compromised along with him.[40] And so he justified the use of 'extraordinary measures':[41] 'The position in which the uprising in Italy has placed us is of such a kind that extraordinary measures can be justified before the world. If it were not a matter of the highest and most sacred interests of the dynasty, of the integrity of the Monarchy, I would not object to legalities. But how can we limit ourselves to the law when our enemies employ every law against us and use means which have never before been used in war either in civil wars or in the Iberian Peninsula?' He continued: 'What has happened here is – I grant it – an attack on personal freedom, but what does this arbitrary action amount to in face of the means that are presently employed against us? An uprising is an uprising whether it is undertaken against a constitutional or an absolute monarchy. Every state has the right to take preventive measures against one.'

On 6 May the new War Minister, Latour, informed Radetzky that the four counts were to come to Vienna but that the thirteen others would be kept in Innsbruck.[42] By then, however, Radetzky, who had heard that the thirteen were to be released on their word of honour, had once again turned to the Archduke John whom he asked to suspend the relevant legal procedures. He warned him:[43] 'If I cannot secure the repeal of this measure, I owe it to myself, the German nation, my honour, the many remaining [faithful] subjects of His Majesty and the army, to make it known publicly that it is not I who have let them down along with their wives and children, and delivered them to the despotism of their enemies.' Latour, on 14 May, wrote from Vienna advising the Field Marshal that in future he would be well advised to keep those whom he regarded as particularly dangerous within his own custody.[44] Vienna was placing its faith in *Pacifikationswerke*. Radetzky, therefore, entered Milan not only in the conviction that the time was ripe to wage a class war against the Italian aristocracy; by this time he had yet another score to settle with them.

Radetzky's class war, 1848–1849

On 23 September 1848 Montecuccoli informed his subordinates, just as Radetzky was informing Latour, that the Lombard provinces could not be separated from 'their dependence on the military authorities even with respect to the civil government' and that 'in accordance with the decision taken by His Excellency Count Field Marshal Radetzky' he would take up his post as from 1 October 'at the Marshal's side and with his agreement'.[45] From 1 October, therefore, all documents relating to the civil administration of the provinces were to be sent to him as 'Imperial Commissioner Plenipotentiary *a lato del sig. Maresciallo Radetzky*'.[46]

That such a position was a contradiction in terms was made evident five days later when Count Pachta, now General Intendant of the Army, issued a proclamation informing the Italians that as from 1 October the General Intendancy of the Army as 'the institution of the supreme military government' would be in charge of matters relating to the police force, the postal services, employment in both these services, the gendarmerie, public security, passports, political events, etc. Moreover, it would continue to be in charge of matters relating to the accommodation, feeding and outfitting of the army.[47] In effect, therefore, Pachta became Civil Governor of Lombardy-Venetia, but since the whole country was under a state of siege and the army had to live off the land, this new arrangement was a fairly logical one. It was certainly not ambiguous: henceforth Radetzky and Pachta, not Montecuccoli, would run Lombardy-Venetia. The situation in which Montecuccoli found himself was described by the British Ambassador in Turin to Lord Palmerston:[48]

Count Montecuccoli is still in Milan, where he arrived to exercise the functions of a Civil Governor but the old Marshal has no idea of sharing power and he, therefore, distinctly states that since they will send him no money from Vienna he must get some for himself in a summary and military manner and that for such an object he has no cause for the aid of a civil governor and that consequently he intends to keep united in his own person the civil and military administrations of the Italian provinces. He, therefore, places Montecuccoli very gently on the shelf.

It should be remembered no doubt that Montecuccoli himself had given Radetzky permission to do this. On the other hand, the Commissioner had never expected that the Marshal would go so far.

Radetzky himself, according to one report, now 'assumed the tone and manner of a veritable sovereign'.[49] He occupied royal palaces – the royal villas at Milan and Monza – and surrounded himself with a splendid military court. He held great banquets and often did the sons of the former Archduke-Viceroy the honour of inviting them to dinner, on which occasions they sat on his right.[50] As for Pachta, very little is known about him, but none of it is good. On 2 October 1848, for example, Doblhoff, the then Minister of the Interior, wrote to Latour in connexion with a request from Radetzky that Pachta should be decorated. The Minister, for a number of reasons, was not disposed to accede to this request. Of Pachta's pre-March services to the Lombard government, he wrote:[51]

... It was known even then that, especially in the light of his position, the reprehensible and notorious disorder of his financial circumstances, the slanderous gossip which surrounded them, and the persistent disrespect in which he was commonly held, rendered his social position in the Kingdom of Lombardy-Venetia untenable. His Majesty, therefore, decided in 1838 to transfer him to Lemberg, which transfer, however, never took place and remained in fact *in suspenso* to await new orders from His Majesty, which orders were never given.

The Minister then quoted from a recent report which he had received from Montecuccoli:[52] 'Lombardy today', it ran,

remains under military rule and all government business is entrusted exclusively to the Army Intendant, Count Pachta. Count Pachta is only too well known for me to have to describe him in detail. If, on the one hand, one cannot gainsay his services to the army, it is only too certain, on the other, that he is in no way suited to head the administration of the country. Nothing but complaints are heard in this respect ... and [these] remove the confidence which we mean to win. I myself have come to Milan in order to speak to the Field Marshal on this subject.

Doblhoff apparently believed that Montecuccoli had succeeded in putting Pachta in his place, and therefore said no more about the man in relation to civil administration. But clearly he did not think much of him even as a 'clever Army Intendant' for he quoted Montecuccoli's verdict with approval, that 'up till now the [army's] needs have been covered by riotous requisitioning and the uncontrolled levying of taxes of all kinds on the municipalities'.[53] Pachta therefore failed to get his decoration,[54] but he was encouraged by Radetzky to continue his programme of requisitioning and super-taxes. The rationale behind this was both practical and ideological: practical in the sense that the army needed to maintain itself; ideological in the sense that it planned to do so by ruining the aristocracy. Radetzky's prejudices could now be given full vent and the army's solution to the Italian question could now be put into operation. It was General Hess, Radetzky's Chief of Staff, appropriately enough, who best summed up the military point of view. With reference to a proposed general amnesty, he replied:[55] 'Never. It would not accord with Austrian policy to pardon rebellious subjects. Their punishment must be, not death, but poverty. The people love us; the nobles, the rich landowners, hate us; we must, therefore, annihilate them.'

Radetzky began as he meant to go on. Pachta announced on 7 August that there would be no collection of outstanding taxes; on the same day it was also announced that the price of salt had been reduced and that the poll-tax had been abolished.[56] Reforms were made regarding stamp duty; other taxes were suspended; and the old *tassa di navigazione* paid at the Porta Ticinese later disappeared.[57] On 15 August 1848, the city's priests were urged to undertake charity work in aid of the poor and on 27 October, Montecuccoli announced the establishment of an 'Extraordinary Commission for Public Relief'[58] whose 'only task [would] be to provide the greatest possible relief of poverty, need and infirmity amongst the poor and unfortunate of the city of Milan and the Corpi Santi and to do so either by means of subventions of money, bread, firewood, etc. or through useful occupations as well as by shelter in charitable institutions in accordance with the respective statutes'. The introduction to this proclamation was thoroughly propagandistic and echoed a previous effort of the Commissioner's published on 17 August which had been positively gushing:[59]

Italians of the Kingdom of Lombardy-Venetia! See what Austria is doing for you! She does it at a time when her valiant armies disperse as dust those who misled you by taking advantage of your credulity; when her victories signal her re-establishment in the splendour of her might. But she has no use for this might but to make you happy. Already she has spontaneously released you from considerable debts and several million livres of rent, not only to the profit of the less well-off but to the advantage of all in order to soften as much as possible the evils created by a war which she certainly did not provoke.

The rich, on the other hand, had no cause to be grateful. With Radetzky's entry into Milan, the homes of the most distinguished families were converted into barracks:[60] the army's headquarters were in the Palace Litta; the Palace Borromeo was made into a hospital. In the house of the Marquis Trivulzio precious archives were thrown into the courtyard to make room for soldiers; soldiers, too, were lodged in the Institute for Young Noble Ladies; the homes of the Marchioness Buscha and the Duchess Serbelloni were turned into barracks; and the houses of the families of Belgiojoso and Uboldi were ransacked for arms on account of the arms museum there. Pillage and plunder took place everywhere.

Radetzky must have taken great pleasure in all this. In June he had written to Latour from Verona saying that he had employed the threat to sequestrate and pillage 'in order to prevent the exit in droves of the rich inhabitants from the cities'.[61] after October 1848, he could carry out his threats while they were still there. Abercromby once again described how the system was operating:[62] 'Marshal Radetzky', he wrote,

can get no money from Vienna for the current expense of the Austrian army in Italy. He is, therefore, obliged to raise it in the Italian provinces and a new contribution for the month of October of 8 centimes upon the *rente fonciere* has just been imposed upon Lombardy. This last contribution makes a total of 19 centimes raised since the return of the Austrians. The amount of the usual yearly contribution, or the *rente fonciere* is about 18 centimes, so that they will have raised a whole year's contribution in the space of a few weeks. This practice coming after the squeezing of the Provisional Government, comes pretty hard upon the Lombards. There is this, however, to be said in defence of the measure, that it will relieve the peasants and rural inhabitants from paying contributions in kind for the supply of the army, the money now to be raised being applied to the payment of contracts entered into for the provisioning of the troops.

Radetzky, in other words, was aiming to squeeze the landowners in order to secure the money with which to pay the peasants to feed his army of occupation. However, if the Ambassador believed that the Field Marshal's motive were more practical then ideological, he was making a mistake. On 24 November, the British Vice-Consul in Milan drew up for Palmerston a statement of the sums raised by Radetzky since he had reoccupied the city:[63] the total amount was 31,836,000 Austrian livres, or upwards of £1,060,000 for two months.[64] The Vice-Consul commented:[65]

It may be proper here to observe that the ordinary predial tax is about 3.5 per cent. Since the return of the Austrians it has amounted from the imposition of extra taxes to about 8 per cent. This is independent of the communal tax, amounting generally to 2 per cent which is applied for the support of public schools, the repair of roads, bridges, etc. I learn from undoubted authority that the extra taxes in the communes where soldiers are now quartered amount to 20 per cent, which together with the ordinary predial tax makes in all 23.5 per cent on landed property. This does not include the large contributions which have been raised on the many insurgent districts as a punishment.

Even this, however, was not enough to maintain the Austrian army. On 5 December Montecuccoli announced that the cost of keeping it between 1 October and 31 December would amount to 18 million livres; but since the ordinary extra tax would produce only 16.5 million livres, there would be a deficit for 1848 alone of 1.5 million livres.[66] The army was thus costing an extra 72 million livres per annum over and above the 44 million livres collected from the land-tax. In December, therefore, another 6.5 per cent of 32 centimes per scudo for the 266,000,300 scudi or 1,130,000 Austrian livres of landed property was levied in Lombardy-Venetia, so that by the end of 1848 the tax on landed property had reached 30 per cent in a period of five months, whereas it had previously stood at 3.5 per cent over a year.

Finally, in order to ensure that landowners or property-owners did not recoup any of this loss from tenants or leaseholders, the Field Marshal issued the following proclamation which served to clarify his thinking:[87]

In keeping with the orders emanating from His Excellency Field Marshal Count Radetzky, all extraordinary super-taxes on land or of any other kind, decreed or still to be decreed, for the purposes of the army are not to be levied on lease-holders or tenants but are to be borne by proprietors alone, irrespective of any agreement or contract whatever which may exist between the said lease-holders and tenants and their respective proprietors.

All in all, between October 1848 and March 1849, Austria raised from Lombardy no less than 65 million livres in order to maintain her army there[68] – and most of that money came from the landowning classes.

Radetzky's proclamation of 11 November 1848

The imperial manifesto of 20 September with its armistice and a promise of liberal institutions for Lombardy-Venetia within the Austrian Empire signally failed to impress educated Italians; they did not wish to remain within the Empire; they resented that the document had first been published in Vienna; they were more impressed by the daily realities of military rule; and the amnesty they interpreted to cover only the period since March 1848.[69] On 11 November, however, a proclamation was published under Radetzky's signature which really made them sit up and take notice. It read:[70]

Since by the valour of my soldiers I have restored these provinces of the Lombard-Venetian Kingdom to their legitimate sovereign, it has been my chief care to establish order so that by the security of person and property, public confidence should be resumed, trade should be revived and families should be in the enjoyment of that tranquillity which the government of His Majesty, our Emperor and King, has always maintained and secured in so long a course of years.

But it is not less my duty to obtain an indemnification for the serious public and private injuries resulting from the revolution and the war injuries which were caused by the most active promoters of the former as well as by those who by their aid and means contributed to the same; and so much the more since many of them, paying no attention to the pardon which His Majesty, in his inexhaustible clemency has vouchsafed to grant to his rebellious subjects, continue to remain abroad, employing there the production of this country in other revolutionary acts and *bringing the class of workmen and labourers of these provinces to (that) distress and misery, against which it must be my care to provide.*

Having reflected that the dictates of humanity, justice and equity demand that the innocent shall not suffer with the guilty, that the deceived shall be treated with greater mildness than the deceiver, and *particularly that the honest trader, the peaceful artisan, the peasant and the labourer, who generally, not of their own impulse but by a blind concession to the force of circumstances, bore a part in the political disturbances, should be treated with every possible consideration;*
I have resolved that extraordinary contributions shall be demanded from

1. The members of the late Provisional Government;
2. Those who took a principal part in the so-called Comitati;

3. Those who have placed themselves at the head of the Revolution, or who have aided in it by their acts or with their material or intellectual means.

The proclamation did not end there. It went on to say that the fortunes of those involved would be duly assessed and that an individual sum would be demanded from them by way of indemnification to the army, which sum would have to be paid in full to the 'respective military chest' within six weeks. Otherwise:[71]

At the expiration of the above term the goods of the party called upon shall be placed under sequestration and guardianship in the most ready way in order that from the profits of the goods and the sale and the produce of the same, payment may be made of the amount assessed; and those goods also shall be seized which each contributor possessed on the 18th day of March last, without regard to any alienation of or claim to the same which may date after that period.

From these contributions, when paid, *succour shall be given to those in need,* in the mode and to the amount which shall hereafter be determined.

The proclamation contained all the essential elements of the Austrian army's thinking in regard to Lombardy-Venetia. It was an open declaration that their version of the class war, their particular solution to the Italian question, was about to enter its final phase. Or so it was hoped.

The proclamation, not surprisingly, provoked reactions of astonishment from almost every quarter of every establishment, save the military one. 'You will be shocked with the open way in which Radetzky endeavours to rouse the passions of the lowest orders against the rich and preaches the purest doctrines of Communism and Socialism', wrote Abercromby to Palmerston,[72] and just in case he was not, the Ambassador took the unusual step of writing officially to the British Prime Minister informing him of the proclamation in much the same terms but reminding him of Austrian behaviour in the past:[73] 'The decree contains', he wrote, ' . . . the expression of such an odious principle, the stirring up of the passions of the poor against the rich, that with the example of the policy adopted by Austria of late in Galicia before their eyes, the unfortunate proprietors of Lombardy are naturally painfully alarmed.' In short, he concluded 'it was hardly possible to have devised a measure better calculated to enable the Marshal to work the ruin of the aristocracy of Lombardy, if such should be his will, than the one he has now published.'

Palmerston *was* shocked. The proclamation, he claimed, had been concerned 'in the spirit of the most odious oppression and enunciated by doctrine which belong[ed] only to the disciples of Communism and which [were] subversive of the very foundations of social order'.[74] Nor was his reaction in any way exaggerated, for the Field Marshal had issued along with his proclamation a list of over 200 persons and the contributions demanded of them.[75] The list, predictably, was more or less a roll-call of the Milanese aristocracy – husbands, wives and children were all severally assessed – and each of those appearing on the list was fined at sums which ranged from 20,000 to 1,000,000 livres. The only conclusion that anyone could draw from this was that Radetzky must indeed be aiming to 'annihilate' the Italian aristocracy. He would certainly 'impoverish' them, for the sums he was asking for amounted to hundreds of millions of livres. The Consulta Lombarda, the name given to the provisional government now in exile in Sardinia, could argue persuasively that if the scheme were ever carried through not only the aristocracy would meet with ruin; Lombardy-Venetia would be so starved of specie that irrespective of whatever effects were suffered by the land market the country as a whole would also be ruined since trade and commerce would come to a stop.[76]

According to Metzburg,[77] the proclamation was the third edition of one which the Field Marshal had hoped to publish at the beginning of October. The publication of the imperial manifesto at that time, however, had pre-empted him from doing so – hence his anger when he heard the news. But after the suppression of the Vienna revolution, the subject of an extraordinary war-tax was once again aired and Radetzky told Montecuccoli that he had been empowered to levy it. The latter apparently had made no objection but had drafted a proclamation, the terms of which in no way conflicted with the Emperor's pardon – the tax, in short, was to be levied only on those who intended to remain in exile and would not profit from the manifesto. The Field Marshal, however, had disliked this plan and on 11 November had published his own proclamation, which in Metzburg's opinion went so far beyond what Montecuccoli had had in mind that it represented a 'repudiation of the intention of His Majesty'.

Montecuccoli was of the same opinion and, after he had read the Field Marshal's proclamation led a deputation to Radetzky's headquarters to protest at what had happened.[78] The deputation, which included the new Mayor of Milan, Count Bassi – Casati's brother-in-law – as well as several others who were in obvious danger of being themselves proscribed and which was led by a man whom the Marshal had understood to have agreed to his measures, was guaranteed an unfriendly reception. Moreover, the extraordinarily lengthy and thorough legal analysis of the measure by Hofrat Pederzani, which the deputation brought along with it and which maintained that the tax was unjustifiable either as a tax or a compensatory measure or even as a preventive measure – quite apart from the fact that it contradicted the imperial manifesto – was likewise calculated to upset Radetzky who, needless to say, was furious but unconvinced. Writing to Wessenberg after the interview he informed him that with the natural exception of those involved, the measure had 'in general been favourably received' and that it had been 'all the more surprising, therefore, to encounter opposition where [he] least expected it'.[79] Montecuccoli, according to Radetzky, had 'suddenly altered' the views which he had 'previously expressed to him both in speech and writing'.[80]

Radetzky had not attempted to give a detailed or legal refutation of the views which had been presented to him. He merely pointed out that nobody was paying any attention to the imperial amnesty; that Montecuccoli himself complained continually that the income of the land could not support the army; and that the truth of the proposition that those most guilty for the war should be made to pay for it was so self-evident as not to warrant argument. He also told Wessenberg:[81]

With my usual military frankness, I cannot conceal it from Your Excellency that the only-too-evident striving after popularity on all occasions of Count Montecuccoli, who become ad latus to me as a result of my initiative, very much impedes my work here, while the Italian party inside and outside the country which is opposed to it, fastens on to [his] too publicly known opposition, so that all sorts of obstacles arise which can only have the most disadvantageous results for the good of the imperial service.

On 17 November, Radetzky received a plea from the city of Milan imploring him to rescind the measures he had taken. He replied that he could not 'at the present moment either withdraw or suspend the execution of the orders given'.[82] Next day, a conference was held attended by himself, Montecuccoli, Marzani, Metzburg, as well as Hofrat Pederzani who at great length persuaded the Field Marshal that his measures were of doubtful legality.[83] The decision arrived at by this meeting, therefore, was 'to uphold the 20 September amnesty unaltered' and to apply 'well-deserved punishment' to those who persisted in opposing the regime from abroad. It was hardly a compromise. Radetzky had backed down.

The Field Marshal extracted himself from the position in which he was now placed at the cost of much embarrassment. On 23 November, a poster – or rather, very few copies of a poster – went up in Milan, some of which were signed by the Military Governor of the city, Count Wimpffen. The Governor explained that since the 11th of the month 'alarming and unfounded doubts' had arisen in the public mind 'as to the application of the relative determinations' of the Field Marshal's proclamation.[84] He had, therefore, been instructed to inform the people that (*a*) those who were abroad with official permission and who did not oppose the government; (*b*) those who had remained in Lombardy but were now behaving with political propriety; as well as (*c*) those who had returned from abroad in accordance with the amnesty arrangements, would not come under the terms of the war-tax. The latter would be applied to two groups only, namely those who had remained abroad to oppose the government and those who continued to oppose the government from inside the Monarchy itself.

This proclamation was not, in fact, the end of a problem but the beginning of a new one, as the military authorities forced the civil ones to take a stand on the question of the emigration. The whole affair, however, had led Montecuccoli to despair completely of military rule and he complained to Wessenberg:[85] 'It is high time that a complete end was put to [their] interference in administrative business; I should have no objection even in the present condition of the country to fully restoring the civil administration, especially, as is the case here, where there is a large army ready at its side to lend support.' The imperial Commissioner, however, was to receive no support from Vienna for this proposal. On the very same day that he had written to Wessenberg, the latter had been replaced as Prime Minister by Prince Felix zu Schwarzenberg.

The year 1849

Schwarzenberg's government was approved by the Emperor Ferdinand on 21 November 1848. On 27 November the new Ministry published its programme and on 2 December the new Emperor Franz Josef ascended the throne. He, too, approved the government's programme, one point of which read:[86] 'With the re-establishment of peace, the Kingdom of Lombardy-Venetia will find in its organic union with constitutional Austria the best guarantee of its nationality. The advisers responsible to the Crown . . . hope that in the not too distant future the Italian people, too, shall enjoy the benefits of a constitution which must unite all the different races by the absolute similarity of their rights.' What Schwarzenberg meant by this is not absolutely clear. He was probably hoping that a few Italians would participate in the Kremsier Reichstag, thus showing the world at large that Lombardy-Venetia still wanted to be integrated into the Habsburg Monarchy. There is no reason to believe, however, that he ever intended to take the Kremsier Reichstag seriously. In any case, the Italians themselves had no intention of falling in with his plans so that when Montecuccoli on 3 January 1849 requested the provincial congregations of Lombardy-Venetia to send deputies to Kremsier[87] in order that the imperial government might 'profit by their advice' the vast majority of the Congregations – seventeen out of nineteen – refused to comply with the request, the deputies of the Provincial Congregation of Milan declaring that they would never willingly send representatives to Austria.[88] Austrian sensitivity had hardly been demonstrated by issuing the invitation on the anniversary of the Tobacco Riots; moreover, while the Milanese were wearing mourning, Radetzky was holding a magnificent ball at the Theatre della Scala.[89]

The Austrians were none too pleased, however, at this rebuff which Metzburg explained away by saying that nothing could be done 'as long as the inhabitants of this land continue[d] to believe that Austria (was) only in temporary possession of the Kingdom of Lombardy-Venetia'.[90] More ominously, he believed that the imperial programme had been thwarted by the emigration, the activities of which were responsible for sustaining the inhabitants' over-optimistic views of their political prospects. Field Marshal Radetzky, of course, wholeheartedly agreed with him.[91]

Towards the end of 1848, the Lombard emigration had been getting 'seriously alarmed as to the fate of their properties.'[92] The effect of Radetzky's decree, in Abercromby's words, had been to give him 'an opportunity of breaking down for ever the power and influence of the nobles' and no one seriously expected him to refrain from using it.[93] On 30 December he confirmed how right they were:[94] a proclamation was issued which demanded that all emigrants 'whose complicity in the revolution' was not 'notorious' should return to Lombardy-Venetia by the end of January 1849. Since the Marshal failed to provide any definition of 'notorious complicity' the inevitable result was that nobody returned. By the end of January 1849, therefore, arrangements had been made to put Radetzky's schemes into operation and on 20 January he sent 'very urgent' orders to communal deputations by which they were instructed to 'transmit to him a list of individuals absent abroad without a legal passport but who possess[ed] property worth more than 10,000 livres annually, along with notes on those individuals amongst these who since the amnesty of 20 September [had] been guilty of crimes of high treason or [had] abetted such crimes either by material or intellectual means'.[95] In this way, the Italians were themselves given the unpleasant task of drawing up the lists of those properties which would be sequestrated. The overall supervision of this enterprise, however, was entrusted by the Marshal to a Commission headed by Count Wohlgemuth, now Military Governor of Milan, and by 31 January the first list had appeared containing twenty-three names of individuals whose total fines amounted to 5,770,000 livres and whose agents soon received letters on their behalf which ran:[96] 'As notwithstanding the letter of —— which intimated your being fined the sum of —— you have allowed the term to elapse for the payment thereof; notice is hereby given to you that Signor —— is appointed to proceed to the necessary acts in order to obtain the said payment.'

If personal property was insufficient to cover the sums due, the agents of the military government received positive orders to sell a portion of the landed property and indeed, the whole, if necessary, to make up the amount.[97]

The Commission, however, got off to a shaky start – almost all of its Italian members refused to serve and were prevailed upon to do so only by the threat of facing 'a council of war as in times of war'.[98] Signor Ratti, on the other hand, the only Italian who had actually agreed to serve, came under pressure of a different kind – his effigy was found hanging by the neck near his home with the words pinned on it, 'this time in effigy only, another time in reality'.[99] The opposition to the Commissions – there was one for both Lombardy and Venetia – grew so intense that Radetzky himself was forced to issue a special proclamation before the end of February which ended with these instructions:[100]

That whatever shall be ordered by [the sequestration commissions] must be carried out and attended to impartially; that the engineers elected by the said Commissioners as trustees are bound to accept this office under heavy punishment in case of refusal, unless they be dispensed with on just grounds; that whoever may throw obstacles in the operations of the trustees or insult them, shall be dealt with according to martial law; that [in the case] of any plots whatever against the execution of the ordered sequestrations, the inhabitants of the place where such may be perpetrated shall be held responsible, unless they have by every means endeavoured to prevent them, and unless the authors thereof have been immediately denounced to the authorities and published accordingly; that whoever are or may be debtors for whatever title or cause towards those subject to the contribution are hereby warned to continue the payment of their debts during the sequestration only into the hands of the trustees, under the penalty of paying double; and that all military commandants and all civil authorities are bound to afford the trustees whatever assistance they may require.

Nevertheless it was due to practical difficulties – largely the non-cooperation of Italians inside and outside the administration – that the Commissions failed to get off the ground before they were overtaken by events in the shape of the second war with Sardinia.

In the negotiations at the end of that war, the British and the French tried hard to get the Austrian military authorities to change their policies with respect to the emigration and the sequestrations, but it was to no avail. Abercromby told Palmerston:[101] 'We found General Hess to be imbued with opinions and sentiments most hostile towards the Upper Classes of the Lombards and those who took part in the late revolutionary movement in Lombardy. His language was both harsh and uncompromising and plainly showed that in his opinion the only way of governing Lombardy was by ruling it with a rod of iron and by completely renouncing all attempts to conciliate or gain the good will of the Italians.' He continued: 'The General put forward the old and hackneyed argument for the exercise of severe measures that it was necessary to prove to the inferior classes of society that those in the upper grades were also subjected to punishment when guilty of any fault and he would not admit that it would be expedient, where emigration had been carried on to so great an extent as had been the case in Lombardy, to adopt a course of conciliation and pardon.'

Radetzky himself was of exactly the same opinion, convinced even that Haynau's notorious treatment of the city of Brescia was in no way unwarranted.[102] His general attitude was communicated to Schwarzenberg in a letter of 13 April. He wrote:[103]

. . . I am thoroughly convinced that it is high time to stop bestowing favours on a country which all too often abuses them; that it is much more necessary and imperative to let the country feel the punitive hand of its mighty and much offended lord, since everyone knows that the Italians fear a strict but just ruler and will do his bidding, while they abuse and despise a good and indulgent one.

In my opinion this wantonly wealthy land can only be punished most severely by the removal of those means which have seduced it into obstinacy and disobedience, for what is exile to the rich if they can take their money abroad and use it to create more trouble?

To humble the refractory rich, to protect the loyal citizen, but *in particular to exalt the poorer classes of the peasantry as in Galicia*, should be the principle on which from now on the government in Lombardy-Venetia should be based.

I am firmly convinced that directly after the conclusion of a peace or as things become absolutely hopeless for the revolutionary party, ringleaders like Casati and Borromeo and others, as well as the greatest part of those who have experienced punitive justice, will petition for clemency regarding their flight and that the government shall smother them in it. The aim of my present letter is, therefore, to beseech Your Excellency beforehand, to set aside any futile clemency and let justice run its course completely, that is, even with regard to the rich aristocracy and the larger cities, who have sinned so severely against the imperial, royal government.

A few days later, on 17 April, Radetzky issued another proclamation which gave notice that all fines which had not already been paid would have to be paid by 1 May 1849;[104] on 3 May he refused to pass on to Franz Josef a petition from the city of Milan which requested a return to normal civil government, maintaining that the tenor of the petition was not 'in his opinion, sufficiently respectful'. The Commission under Wohlgemuth, however, never ever emerged from its bureaucratic morass; it was still encountering the most determined resistance from all Italians; there was probably also some resistance from Vienna; but most important, Radetzky's attention was primarily fixed on the possibility of renewed hostilities with Piedmont.

The Field Marshal's next move was delayed until 12 August when another proclamation of his excluded from the amnesty thirty-two *émigrés* from the province of Milan and fifty-four others from the rest of Lombardy-Venetia.[105] These included all the 'big names' – Borromeo, Casati, Litta, Rosales, Belgiojoso, Pallavicini – and even Count Marco Greppi, who had returned to Milan to profit from the amnesty, had to flee a second time to escape the consequences of his confidence.[106] The proclamation could, nevertheless, state that 'several of those who had removed themselves from the country [had] already returned to the Kingdom without having in any way been harassed'. But a warning was given to those who did return that if they were subsequently held to have involved themselves in any trouble, they would be liable to the full penalty of military law. Events inside the kingdom in any case were in no way encouraging for anyone who was contemplating a return; more blood was spilt on the occasion of the Emperor's birthday on 18 August; and when Venice was retaken on 22 August, fifteen traders were caned in public and fourteen nobles and merchants were condemned to imprisonment in irons.[107]

Montecuccoli, meanwhile, was trying to put a stop to all this and on 20 September he went so far as to publish a letter patent increasing the land tax by 50 per cent over its 1848 value, but at the same time promising in return that both military requisitioning and the levying of extraordinary taxes would come to an end.[108] He even promised compensation for property damaged in the course of the war. However, the military took no notice of him, and a few days after these promises had been posted up throughout the country, Mantua had an extraordinary tax of 400,000 livres imposed upon it and Brescia, which had already been milked of 6,500,000, one of 90,000.[109]

Between 8 September and 21 October Radetzky visited Vienna and rumours began to spread that the war would once and for all be regarded as over and that there would at last be a return to civil government. The Field Marshal himself added credence to these rumours by publishing on his return a proclamation which informed the Italians that the Emperor had agreed to a 'provisional' reorganisation of the administration along lines which would accord 'with the principles of the constitution and the needs of the country'.[110] All this, in fact, meant only that the civil and political administration of the country was being put under a civil and military governor who would be responsible to the Ministry in Vienna and that the administration would be divided into two independent departments, one for civil and one for military affairs. However, since Radetzky himself was given the top job, the Italians were hardly impressed by the new arrangements. Nor, in fact, did these do much for Montecuccoli; it is true that he was put in charge of the civil department, but he was given Radetzky's son-in-law, Michael Strassoldo as his deputy. Pachta, on the other hand, was retired on a pension of 4,000 fl. and the General Intendancy of the Army was at last dissolved; yet all in all, the new arrangements constituted a prime example of 'plus ça change, plus c'est la même chose'.[111]

The Field Marshal and the peasants

Radetzky's relations with the Lombard-Venetian peasantry depended primarily on his treatment of two groups of men – the deserters from his Italian regiments and the peasant youths who were liable to conscription. If he wanted to win over the peasantry for Austria, he needed to be exceedingly delicate in his handling of the Italian troops of the Austrian army. However, despite the fact that the Field Marshal was very aware of the issue involved, the Austrian had no more success with the peasants than had the provisional government.

Radetzky tried hard to win the confidence of the rural population. On 3 September 1848 he issued a general pardon to all troops from the rank of sergeant downwards who had deserted from the colours or who had fought for the enemy after 18 March, so long as they were guilty of no other crimes.[112] Their military record or length of service, he promised them, would in no way be affected if they gave themselves up within three weeks; if they could legally prove that this was impossible, the period of grace was extended to two months. The pardon, in fact, was prolonged from time to time so that it covered more or less the whole of the period up to March 1851.[113]

Latour and Radetzky had been pressing the Emperor to accept such a policy since the reoccupation of Milan, and on 8 August the Field Marshal had granted an amnesty to those in the countryside who would surrender their arms.[114] The War Minister and the Field Marshal had also been concerned to reward in some tangible fashion the Italian troops who had remained loyal to the Emperor so that on 9 September, Latour had suggested to Ferdinand[115] that two years be subtracted from the 'capitulation'[116] of those who had served in Italy and that one year should likewise be deducted for those who had served elsewhere in the Monarchy. Such a move, he wrote, would 'have to have the most advantageous effect in the countryside as well as amongst the persons concerned'. He then wrote to Radetzky predicting with confidence that his advice would be accepted and advising the Field Marshal to send home on leave the deserters who had meantime returned to their regiments.[117] On 8 August, meanwhile, Prince Felix zu Schwarzenberg, then Military Governor of Milan, had scotched a rumour of an impending call-up with the words, 'the Austrian government does not require such a levy, which [in any case] it never had the least intention of proposing',[118] so that altogether, it appeared that the Austrian military authorities were displaying unusual wisdom in their policy decisions.

Yet things began to go awry. By 27 September Radetzky was informing Latour that the measures taken had 'aroused the greatest discontent amongst the Italian soldiers who [had] remained loyal' and was pleading for quick remedial action. Indeed:[119] 'The position of the officers with the Italian troops, which up till now has been most uncomfortable, will from now on, with respect to the good but highly discontented troops, became almost untenable. It is even to be feared that many of those who have up till now remained loyal, will desert the colours at the first favourable opportunity, calculating that not punishment but leave will follow treason once committed.' The Field Marshal continued:[120]

The granting of leave to soldiers who deserted has made a totally bad impression in the countryside. The calling-in [i.e. of deserters] was generally approved and the moderation shown thereby was appreciated. People, recognize, however, that the calling-in is useful precisely because many breadless persons are constrained from wandering around the countryside and living off others in every way. In a country where order has not yet been restored, one cannot discover who is without means of support and many prefer to rob than to submit to our strict discipline or else they turn to the first possible troublemaker for greater freedom and more money. I do not know what reasons have motivated Your Excellency to adopt the measure in question, but I can only hope that the arrangements which I shall execute immediately regarding this matter, will not conflict with Your Excellency's intention.

Radetzky intended to publish a proclamation to his Italian troops stating that with regard to leave, first preference would be given to those who had participated in the campaigns and who were needed at home; second preference would go to newly enlisting men from poor families; and only then would the deserters be considered and only in so far as leave would be given to those 'who were disloyal [but] who [could not] be usefully employed with the troops until further arrangements [could] be made'.[121] Radetzky ended his proclamation:[122] 'I take this opportunity to make known to the Italian troops who remained loyal that I have already beseeched the Ministry of War in a report on all present arrangements to give appropriate recognition to your fidelity and dutiful devotion to His Majesty, Our Emperor.' However, Latour's advice to the Emperor was not accepted and the War Minister, therefore, objected to Radetzky's plans to reorganise the Italian regiments. He replied to the Field Marshal stating,[123] 'we are not yet certain in which form we shall retain the provinces, far less – and the question of military service is relevant here – are we able to proceed to determining their internal administration'. There was also the possibility that hostilities might break out once again with Piedmont and in such an eventuality 'half-organized native troop detachments made up of unreliable men . . . would only add to all [our] difficulties'. Latour, however, was prepared to accept a compromise. His previous despatch, he wrote, did not exclude 'the gradual granting of leave to the loyal Italian troops and their replacement by the enlistment of those who [had] registered under the General Pardon'. The main point was simply that care should be taken to ensure that if leave was granted to loyal troops, those who remained should still outnumber the former deserters in any regiment. In this way the War Minister hoped to dispel the 'evil impression' that the loyal were being punished and the faithless rewarded.

However, for reasons which are not altogether clear, the Field Marshal did not publish any plans in this regard until February 1849. Meanwhile, as Italians became ever more convinced that conscription would be reimposed, unrest in the countryside intensified and the Austrians were forced to take special measures to halt the flight of thousands of peasant youths towards the borders of Switzerland and Piedmont. Campbell reported to Palmerston on 26 January 1849 that military cordons surrounded the borders of the kingdom, adding:[124] 'An emigration of the Lombard peasants into Switzerland and Piedmont has for some time past been going on but it has lately increased to such an extent that in the provinces of Brescia, Sondrio and Como, the military commandants in those quarters have made the communes and the heads of families responsible under the penalty of fine and imprisonment for those who leave their respective communes for other states without permission.'

One cause for the growing unrest was the fact that between 16 November and 23 January arrangements had been instituted to compile a list of those eligible for conscription among those born between 1824 and 1828.[125] The Military Governor of Milan on 23 January 1849 had informed the Lombards that this was 'in fact only an administrative measure' and that the story that it was a preliminary to conscription was 'the work of evil-minded persons who [wanted] to render the people apprehensive and fearful';[126] but his powers of persuasion proved less than irresistible. By mid-February, in any case, Radetzky himself appeared to have saved the situation. The local authorities were made to publish a proclamation which promised that 'no levy [would] be imposed this year on the Lombardo-Venetian Kingdom'[127] while the Field Marshal himself in a proclamation dated 9 February but published on 17 February instituted new arrangements to bring his army up to strength by incorporating elements of the plans which he had previously discussed with Latour.[128] Thus company strength among the loyal Italian regiments was to be fixed at a nominal 140 men, but in practice would remain at 120 since 20 men in each company would be allowed to go on what appears to have been meant as indefinite leave. Moreover,[129] 'These 20 men shall be chosen from those who participated in the campaign and who have conducted themselves well. Special consideration shall be given to those soldiers who belong to poor families and can help them with their work. I repeat, that these 20 men shall be entirely freed from the obligations of military service.'

Radetzky promised similar treatment for the other troops who had remained loyal if circumstances should permit. In the meantime, he once more called upon deserters to return to their colours, providing them this time with the incentive of knowing that if they did not their families or the local commune would have to provide a substitute who would serve out the remaining period of their capitulation. The results were promising:[130] 'On the faith of these repeated assurances that no extraordinary levy would be made [that] year, the greater part of the deserters from the army gave themselves up and rejoined their regiments while most of the emigrant peasants returned to their families.' Yet the Field Marshal was still not satisfied and in his determination to account for every man who had deserted either by having him return or by securing a substitute on 10 March he had the delegations set up local 'conscription committees' to compile lists of the 1824–8 conscription classes in order to discover which youths were liable to be called up as substitutes.[131] This meant, of course, that the whole bureaucratic procedure of a normal levy had to be carried through, and to get it over with as quickly as possible the authorities were told on 29 April that the process should be completed – even to the extent of having transferred the substitutes to the army – by 20 May. Not unnaturally, this created the impression in the minds of the Lombards that the army was deceiving them and Campbell reported to Palmerston on 7 May[132] that

the indignation among the people chiefly among the peasantry, at the gross breach of good faith on the part of the Austrian Government is such that I greatly fear there will be some serious outbreak shortly. I can assure Your Lordship that there is not a village large or small in Lombardy where symptoms of this indignation have not manifested themselves. In many the authorities could not even cause the usual official notices to be posted up. In others the curate and the local authorities were prevented by proceeding in the drawing [i.e. of lots to determine those liable to be substitutes] by the threatening attitude of the peasantry.

On 9 May, therefore, the local authorities suspended these measures and on the following day Radetzky 'completely annul[led] all ordinances on this matter' arguing that his intentions had been thoroughly misunderstood.[133] On 22 May he issued a proclamation in which he let it be known that since most deserters had returned anyway, all previous regulations relating to the families and communes of deserters would cease to have effect from 1 June and that the Italian regiments would henceforth be brought up to strength 'in the usual way' – i.e. 'when it shall please His Majesty to order a new levy'.[134]

Radetzky, despite all his calculations, therefore, had hardly succeeded in winning the affection of the Italian peasantry. Moreover, since most of the poor, whether in town or country, were in some way dependent on the prosperity of the landowning and commercial classes for their livelihoods in any case, his policies towards the upper classes were ultimately destined to alienate the majority of the population. His strategy, in short, came close to killing the Italian golden geese. On 26 January Abercromby had sent Palmerston a report on the situation which, although composed only at the start of the year, can be taken as a prescient description of social developments in Lombardy-Venetia over the course of the following months. He wrote:[135]

It is the policy of the Austrians to declare openly that only one class of their Italian subjects, namely the nobles, are really disaffected towards them and that the measures which have been adopted are calculated only to break the spirit of the revolt in that portion of the population, and to enable them to confer that happiness and contentment upon the rest of the inhabitants which it is asserted they are perfectly ready to receive at the hands of their Austrian rulers.

The information which I have received leads me to form a totally different conclusion. From the reports which have been made to me by persons who have had the opportunity of studying this point I believe that one feeling of deep-rooted hatred of the Austrian name pervades the minds of every man, woman and child throughout Lombardy; and that this feeling has immeasurably increased since the reoccupation of her provinces. . . . The people may be kept down by force of arms and military despotism, but Austria will not obtain the affections of the inhabitants or render the Lombard Provinces a source of wealth or power to the Imperial Crown.

The final try

In Vienna, Radetzky, it would appear, secured the full backing for his policies of Schwarzenberg, who after 1849 gave him a pretty free hand in running the internal affairs of Lombardy-Venetia.[136] Certainly the Minister President shared the Field Marshal's views on the question of the emigration, for when the Sardinian government raised the issue on 26 November 1849, he took a very firm stand behind his former chief.[137]

The question raised by the Sardinian government was the exact legal status of three Lombard exiles, Raffi, Caulini and Caldirola. This initial enquiry, however, was brushed aside by Vienna with the advice that, although the amnesty had now expired, individual petitions might still be submitted to Radetzky. The Sardinians, on the other hand, were determined to force the issue and thus Schwarzenberg, who, as it happened, had just received a report on the matter, was informed from Turin, that a special envoy, General Dabormida, would visit Radetzky to take up the matter on a general level. The Minister President was none too pleased. He forecast in a letter to his Ambassador in Turin that Dabormida would 'secure no modification' in the system 'which the Marshal [had] followed up till [then]' with regard to the emigration.[138] In any case, in order to thwart the Sardinian envoy, he had already taken the trouble of writing to Radetzky to 'beseech' him 'to stick to the system already adopted',[139] explaining:[140] 'The course which the Sardinian government plans to follow seems fairly clear to me. It intends to get rid of the greatest number of the Lombard refugees who belong to the poorer classes as quickly as possible, while at the same time offering the prospect of Sardinian citizenship to the rich through the royal decree of the 4th of this month. . . . Under such circumstances, there is no reason to show any particular indulgence to the Sardinian government on this question.'

Schwarzenberg's letter – which indirectly confirmed the failure of Radetzky's peasant policy – had reached Radetzky just in time, for Montecuccoli, who had had prior warning of Dabormida's visit from sources in Turin, had just been to see the Field Marshal on the question of the poorer emigrants.[141] The outlook of the Commissioner was radically different from that of Schwarzenberg. He would have agreed that Sardinia's motives were as Schwarzenberg described them, but his sympathy for the Lombard peasantry was stronger than his desire to win a diplomatic point. He told Radetzky:[142] 'A man must have a homeland. He cannot run around without a home. If people leave him to wander about like a wild animal he will eventually become a thief or a robber and will be much more dangerous to society than if he were taken into his homeland and kept under watch.' And he added: 'These are people who, so long as they are abroad, will undoubtedly be more dangerous to our government than if they had been accepted again, because they find themselves in a position of such bitterness and despair that they will support any wild scheme and will thus join our enemies at the first opportunity.'

Radetzky, of course, still retained all his old notions about the Italian peasantry, however confounded they had been, and had been sufficiently impressed by what the Commissioner had had to say as to reach an agreement with him; Montecuccoli was to write to Apponyi in the Field Marshal's name instructing the Ambassador to settle with Turin. The settlement which was envisaged was that groups of about forty to fifty poorer emigrants were to be allowed to cross back into Lombardy under military supervision so long as they had been given the necessary documents beforehand by the Sardinians. Before Montecuccoli could sit down to write his letter, however, a Major Langwider arrived from Radetzky informing him that the Field Marshal had changed his mind about the arrangement and that he 'no longer wanted to occupy himself with this question' since, having received the letter from Schwarzenberg, he now regarded the whole affair as a diplomatic one between Vienna and Turin.[143] Orders were given, therefore, that none of the regulations regarding emigrants were to be changed; Radetzky refused to meet Dabormida on the ground that he could not discuss the matter 'in general'; and Montecuccoli, instead of writing to Apponyi, wrote instead to a M. Zulauf, whom he asked to pass on his views to the Ambassador in the hope that they might thereby reach Vienna.[144]

Apponyi duly related everything to Schwarzenberg for which he was told, 'you have done well';[145] but Schwarzenberg was not at all impressed by the views of Montecuccoli, which he described as 'singular', arguing:[146] 'These people have sufficiently evinced the disaffection which consumes them by the obstinacy with which they have refused to make use of the amnesty granted to them in spite of the extension of deadlines. Moreover, the vagabond's life which they have been leading since they left their homeland and the pernicious influences to which it has exposed them, does not lead one to expect that on their return home, they would turn into peaceful, law-abiding citizens.'

To clarify the legal position of the emigrants, the Minister President referred the matter to Dr Alexander Bach, the imperial Minister of Justice.[147] Bach, however, replied that no legal arguments were necessary since, given the obvious threats to Austrian security involved in the question, the imperial government was supported by 'natural law',[148] 'The disadvantages and dangers', he wrote, 'which would arise for the still insufficiently protected public order and security of the Lombardo-Venetian Kingdom from the transplanting of so many proletarian and revolutionary elements are so obvious that the Austrian government should feel no compunction in decisively rejecting the Sardinian government's objective of repatriating the refugees which are a burden to it.' The former radicalism of the Justice Minister was evident only in the following passages of his report:[149] 'With regard to that part of the emigration which has wealth', he wrote, 'I can well sympathise with the government over the loss of their persons. However, I cannot remain indifferent to the fact that the fortunes belonging to the same will be taken abroad. Above all, therefore, it appears necessary that these fortunes should be sequestrated and I should think that the Civil and Military Governor should be instructed to introduce this measure where up till now it has not taken place.'

Bach's advice, however, was not really adopted until February 1853, when, after an uprising in Milan, the landed properties of all the prominent emigrants were sequestrated by the military. Something was done for the 'vagabonds' in the course of 1850,[150] though how many of them benefited thereby, it is difficult to say. Meanwhile, inside the Kingdom of Lombardy-Venetia, rich and poor suffered equally under the Austrian yoke so that when Sir James Hudson, British Ambassador in Turin in 1853, came to describe the abortive uprising of 6 February of that year to the British Foreign Secretary, Lord John Russell, he laid particular emphasis on the social aspect of events:[151]

Heretofore the movements in the Lombardo-Veneto were set on foot by the upper classes and the lower orders were almost neutral in the countryside although they followed in the towns; they were supposed to dislike the Austrians but not to love their own upper classes:– in the rural districts they took but a small share in the events of 1848–9.

But on the 6th instant it was the lower classes – exclusively (commonly called at Milan the Barabbas) who attacked knife in hand the Austrian outposts and the Chateau.

The difficulties of the Austrian Government in administering the Lombardo-Veneto would appear, therefore, to be rather increased than otherwise.

It was easier to deal with Revolution when certain recognised chiefs, fighting for certain fixed principles were known, than it can be to deal with the same spirit of revolt which animates the masses to attack their rulers with no other weapon than the knife and with no other organization than that afforded by a spirit of common hatred.

Radetzky's plan, in other words, had thoroughly backfired. His financial measures had led to misery, unemployment and higher prices;[152] his class policies of 'divide and rule' had brought about universal hatred and resistance.[153] After five years, rich and poor alike detested the Austrians.

Conclusion

The social body which was the Austrian army was severely tested in Italy in 1848, the corrosive impact of the revolution revealing its strengths and weaknesses. The social forces which bound officers together, but which separated officers from men, and men from men, were suddenly exposed and the cohesiveness of the army undermined. Thus, if the sense of *Kaisertreue,* the thirst for ennoblement and promotion,[1]* not to mention the feeling of security provided by the pension system, all served to retain the devotion of the officer corps for the Emperor, the revolutionary atmosphere, the lack of coercive power on the part of officers, the anti-Habsburg stand of the Church, and the keenly felt fear of being sent or kept away from one's homeland, meant that thousands of troops deserted their colours, accompanied, it would seem in many cases, by these, perhaps key figures, the N.C.Os. The army, in short, approached the brink of dissolution as the political divisions of the Monarchy as a whole were reflected within its ranks. It may be true that it was spared an internecine struggle between Hungarian and South Slav troops, but even in Italy the problems created by these peoples were huge and threatened the army's very survival. Nor was it clear for many months that it would be able to overcome them.

That it did so eventually was also due in a curious sense to the way in which it mirrored society. For just as the Monarchy was run by a small group of old men, so too was the military. The difference was that the leading gerontocrat in the army, unlike the Habsburg Emperor, was a man of sense and resolution who applied a policy of 'impartiality' to the Hungarian question instead of one of deception. This did not have to be the case – the army's selection processes at the top were no more rational than those of hereditary monarchy – but by happy chance – at least from the imperial point of view – it happened to be so. The result was that the army in Italy was held together, not by any system of 'divide and rule' (the expedient to which the dynasty so often resorted) but by its very opposite. In fact, there had never really been a policy of 'divide and rule' at work within the Austrian army anyway, the Habsburgs never having worked one out or having felt the need to do so. The process of moving regiments around the Empire was simply the logical consequence of the need of a European great power to maintain a centrally organised fighting force. The Habsburgs knew, of course, that if unrest broke out it would most likely be suppressed by troops of various nationalities, but those who believe that a sophisticated or diabolical system of divide and rule was operated will have to

---

* Notes to this chapter are on pp. 279–80.

show why, if this was the case, so many regiments in 1848 were to be found at the wrong place, at the wrong time and had been there for so long.

So much then for the social background of the Austrian army in Italy in 1848. As far as civil–military relations are concerned, one fact stands out above all others: that Radetzky personally was determined to save Italy for the Monarchy. There were two reasons for this. First, because as he put it,[2] 'What [would] become of our Monarchy without Italy?' It was not difficult to foresee that if the Habsburgs were forced out of Italy they would also be forced out of Germany and reduced to taking up residence in Hungary. Radetzky had simply no desire to see the Empire so transformed. The Field Marshal was also determined to redeem his personal reputation. The Austrians may well have had, in Talleyrand's phrase, 'the annoying habit of always losing battles',[3] but Radetzky belonged to a different tradition. His honour, however, had been compromised by his retreat from Milan and he was at pains to end the scepticism with which his efforts were being greeted in Vienna. The legend that he saved his reputation through disobedience, on the other hand, is one which is simply not grounded in reality.

There is no evidence at all that Radetzky's success was based on disobedience. Indeed, given the position in which he found himself after almost twenty years as commanding general, given his age and given the absolute nature of the assurances which he had previously passed on to his superiors, what impresses the historian today is not merely his resolve to reverse the humiliation of his initial defeats but the patience with which he set about his task. And yet there is nothing really surprising about it: he had, after all, displayed remarkable calm throughout the critical winter of 1847–8 and the – in all probability unforeseen – results of reinforcing the garrison at Ferrara had no doubt sustained his belief that the army's role should be a secondary one. The fact is that Radetzky, for all the bluster which was an essential part of his character, deferred regularly to the views of the civil authorities, accepting even in November 1848 their objections to his extraordinary war-tax.

On the other hand, his powers of persuasion were very often effective: the Hummelauer proposals were abandoned; he received the permission which he sought to fight the decisive battle of Custozza; and eventually it was recognised that he should head the administration of Lombardy-Venetia (which he did till 1857). His most powerful weapon in this respect was not, however, the threat of insubordination but, rather, the threat of resignation which he employed on more than one occasion. After 1848 this was never used again although it should not be thought that there were never any differences between himself and Schwarzenberg: the latter was critical, for example, of the armistice which Radetzky arranged with Victor Emmanuel in 1849 and was eager to break off the negotiations which ensued; Radetzky, however, persuaded him not to do so.[4] He also refused to make troops available for the Hungarian campaign.[5] On the other hand, the general outlooks of both men were very similar and for this reason there was no need for the Field Marshal to interfere with Schwarzenberg's policies regarding the rest of the Empire; Schwarzenberg, in turn, could give Radetzky a fairly free hand in running Lombardy-Venetia.

Both men, in fact, believed that the trouble in northern Italy had stemmed from the role of the nobility there[6] and would have liked to win over the local population for Austria through a policy of impoverishing the *signori* and appeasing the peasantry. There were grounds for expecting that such a policy might work: the Austrian record at the time of the Great Depression of 1814–18 had been a good one;[7] prices during the following decades had been very stable;[8] and the record of the provisional government had been disastrous as far as the peasantry was concerned. Yet this policy failed. The peasants had a natural distrust of governments and misunderstood what the Austrians were up to; the priesthood was opposed to the military regime; and, most important, the country as a whole suffered from measures against the landowning classes. The general needs of the imperial exchequer after 1849 meant that taxes everywhere would be high; but as it was a principle of the imperial government that those who had caused the trouble should pay for it, the situation in Italy was especially desperate. Lombardy in 1854, for example, provided the imperial treasury with just less than 80 million lire or one-ninth of the Empire's total revenue.[9] Venice was forced to pay the total cost of her resistance by herself with the result that one English economist could write in 1850 that the city was economically 'dead'.[10] Steps were taken in 1851 and 1852 to retrieve the situation, but with the Peace of Villafranca in 1859 and the Franco-Prussian Trade Treaty of 1862 it again deteriorated. The city did not really recover until the 1880s.[11]

Events in Italy, as interpreted by the army, finally, were also to have consequences for Austria itself. For having established himself in Vienna as the Empire's leading political figure, Schwarzenberg proceeded to deprive the nobility as a whole of any role in governing the Monarchy. Windischgraetz's schemes to establish aristocratically dominated Diets were quickly brushed aside and the rest of the Monarchy, like the Italian provinces in the 1850s, was run by soldiers and bureaucrats from the centre. The reason for this was that Schwarzenberg had convinced himself that the nobility could no longer be trusted. It had made the revolution in Italy and from passages in his letters to Windischgraetz we discover that he held a similar view of events in Hungary. He wrote:[12]

The Hungarian aristocracy is a politically and morally degenerate body: if the government wishes to rely on the nobility in that country it can hope for no support. The role which the nobility has played in the political history of Hungary – particularly in recent times – shows clearly its true spirit. I do not believe in political conversions and since the nobility in Hungary made and executed the revolution there, I find no guarantee of its future effectiveness. One can be of old lineage, have an old title and call oneself an aristocrat but still be a supporter of revolutionary subversion.

Is it at all surprising, therefore, given his views on Italy and Hungary, that Schwarzenberg should have arrived at the following conclusion – once again while writing to Windischgraetz:[13]

I know of not a dozen men of our class with sufficient political wisdom or with the necessary experience to whom an important share of power could be entrusted without soon having to fear for it. I have thought a great deal about how to constitute the aristocracy of Austria as a body so as to maintain for it an appropriate political influence but the elements out of which this body consists, I have been unable to find. Democracy must be fought and its excesses must be challenged but in the absence of other means of help, that can only be done by the government itself. To rely on ally as weak as our aristocracy unfortunately is, would be to damage our cause more than to help it.

The Habsburg Empire in the 1850s, therefore, was to rest on narrower bases of support.

The Articles of War for the imperial-royal army of Austria

1. *Violence to Superiors* – Whoever shall violate the laws of obedience, by a forcible opposition to his superior in service, whether the said superior is thereby injured or not, shall be punished with death, by means of powder and ball, both in time of war and peace.
    Should this extreme insubordination take place in public, and be of such a nature as to create an impression on the minds of others prejudicial to the service, it shall be tried on the spot by a drum-head court-martial.

2. *Disobedience of Orders* – Whoever shall disobey the command of his superior (although not forcibly, yet by behaving with unseemly forgetfulness of the respect that is due to him), or who shall not carry into effect the said command, either from evil intention, or from gross carelessness, shall according to the degree of the mischief produced to the service by the disobedience (especially when evil intention is proved), be punished with death, by means of powder and ball.
    The obedience to orders enjoined by this article not only comprises such as relate to all the common duties of a soldier, but also to those services he is capable of rendering his monarch by his trade, handicraft, or skill. Furthermore this article of war compels all inferiors to pay the respect due to their superiors on *all* occasions. – Only when the commands of a superior are manifestly against the rules of the service, and in opposition to the allegiance sworn to the monarch, or clearly have for their object some bad end, is it permitted to an inferior (and then does it become his positive duty) to remonstrate against, or even not obey the said commands. But likewise in this case must the remonstrance invariably be made with moderation and respoect.

3. *Superiors causing Insubordination* – Any superior who by unjust, cruel, or intemperate conduct, shall have occasioned an act of insubordination, shall be most severely punished, according to the aggravation of the circumstances.

4. *Mutiny* – Whoever shall excite any mutiny, or take part in one, or who shall permit himself words, writings, or acts, tending to cause mutiny, shall according to the importance of the circumstances be severely punished, and in war time suffer death, by means of powder and ball.
    Should the intended insurrection have commenced, or be on the point of breaking out, it shall in time of war, as well as of peace, be immediately brought before a drum-head court-martial.
    The crime of mutiny is said to be committed when a man at a meeting of

few or many holds language concerning his superiors disadvantageous to the Service, the State, or Monarch; and animadverts upon them, so as to leave a bad impression on the minds of those listening. Also, by endeavouring to set prisoners at liberty, or to hinder executions. Also, by more than two men designedly going to their superior to demand relief from a hardship, or by one or more men complaining when in the ranks, or even in the presence of others, of their superior, in so impetuous a manner as to make it likely they might be seduced into participation.

5. *High Treason* – Whoever shall be guilty of the crime of high treason shall be punished with death, by hanging, as well in peace as in wartime. This crime is committed by all such as attempt the personal safety of the monarch; or undertake anything that is planned upon a violent change of the constitution; or upon attracting or increasing danger to the State from without. Any man designedly omitting to prevent, or give notice, of a concerted high treasonable undertaking, shall himself be punished for high treason.

6. *Spies, &c.* – Whoever shall be detected in correspondence with the enemy, likewise all spies and traitors, with their abettors, shall be executed by means of hanging.
    In accordance with this article, which properly treats of treasonable understanding with the enemy, whether it be by writing, by word of mouth, by signs, or by any other means whatever; all correspondence even on the most indifferent matters without previous authorised consent, is forbidden and punishable. All letters, therefore, both going to, and coming from, the enemy, must be notified to the commanding officer. Furthermore, all those infringe this article who, by spreading bad news, cause faintheartedness among the soldiers, citizens, or country people; and, likewise, such as having knowledge of treachery shall not report it.

7. *Offenders against Religion* – Whoever shall permit himself words or acts blasphemously setting at nought the reverence due to God, or openly offend him, shall be very severely punished. This article of war extends also to those who depreciate religion, either by mockery, or levity in sacred matters; or by disseminating doctrines and writings tending to undermine religion and morality; or lastly, by wantonly exciting hatred between different sects.

8. *Perjury* – Whoever shall take a false oath shall have a heavy punishment inflicted on him, and more especially if any man, with an intention to accuse another of a crime not committed, perjure himself, and by means of the said perjury cause the accused to be punished by death, shall himself suffer death.

9. *Resisting Patrols, &c.* – Whoever shall forcibly resist a guard, patrols, rounds, or safeguard, shall be most severely punished, and according to the circumstances, in wartime, suffer death by means of powder and ball. Likewise, those shall be severely punished who indiscreetly do not submit themselves to an arrest imposed upon them, as well as those who designedly omit to answer the challenge of a sentry.

10. *Escaping from Arrest* – Whoever shall attempt to make his escape from a

guard when he is put under arrest, shall, when no other means of preventing him are at hand, be shot down upon the spot; should he, however, otherwise be prevented, he shall be most severely punished. He also shall be shot down who forcibly resists a guard and breaks away from it, or makes himself suspected when on a dangerous post, more especially on one threatened by the enemy, and runs off without heeding the challenge of the sentries.

11. *Permitting Prisoner to Escape* – Whoever shall afford another who is under arrest an opportunity of escaping, more especially a sentry permitting a prisoner to get away, shall be severely punished, and according to circumstances, particularly if done designedly, or when the prisoner shall have been known as a state or otherwise dangerous criminal, or shall have been given over as such to the sentry, shall suffer death by means of powder and ball. Likewise the commander of the guard, if he shall not have acquainted his men with the importance of a dangerous prisoner, or has not used all requisite means of precaution, is, according to the sense of this Article of War, liable to punishment.

12. *Sleeping on Sentry, Drunk on Guard, &c.* – Whoever shall be found asleep on sentry, or leave his post of his own accord before being relieved, or get intoxicated when on guard, or come to the same drunk; furthermore, whoever shall neglect his guard or post, or not conduct himself thereon conformably to his duty, shall be most severely punished, and in wartime shall, according to the importance of the circumstances, and the inconvenience thereby produced to the Service, suffer death by means of powder and ball.

When anything is the matter with a sentry, or if he is not relieved at the proper time, he must call to the sentry on the next post who passes the word on to the guard-room furnishing the relief.

Every sentry must give his full attention to the watchword, for should he give the rounds or patrols a wrong word, he must be immediately relieved, and according to circumstances, especially when danger from the enemy is apprehended, be punished most severely.

Moreover, no sentry shall presume, on any account, to allow himself to be relieved without the presence of the corporal.

The foregoing Article of War concerns as well all superiors as subordinates, and more especially every commander of a post.

13. *Surrendering Posts, &c.* – A commandant surrendering a post, without having resisted to the uttermost, as well as all officers subscribing to such faithless surrender, shall be executed by means of *hanging,* as men without honour; and the troops likewise shall, if equally guilty, be *decimated* and *hanged.*

Those who are convinced that the commandant of a post intends surrendering from faint-heartedness or want of loyalty, but more particularly those next to him in rank – shall, in the first instance, make him, with all due order and moderation, the most expressive remonstrances; should these, however, prove ineffectual, and it is conjectured with reason that the surrender has been determined on, either without necessity or from treachery, they will not permit it, but place under arrest the commandant, and under the new orders of him on whom the command by seniority of service next devolves, shall, with united powers, endeavour to defend the place.

14. *Disheartening Language* – Whoever shall hold faint-hearted or dangerous language concerning the surrender of a post, shall, according to the importance of the circumstances, be tried by a court-martial, or even be brought before a drum-head court-martial, and be removed from the eyes of his brave comrades.

15. Whoever shall decline engaging with the enemy, or who during an action shall remain in the rear in a cowardly manner, or who shall run away, shall be executed by hanging. Likewise is every officer bound by his honour, in those cases where the disgraceful running away of a soldier might cause immediate danger to the army, to cut down the coward on the spot.

16. *Cowardice* – When bodies of troops do not do their duty in action, or abandon field-works, redoubts, fortresses, or other posts in a cowardly manner, without having made as great resistance as possible – or mutiny, every tenth man, and likewise every officer who is in any way guilty, shall be executed by means of *hanging*. A cowardly regiment declining to fight shall also lose their colours until they next distinguish themselves; and smaller bodies shall be divided among other regiments.

17. *Plundering, &c.* – Whoever in wartime shall be found plundering before it is ordered or permitted, shall be most severely punished, and should the plundering become of a violent nature, it shall be treated by drum-head courts-martial; and, moreover, when it can only be restrained by an immediate example, the officer shall cut down the offender on the spot.

18. *Desertion* – Whoever shall (without regard to his oath, and faithless) desert and be brought back by the military, shall, according to the nature of the circumstances, especially when he has before deserted and been brought back, be executed by hanging.
    Further, the present article refers to all such as desert, whether they enlist into any other regiment, or, without taking service, remain in the country; likewise to such as return of their own accord and report themselves, except in the case of a general pardon being promulgated. All these shall in proportion, and according to circumstances, have a suitably heavy punishment inflicted. Moreover, it is necessary to cause the existing circumstantial orders to be observed, by frequently making known the sentences pronounced on deserters.

19. *Persuading to Desert* – The soldier who persuades two or more of his comrades to commit perjury by deserting, shall, as author of a plot, be punished the same as a deserter, whether the plot shall in fact succeed by the desertion taking place, or be prevented.

20. *Foreign Enlistment* – Whoever shall levy troops for a foreign service, or impress by force any subject for that purpose; furthermore, whoever shall enlist any man belonging to any military body, although only for the purpose of settling in foreign countries, or forcibly entrap him for any other purpose whatever, shall be immediately brought to trial before a drum-head court-martial, and be executed by hanging.

21. *Breaking Quarantine* – Any man breaking quarantine shall be severely punished; or who, when once a close cordon is drawn, shall not turn back on being challenged, shall be shot down by the guard; but he who breaks through the cordon by using force against the guard, or who clandestinely evades it, shall be tried by a drum-head court-martial, and be executed by means of powder and ball.

22. *Selling Necessaries* – Every soldier shall, on pain of heavy punishment, keep in good order his arms, ammunition, and equipments, and take good care, on any account whatever, not to pawn or sell them.

23. *Booty* – Prisoners of war, artillery, arms, ammunition, colours, standards, horses, magazines, military chests records, and such like, taken from the enemy, shall, on pain of severe punishment, be delivered, whenever the General commanding shall direct.

24. *Breaking out of Barracks* – Nobody shall go in or out of any fortress, post, or other work, by other than the usual entrance, on pain of heavy punishment.
    Those likewise infringe this article who break out of barracks, or other quarters, or climb over the walls or roofs.

25. *Injuring Buildings, &c.* – Whoever shall wantonly injure public buildings, works, hedges, avenues, fruit trees, fields, gardens, and such like, shall, whether it be an enemy's or friendly country, be severely punished.

26. *Open Violence* – All acts of open violence shall be severely punished; and in wartime, according to circumstances, be punished with death by means of powder and ball.
    This article includes all such acts of violence as are perpetrated to the prejudice of the peace and security of others, very especially also such as are committed without authority in an enemy's country.

27. *Misconduct in Billets* – Whoever shall ill-use his landlord in billets, or permit himself any extortion whatever beyond his due, shall be most severely punished. This article refers also to all unjust and forcible cantoning, as well as to all exactions of horses, guides, or forage, which may be practised against citizens or country people.

28. *Ill-using Public Officers* – Whoever shall ill-use, by striking, either a nobleman, public officer, or any other person distinguished by public office, shall be severely punished; and any officer guilty of such misconduct shall, according to circumstances, be cashiered, or be even still more severely punished.

29. *Duelling, &c.* – All insults, challenges, duels, as well as those assisting in them as seconds, shall, according to the circumstances of the original provocation, be severely punished.

30. *Murder* – Every murder is punished by *hanging,* in war as well as in peace time. Whoever with deadly intention acts towards a man so as to cause his death, renders himself guilty of the crime of murder. More especially the worst species of murder are assassinations effected by poison, or otherwise treacherously. Murder accompanied by robbery (which is committed with the intention to appropriate the property of another by

using violence to the person), also provocation to murder, where any one is compelled, or in any other way induced by a third, to commit the act. Of the last-mentioned nature is the immediate murderer as much to be punished with death, by means of hanging, as he who has prompted the deed.

31. *Manslaughter* – Every blow occasioning death, is most severely punished, and in wartime, according to the nature of the circumstances, visited by death by means of powder and ball.
    A death blow is when the act whereby a man loses his life has been committed with hostile purpose, although not intended to kill him. Likewise causing death of a man, either by inattention or carelessness, shall be punished according to the proportion of guilt.

32. *Arson* – Whoever shall wilfully burn, either in friendly countries, or in an enemy's, without orders, or unless justified in so doing by necessity, shall be punished by means of hanging.

33. *Theft* – All thefts are severely punished, and in war time, when the theft amounts to more than the sum of 100 Guldens (about 10 l.), it is punished by *death* by means of hanging.

34. *Stealing Regimental Property, or from Comrade, &c.* – Whoever shall steal artillery, ammunition, arms, accoutrements, stores, or other military property, or who shall take with dishonest intention money belonging to any regiment, squadron, or company, or appropriate to his own use, in a faithless and dishonourable manner, any military money, or other articles of commissariat intrusted to his care, or who shall steal property that he is ordered to guard, or shall wilfully allow it to be stolen; also one comrade thieving from another, a servant from his master, or a theft committed at the time of a fire, inundation, or other public calamity; and those persons guilty of theft against whom, by reason of their free entrance and particular business, it is not so easy to guard; also those thefts where the offender has been provided with arms, or other instruments dangerous to personal safety, or which have been effected by means of breaking into, or climbing over places; furthermore, a theft committed with sacrilegious profanation of the holy service of religion, in any place dedicated to the worship of God, or of any article immediately consecrated thereto; in fine, every theft, the perpetrator of which has already been twice punished for the same offence, shall without consideration of the amount, be visited at all times most severely, but in war time, when the act is aggravated by the concurrence of any of the aforesaid circumstances, be punished with death by means of hanging. Those also offend against this article who withhold from the soldier his pay, or provisions, or who arbitrarily deprive another of booty legitimately acquired.

35. *Robbery* – Every robbery is, in time of war and peace, punished by *hanging*. Every one who does violence towards a person in order to possess himself of his (or, indeed, of anybody else's) property, renders himself guilty of the crime of robbery, whether the violence is committed by actual ill-treatment, or only by threatening; whether in the open street, in houses, or in any other place whatever; whether in a friendly or enemy's country; whether by a single person, or by many.

36. *Petty Frauds* – All petty frauds, such as when any one with interested intentions forges, or counterfeits, seals, writings, and such like, or attempts to pass current a second time any bond already paid, or breaks open or suppresses letters, or represents the person and character of another; likewise all false players are punished severely as thieves, and in wartime, according to the nature of the circumstances, *hanged*.

37. *Forgery* – Whoever shall forge illegal coin, or counterfeit genuine pieces of money, shall be most severely punished; and whoever shall counterfeit public bank notes which are current as money, or bonds issued from any public bank, by means of instruments made for that purpose, so likewise every one who in any way whatever assists in this crime, or participates therein, shall, both in time of war and peace, be executed by hanging.

38. *Officers Missing Muster* – Any officer who shall wilfully miss muster or review shall be cashiered, accompanied by an explicit declaration of his unworthiness to serve in the Imperial Royal Service, and, according to the nature of the circumstances, even be further most severely punished.

39. *Rape, &c.* – Rape, incest, and such like impure acts, the crime of bigamy, the forcible abduction of any woman, and all other crimes of the same nature, not expressly quoted in this Article of War, are, according to the laws existing for the Imperial Royal Army, severely punished.

40. *Concealing Criminals* – Whoever shall wilfully harbour and conceal any criminal or offender against the foregoing articles shall be punished most severely, in proportion and according to the crime committed.

Remarks

The Articles of War must frequently be read from beginning to end, and clearly explained to the soldiers; more especially to recruits, on joining, in their native language; likewise also must they be read out at all musters.

The promulgation of any Article of War which may henceforth be altered in any particular, or any new one added, must be solemnly performed with beat of drum, or sound of trumpet.

Radetzky's report of 5 April 1848

Kriegsarchiv, Ministerium des Kriegswesersakten (1848), No. 302

List of troops lost by the army in the various catastrophes

Jäger

Four companies of the 8th Battalion – deserted at Rovigo St Maria Maddalena.

Grenzer

Warasdiner Kreuzer Battalion – is supposed to be fighting its way to the Tyrol from Como.

Warasdiner St Georger – remains surrounded in the citadel of Ferrara.

First Banat Battalion – allowed to withdraw behind the Isonzo through the capitulation of FML Ludolf.

Peterwardeiner – allowed to be shipped to Trieste through the capitulation of Venice.

Second Banat Battalion – Two companies allowed to withdraw behind the Isonzo through the capitulation of FML Ludolf.

Infantry of the line

Von Geppert: Two companies of the 3rd Battalion of the garrison of Pizzighettone deserted – whereabouts of three companies of the 2nd Battalion of the garrisons of Lecco, Morbegno and Sondrio unknown. Apart from this, the regiment has lost 700 men on the retreat from Monza.

Archd. Albert Infantry: Two battalions of the garrison at Cremona deserted.

3rd Battalion Ceccopieri: Deserted with the garrison at Cremona.

3rd Battalion Ferdinand Victor d'Este: Garrisons at Udine and Palma Nuova deserted.

3rd Battalion Zanini: The garrison at Treviso deserted.

3rd Battalion Wimpffen; *Angelmayer Grenadiers*; *5th Garrison Battalion:* Deserted with the garrison at Venice.

3rd Battalion Haugwitz: Has lost about one-third through desertion.

Kinski Infantry, 2nd Battalion: Enabled to be shipped to Trieste through capitulation of Venice.

Franz Ferdinand d'Este Infantry: Four companies of the Parma garrison cut off in Colorno.

Cavalry

Windischgraetz Chev. Leg.: One squadron of the Parma garrison cut off in Colorno.

Artillery

Foot Battery No. 7 of the Cremona garrison taken – men and equipment.

Losses consist of 17 battalions, 2 squadrons (*sic*), 1 battery.

Radetzky then gave his army as consisting of:

Infantry

	Battalions
2nd Battalion Kaiser Jäger	3
10th Jäger Battalion	1
11th Jäger Battalion	1
9th Jäger Battalion	1
Combined 8th and 9th Battalion (one-third 8th, one-third 9th)	1
Oguliner Grenz Battalion	1
Graciscaner Grenz Battalion	1
Ottochaner Grenz Battalion	1
Brooder Grenz Battalion	1
2nd Banat Grenz Battalion (4 comp.)	1
Szluiner Grenz Battalion	1
Prohaska Infantry	2
Geppert Infantry (made up from 3 battns)	2
Reisinger Infantry	2
3rd Battalion Archd. Albert Infantry	1
Sigmund Infantry	2
Gyulai Infantry	2
Bukovina Infantry	2
Paumgarten Infantry	2
Grenad. Battalion d'Anthon	1
Grenad. Battalion Weiler	1
Kaiser Infantry	2
Hohenlohe	2
Archd. Franz Carl Infantry	2
Haugwitz Infantry (3rd Battn 500 men)	3
Archduke Ernst Infantry	2
Archduke Franz Ferd. d'Este (2 battns of 4 comp.)	2
6th Garrison Battalion	1
Pioneer	1
Pinet Infantry	2
Total infantry	47

Cavalry

	Squadrons	Batteries
Sardinian Hussars	8	
Reuss Hussars	7	
Windischgraetz Chev. Leg.	7	
Liechtenstein Chev. Leg.	6	
Kaiser Uhlans	6	
Baiern Dragoons	6	
6 lb. foot batteries [1 complete batt. lost in Cremona]		8
6 lb. cavalry batteries		5
12 lb. batteries		2
Rocket Batteries		2
New Haublitz Battery (being formed)		1
Total troop strength:	47 battalions	40 squadrons	18 batteries

From this subtract as occupation forces:

	Battalions	Squadrons	Batteries
at Mantua	10	2	2
at Verona	10	4	2
at Legnago	1	–	–
at Peschiera	1	–	–
Italian troops	10	–	–
Pioneer Battalion	1	–	–
Total	33	6	4
Troops left to be deployed	14	34	14

Criminals in the Ranks: the case of the Infantry Regiment Archduke Ferdinand d'Este
Welden to Nugent, Innsbruck, 13 February 1848

Kriegsarchiv, Ministerium des Kriegswesensakten (1848), No. 42.

With respect to a note of the United Court Chancery to the Hofkriegsrath about a previous break-down of public security in Innsbruck due to the large number of trouble-makers still unfortunately to be found in the Infantry Regiment Archduke Ferdinand d'Este, it pleased Your Excellency to order me by directive no. P319 of 9th February to report on the present state of order, morality and discipline prevailing in this regiment.

Given the detrimental situation revealed by the list of 284 partly very dangerous criminals incorporated in the 12 companies of this regiment which is recruited from foreign districts in Italy; given the influence they had to exert on regimental morality, the higher authorities decided at least to stop the delivery of such criminals directly from the jails. Meanwhile, about 100 of these trouble-makers have been released in accordance with the existing conscription regulations; on the other hand, 25 real criminals and 40 released *ab in stantia,* that is to say 65 trouble-makers in all, were assigned to the regiment in 1846, so that at present there are 269 of these depraved people here, 20–25 of them in each company.

Since 1 January 1846, the regimental court has dealt with 18 cases of theft by forcible entry, 3 cases of robbery with attempted murder as well as 3 cases of theft and 2 of robbery which could not be proven.

If investigations have often been very long drawn out due to the inadequacies of our laws and the cleverness of the Italian criminals; if the desired results have not always been achieved, the administration of justice within the regiment has always been carried out with circumspection and the most severe strictness, the results of which can be seen in the fact that among such a large number of the most hardened criminals, the company, battalion and regimental punishments are almost two-thirds less than in the Tyrolese Jäger Regiment which is supposed to be composed only of selected men and which can hand over its worst criminals to other regiments. The number of desertions is particularly small and yet there are detachments stationed on the Bavarian and Swiss borders. Among the latter not a single man has deserted nor has a single one been punished so long as they have been in Vorarlberg. The same applies to all singly detached companies and proves that where there is not such a large number of troops as here; where they normally live locked up in barracks on account of their dangerousness – [that is to say] in the countryside where the opportunities for criminals are less and where the attractions of the big cities are not at hand – it is better to divide the regiment into small detachments. The good behaviour of these groups of men is based on the excellence of their captains and the greater part of the N.C.Os and leaves no doubt for even a moment that they can be relied upon in any sort of situation. There is spirit and even ambition in the common soldier. Thus very recently, when there were cases of robbery and attempted murder among two companies at the regimental camp at the Granzensreste, the revulsion in the whole division was so great that the one company would have nothing more to do with the other company to which the two criminals belonged. Since recently there have been many thefts here which have been ascribed to trouble-makers in the regiment, but which have not been sufficiently quickly solved, I have ordered the tattoo to be beaten at sunset solely for the Este regiment. The men of the regiment requested that the tattoo should be beaten not by the main watch but in the barracks so as to spare them being shamed in front of the inhabitants. However, this will not happen so long as the thefts go unsolved and unpunished.

It will always be good to keep these troops, as has been said already, in not too large bodies and mixed with others; upon which [principle] my accompanying humble proposals for the distribution of troops in the Tyrol has been based, partly in order to have them readily disposable, partly in order to secure more peace in the countryside.

Welden F.M.L.
mfp

A Desertion Report
To the Regimental Command of the 26th Infantry Regiment (Archduke Ferdinand d'Este)
Innsbruck, 5 April 1848

Kriegsarchiv, Ministerium des Kriegswesensakten (1848), No. 538

With respect to the desertion of the second transport of reserves, the following report will describe its causes and the clumsy means taken to prevent it.

On 18 March of this year the undersigned set out from Udine with the second reserve transport of 380 troops two days after the Constitution had been proclaimed with all possible sensation. The experience showed what a transformation took place in the hearts and minds of the Italians from that moment on and how the flames of rebellion spread like wildfire through the Venetian provinces also. The undersigned must call attention to this fact for herein lay the source of the evil and the cause of the desertion.

Daily, hourly almost, the revolution won ground in all provinces, which were denuded of troops and administered by weak or treasonous officials. In all the places through which the transport passed, the royal officials had been dismissed and had been replaced for the most part by the most enthusiastic supporters of the overthrow of the existing order. The priests displayed the worst attitude of all and placed themselves with incredible insolence at the head of the revolutionary movement. It was they who were most responsible for inciting and influencing the lowest classes, in particular the peasants. All symbols of imperial authority were destroyed and in their place was planted the tricolour Italian flag. In all places the men of the transport were received with shouts of joy and shouts of *Eviva gli italiani – Eviva l'Italia, l'indipendenza, Eviva Pio IX,* etc. The richest people as well as the beggars, the Bishops as well as the meanest monks were all wearing the Italian cockade. The men, as native sons, were everywhere given bread and wine and there were even inns where the men were given food and drink free. False, totally unfounded rumours calculated to upset people or to strike up enthusiasm in others, circulated from mouth to mouth – secret emissaries doggedly followed the transport and sought by all sorts of misrepresentations and even with money to undermine the spirit of the troops. In such circumstances the undersigned had to make his way with native sons through the provinces of Friaul, Treviso and Vicenza with only one officer and with N.C.Os all of whom were unknown to him. In Lomegliano three men attempted to murder him and he saved himself only through presence of mind. At the moment of entering Bassano the news arrived of the capitulation of Venice, of the proclamation of the Republic, of the retreat of the second Army Corps, of the fall of Treviso and Padua, of the Piedmontese invasion of Lombardy, of the crossing-over of most of the Italian troops and of the third battalion of the regiment itself – in open places the Venetian Republic was proclaimed with the greatest celebration and delirious joy. The Civic Guard, armed with the rifles of the disarmed *Finanzwache* and preceded by the great tricolour flags went shouting through the streets. The leaders of the Civic Guard, priests and emissaries went to the two barracks in which the men were quartered and read them the latest Milanese and Venetian newspapers, seditious writings, poems, etc.; formal sermons were held; and money was distributed. Civilians hauled off ten or more men at a time and held the most engaging discussions with them.

The men were asked not to march further but to remain in Bassano, where they would all be handsomely looked after. Attempts were made to frighten them by telling them that they would be sent to Germany as hostages, that the time they had served would be forfeited, that they would be killed in revenge for the German troops who had fallen in Italy. They were told that their homeland needed them for its own defence, etc., etc. The undersigned went immediately to the barracks with Lieutenant Hawik and removed the civilians only with the greatest difficulty for two priests in particular could only be got rid of with threats. In a short forceful speech the undersigned exhorted the men to remain loyal to their sovereign and flag, to remember their oath and, as men of honour, to resist the thousand kinds of sedition they would experience with manly firmness. At the end of his speech the undersigned asked the men whether they would leave their commander faithlessly in the lurch and as if from one mouth came the reply that they would not but that they would defend him with their life.

Shortly after the undersigned had entered Bassano, a deputation of the Civic Guard came to him with the demand, based on the Capitulation of Venice, that the Italian troops should not leave Bassano as planned but should stay there in the pay of the town to defend it. It would require too many details to give an account of negotiations here. The result was that several delegations came and besieged the undersigned and according to their talents, requested, promised or threatened him to get their way; in the end negotiations broke down.

People tried formally to waylay the undersigned and Lieutenant Hawik; it was said clearly in all open places that if taken they would be hanged. They were always followed in the open street by bands of the most suspicious people; finally, it was decided to have both officers shot by hired guns as they were marching out of Bassano at the head of the column. People counted on the participation of the men; the streets out of town were supposed to be barricaded and the march prevented by force. Another plan was to disarm the men in their barracks. The steps which had to be taken were obvious.

The transport was supposed to have a day of rest in Bassano [but] the dangers of a longer stay were apparent and grew from hour to hour. The undersigned was [therefore] ready to leave immediately. Yet all sorts of obstacles had to be overcome. One did not want to lend a hand in helping supplies disappear so that one put it around that the troops were resting in Bassano and that the bread required from Vicenza had not yet arrived. (Bread for Bassano came from Vicenza.) In short, one thought of all possible obstacles. Nothing would have moved the undersigned from his decision if one circumstance had not emerged to force him to keep the rest-day. A detachment of the Second Banat Border Regiment consisting of one officer and sixty men had remained behind in Bassano – the detachment had run out of bread; the quartermaster-sergeant did not wish to give any away and was nowhere to be found. No one spoke

Italian – the officer, without news or orders, was in the saddest situation.

The day the transport reached Bassano was a great market-day and thousands of peasants were swarming into the town – most of them armed, albeit only with cudgels – to supply it. In the evening the main watch, which was in a most uncomfortable position and comprised 24 Croatian troops, was supposed to be attacked. In such a position, the undersigned could not leave his brothers-in-arms in the lurch. He had the commander of the latter come to see him (Lieutenant Ziokovich), let him know of the danger, advised him to concentrate his detachment, to forget about the main watch, to supply his men with a bread ration and offered him the co-operation of the men in his own transport. Since the undersigned, in any case, had made up his mind to push ahead on 25th of the month without awaiting greater danger with the transport, he sought to persuade the detachment not to sacrifice itself for nothing, but to march forward that very day to the main body of troops at Vicenza – which is what happened.

On 24th when orders were being given out in the afternoon, it was discovered, by a crowd of spectators, that we would be setting out the following day at 5am. for Primolano. That evening at 11pm. the undersigned went to one of the barracks and sent Lieutenant Hawik to the other and with the greatest silence had the men wake up, fix rifles, load them will ball, fix bayonets, form the appropriate formations and at 12 midnight punctually marched out of Bassano in the greatest silence and without drum-beat. Baggage and equipment was left behind under the supervision of a sergeant who had orders to follow on as soon as possible. Many people came running out of their houses and gathered in armed groups, but everyone was obviously taken by surprise, the men's behaviour obviously commanded respect. The march out took place without incident; only it was immediately recognised that it was an extraordinary detachment commander who had taken the necessary measures immediately.

Having arrived in Trent, the undersigned was informed officially that people intended to win over the men and to stage an uprising with their help.

Under the excuse of military preparedness, all the troops were consigned to barracks. No one was allowed to enter or leave. The transport was now joined by Lieutenant Tukovich, a sergeant and a drummer. An officer always held inspections at the barracks' door. The city of Trent gave the men wine, bread and cheese free of charge. This was distributed by an officer. In the evenings several hundred men gathered in front of the barracks and shouted *Evivas* to individual soldiers and asked them to make common cause with them. They sang revolutionary songs. The undersigned and the two officers attempted to disperse these people but to no avail; the undersigned went directly to the town commander and reported the matter. The town commander who lacked troops, had the civic guard restore order. The undersigned received orders to lead the transport to Innsbruck. It left Trent in good order and proper fashion at midnight. It reached Neumarkt in good time on the 28th. The march out was set for 5am. on the 29th but the undersigned intended to set off at midnight. All men were present to receive their pay that afternoon and all appeared to be orderly. At 7.30pm. the tattoo was beaten. Half an hour later, the undersigned intended to make the usual count with both officers to ensure that all the men had retired, when at that very moment some corporals came hurrying with the report that the greater part of the troops in the transport had loaded their rifles, fixed them with bayonets and were withdrawing towards the mountains. The undersigned and the officers sought from house to house to find enough men to make up a patrol. But there was no one to be found. A general fear had spread among the men and the well disposed had hidden themselves so as not to be swept along with the crowd. Two hundred and twenty-four men altogether – the two patrols which had been assembled with such difficulty as well as two orderlies who had been assigned to watch the undersigned's baggage and who had pilfered his wash and an under-shirt – deserted and made their way home through the Flams valley via Cavalese. Several N.C.Os who tried to stop people were held back with shots which, on account of the darkness, missed their mark. The undersigned hurried immediately to the local court and requested the aid of such armed peasants as could be mustered as well as requesting that the local authorities at Cavalese be informed, in order to ensure the arrest of some deserters at least. The kk. provincial authorities at Botzen were likewise informed.

On 29th, the transport arrived at Botzen and was met by a large crowd of people shouting 'Eviva i bravi, eviva gli fedeli!' In Botzen five men returned voluntarily (one had been taken along by force), all of whom had risked their lives by leaving their mutinous comrades. On the 30th the march out of Botzen took place amidst great publicity and caused a visible impression so that those who had remained loyal fulfilled their duties till the end.

Although the transport approached the Italian border from time to time near Brixen in order to send many communications to Italy, no more desertions took place, however. The men were in the best of spirit and order and discipline was maintained.

The undersigned, like each of the other officers, feels himself to be in no way responsible. One sought persistently without heed to life or health to do one's duty. For ten days the undersigned remained in the same clothing and several nights [sleep?] were sacrificed. The proven affection and devotion of the men as well as the testimony of all those who came through offers the best justification of the undersigned's behaviour and of that of his officers. The undersigned can say without fear of contradiction that it was only out of devotion that the men did not desert him in Bassano and that it was out of devotion too that several who were very tempted to make off, remained with him till Innsbruck.

Had the transport left Udine on the 16th of the month as planned, instead of on the 18th perhaps the greatest part of the troops would have remained with the regiment.

Baron Aichelberg
Hauptmann   mfp

An Appeal to Loyalty
To the soldiers of the Este Regiment

Kriegsarchiv, Centralkanzleiakten, Präsidialreihe, 1848, No. 1085

For many years now you have given proof of your loyalty and devotion not only to the army but also to my person. Thus I acknowledge and I thank you for it.

It is a great satisfaction to win the affection of one's subordinates and to maintain it even in these days of great danger and distress which disloyalty to the state has produced.

I give you my word of honour, never to lead you against your fellow countrymen. Therefore resist every temptation put in your way by the many evil individuals in your midst and without. Seize these traitors and turn them over for speedy justice. Refrain from deserting your colours. This will be severely punished and in order that no misapprehension should remain, allow me to explain clearly to you, martial law is being declared throughout the land.

I would very much regret to have to make use of it or to hear that a deserter had been killed by peasants – as was partly the case with your comrades who deserted.

The day after tomorrow 160 men of the 2nd Reserve transport of Este Infantry will join their loyal comrades again, having under the leadership of only two officers, firmly and faithfully resisted the evil example of their mutinous comrades who from Neumarkt on, used every means possible to incite them to desert – yet they resisted even at Brixen from where they could have reached their homeland. I declare my respect for them today and look forward to having the pleasure of meeting them on 8th May.

You should receive those who have been loyal with celebration on their return and for this purpose, I am giving you a small sum of money so that your brothers will be heartily glad to see you and will feel the joy of having done their duty.

A Revolutionary Catechism
Soldiers and Citizens!

Kriegsarchiv, Centralkanzleiakten, Präsidialreihe, 1848m No. 413

Q. Are you Italians?

A. We are by the Grace of God.

Q. What does it mean to be Italian?

A. It means to be born on Italian soil, of an Italian mother, by an Italian father.

Q. What is the distinctive exterior sign of the Italian?

A. It is hatred of the German tyrant, hatred which must show in the face, in the bearing, in our words and actions.

Q. What are the distinctive interior signs of the Italian?

A. There are three: memory, intellect and will.

Q. What does memory effect in us?

A. It ensures that we always bear in mind the gold and the blood that the German Vampire sucked from us.

Q. What does will effect in us?

A. It unites all clergy, nobles and plebeians in one people, in one soul, directed to one end: Italian Unity.

Q. What are the articles of the creed?

A. There are five: First: I believe firmly in the imminent, irrepressible regeneration of Italy. Second: I believe that Italy has in it all the elements necessary to raise itself to a lasting and powerful level of nationality. Third: I believe that the unification and nationality must be a fount of riches, of power and happiness for her children and that it is a condition *sine qua non* of the European equilibrium. Fourth: I believe in the apotheosis of all those who encounter suffering and death for the redemption of Italy. Fifth: lastly, I believe that the Italians must, can and wish to do everything by themselves.

Q. Must we not trust in an Italo-foreign intervention?

A. No! No! No!

Q. How many cardinal virtues of the Italians are there?

A. There are four: prudence, justice, strength and temperance.

Q. Why are they called cardinal?

A. Because they are the fount of good and fortunate undertakings.

Q. Say what is the purpose of these virtues.

A. Prudence makes us considerate and cautious in order that we are not tricked by our tyrants, nor by traitors without or within; 'timete Danaos et dona ferentes!' Justice commands us to repay to its utmost all the evil we receive from our oppressors: 'Carthago autem delenda.' Strength fills us with the sentiment of our dignity to look down on them and courage to exterminate them. Temperance makes us moderate in food and drink; content with ladies and abstemious in all diversions which make us forget our hard servitude; and all this serves to strengthen our bile and necessary robustness. Besides it makes us averse to German tobacco, to all objects of luxury so that rapaciousness does not arise from indigestion but from hunger.

Q. What are the works of spiritual mercy which we must perform mutually?

A. There are seven: First: to rouse from lethargy the depressed. Second: to put new strength into the faint-hearted. Third: to illumine the blind. Fourth: to convert the obstinate. Fifth: to inflame the unfortunate. Sixth: to forget offences and private rancours. Seventh: to honour the memory of our martyrs.

Q. Why is there no mention here of patience?

A. Because where liberty is in question, that is the virtue of the ass, not of man.

Q. But do you not fear the vaunted cavalry and infantry of the German Pharaoh?

A. The Red Sea is deep enough for all of them.

Q. What will be the Germans' Red Sea?

A. Their own blood.

Q. What is the best work of mercy that the Italian can perform towards the German?

A. To celebrate Sicilian Vespers for him.

Q. And what of an Italian who bears arms for the Tyrant against his own father, his own mother, his own brother, against the Italians?

A. He is a Cain.

Q. How does God punish a Cain?

A. With his life.

Q. And what of an Italian who betrays another Italian with a kiss of friendship and gives him into the power of the German Pharisees?

A. He is a Judas.

Q. How does God punish a Judas?

A. With Death.

Q. And both of them?

A. With eternal damnation.

Q. And what of Italians who do not believe in and profess this present catechism?

A.   They are pseudo-Italians.

Q.   What fate awaits them?

A.   That to which Christ condemns the unfruitful tree: they will be rooted up and thrown on the fire.

Q.   And when shall we be able to call ourselves blessed in our nationality?

A.   When we shall have drunk the blood of the Germans in the skulls of Metternich and Radetzky.

Choir: Amen.

The National Catechism

Q. Who are you?

A. Italians by the Grace of God.

Q. Who is your God?

A. The one who drowned the Pharaoh and rained fire on his enemies.

Q. How many principal enemies do we have?

A. Two: one visible; one invisible.

Q. Which is the invisible one?

A. The Devil.

Q. Which is visible?

A. The Emperor of Austria, Vicar of the Devil here on earth.

Q. How many natures does he have?

A. Two: one human; the other infernal.

Q. How many Emperors of Austria are there?

A. Only one, but divided into three persons.

Q. What are the names of these three persons?

A. Ferdinand, Metternich and Radetzky.

Q. What are the attributes of the first?

A. Despotism, Arrogance and Barbarity.

Q. What are the attributes of the second.

A. Treachery and Infamy.

Q. What are those of the third?

A. Robbery, a thirst for Italian blood and ignorance.

Q. What inspires Ferdinand?

A. Sin.

Q. What inspires Metternich?

A. Ferdinand.

Q. And Radetzky?

A. The Fornication of Both.

Q. So, there are three of them?

A. No, only one monster with three tails.

Q. Why is this?

A. It's a mystery.

Q. Which of the three is most wicked?

A. They are all equally so.

Q. And who are the Germans?

A. Half bears, half men, all beasts.

Q. How do they harm us?

A. They destroy Italian freedom, and try to deprive us of our souls, our thoughts, our homeland and even our memory of God.

Q. Shall we be able to get rid of them?

A. It is at least time to hope so.

Q. How?

A. In union with our brothers and with faith in our sovereigns and in their armies.

Q. What punishment is merited by an Italian who mocks his name by identifying with the Germans?

A. Death and infamy, in the name of
     Pius IX,
     Charles Albert,
     and Leopold II

Infamous Catechism of the Austrian Soldiers

(written in pseudo-Teutonic dialect)
British Library Catalogue No. 804k.13/236.

Q. Who are you?

R. We are valiant Austrian soldiers.

Q. Where are you going?

R. We are going to slaughter the Lombardo-Venetian fox, the Piedmontese pig, and those from Venice, Rome, Tuscany, Switzerland, all of them, all. . . .

Q. Why are you going to war?

R. Because the Kingdom of Lombardy-Venetia no longer wants the yoke, because the Italian Devil no longer wants us to eat macaroni; because everyone shouts 'Viva Pius IX'; 'Viva Carlo Alberto and Leopoldo', 'Viva Gioberti' and not 'Viva' for the poor good Austrians – because the Italians no longer want us in Italy; because we are hungry, because we have nothing to eat.

Q. And if you are slaughtered?

R. If we are slaughtered, we shall no longer be hungry.

Q. And if you are taken prisoner?

R. If we become prisoners, Charles Albert will give us bread.

Q. And if you win the battle?

R. If we win, we shall enter Milan and eat macaroni; if we win we shall get gold and go around in gangs killing and smoking; if we win, we shall eat and eat and drink, drink and always drink good wine.

Q. Who is your leader?

R. Our leader is Hunger.

Q. Do you like Radetzky?

R. No, because Radetzky is a rogue.

Q. Do you like Metternich?

R. No, because Metternich is infamous.

Q. Do you like your Emperor?

R. No, because the Emperor does not pay us and makes us die of hunger.

Q. Where is your homeland?

R. Where we can eat.

Dialogue Between Radetzky and Satan

(written in pseudo-Teutonic dialect)
British Library Catalogue No. 804k.13/327.

Satan: General Radetzky, we are all at your command.

Radetzky: Bravo! You are a gentleman, but I have a favour to ask of you.

Satan: I have come to the gates of Hell in order to oblige you.

Radetzky: I want you to suggest some means to me how I can get my revenge on this Italian pig who has burned all my good cavalry by throwing buckets of oil on their heads and backs.

Satan: My dear, you have asked me too late. There is no more time. Nor do I know what weapons to suggest to you in this situation apart from those of desperation!

Radetzky: And what are the weapons of desperation?

Satan: The weapons of desperation are to take to flight as quickly as you can, to go down a well head downwards, to blow your brains out, etc., etc.

Radetzky: Bravo! What good suggestions. You rascal of a Devil, is the imperial cause lost then?

Satan: Lost beyond repair. Don't you see that the Italians are triumphant? That they advance, advance, advance and you retreat, retreat, retreat?

Radetzky: A plague on you, you accursed beast! Would that I could use my sword on you! Away with you; even you have abandoned me.

Metternich's Aid for Radetzky. A Dialogue

(written in pseudo-Teutonic dialect)
British Library Catalogue No. 804k.13/327.

A sentry on the bastions of Verona: To arms! To arms! A traitor has dared approach the fortress while I am on watch!

Metternich: Quiet, Croat dear, and instead of shouting for arms, do your duty and present arms to Prince Metternich!

Sentry: The devil! . . . you are Metternich?

Metternich: Yes, Croat, I am Metternich!

Sentry: And why have you come to this evil place at a time when all poor Germans are dying of hunger? . . . You have played your cards very badly.

Metternich: I have come to help Radetzky and then to flee.

Sentry: Bravo! To help Radetzky – and have you no help for us other poor soldiers?

Metternich: Yes, for you too.

Sentry: Have you brought bread?

Metternich: No.

Sentry: Then to the devil with you! You don't know what to do!

Metternich: But Radetzky knows what to do with me. Call Radetzky. I'd like to talk with him.

Sentry: General! General!

Radetzky: What do you want?

Sentry: Metternich stands below the fortress and wants to speak to you.

Radetzky: Come Metternich, Come. (Metternich climbs up on to the bastion).

Metternich: Greetings Radetzky. I knew that you were besieged here. I knew of your misfortunes and I have brought you aid.

Radetzky: So many misfortunes. We have nothing to eat. Have you brought food?

Metternich: No, why? . . . It took me all my time to get here without falling into the hands of the Piedmontese. And I could not bring bread when I had no money left.

Radetzky: Have you come without a sword? Have you brought me a sword?

Metternich: Where did you lose your sword? I lost mine too. I regret that you are without one, but I am without one too.

Radetzky: But what help have you brought then?

Metternich: I knew that when you fled from Milan you lost your chamber-pot as well as your sword and so I brought it to you immediately.

Radetzky: Bravo! Bravo! This is marvellous. I do so look forward to using it. Please give it to me.

Metternich: Here it is! Here it is! Glad to have been of service.

Radetzky: Oh good, good dear Metternich, you are my loyal friend. Now thanks to you I shall lack nothing but bread. A sword which is sheathed is no good. But having received this blessed chamber-pot from you! Now I can die content since at least I can get rid of the shit I have taken from these Italian pigs!

Metternich: Goodbye Radetzky!

Radetzky: Goodbye Metternich, thanks!

Metternich: Where shall we meet again?

Radetzky: Either in Genoa as victors, or in Hell!

Metternich: Very well! In Hell! In Hell!

The Triumph of Charles Albert over Radetzky

(written in pseudo-Teutonic)
British Library Catalogue No. 804k.13/52.

Italy: In the long succession of centuries, through the various revolutions of the seasons, amidst all the catastrophes which have occurred in this poor, desolate land, the period which will receive most mention in the history books, the one which will stand out, is 1847 which will, on the centenary of the defeat of the Austrians in Ligura, produce great events worthy of the great man who first began the Risorgimento. Remember, Charles Albert, it was you who unchained and freed me when I was downtrodden and oppressed, you too, who wielding the sword of the great Pius gave proof of your greatest valour against the tyrants and oppressors. To you alone was vouchsafed the glory of the ancient House of Savoy, the only house in all my vast territories to exalt in the sacred name of Italy. An end to tyrants who have destroyed this land through pillage! An end to tyrants who even now oppress their subjects and who sacrifice the blood of innocents who justly seek their own emancipation! No more doddering old Ferdinands, no more pitiless Bourbons! But destiny has chosen you Charles Albert; Italy honours you alone and I hope through you to see Italy rise from her long abasement in which for centuries she has lain under the yoke of the tyrant.

Charles Albert: I am grateful, Italy, for all your fulsome expressions, and on the battlefields of Lombardy, I will give you proof of that Italian valour which you have recognised in me. Here, Italy, is the greatest of your oppressors, already lying beneath my feet.

Emperor: Let me go, Charles Albert. Show respect to the imperial crown and, let me have your demands.

Charles Albert: Your subjects have had the impudence of painting me as in your pocket, meaning to imply that I will always be your inferior and that Austria will always rule, will be an empire and will be in control. Well the tables have now been turned. I am no longer in your pocket but you are at my feet. But you will not be able to pay for your disregard [with money alone].

Emperor: Have pity Charles Albert, I am innocent. If my ministers did not take sufficient action, how am I to blame?

Charles Albert: How? If you wish to be a despot, an absolute sovereign, why do you allow yourself to be guided by ministers? Here is the price you have to pay for their skulduggery.

Emperor: The infamous Metternich who ruined me has now been kicked out and my wife who used to boss me was not aware of his trickery. For pity's sake, forgive me, I will get a new minister and put matters right.

Charles Albert: Any such attempt would be futile since you are already ruined. Your throne is shaking, your Empire is crumbling. And now, before you can get up you will have to concede what I shall demand of you in the name of Italy.

Emperor: Explain yourself: what does Italy want? I shall tell my wife and she will take the decision.

Charles Albert: What wife? What wife? You have to decide now and I have to promise to liberate Italy from your barbarian troops, from Radetzky and his Croats who have robbed her. Henceforth, you must abandon any thought of dominating her, since she wants her rights to liberty, unity and independence to be recognised.

Emperor: I cannot act alone; I need my ministers.

Charles Albert: Your Ministers have abandoned you.

Emperor: Is there no one who will help me? Have pity! Let me breathe, help!

Radetzky: Ah! My emperor is in danger. Now you are going to pay for your audacity, Charles Albert. My sword shall pass through your stomach.

Charles Albert: Take that you insolent coward! How dare you throw yourself against my sacred sword as once you threw yourself against our sacred temples. Now die and with you all tyrants.

Radetzky: I recognise your strength. Austria cannot resist it. My emperor shall concede your demands.

Emperor: Given that I have now lost the most loyal of my generals, so that my troops can no longer exist, I promise in front of your heroic champion, that within a month, Italy shall be free of all foreign domination.

Litany of the Lombard Pilgrims

'The whole of Italy is our homeland and we shall be exiles until this soil of ours is Italian. Yet we are also pilgrims who have taken vows to enter the Holy Land, that is liberated Lombardy.

    Kyrie eleison
    Christe eleison
    Christe audi nos
    Christe exaudi nos.

Father in Heaven who freed your people from their captivity in Egypt and led them back to the Promised Land,
    Lead us back to Lombardy.

Son of God, who climbed Calvary to redeem us, who wept on Golgotha and who died on the Cross,
    Resurrect Lombardy.

Virgin Mary, Mother of Sorrows, protectress of the persecuted, mediatrix of the martyrs,
    Save Lombardy.

Saint Ambrosius, Patron Saint of Milan,
    Pray for us.

Saint Mark, Patron Saint of Venice,
    Pray for us.

Glorious Pius IX, Apostle of Charity, Patron of Italy,
    Pray for us.

From the Austrian invasion,
    Deliver us, O Lord.

From Austrian servitude,
    Deliver us, O Lord.

From the scourge of the presence of Austria,
    Deliver us, O Lord.

We pray thee, Lord of armies, listen to us; Lord of Glory, triumph with us; God of vengeance, help us grind our tyrants in the dust.

    Kyrie eleison
    Christe eleison
    Christe audi nos
    Christe exaudi nos

In the name of the Father, the Son and the Holy Ghost, Let it be.'

The Pater Noster of the Lombards

British Library, Catalogue No. 804k.13/64.

Our Father which art in Heaven. Have pity on our sorrows, Lord, so long and fierce and save us from the cruel nails of the foreigner.

Hallowed Be Thy Name. As many times and as much as that of Satan is cursed and blasphemed.

Thy Kingdom Come, a kingdom of Love, which Pius has aspired to imitate on earth, which exalts virtue and opposes all injustice.

Thy Will be Done, if that day of vengeance and redemption, which will see Italy and Lombardy bound together is still delayed.

In Earth as it is in Heaven, on this day, it is written, that the snake and the lion, united in liberty, will have won their rights by force.

Give Us This Day Our Daily Bread which the foreigner steals from our very lips. Milan's cup of sorrows is full and henceforth shall overflow.

And Forgive Us Our Debts as We Forgive Those who lay traps for us in Vienna and Verona.

Lead Us Not Into Temptation but give us strength in heart and mind to win convincingly on the day of battle.

But Deliver Us From Evil and from the Germans. Nay! Save unhappy Lombardy from the Aulic Council and Radetzky.

Let it Be.

M. Maggioni

Proclamation of the Lombard Provisional Government to the Hungarians (April 29 1848)

British Library Catalogue. No. 804k.13/324.

To noble and generous Hungary we offered in the first days of our liberation the sincere salute of men who knew the cost of conquering national independence.

And we sent back to the heroic Magyar people some of the prisoners from their native land whom the fortunes of war had placed in our hands in the hope that they would return safe and sound to their firesides where they could tell you of the cruelty of our common oppressors, of our valour in battle and of our humanity in victory.

This great people replied to our address immediately under the impetus of true fraternity; and today we are proud to publish to all Italy their most noble reply.

It was what we yearned for and as a testimonial we can do no better than to publish it in the same form in which it reached us.

The fraternal greetings of the Hungarians are like the announcement of a victory for us!

'Italian Brothers!

'For a long time now foreigners have disposed of our finances and our blood and the people of Hungary have complained of it greatly. These complaints have been echoed in incessant requests and remonstrances that our troops should not leave their native soil. But political intrigue and tyranny has always opposed our just desires. Thus recently, when the trumpet of Italian independence resounded on the field of battle, those Hungarian soldiers, who form part of the paid troops of Austria, were employed as a blind instrument against the development of your freedom and forced to fight against your defenders of the trampled rights of the people.

'From the very first, we did not stop petitioning our ministers to have our troops recalled from the theatre of war, telling them that this compromised our national honour and interests. And we were already looking forward with impatience to the satisfaction of our desires when your proclamation arrived. Our indignation was universal and in each and every one of us arose the thought and cry: that we could no longer support this state of affairs.

'We do not doubt that the wishes of our ministers correspond fully to the desires of the nation. If, however, the Austrian bureaucracy is capable of creating difficulties in this respect, we can declare in the name of the people of Hungary that he who continues to fight against the cause of freedom will no longer be considered a son of this free land.

'Italian Brothers! Do not doubt the friendship of the Hungarians – in their fight for freedom our soldiers cannot nurture any true feeling of hatred against you, who have spilled your blood in these glorious encounters. We will never take up arms against the immortal image of Pius IX, that symbol of salvation and hope with which you adorn your breasts. We should be aghast to give our support to those who will have nothing to show from these glorious days but the sad sarcophagi of the freedom fighters who were sacrificed by them.

'God cannot permit tyranny to triumph over eternal right. This is our faith, our hope! Therefore, be assured that our most ardent wishes are that your freedom shall shine as a splendid star in the firmament and that Italy and Poland shall become free for their own sake and in the interest of the whole of Europe.

'Long Live Italy! Long Live Liberty! Long Live Equality, Long Live Fraternity!'

From the Committee of the City of Pest.

Appendix 15

D'Aspre's Critique of Radetzky's Leadership in Italy

Kriegsarchiv, Nachlass B349/7 (Nachlass FML. Freiherr d'Aspre)

It should not be necessary to investigate the causes of the great losses suffered in Italy during the revolution.

(a) These in my opinion may be attributed to the way in which the army was administered ('in den Geschäftsgänge gesucht werden').

The Army Command in Milan was subordinate to the Commander-in-Chief and to the General Command in Verona.

The orders emanating from both sides were often contradictory and because it was necessary to question them, always delayed.

The Second Army Corps Command received orders from the High Command either through its representatives in the General Command or directly.

All troop commanders were subordinate to the Corps Commands – as were, however, also most garrison (*Stadt*) commanders – and as such came under the orders of the General Command. In this way, the same individual found himself subordinated to two different authorities, whose orders were often contradictory.

For example: a battalion was due to go on the march. The corps commander naturally ordered it to depart as strong as possible. The garrison commander, on the other hand, kept all those so commanded behind.

When several such marches were ordered at the same time, there remained behind in most towns a whole host of people who, as a result of frequent garrison changes, belonged to various regiments and whose numbers depended on the requirements of the branches of the forces to be found in a [given] garrison. These people could not then be released since they were kept by these branches for their own use.

When on account of pressing circumstances, a battalion of Franz Carl Infantry had to leave quickly for Ferrara, it had, despite the insistent intercession of its commander Colonel Kavanagh, to leave 200 men behind in Verona. I complained over the matter pointing out that such an unsatisfactory state of affairs could only be remedied, if an urgent command were issued, to the effect that when troops had to depart, not a single man could be kept behind for whatever reason or else the local commander would be held to be strictly accountable. I was told by the General Command 'that I should refrain from giving advice'.

Given that, with the outbreak of revolution the only salvation of the army was a quick concentration of troops, those people who remained in the cities or who followed on in small detachments – were captured or lulled by the insurgents.

(*b*) Under such circumstances several detachments of troops – namely, eight companies of Borderers – which were stationed in various garrisons of the north Venetian provinces, received orders directly from the General Command; received other orders directly from myself; and finally, they received orders from FML. Ludolf on his own authority.

The confusion which must have arisen, can be imagined. The result was that these eight companies of Borderers which were supposed to have set off for Treviso, never reached it. The fall of Treviso ensued and frustrated my intention to withdraw half of the Italian battalion stationed there.

The battalion's commander Major Frank had let me know personally that he feared this battalion would not willingly withdraw. The presence of the Borderers, however, would have ensured good behaviour, the (Italian) battalion would have been split, a part of the Borderers would have remained in Treviso and, with four companies of the same sent by rail to Venice, my communications with that city would have been secured.

The troops in Venice stood under my command; however, all detachments on duty were under the orders of the fortress commander FML. Count Zichy who gradually withdrew them from all posts they occupied and replaced them by national guards and who had them locked up in their barracks along with their officers. I received no word of this either from him or from Brigadier-General Culoz until the shameful capitulation of Venice was concluded.

FML. Zichy was an upright, brave soldier, but one of those for whom everything is fine so long as they have peace. The chief of the artillery section had and, moreover, sought, no influence.

The chief of the artillery was a nonentity – a brave, talented officer, he would never have opposed the fortress commander under any circumstances. And so, Venice fell. I was only two hours away (by rail) but could exercise no influence.

I feel all the more obliged to mention these matters since even now on 3rd December 1849, when given present conditions I could be ordered to march out from one day to the next, the town and fortress command of this place – such a strategic point as Piacenza – has been entrusted to FML. Count Ata. The latter may also be an upright, brave soldier but is also incapable under any circumstances of acting with force or insight or even of behaving independently. This has been known by the Army High Command for ages so that any further discussion of the matter would be redundant.

I shall similarly restrict my observations on the distribution of the 6th Army Corps presently under my command.

The Division which was formerly under the command of His Highness the Archduke Albert was entrusted a few months ago to FML. Baron Rath. Shortly afterwards he had to take over the other Division of my army corps, the first being given to FML. Prince Liechtenstein.

(*c*) All his troops were taken away from G.M. Count Stadion. They were sent to Bologna to the 8th Corps on active service and for economic reasons and placed under a general I do not know.

(*d*) Count Stadion, on the other hand, received another brigade and a cavalry battery.

(*e*) G. M. Count Kolowrat lost the Franz Karl Regiment.

(*f*) The Gyulai Regiment came to Milan to the 5th Corps – the 6th received the Geppert Regiment in return.

(*g*) When G.M. Wimpffen became FML. his brigade was broken up. G.M. Draskovich is in Cremona – the Török Brigade is stretched out from Modena to Piacenza.

I remain at headquarters with the artillery reserve at the most extreme limit of the corps at Piacenza with a chief of the General Staff who is unknown to me. Most orders come to me to be issued or by way of information but most also go direct from Headquarters to the troop detachments below, as a result of which fairly many marches and counter-marches ensue.

The second Army Corps, now called the sixth, fighting either by itself or with another corps, won all the battles it took part in in the last two campaigns. At the head of it, I believed that I could undertake everything, but I must now declare that I have lost this faith completely. I can also definitely declare, that this confidence no longer exists in this now completely dismantled corps.

Appendix 16

A Plan for Class War

Vienna, Haus-Hof- und Staatsarchiv, Kabinettsarchiv, Geheimakten, Karton 11 (Schwarzenberg Nachlass V, No. 274).

Hartig to Schwarzenberg, Vienna, 21 March 1849.

An unnamed person, who probably does not know of my retirement, has sent me the enclosed draft of a law for the Kingdom of Lombardy-Venetia, which would, in his opinion, prevent the restless *Possidenti* there from intriguing against the Austrian government and which might also persuade their *Coloni* to link their personal interests with those of the government.

The enclosed draft ran as follows:

The pacification of the Kingdom of Lombardy-Venetia is most important and urgent. The more the revolutionary party uses every means – even the most abominable – to achieve its ends, the more the government must feel itself obliged to resort to every legal means which it on its side has at its disposal. One such means which would be both useful and which would promise the best results for Austria would be the following: the *Coloni* of the Kingdom of Lombardy-Venetia are viewed naturally merely as labourers hired for a certain length of time by those who provide their work, namely the *Possidenti* on whom they are entirely dependent and who use them for their own ends. However, since the hatred of the *Coloni* for Austria does not originate in their own minds but is implanted there, it should not be so difficult to remove it altogether and to organize them in the interest of Austria. This could be brought about by passing a law according to which those *Possidenti* who in future commit treason against Austria, as well as those who conspire against Austria abroad and refuse to return to their estates within a certain number of days to be calculated from today onwards, would lose their properties, which would be made over in perpetuity to those who up till now have worked on them, so long as they conduct themselves lawfully. Such a measure would be *just* even although the State, according to articles 1295, 1302, and 1324 of the Imperial Law Book must fully compensate those who are to be punished. No complaint of illegality could be made since these arrangements would be made known beforehand and would only be used in serious cases. The state has the right in any case, when compensation has to be paid for estates which fall to it, not to sell these – which brings little profit politically – but to exploit them by making over the enjoyment of the land to the *Coloni* as opposed to the hereditary owners and by ensuring that the former pay the land-tax previously paid by the *Possidenti* and that they pay the state a fixed yearly rent under article 1122 of the Law Book. This measure would also be highly politic; for from the moment such a law was made known mistrust would spread among the people and that too in accordance with the axiom 'divide and rule'. The people would be divided into two classes: the

Coloni and the *Possidenti*. The *Coloni* whose condition at present is so wretched would watch every step of their masters with argus eyes in the hope of becoming self-reliant. In this way, the Austrian government would not only be sure to hear of any intrigue immediately, but this whole section of the population would be won at a stroke for Austria, since only under this government could they have the hope of becoming self-reliant or of not losing their self-reliance should it already have been won. The dangerous classes of the people as far as state security is concerned are those without property and those with too much. The middle class is the pillar of the state: but it has too much property not to be in danger of losing some; and too little not to rule out hopes for more. This middle class (*Mittelclasse*), which intends to enjoy the income necessary to meet its needs in peace, must endeavour to support the government. In the Kingdom of Lombardy-Venetia, no such class really exists, which also explains the provocations of the nobles aided by their exploitable proletariat of *Coloni*. If these *Coloni* were to enjoy the benefits of the land they worked in a manner similar to German Austrian peasants, they would be reliable supports of Austria. Just as the Galician peasants proved themselves so grateful to a government which accorded them only the usual protection of the law, so too would the Italian peasantry – since it would owe its very existence to Austria. The *Possidenti* would be obliged by such measures to behave very loyally towards the Austrian government in order not to be suspected and endangered as be no longer in question. If any measures should be taken by the *Coloni* against their rightful, loyal landowners, the protection of the state would have, of course, to intervene. In the above manner, *soldiers* who had distinguished themselves could also be *rewarded*.

Abbreviations used in the notes

B.F.S.P. British and Foreign State Papers.

Carte Segrete Carte Segrete della Polizia Austriaca in Italia, Estratte dell'Archivio di Venezia e pubblicate per Commissione di D. Manin, 3 vols, Capolago, 1851.

C(1) Federico Curato (ed.) *Le Relazioni Diplomatiche fra Gran Bretagna e il Regno di Sardegna,* Vol. 51 in the series Fonti per la Storia d'Italia, Rome 1961.

C(2) Curato, op. cit., Vol. 52.

F(1) Angelo Filipuzzi, *Le Relazioni Diplomatiche fra L'Austria e il Regno di Sardegna e la Guerra del 1848–49* (2 vols). Vol. 53 in the series Fonti per la Storia d'Italia, Rome, 1961.

F(2) Filipuzzi, op. cit., Vol. 54.

H-H.SA.S.K. Vienna, Haus-Hof- und Staatsarchiv, Staatskanzleiakten, Kriegsakten.

H-H.SA.S.P.L-V. Vienna, Haus-Hof- und Staatsarchiv, Staatskanzleiakten, Provinzen, Lombardo-Venezien.

K. Karton.

KA.CK. (Präs.) Vienna, Kriegsarchiv, Centralkanzleiakten, Präsidialreihe.

KA.F. Vienna, Kriegsarchiv, Feldakten.

KA.M.A. Vienna, Kriegsarchiv, Memoiren Abteilung.

KA.M.K. Vienna, Kriegsarchiv, Ministerium des Kriegswesensakten.

Max. 1. 'Blick auf Italien im Herbst 1847', KA.F., Krieg im Italien, Hauptarmee, Fascicle 213.

Max. 2 'Blick auf die Lage des Lombard-venezianischen Königreiches, Anfangs 1848', KA.F., Krieg im Italien, Hauptarmee, Fascicle 214.

Max. 3 'Blick auf die Lage Italiens, Anfangs 1848 (Nicht Unwendbar)', KA.F., Krieg im Italien, Hauptarmee, Fascicle 214.

Max. 4 'Über die Nothwendigkeit dass Österreich die Lombardie behalte.', KA.F., Krieg im Italien, Hauptarmee, Fascicle 214.

Max. 5 'Ein Wort für die Gegenwart', KA.F., Krieg im Italien, Hauptarmee, Fascicle 214.

O-E.A.(IV) Vienna, Hans-Hof- und Staatsarchiv, Österreichisch-Estensisches Archiv (IV).

P.R.O., F.O. Public Records Officer, Foreign Office.

V(1) Franco Valsecchi (ed.), *Le Relazioni Diplomatiche fra l'Austria e il Regno di Sardegna,* Vol. 66 of the series Fonti per la Storia d'Italia (Vol. 3 in Series III, 1848–60), Rome, 1963.

V(2) Valsecchi, op. cit., Vol. 67 (Vol. 4 in Series III).

Raccolta Raccolta degli Atti ufficiali dei Proclami ecc. emanati e pubblicati in Milano dalle diverse Autorità durante L'I.R. Governo Militare, Vol. 1 (6 Aug. 1848 to 31 Mar. 1849), Milan 1849?

Notes

Notes to introduction

1. A. J. P. Taylor, *Europe: Grandeur and Decline*, London, 1967, p. 127.
2. William Roscoe Thayer, *The Life and Times of Cavour*, London, 1911, Vol. I, p. 153.
3. This point is well supported by the standard account of Hungarian diplomacy in the spring and summer of 1848; István Hajnal's *A Batthyány-Kormány Külpolitikája*, Budapest, 1957.
4. The Baroness Blaze de Bury, *Germania: Its Courts, Camps and Peoples*, 2 vols., London, 1850, Vol. II, pp. 144–55, fn. 2.
5. See below, Note 21, Ch. 4 (p. 87).
6. Quoted by M. Hartley, *The Man who Saved Austria*, London, 1912, p. 185. But cf. Note 9.
7. 'Field Marshal Radetzky had taken command of all troops in Lombardy-Venetia in 1831. From then on he kept a calm but steady eye on political events and since the progress of the revolutionary party did not escape his attention he was actively concerned through both tactical and moral means to give the army the necessary strength to restore the law and order which treason was subverting. His zeal was not merely restricted to military administration but extended to political matters and indeed in the latter stages he attempted to rouse the highest governing organs from their unconcern and to make them take action against the looming storm in the Kingdom of Lombardy-Venetia. His efforts, however, were not always crowned with the desired success.

'If, therefore, the army in Italy was unable to face the revolution completely armed, and if the defence of fortified places was incomplete, the blame was in no way the Field Marshal's but that of the governing authorities, which, blinkered by preconceived ideas, held his reports on the condition of Italy to be exaggerated, attributed his demands to excessive fears, and found them insufficiently worthy of attention.' (*Der Feldzug der österreichischen Armee in Italien im Jahre 1848*, Vienna, 1854, p. 4.)
8. 'The Field Marshal had always had the intention of organising his forces into two easily concentrated main parts but found this strenuously opposed by the local political authorities, which maintained that they could only maintain order and carry out their functions under the protection of bayonets. They were against the diminution of this or that garrison with the result that the army remained dispersed, often in insufficient numbers for garrison duty and lacking sufficient strength at the mercy of events.' (*Der Feldzug*, pp. 8–9.)
9. 'If the Field Marshal had been given the powers he demanded earlier on, before the weight of events forced him for the good of the state to take the power of governing into his own hands, it is certain that the timeous deployment of his forces would have brought about a different outcome in Milan. However, once the resistance could reach such a level unhindered, each display of force, given the means available, came too late and was too weak.' (*Der Feldzug*, p. 11.)
10. 'The bitterness of the military was, therefore, aroused to the same degree and more since it could not escape notice that the civil authorities witnessed those manifestly revolutionary activities with complete passivity, nay even supported them. . . . From these and many other symptoms it was easy to see how the spirit of revolution had already infiltrated the organs of administration and what progress it had made.' (*Der Feldzug*, pp. 6–7.)
11. *Der Feldzug*, p. 7. But cf. ibid., pp. 10–11, when the author, writing of the independence movement writes: 'This was the ambition of the leaders of the movement in Lombardy-Venetia who belonged to the first families in the land. Only a few capable men of the lower classes were used as instruments in order, with their support, to influence the people.'
12. I quite accept the point that 'it is not through what armies *are* but what they *do* that the lives of nations and of individuals are changed'. (John Keegan, *The Face of Battle*, New York, 1977, p. 30),

but armies often do or do not do things because of what they are. That is the point of this book. Moreover, a reliable battle history of 1848–9 already exists, See Note 21, Ch. 4.

13. In fact there is only one outstanding contemporary account and that is Freiherr Fenner von Fenneberg's *Oesterreich und Seine Armee,* Leipzig, 1847(?) which has to be supplemented by Moriz Edlen von Angeli *Wien nach 1848, Aus dem Nachlasse von Moriz Edlen von Angeli*, Vienna and Leipzig, 1905.

14. See Note 13, Ch. 4.

Notes to Chapter 1

1. Wiener Neustadt and the Engineering Academy between them put out only 90–120 graduates each year, i.e. 3,000–4,000 officers during the period 1815–48. In the period 1815–29, therefore, some 1,500 such officers had joined the army. In 1829 the peace establishment of the Austrian army included *c.* 27,000 officers, which meant that academy graduates formed only 5.6 per cent of the army as a whole and 2.9 per cent of the infantry and cavalry if one disregards the technical corps. True, these figures do not account for graduates among the veterans, but even so, by 1848 Wiener Neustadt could only have accounted for about 3 per cent of infantry and cavalry officers. References: von Angeli, *Wien nach 1848, Aus dem Nachlasse von Moriz Edlen von Angeli,* Vienna and Leipzig, 1905, p. 96; Fenner von Fenneberg, *Öesterreich und seine Armee*, Leipzig, 1847 (?), p. 43; Capt. Basil Hall, 'Notices on the Austrian army', *United Services Magazine,* Sept. 1835, p. 29, Table 3.

2. I shall devote most of this section to Wiener Neustadt Military Academy for the simple reason that the other military training schools had little influence on the army as a whole. The Engineering Academy, for example, produced only five to ten officers per year.

3. Baron Antoine de Mollinary de Monte Pastello states in his memoirs, *Quarante-six Ans dans L'Armée Austro-Hongroise, 1833—79,* Paris 1913, Vol. 1, p. 27, that Tulln was the third school in the land after the two academies.

4. Mollinary, op. cit., p. 33 says that at some point during this period it had been established that the two top students at Tulln should enter the army as second lieutenants in the same way as academy graduates. However, this rarely happened. Görgey, the man who was to achieve so much for the Hungarians in 1849, was not allowed to enter the army as a second lieutenant although he was first in his year at Tulln.

5. According to von Fenneberg the General Staff was less influenced by nepotism than the infantry and cavalry: 'Although high birth and powerful patronage may ease entry into this corps also, in general both a strict scientific education and wide knowledge of military science are regarded as a *conditio sine qua non* for assignment to the Bureaux or appointment to this excellent corps.' Officers of outstanding intellect were rare in the Austrian army according to von Fenneberg, but where possible an effort was made to bring them into the General Staff – as much as anything to rid the regiments of their unwelcome presence (von Fenneberg, op. cit., pp. 140–2). Bright N.C.Os were also recruited to work in the staff offices. By the end of the 1840s officers recruited to the staff were made to sit a sort of nominal exam. But the real test came when they were assigned their tasks. Then the incompetent were soon found out (von Fenneberg, op. cit., pp. 156–7). The corps, however, consisted of only fifty-nine men, and other observers, it should be noted, took a less sanguine view of it than did von Fenneberg. See pp. 10, 87 above.

6. See von Fenneberg, op. cit., p. 30. However, von Angeli, op. cit., p. 99 says that the foundation was established first for the sons of poor noblemen and only monopolised thereafter by the sons of poor subalterns when the first group did not make use of it.

7. Von Fenneberg, op. cit., p. 30.

8. A *Feldmarschalleutnant* (FML.) commanded a division, sometimes an army corps.

9. See von Fenneberg, op. cit., pp. 49, 156. There were only 60–80 private and permanent endowments out of 340 places in Wiener Neustadt.

10. Von Angeli, op. cit., p. 99.

11. Von Angeli, op. cit., p. 99.

12. Von Angeli, op. cit., p. 100.

13. Von Angeli, op. cit., p. 105.

14. Dorothea Gerard, *The Austrian Officer at Work and Play*, London, 1913, p. 195.

15. These watchdogs were known as 'rags' and were not allowed to swear at the boys who were regarded, in this instance at least, as future officers.

16. Gerard, op. cit., p. 192. There was no such thing as ball-games or the like and it was forbidden, of course, to walk on the grass. The paths themselves reflected the official Austrian mind quite

admirably: one was called 'the big path', the other 'the little path'.

17. Homosexuality is at least implied here and it must have taken place. These boys were locked away from everybody but themselves from the age of eleven to eighteen. Indeed, most of them were not allowed out of the Academy during their whole seven years there. Once they entered the army conditions also encouraged such behaviour. Only one-sixth of the officers were allowed to marry and according to Mollinary, op. cit., p. 80, the soldiers slept two in a bed.

18. If he were really lucky, of course, a rich nobleman would adopt him as his son and set him on the road to a wonderful career.

19. Gerard, op. cit., p. 195.

20. Von Angeli, op. cit., p. 109.

21. Von Angeli, op. cit., p. 109.

22. For these rules, see von Angeli, op. cit., pp. 110–11.

23. The Vienna–Wiener Neustadt railway opened in 1841.

24. See Gerard, op. cit., pp. 195–203.

25. Von Fenneberg, op. cit., pp. 32–3.

26. This no doubt included a course on the horribly sycophantic style which fills military documents of the period; see von Fenneberg's remarks on this, op. cit., pp. 51–2 and p. 13.

27. Note the difference.

28. Only superficially. The Engineering Academy was the place for this.

29. That is, into the courtyard of the Academy – not outside its walls.

30. See von Fenneberg, op. cit., pp. 39–40.

31. Von Fenneberg, op. cit., pp. 39–40.

32. See von Fenneberg, op. cit., pp. 150–5.

33. For the quotations in this paragraph see von Angeli, op. cit., pp. 101–2.

34. Von Angeli, op. cit., p. 102.

35. Von Fenneberg, op. cit., p. 29.

36. The only complete failures were those with a record of endemic insubordination.

37. Von Fenneberg, op. cit., p. 34.

38, 39. Von Angeli, op. cit., pp. 113–14, says that the rest of Wiener Neustadt 'was as unknown to them as any place in Hindustan or Zululand'.

40. German for 'teens', the age leading up to puberty, adolescence.

41. See part II.

42. A common moulding process began at the Academy when boys would refuse to 'squeal' on one another, and where a common sign-language evolved. In the 1850s fixed bayonets had to be used to storm barricades set up during a student revolt.

43. See von Fenneberg, op. cit., p. 43.

44. Mollinary, op. cit., p. 32, fn. 1. There were six places per regiment reserved for imperial cadets in the infantry and cavalry regiments. The Bombardier Corps reserved thirty.

45. Mollinary, op. cit., p. 23. Also see p. 21, where Mollinary says of his own family. 'It was a real family of soldiers, the sons knew no other profession but that of the officer. They had no other ambition but to serve the Emperor in his army as their fathers had done.' See also von Fenneberg's comment, op. cit., p. 31: 'through this almost exclusive system a separate caste is being formed in the army'. He was referring to the training institutions as a whole.

46. See: von Angeli, op. cit., pp. 116–17; von Fenneberg, op. cit., p. 44.

47. See von Fenneberg, op. cit., pp. 43, 117. Every third officer's position which fell vacant had to be given to an imperial cadet.

48. *Expropriis-Gemeine* 'were volunteers who did not want to enlist as privates. They wanted to become officers. There were treated just the same as regimental cadets, but the latter could only be appointed with the express permission of the regimental colonel-proprietor and had to be soldiers' sons.

49. One-fifth value must be added to C.M. to give its value in rhennich. C.M. (Konventmünze) was the currency system used in Austria.

50. German for 'uniform money'.

51. Von Angeli, op. cit., p. 119.

52. Von Fenneberg, op. cit., p. 118.

53. Foreigners were able to join any branch of the Austrian state service.

54. Von Angeli, op. cit., p. 119.

55. Von Angeli, op. cit., p. 119.

56. Von Fenneberg, op. cit., pp. 115–16.

57. Von Angeli, op. cit., p. 119.

58. Vienna, KA.M.D., Section 28, Miscellaneous 1846.

59. Von Angeli, op. cit., p. 119, agreed with this sort of description. According to him – and his book is written much more from the viewpoint of the officers than the common soldiers – the infantry regiments at this time were supplied by what he terms, 'more or less the *beaux restes*', the argument running that the better people joined the cavalry.

60. The post of ensign was abolished in 1838. Holders of that rank were then made second lieutenants.

61. Von Fenneberg, op. cit., p. 117. These were kept for imperial cadets.

62. Peter Evan Turnball, *Austria*, 2 vols, London, 1840, Vol. 2, Ch. 10, p. 286.

63. For example, the Radetzky Hussars.

64. Such nominations were intended to be purely honorary anyway.

65. Hall, op. cit., p. 23.

66. See von Fenneberg, op. cit., p. 165. Usually the soldiers were asked to contribute to this fund to help offset heating and lighting expenses. They were therefore deprived of money by a fund which supposedly had been set up to help them.

67. There was usually a shortage of cloth.

68. C. A. Haillot, *Statistique Militaire et Recherches sur l'Organisation et les Institutions des Armées Étrangères*, 2 vols, Paris 1846, Vol. 1, p. 78.

69. Von Fenneberg, op. cit., p. 171.

70. Von Fenneberg, op. cit., p. 171.

71. Von Fenneberg, op. cit., p. 171.

72. See von Fenneberg, op. cit., p. 172.

73. Von Angeli, op. cit., p. 127.

74. Von Fenneberg, op. cit., p. 172.

75. Von Fenneberg, op. cit., p. 173. He did not regard such people as 'fools and idiots who without such patronage would have got nowhere, but [did] assert that "the majority are *lumina mundi*."'

76. Gerard, op. cit., p. 216.

77. Mollinary, op. cit., p. 37.

78. See von Angeli, op. cit., p. 123.

79. Von Angeli, op. cit., pp. 123–4.

80. This, at least, is the view of Hall, op. cit., p. 23. Turnball, op. cit., p. 236 disagrees with him. Other sources only discuss the system of conventions, which perhaps implies that they are on Turnball's side.

81. In equivalent British money £200 and £300.

82. See von Angeli, op. cit., p. 122. It is his view that by retaining the system the Archduke continued the supply of better officers. But he must have lost out, too.

83. Von Fenneberg, op. cit., p. 174.

84. Von Fenneberg, op. cit., p. 175.

85. Turnball, op. cit., p. 287.

86. Turnball, op. cit., p. 237.

87. Outsiders, literally 'shoved-ins'.

88. Turnball, op. cit., pp. 287–8.

89. See von Fenneberg, op. cit., p. 178.

90. Von Fenneberg, op. cit., p. 125.

91, 92, 93. See von Angeli, op. cit., pp. 125–6.

94. See von Angeli, op. cit., p. 127.

95. Oscar Regele, *Feldmarschall Radetzky: Sein Leben, Leistung und Erbe,* Vienna, 1957, p. 482.

96. The pay scales which follow are taken from Hall, op. cit., pp. 170–1. He also calculated them in the equivalent British figures using the official exchange rate for 1835, namely 2*s*. 1*d*. to the florin.

97. Hall, op. cit., p. 117.

98. Pay for Jäger was everywhere the same.

99. Pay in the artillery was highest of all.

100. The Austrian term for garrisons in different lands.

101. See Hall, op. cit., p. 171.

102. 1 June 1856 was the great day for officers because their pay was ordered to be brought forward. They were paid, therefore, on 20 May and 1 June.

103. This allowance is included in the tables.

104. See von Fenneberg, op. cit., pp. 235–6.

105. See von Fenneberg, op. cit., p. 233.

106. Von Fenneberg, op. cit., p. 238.

107. After the pay increases of 1840.

108. See von Angeli, op. cit., pp. 131 and 146.

109. Von Angeli, op. cit., p. 134.
110. Turnball, op. cit., p. 290.
111. See von Angeli, op. cit., p. 134.
112. Von Angeli, op. cit., p. 149.
113. Later it was reduced to one-third of the increase.
114. Haillot, op. cit., pp. 64–5, says that the price of a horse was between 110 and 160 fl., depending on the type required.
115. See von Angeli, op. cit., p. 150.
116. See Ch. 3.
117. See below, pp. 27–8.
118. See von Angeli, op. cit., pp. 138–9.
119. See von Angeli, op. cit., p. 139. But see also Gerard, op. cit., pp. 279–80: 'The Jew does not wait to be sent for. Scarcely has a regiment marched into a new station than there is a swarm of usurers about it with their pockets full of banknotes which they literally press upon even reluctant receivers well aware that however long the harvest may be in coming the severity of Austrian military laws will cause the family in question to strain every possible resource in order to cancel the debt and thus save young Hopeful's career.' Gerard, the wife of an Austrian cavalry officer, is only reflecting the widespread anti-Semitism of the Austrian army as a whole. Her most purple passage comes on page 286:

> It is well known that regular registers are kept of the financial position, not only of every officer, but also of his parents and relations in various degree no matter in what part of the Empire they live in order to be referred to in the interests of money-lending. Naturally, however, this secret service embraces many other fields of business. Incredible things are told of the Galician Jew's omniscience – incredible, however, only to those who have not seen him at work. By what secret channels information is circulated, it is impossible for an outsider to say; but that some such secret service exists and is far more perfectly organised than that of the secret police of any country, it is impossible to doubt.

120. See von Angeli, op. cit., pp. 150–7.
121. Hall, op. cit., p. 173 and Turnball, op. cit., p. 299 give the figure as one-third. They are both wrong. Turnball is merely copying Hall in any case. French and Austrian sources always cite one-sixth. For example, von Fenneberg, op. cit., p. 60 and Haillot, op. cit., p. 82.
122. Hall, p. 173 gives a table of cautions listing 10,000 fl. for field officers and 8,000 for lower officers in 1835. Turnball says the same. Von Fenneberg always refers to a sum of 6,000 fl. for subalterns and is probably right, since he served in the army during this period. Again, according to these English sources, a cash sum was not always necessary, but a property could be purchased at a price which could guarantee an annual rent of 600 or 400 fl. instead of interest.
123. See von Angeli, op. cit., pp. 144–6.
124. The name given to their dress uniform.
125. See von Angeli, op. cit., pp. 140–2.
126. Radetzky was eighty-two in 1848 and still in command of the army in Italy. In 1855 the War Minister had personally to take over the command of a regiment whose colonel was 100 years old. See Antonio Schmidt-Brentano, *Die Armee in Österreich, Militär, Staat und Gesellschaft, 48–67*, Boppard am Rein, 1975, p. 411.
127. This was true at least for artillery officers. Officers in other branches of the service received the same treatment only if they were classified as 'real' invalids and were the oldest members of that rank in the corps. Hall, op. cit., p. 172.
128. Hall, op. cit., p. 172.
129. Von Fenneberg, op. cit., p. 317.
130. See von Fenneberg, op. cit., Ch. 10.
131. Von Fenneberg, op. cit., pp. 311–16.
132. Von Fenneberg, op. cit., p. 318.
133. Gerard, op. cit., p. 7.
134. Von Fenneberg, op. cit., pp. 73–4.
135. See von Fenneberg, op. cit., pp. 4–5. One regulation in force under Maria Theresa read 'The captain must be sober on at least one day during the year, namely when recruits are broken in.'
136. See Gerard, op. cit., p. 252.
137. According to von Fenneberg, op. cit., p. 18, 45,000 gulden could be won or lost in a night. Middling officers could lose three months' pay. At manœuvres, 'there is a passion for gambling'.
138. See von Angeli, op. cit., p. 148 and pp. 158–63.
139. A document drawn up by two officers saying that the man had resigned of his own volition.
140. They also took over the debts of officers who committed suicide.

141. See von Fenneberg, op. cit., pp. 124–7.
142. Socialists suffering from the same kind of illusions call each other 'comrade' or 'brother'.
143. See Gerard, op. cit., pp. 293–6. There were two main types of duel: 'with advance' or 'free shot' duels. The first had the antagonists placed 35–40 paces from each other. At the order 'advance' they went forward and had to shoot before they were 20 paces apart. This was standard practice. Alternatively the 'free shot' duel saw them 30–35 paces apart at fixed points. They had to shoot within 30 seconds of the order 'shoot'.
144. See von Fenneberg, op. cit., pp. 136–7: 'I take the view that it is an eternal stain on the government if it is not in a position to protect the existence of those who obey its laws and the dictates of reason and humanity.'
145. Von Fenneberg, op. cit., p. 315.
146. Gerard, op. cit., p. 129. But note that in the cavalry where almost everyone was aristocratic, social intercourse with cadets was more acceptable.
147. Von Fenneberg, op. cit., p. 122.
148. Von Fenneberg, op. cit., p. 122.
149. Turnball, op. cit., pp. 292–3.
150. Nikolaus von Preradovich. *Die Fuhrungsschichten in Oesterreich und Preussen, 1804–1918, mit einem Ausblick zum Jahre 1945,* Wiesbaden, 1955.
151. Von Preradovich, op. cit., pp. 5–7 gives explanation of the different categories.
152. See von Fenneberg, op. cit., pp. 120–1 and von Angeli, op. cit., p. 96.
153. Von Fenneberg, op. cit., p. 6. He refers to its 'almost democratic constitution'.
154. See von Fenneberg, op. cit., pp. 47–8.
155. See von Preradovich, op. cit., pp. 6–7. Other people who experienced systematic nobility were holders of the Order of the Iron Crown III Class or the Knight's Cross of the Leopold Order; holders of all grades of the Maria Theresa Order: the Freiherr class recruited holders of the Order of the Iron Crown, Classes I and II, proprietor-colonels and Commanders of the Great Cross of the Leopold Order and Knights and Commanders of the Royal Hungarian Stephen Order.
156. Von Fenneberg, op. cit., pp. 59–60.
157. See Schmidt-Brentano, op. cit., p. 448, fn. 166.
158. The Austrians lost fewer officers during the period 1618–1913 than the French lost during the Revolutionary and Napoleonic Wars.
159, 160. See von Fenneberg, op. cit., pp. 41–6.
161, 162. See von Fenneberg, op. cit., pp. 141–6.
163. Von Fenneberg, op. cit., p. 68. 'My soldiers should read what they want as long as they fight bravely.'
164, 165. See von Fenneberg, op. cit., pp. 55–6.
166. See Gerard, op. cit., pp. 5–6.
167. See von Fenneberg, op. cit., pp. 177–80.
168. Burial taxes only operated when losses allowed, no charge being made for men from sergeant downwards. Generals and staff officers paid at their discretion. Christenings were free. The pay received by doctors was, by contrast, meagre. Most officers (subalterns) were treated free of charge. The regimental doctor himself was a lieutenant but could be buried as an *Oberleutnant*.
169. See *Unserer Armee vom Verfasser des 'Deutschen Soldaten',* Vienna, 1850, pp. 352–3.
170. See Haillot, op. cit., pp. 83–4. Some regiments contained not a single decorated man. Decorations had to be earned. They were also worth a considerable sum of money to their owners. Pensions awarded to holders of the Maria Theresa order, for example, could be worth as much as 1,500 fl.
171. See Gerard, op. cit. p. 215.

Notes to Chapter 2

1. Gunther E. Rothenberg, 'The Austrian army in the age of Metternich', *Journal of Modern History*, 40 (1968), 155–65, 160.
2. Capt. Basil Hall, 'Notices on the Austrian army', *United Services Magazine*, Sept. 1835, p. 176.
3. It is difficult to establish whether the militia existed or not for the whole Vormärz period. Hall and Turnball writing in the mid 1830s assumed that it did, although Turnball adds (*Austria,* 2 vols, London, 1840, Vol. 2, Ch. 10, p. 282) 'The *Landwehr* unless embodied, which it never is in ordinary times of peace, receives no pay and exists only on paper, but this paper existence is with

very little trouble or delay convertible at any time into corporeal reality; as the registers are excellently kept and each battalion has its full establishment of officers marked out, who from the retired or supernumerary list, are held ready to join at a day's notice.' Hall implies that the Landwehr had a more tangible existence which my narrative also assumes. Rothenberg, however, states (op. cit., p. 159) that 'although the Landwehr had acquitted itself rather well in 1809, it was not an institution which recommended itself to the authorities, and it was progressively dismantled and completely shelved [he later refers to its "abolition"] in 1831'.

It would seem, in fact, that Rothenberg has simply misread his sources. His reference to Vol. I, p. 48 of Alphons von Wrede's 'Geschichte der k.u.k. Wehrmacht' (5 vols., Vienna, 1893–1900) turns out to be a reference not to the *abolition* of the *Landwehr* but to its *activation* in 1831.

4. See Robert Endres, *Revolution in Österreich 1848*, Vienna, 1947, p. 27. But various sources give different categories of exemptions.

5. See Rothenberg, 'The Austrian army', p. 160. Also cf. Appendix 3.

6. See Johann Springer, *Statistik des österreichischen Kaiserstaates*, 2 vols, Vienna, 1840, Vol. II, p. 254: 'In peaceful times it is usual for a third or even a greater part of the men to be on leave and to keep only those who are indispensable for duty. In particular, the peaceful years 1816–29 allowed no greatly extended use of this system, which is occasioned by economy and industrial considerations, that is in each of the years, 1825, 1826, 1828 almost one half of the men were on leave.' Turnball (op. cit., p. 281) states: 'The usual mode of increasing or diminishing the force is not by altering the number of regiments [although this has also been done in regard to two or three since the peace of 1814] but by augmenting and reducing the number of men in each, and placing the corresponding number of officers on the list of full pay or of retreat.'

7. Rothenberg, 'The Austrian army', p. 160.

8. Maximilian Bach, *Geschichte der Wiener Revolution im Jahre 1848*, Vienna, 1898, pp. 290f. Quoted by Endres, op. cit., pp. 27–28. The account clearly refers to the period 1845–8.

9. Bach, op. cit., pp. 27–8.

10. Hall, op. cit., p. 173. It is possible that Hall means that substitutes had to be under the age of twenty-five (which would make more sense) but I have found no evidence to contradict him.

11. Antonio Schmidt-Brentano, *Die Armee in Österreich, Militär, Staat und Gesellschaft, 1848–67*, Boppard am Rhein, 1975, p. 408.

12. Schmidt-Brentano, op. cit., p. 409.

13. Schmidt-Brentano, op. cit., p. 408. Schmidt-Brentano argues that the Austrian soldiers *were* better off on the ground of these figures which are taken from (FML.) Karl Moering's *Sibyllinische Bücher*, Vol. 2, p. 64.

14, 15. Moriz Eldlen von Angeli, *Wein nach 1848*, Vienna and Leipzig, 1905, p. 129.

16. Distributed every five days – author.

17, 18. Von Angeli, op. cit., p. 129.

19. Von Angeli, op. cit., p. 130.

20. The figures are taken from Endres, op. cit., p. 46.

21. Endres, op. cit., p. 29. There were 60 kr. to a florin.

22. See Schmidt-Brentano, op. cit., p. 408; cf. Turnball, op. cit., p. 297.

23. Turnball, op. cit., p. 297. But see also Baron Antoine de Mollinary de Mente Pastello, *Quarante-six Ans dans L'Armée Austro-Hongroise, 1833–79*, Paris, 1913, Vol. I, p. 33; and Rothenberg, op. cit., p. 160.

24. Fenner von Fenneberg, *Oesterreich und seine Armee*, Leipzig, 1847(?), pp. 142–3.

25. Von Fenneberg, op. cit., p. 142.

26. Von Fenneberg, op. cit., p. 142.

27. Hall, op. cit., p. 173.

28. Mollinary, op. cit., Vol. I, p. 33; Rothenberg, 'The Austrian army', p. 160.

29. Von Fenneberg, op. cit., p. 326.

30. Hall, op. cit., p. 173.

31. Hall, op. cit., p. 175.

32. Von Fenneberg, op. cit., pp. 326–7.

33. Von Fenneberg, op. cit., p. 330.

34. Von Fenneberg, op. cit., pp. 332–3.

35. Von Fenneberg, op. cit., p. 333.

36. Von Fenneberg, op. cit., p. 333.

37. Von Fenneberg, op. cit., pp. 45–6.

38. Von Fenneberg, op. cit., pp. 61–2.

39. For the previous few sentences, see von Fenneberg, op. cit., pp. 61–5, 71–3, 142–3.

40. Von Fenneberg, op. cit., pp. 17–26.

41. See Appendix 1.
42. Hall, op. cit., p. 178.
43. For punishments see Hall, op. cit., pp. 178–80 and von Fenneberg, op. cit., pp. 160–4 and 297ff.
44. Hall, op. cit., p. 179.
45. See *Oesterreichs innere Politik,* Stuttgart, 1847, p. 182, fn. The author added that running the gauntlet was 'the type of punishment most frequently employed'.
46. *Oesterreichs innere Politik,* p. 182, fn.
47. Von Fenneberg, op. cit., pp. 66, 71, 75–6, 107–10.
48. Von Fenneberg, op. cit., p. 69.
49. Von Fenneberg, op. cit., p. 69.
50. See Note 47, above. An article in the journal *Unserer Gegenwart und Zukunft,* 2 (1846), Leipzig, made the same points.
51. Hardegg to Lederer, Vienna, 7 Jan. 1848, KA.CK. (Präs.), 1848, No. 40.
52. Op. cit. KA.CK. (Präs.), 1848, No. 40.
53. Op. cit., KA.CK. (Präs.), 1848, No. 40.
54. Von Fenneberg, for example, refers to arrests in Galicia in 1840 and 1844–5. See von Fenneberg, op. cit., pp. 83, 88–9.
55. This is the conclusion which I draw, having worked through all the files of Metternich's correspondence on Italy which survive in the Haus-Hof- und Staatsarchiv in Vienna.
56. The police in fact had little trouble from the secret societies. They possessed *inter alia* the key to the secret code used by Mazzini's 'Young Italy', a list of subscribers to its publications and a list of members of all masonic lodges in Lombardy-Venetia. See Note 55, above.
57. Vienna, H-H.SA.SP.L-V., K. 17, Correspondence with Hof. Ritter von Menz 1833, extract from report of Milan Police Director Hofrath von Torresani, 23 Aug. 1833, No. 947 Secret.
58. Hartig to Metternich, Prague, 31 Aug. 1833, H-H.SA.S.P.L-V., K. 17.
59. Von Fenneberg, op. cit., pp. 131–2.
60. Correspondence with Radetzky and Frimont, 1830–48, Frimont to Metternich, 14 Sept. 1830, H-H.SA.S.P.L-V., K. 24.
61. Radetzky to his daughter, Friedericke, ?March 1847, in Bernard Duhr (ed.), *Briefe des Feldmarschalls Radetzky an Seine Tochter Friedericke, 1847–57,* Vienna, 1892, p. 41.
63. Radetzky to Hardegg, Milan, 5 Jan. 1848, KA.CK. (Präs.), 1848, No. 56.
64. Op. cit., KA.CK. (Präs.), 1848, No. 56.
65. Castiglione to Zanini, Cracow, 30 Mar. 1848, Vienna, KA.M.K. (1848), Nos. 336 and 394.
66. The statistics and tables used in the following section have been compiled from a variety of data which can be found in von Fenneberg, op. cit.: Rudolf Kiszling, *Die Revolution im Kaisertum Österreich, 1848–9,* 2 vols, Vienna, 1849, Vol. I; C. A. Haillot, *Statistique Militaire et Recherches sur l'Organisation et les Institutions Militaires des Armées Étrangères,* Paris, 1846, Vol. I; *Oesterreichs Heerwesen in neuester Zeit von einem österreichischen Officiere,* Leipzig, 1846; Johann Heinrich Blumenthal, 'Vom Wiener Kongress zum Erster Weltkrieg', in *Unser Heer, 200 Jahre österreichisches Soldatentum in Krieg und Frieden,* Vienna, Munich and Zürich, 1963; and Major Alphons Freiherrvon Wrede, *Geschichte der k.u.k. Wehrmacht,* 5 vols., Vienna, 1898–1905, Vol. I, Vienna, 1898.
67. Oscar Jaszi, *The Dissolution of the Habsburg Monarchy,* Chicago, 1966, p. 82.
68. Gunther E. Rothenberg, 'The Habsburg army and the nationality problem in the nineteenth century, 1815–1914', in *Austrian History Yearbook,* 1967, Vol. 3, Part I, pp. 70–87, p. 72.
69. Rothenberg, 'The Habsburg army', pp. 70–87, p. 72.
70. I should stress that there is no implication here that Professor Rothenberg has tried to deceive his readers, only the suggestion that he has mis-cited a footnote, a common enough slip made by academics. Professor Rothenberg, I hasten to add, has an excellent claim to be the world's leading authority on the Habsburg army. However, for the articles by Kiszling see Rudolf Kiszling, 'Habsburgs Wehrmacht im Spiegel des Nationälitätenproblems 1815 bis 1918', in *Gedenkschrift für Harold Steinacker,* Buchreihe der Südostdeutschen Historischen Kommission, Munich, 1966, Vol. 16, pp. 240–53, and 'Das Nationalitätenproblem in Habsburgs Wehrmacht, 1848–1918', *Der Donauraum,* 4 (1959) Pt. II, 82–92.
71. See Note 75, this chapter.
72. See the order of battle of his troops for beginning of 1848 reprinted in G. F-H. and J. Berkeley, *Italy in the Making, January 1st 1848 to November 16th 1848,* Cambridge, 1940, pp. 6–9. The authors wrongly assume, however, that Slavonia was inhabited by Slovaks. I have, therefore, adjusted their figures where necessary.
73. Latour to Lederer, Vienna, 3 May 1848, KA.M.K. (1848) No. 999.

74. Von Fenneberg, op. cit., p. 93.
75. Aladár Urbán, 'A Magyarországi Osztrák Hadszervezet és a Hazánkban Allomásogó Katonaság 1848 Aprilisban', *Hadtörténelmi Közlemenyek*, Pt. 2 (1963), 145–69, 154.
76. *Oesterreichs Heerwesen*, p. 108.
77. These records can be found in the appendices to von Wrede, op. cit.
78. For von Fenneberg's description of the nationality problem, on which the next few pages are based, see his op. cit., pp. 76–106.
79, 80. Von Fenneberg, op. cit., pp. 82, 103.

Notes to Chapter 3

1. Count Hartig, 'Genesis or details of the late Austrian revolution by an officer of the state', appended to Archdeacon Coxe's *History of the House of Austria*, London, 1853, p. 65, fn.
2. Hartig is probably referring to his own doubts here as expressed to Metternich in 1833. He may have repeated them later.
3. Radetzky to Hardegg, Milan, 4 Jan. 1848, KA.CK. (Präs.), 1848, No. 46.
4. Radetzky to Hardegg, Milan, 12 Dec. 1847, KA.CK. (Präs.), 1847, No. ?
5. KA.CK. (Präs.), 1848, No. 997.
6. FML. Gehardi to Welden, Vienna, 27 Mar. 1848, KA.CK. (Präs.), 1848, No. 1078. [Author's italics.]
7. Welden to Hofkriegsrath, Innsbruck, 30 Mar. 1848, KA.CK. (Präs.), 1848, No. 1034.
8. Welden to Count Lichnowsky, Innsbruck, 30 Mar. 1848, KA.CK. (Präs.), 1848, No. 1034.
9. See Appendix 2.
10. Radetzky to Friedericke, Verona, 27 Apr. 1848, in Bernard Duhr (ed.), *Briefe des Feldmarschalls Radetzky an Seine Tochter Friedericke, 1847–57*, Vienna, 1892, p. 80.
11. Radetzky to Friedericke, Verona, 23 Apr. 1848, in Dunh, op. cit., p. 79.
12. Radetzky to Zanini, Verona, 4 Apr. 1848, KA.M.K. (1848), No. 302.
13. Radetzky to Latour, Verona, 12 May 1848, KA.M.K. (1848), No. 1465.
14. See Appendix 3.
15, 16. Welden to Hofkriegsrath, Innsbruck, 31 Mar. 1848, KA.CK. (Präs.), No. 1064.
17, 18. Welden to Hofkriegsrath, Innsbruck, 30 Mar. 1848, KA.CK. (Präs.), No. 1034.
19. Welden to Radetzky, Innsbruck, 4 Apr. 1848, KA.MK. (1848), No. 86.
20. Op. cit., KA.M.K. (1848), No. 86.
21. Welden to Radetzky, Innsbruck, 4 Apr. 1848, KA.M.K. (1848), No. 86.
22. Archduke John to Zanini, Innsbruck, 23 Apr. 1848, KA.M.K. (1848), No. 693.
23. Welden to Hofkriegsrath, Innsbruck, 26 Mar. 1848, KA.CK. (Präs.), No. 1102.
24. See Kent Roberts Greenfield, 'The Italian nationality problem of the Austrian empire', in the *Austrian History Yearbook*, 1967, Vol. III, Pt. II, pp. 495–99 (on South Tyrol), p. 498.
25. See Appendix 4.
26. Regimental Command to General Command, 5 June 1848, KA.M.K. (1848), No. 2306.
27. General Command to War Ministry, Graz, 5 June 1848, KA.M.K. (1848), No. 2306.
28. Welden to Hofkriegsrath, Innsbruck, 29 Mar. 1848, KA.CK. (Präs.), 1848, No. 1014.
29. Welden to Hofkriegsrath, Innsbruck, 1 Apr. 1848, KA.CK. (Präs.), 1848, No. 1085.
30. See Appendix 5.
31. Radetzky to Zanini, Verona, 16 Apr. 1848, KA.M.K. (1848), No. 384.
32. Regimental Command to General Command, 5 June 1848, KA.M.K. (1848), No. 2306.
33. A great deal of Italian propaganda from this period survives and can be consulted in the Reading Room of the British Library (British Museum). It is catalogued under the general heading 'Lombardy-Venetia'.
34. KA.CK. (Präs.), 1848, No. 413. See Appendix 6.
35. Cf. Appendix 7.
36. See, for example, Appendix 8.
37. See Appendix 9.
38. See Appendix 10.
39. See Appendix 11.
40. See Appendix 12.
41. See Appendix 13.
42. The main secondary sources used in this section were Giuseppe Pierazzi, 'Studi sui rapporti italo-jugoslavi, 1848–49', *Archivio Storico Italiano*, CXXX (1972), Disp. II, 181–249; Gunther

Rothenberg, 'Jellacić, the Croatian Military Border and the intervention against Hungary in 1848', *Austrian History Yearbook*, 1965, Vol. I, pp. 45–68; and *The Military Border in Croatia, 1740–1881. A Study of an Imperial Institution,* Chicago/London, 1966. The background information on the Grenzer in the first few pages follows Rothenberg; the account of South Slav political developments follows Pierazzi. Primary sources are cited where used.

43. The following account of Italian–South Slav relations and of South Slav politics is based on Pierazzi.
44. Zanini to Radetzky, Vienna, ? Mar. 1848, KA.M.K. (1848), No. 118.
45. Op. cit., KA.M.K. (1848), No. 118.
46. Op. cit., KA.M.K. (1848), No. 118.
47. Latour to Emperor, Vienna, 26 May 1848, KA.M.K. (1848), No. 1942.
48. Latour to Radetzky, Vienna, 26 May 1848, KA.M.K. (1848), No. 1942.
49. Radetzky to Latour, Verona, 23 June 1848, KA.M.K. (1848), No. 2863.
50. Op. cit., KA.M.K. (1848), No. 2863.
51. Op. cit., KA.M.K. (1848), No. 2863.
52. See Radetzky to his daughter Friedericke, Milan, 7 Aug. 1848 in Duhr, op. cit., p. 85.
53. *B.F.S.P.,* London 1865, Vol. 44, doc. 32, p. 704.
54. Radetzky to Latour, Verona, 23 June 1848, KA.M.K. (1848), No. 2863.
55. Op. cit., KA.M.K. (1848), No. 2863.
56. Op. cit., KA.M.K. (1848), No. 2863.
57. Latour to Radetzky, Vienna, 28 June 1848, KA.M.K. (1848), No. 2861.
58. Radetzky to Latour, Milan, 3 Sept. 1848, KA.M.K. (1848), No. 4844.
59. Op. cit., KA.M.K. (1848), No. 4844.
60. Latour to Radetzky, Vienna, 8 Sept. 1848, KA.M.K. (1848), No. 4844.
61. Op. cit., KA.M.K. (1848), No. 4844.
62. Radetzky to Latour, Milan, 3 Sept. 1848, KA.M.K. (1848), No. 4844.
63. Vice-Consul Campbell to Palmerston, Milan, 22 Oct. 1848, *B.F.S.P.*, London, 1865, Vol. 44, p. 725.
64. Radetzky to War Ministry, 21 Nov. 1848, KA.M.K. (1848), No. 6070g.
65. Vice-Consul Campbell to Palmerston, Milan, 22 Oct. 1848, *B.F.S.P.,* London, 1865, Vol. 44, p. 725.
66. The main secondary sources consulted for this section were István Hajnal, *A Batthyány-Kormány Külpolitikája,* Budapest, 1957; Lajos Pásztor, 'La Guerra d'Independenza italiana del 1848 e il Problema dei Soldati ungheresi in Italia', in *Atti e Memorie del XXVII Congresso Nazionale, 19–20–21 Marzo 1948,* Milan, 1948, pp. 517–32; and Magda Jászay, (see f. 135). 'L'Italia del Quarantotto nella stampa ungherese del tempo', *Rassegna Storica del Risorgimento* (1968), pp. 226–71.
67. For the first half of this section, unless otherwise stated, I am following the account in Jászay, op. cit.
68. See Hajnal, op. cit., Ch. VII.
69. See N. Campanini, 'I Proclami latini diretti dagli Italiani ai soldati ungheresi' *Rassegna Sorica del Risorgimento* (1919), 543–71.
70. See Appendix 14.
71. See Appendix 14.
72. See Appendix 14.
73. See Hajnal, op. cit., Ch. VII.
74. For the next few pages, the account, unless otherwise stated, follows Pásztor, op. cit.
75. Radetzky to the Emperor, Milan, 7 Feb. 1849, KA.M.K. (1849), No. 1803.
76. Vice-Consul Campbell to Palmerston, Milan, 24 Oct. 1848, *B.F.S.P.,* London, 1865, Vol. 44, p. 725.
77. Vice-Consul Campbell to Palmerston, Milan, 13 Oct. 1848, *B.F.S.P.,* Vol. 44, pp. 720–1.
78. Vice-Consul Campbell to Palmerston, Milan, 22 Oct. 1848, *B.F.S.P.,* Vol. 44, p. 727.
79. Op cit., *B.F.S.P.,* Vol. 44, p. 727.
80. The evidence referred to can be found in scattered reports in the files of the Vienna Kriegsarchiv. The author hopes to use these reports in an article on the subject.
81. Professor Polisensky of Prague is working on this topic.
82. See J. Ravlic, 'Tajno drustvo za osnivanje slavenskog carstva u puku "Karl Ferdinand" br. 51 u Veneciji god. 1844'. Review in *Historijski Zbornik,* Zagreb, XIII (1960), 239–41.
83. See *inter alia,* Stefan Kieniewicz, *Legion Mickiewicza, 1848–49,* Warsaw, 1955; Henryk Batowski, *Legion Mickiewicza w kampanii wlosko-austriackiej 1848,* Warsaw, 1956; Kalikst Morawski, *Polacy i sprawa polska w dziejach Italii w latach 1830–1866,* Warsaw, 1937; Leonardo

Kociemski, *La Legione Polacca di A. Mickiewicz nel 1848 in Italia*, Rome, 1948–9; Ladislas Mickiewicz, *Mémorial de la Legion Polonaise de 1848 par Ladislas Mickiewicz d'après les papiers de son père*, 3 vols., Paris, 1877–1910; and Leonardo Kociemski, 'La Legione Polacca di Mickiewicz nel 1848 a Milano', *Atti e Memorie del XXVII Congresso Nazionale 19–20–21 Marzo 1948*, Milan, 1948, pp. 303–28. What follows is based on Kociemski's article unless otherwise stated.

84. See Teodor Onciulescu, 'Vegezzi-Ruscalla', *Rassegna storica del Risorgimento* (1940), 261.
85. Lower Austrian Command to War Ministry, Graz, 23 June 1848, KA.M.K. (1848), No. 2785.

Notes to Chapter 4

1. See R. J. Rath, 'The Habsburgs and public opinion in Lombardy-Venetia, 1814–15', in E. M. Earle (ed.), *Nationalism and Internationalism: Essays Inscribed to Carlton J. H. Hayes,* New York, 1950, pp. 303–35.
2. Rath, op. cit., pp. 303–35.
3. See Joseph Alexander Freiherr von Helfert, 'Casati und Pillersdorff und die Anfänge der italienischen Einheitsbewegung' *Archiv für Osterreichische Geschichte*, 91 (1902), 44.
4. Helfert, op. cit., pp. 330–1. The letter is dated 20 July 1816.
5. Helfert, op. cit., pp. 330–1.
6. Bolton King in his *A History of Italian Unity*, London 1912, Vol. I, p. 30, argues to this effect.
7. Helfert, op. cit., p. 261 wrote that: 'Among the unparticipating parts of the population sympathy was felt almost only for the students of Pavia because they were regarded as misguided. The lot of the others met with indifference on the part of most people who in no way had a personal interest in events.' Until recently this would have been regarded as merely the Austrian version. But see Angelo Filipuzzi, 'Die Restauration im Italien im Lichte der neuren Historiographie', *Mitteilungen des Institute für Österreichische Geschichtsforschung* 166 (1958).
8. See General K. von Schönhals, *Errinerungen eines österreichischen Veteranen aus dem italienischen Kriege der Jahre 1848 und 1849*, Stuttgart and Tübingen, 1853, p. 14.
9. See his *Statistik des österreichischen Kaiserstaates*, Vienna, Vol. II, p. 254.
10. Schönhals, op. cit., p. 14.
11. Schönhals, op. cit., p. 14.
12. See Fritz Pflegerl, 'Graf Clam-Martinitz als Diplomat und Heeresreorganisator von 1830–1840', unpublished doctoral thesis, University of Vienna, 1928, pp. 7–11. From the way in which Pflegerl quotes documents it is impossible to check his sources.
13. There are hundreds of books in German on Radetzky, but the vast majority are hagiographical. Perhaps the best studies are Oskar Regele, *Feldmarschall Radetzky, sein Leben, Leistung und Erbe*, Vienna, 1957 and Col. Freiherr Wolf-Schneider von Arno's lengthy article in *Militärwissenschaftliche Mitteilungen*, 65 (1934) 162–303.
14. Von Arno, op. cit., p. 167.
15. See Field Marshal Radetzky, 'Aus meinem Leben, 1814–47', *Österreichische Rundschau*, 14 (1908).
16. Von Arno, op. cit., p. 203.
17. Radetzky was not, in fact, the Emperor's first choice. General von Lederer, later to become a central figure in the Hungarian drama, was considered first.
18. Maximilian Freiherr von Kübeck (ed.), *Tagebücher des Carl Freiherrn Kübech von Kübau*, Vienna, 1909, Vol. I, Part II, p. 550.
19. Radetzky arrived in Italy before Frimont returned to Vienna. Their terms of command overlapped for the simple reason that Frimont was supposed to show Radetzky the ropes. Hence, however, the Archduke's mistake.
20 See Rudolf Kiszling (ed.), *Die Revolution im Kaisertum Österreich 1848–9*, 2 vols, Vienna 1948, Vol. I, p. 87.
21. Reasons had to be found for the Austrian victories of 1848–9, although Austrian historians like most other people were no doubt surprised when history offered them this task. Some saw the causes in the Clam-Martinitz reforms of 1838–40, but this is implausible. Pflegerl's thesis (see Note 12, this chapter) despite its intentions shows that the Austrian army could only have been less efficient after these reforms than it had been beforehand. Most of Clam's work had been devoted to changes in uniforms and to increasing the size of the military bureaucracy. The Austrian army in 1848 was much less well organised than is commonly believed, especially in Italy. In seeking the causes of its ultimate success, much weight must be given both to the geographical

position of the Quadrilateral and the deficiencies of the Italians. Radetzky's generalship was first class on the field, but his greatest advantage was undoubtedly the condition of his enemy. See in particular Piero Pieri, *Storia Militare del Risorgimento*, Turin, 1962, as well as Carlo Cattaneo's classic *L'Insurrection de Milan*, Paris, 1848.

22. From the manuscript entitled, 'Ursachen unsere unglücklichen Feldzüge, Vienna, KA.M.A./28 Erzherzog Maximilian d'Este, 1846'.

23. See his *Österreich und seine Armee*, Leipzig (almost certainly) 1847, pp. 17–26.

24. KA.M.A., Nachlass FML. Freiherr D'Aspre, Nachlass B 349/7. See Appendix 15.

25. General von Stratimirovic, *Was Ich Erlebte*, Vienna and Leipzig, 1911, p. 19. The General was stationed in Italy between 1841 and 1843.

26. Schönhals, op. cit., p. 31.

27. Radetzky to Hardegg, 4 Jan. 1848, Vienna, KA.CK. (Präs.), 1848, No. 46.

28. KA.CK. (Präs.), 1848, No. 136.

29. Radetzky to Viceroy, Milan, 9 Feb. 1848, KA.CK. (Präs.), 1848, No. 475. He added: 'The thought that we would maintain Milan by force has just not occurred to them; the firm declaration that we would turn Milan into a battlefield makes no impression. The reason for this incredible blindness lies partly in the ease with which till now the revolution in central Italy has been blessed.'

30. The position of the Austrian army in Italy in the years 1847–8 was analysed by the Archduke Maximilian d'Este in a series of extremely valuable essays written at the time. These are referred to as Max. 1, Max. 2, Max. 3, Max. 4 and Max. 5. Full details are given in the List of Abbreviations on p. 246.

The strategical argument is found in Max. 4 and 5, but see also KA.M.A., XXVIII, Radetzky Nachlass, Fascicle 1 Litt. A. 24, No. 64, and especially Fascicle 1 Litt. A. 31, No. 52, 'Pro desideria in Bezug auf die Vertheidigung Italiens 1840'.

31. See Schönhals, op. cit., pp. 18 and 28–9, where he writes: 'Trust in French conditions returned. The Cabinet began to disarm again. The significant armed force which Austria had assembled in Italy, was, therefore, gradually weakened.'

32. Austrian governments never placed great faith in the army. See below, Chapter 8 and p. 395.

33. Radetzky, in the first *Denkschriften* referred to in Note 30, Ch. 4, above, saw the centre of European revolutionary movements in France. Like the Archduke Maximilian, he believed that they were guided by a *Comité-Directeur* (see for instance, his report to Hardegg of 15 Feb. 1848, KA.CK. (Präs.), 1848, No. 429). Maximilian was more explicit. In Max. 1, he wrote, 'The great Comite-Directeur . . . which resides in London or Paris and which tries always and everywhere to undermine authority and religion (and without which nothing would be the matter in Italy) . . . is again entering into Italian affairs. . . .' In Max. 5 he outlined why Austria became a European necessity: '. . . if Milan is not in the hands of Austria, it is in the hands of France whenever France wants to occupy it, and, with Milan, France has supremacy over the whole of Italy. But can Europe, Germany in particular, remain indifferent to the enlargement of France, the encirclement of Germany from the south? Can England at the same time afford to see its rival rise so high and see it in possession of so much sea-coast?'

34. Vienna felt particularly vulnerable to a French attack after two invasions by Napoleon. Despite the army in Italy this feeling never really wore off. The truth is that neither Metternich, Kolowrat nor the Archduke Charles before he died had any faith in the army. Why had there been no war in 1829? Because the Emperor had had a look at his troops and decided with Prussian agreement that they were not worth the risk. Why had there been no mobilisation in 1840 at the time of the war scare? Because Metternich had arrived at the same conclusion.

35. Heinrich Friedjung, in his *Der Kampf and die Vorherrschaft in Deutschland, 1859 bis 1866*, Stuttgart–Berlin, 1901, Vol. 1, pp. 5 and 8 wrote:

The whole row of rulers and ministers who have determined Austrian policy since the days of Maximilian I have been firmly convinced that the Habsburg Monarchy required strong alliances in order to redeem the luck of war so often denied on the battlefield. The policy of alliances was the continuation of the policy of marriages through which Austria had been established. . . . Austria could not dare risk any kind of military venture which unitary national states were capable of. Her position of power, her existence, rested on alliances.

36. See Max. 2.

37. See Max. 3. Radetzky, on the other hand would never have agreed about the financial argument. He was always complaining that the government's policy was to save thousands now only to lose millions later on. But he would have been forced to agree with the rest of what Maximilian said. There was little doubt that the army was an army of occupation: 'We still rule because the army is loyal and uncorruptible, but we govern no more', wrote Radetzky to Hardegg on 18 January 1848 (KA.CK. (Präs.), 1848, No. 254). On the subject of the strategical limits of the

North Italian forts, Radetzky must also have concurred especially after his report of 5 April 1848 (KA.M.K. (Präs.), 1848, No. 302). All Maximilian's predictions came true. Radetzky reported to the War Minister from Verona that out of the 47 battalions which were left of his army, the following had to be set aside for garrison duties: 22 battalions; 6 squadrons; 2 batteries. This meant that, once he made allowances for certain other factors, which will be discussed later, his active army was reduced to only: 14 battalions; 34 squadrons; 14 batteries.

38. See Radetzky's report to Hardegg, Milan 3 Feb. 1848, KA.CK. (Präs.) 1848, No. 325. He was arguing about the defence of Milan, a topic which will be discussed later. 'There could be no resistance to the few millions needed for it . . . in the whole of the present state budget there is no item which must not be subordinated to this.' He then went on to argue that if Lombardy-Venetia were lost, so too would be the millions which Austria had invested in railways and asked, 'What would become of our flourishing factories and manufactures if they lost this debouche?'

39. See Bolton King, op. cit., Vol. I, pp. 51 and 53.

40. Helfert, op. cit., p. 277 wrote: 'The Kingdom of Lombardy-Venetia enjoyed with complete justification the double reputation: of being the most favoured of all the countries of the Empire and of being the best governed of those of the Appenine peninsula.' For a modern Austrian view see Kiszling, op. cit., pp. 11–12, 'It can today no longer be denied that in the Italy of the Risorgimento, no civil administration was better or more admirable than that of the north Italian provinces of the Empire. Together with Tuscany which was a Habsburg secondo-genitur, the Kingdom of Lombardy-Venetia, with respect to spiritual and economic culture, marched at the forefront of all Italian states.' Heinrich Benedikt, *Kaiseradler über dem Appenin. Die Österreicher in Italien, 1700 bis 1866,* Vienna and Munich, 1964, is of the same opinion. His book is very much a defence of the Austrian record.

41. See Howard R. Marraro, 'An American diplomat views the dawn of liberalism in Piedmont (1834–48)', *Journal of Central European Affairs,* 6 (1946–7), 75–6. The article does not add very much to our knowledge. Even worse is an article in volume 9 of the same journal (Oct. 1949) by A. William Salome, entitled, 'The liberal experiment and the Italian revolution of 1848 – a revaluation', which begins with the curious sentence: 'Against the multiplicity of the Risorgimento, every unilateral interpretation appears unrealistic or absurd.'

42. See Schönhals, op. cit., pp. 21–3. 'Anyone who at that time followed the newspapers but who did not have the opportunity to get to know Italy for himself must have thought that under Austria this country had sunk into barbarism. Nothing more absurd was ever written than this complaint. We saw Italy and her cities when they passed from French into Austrian hands. . . . Italy under Austria flourished to a degree never known before . . . [and after listing many Austrian benefits, he ended] . . . Who then was better off, the Germans or the Italians?'

43. Regele, op. cit., p. 361.

44. Regele, op. cit., p. 361.

45. Schönhals, op. cit., p. 30 and p. 1.

46. Max. 1.

47. See Schönhals, op. cit., p. 2 and 13. On p. 2 he wrote: 'Never at any time did Italy form an independent political whole – not even under the world-rule of Rome which treated it as a conquered province.' Maximilian also wrote (Max. 1) that it was a good thing to have 'Lombardy men' on one's own side because 'they are originally a German stock which then mixed with other blood, but there still remains in the real peasantry traces of German probity and courage which are to be found nowhere else in Italy'.

48. See Schönhals, op. cit., p. 13. 'Long and cleverly-directed efforts were required to set aside to any extent the antagonisms between the various states and cities. Probably these attempts would never have succeeded, had not the hatred found a target in which the feelings of all could come together to one another's aid. This target was Austria and her position in Italy.'

49. See Max. 1.

50. Schönhals, op. cit., p. 24. He added: 'Nor did it possess more [independence] at the time of French rule; its then Ministers were nothing more than French commissars who took their orders from Paris. By setting the Iron Crown of Lombardy on his own head in Milan Cathedral, the Kaiser recognised the independence of the Kingdom to a certain extent. In this coronation lay an acceptance of responsibility for national rights and Austria has in no way encroached upon these rights.'

51. Schönhals, op. cit., p. 25.
The so-called Congregations which consisted of deputations from the nobility and the bourgeoisie took the place of our provincial estates. These estates to be sure did not correspond to modern Parliaments or Diets, they had no galleries, but they did have the right of free discussion and the duty of bringing the wishes and needs of the country before the monarch. We

doubt whether they fulfilled this duty faithfully. They first raised their voices when the Revolution had already penetrated all hearts. It was no longer the voice of truth and duty. It was the voice of rebellion – which perhaps was no longer content to remain behind the example given by their German colleagues.
In fact, the Congregations had tried to get reforms in 1825, but had been thwarted by the government.
52. Schönhals, op. cit., pp. 26. In spite of the pass-system, thousands of 'professors of the barricades' reached Vienna and Milan. 'To what end was the hatred of the people aroused?' p. 27: 'Both these maladies weighed upon the *whole* monarchy with equal severity.' The Italians were no worse off than anybody else.

Notes to Chapter 5

1. Oskar Regele, *Feldmarschall Radetzky, sein Leben, Leistung und Erbe,* Vienna, 1957.
2. *Carte Segrete,* Vol. III, p. 121.
3. See KA.M.K., 1848, No. 1051.
4. Christopher Hibbert, *Garibaldi and his Enemies,* London, 1956, p. 27.
5. Bernard Duhr (ed.), *Briefe des Feldmarschalls Radetzky an seine Tochter Friederike, 1847–57,* Vienna, 1892, pp. 45–6.
6. *Carte Segrete,* Vol. 3, doc. 555, p. 104: '. . . People believe that Radetzky will not tolerate a civil guard or patrols in Ferrara since they say that, according to the treaties, with the exception of the carabinieri which is only entrusted with police work, there can be no other armed force in that town apart from the Austrian garrison. If Radetzky should, therefore, oppose [what is happening in Ferrara] the news would be well received.'
7. Duhr, op. cit., p. 14.
8. See the *Archivio Triennale delle Cose d'Italia dall'Avvimento di Pio IX all'Abbandano di Venezia,* Capolago-Chieri, 1850–5, Vol. I, pp. 14–16.
9. *Archivio Triennale,* pp. 21–2.
10. Carlo Tivaroni, *L'Italia Durante il Dominio Austriaco,* 3 vols., Turin and Rome, 1892–4, Vol. II, pp. 291–2.
11. Count Hartig, 'Genesis or details of the late Austrian revolution by an officer of state', appended to Archdeacon Coxe's *History of the House of Austria,* London, 1853, p. 63.
12. Hartig, op. cit., p. 63.
13. See G. F-H. Berkeley, 'Some fresh documents concerning the Italian Risorgimento before 1849', *Proceedings of the British Academy,* XVI (1940), 241. My own investigations in the *Kriegsarchiv* reveal that when he first received the news of Radetzky's actions regarding Ferrara, Metternich 'declare[d] himself in agreement with the orders given to the Fort Commander, Count Auersperg.' See KA.CK. (Präs.), 1848, No. 1170, 27 July 1848.
14. Metternich to Ficquelmont, Vienna, 22 Aug. 1847, H-H.SA.S.P.L-V., K. 23: 'The occupation of Ferrara presents an incidental question which shall have to be resolved.' A convention, such as existed with many other towns, would have to be signed.
15. Op. Cit., H-H.SA.S.P.L-V., K.23.
16. Ficquelmont to Wessenberg, 22 Aug. 1848, H-H.SA.S.P.L-V., K.23.
17. See The Princess Radziwill (ed.), *Memoirs of the Duchesse de Dino,* 3rd series, 1841–50, London 1910, p. 230.
18. Joseph Alexander Freiherr von Helfert, 'Casati und Pillersdorff, und die Anfänge der italienischen Einheitsbewegung', *Archiv. für Österreichische Geschichte,* 91 (1902), 331.
19. Helfert, op. cit., p. 331.
20. Helfert, op. cit., pp. 484–6 contains a letter from D'Aspre to Captain Huyn of the general staff, part of which reads: 'In Ferrara our rights are trampled on. Our troops – I should say "we soldiers" – maintained our rights (perhaps because we had fought for them with our blood). The bureaucrats (*die Feder*) decided otherwise; we had to give in, give up our rights – after we had clearly demonstrated them before all Europe. Scorn and derision was the result.'
21. Helfert, op. cit., pp. 468–72, Captain Rossbacher to Huyn, 21 Nov. 1847.
22. Helfert, op. cit., pp. 454–6, Count Auersperg to his wife, from whom he did not want to be separated by serving, much less fighting in Ferrara. While he believed it was 'quite right' to stand up to the revolution, he believed that Radetzky was 'confused in his ideas.'
23. Metternich to Ficquelmont, Vienna, 22 Aug. 1847, H-H.SA.S.P.L-V., K. 23.

24. Metternich to Emperor, Vienna, 17 July 1847, H-H.SA.S.P.L-V., K. 38.
25. Op. cit., H-H.SA.S.P.L-V., K. 38: 'With respect to the number of troops required to maintain law and order in the kingdom of Lombardy-Venetia, the number [at present] under the command of Field Marshal Radetzky appears to me to be sufficient to cover this requirement. Among this number I include not only the troops stationed in both provinces but also those reserves at the Field Marshal's disposal outside the area of his command.'
26. *Protokoll* of the meeting held on 20 July 1847 between Metternich, Kübeck and Hardegg. H-H.SA.S.P.L-V., K. 38.
27. Metternich to Ficquelmont, Vienna, 23 Sept. 1847, H-H.SA.S.P.L-V., K. 23. 'I have, therefore, proposed to the Emperor that martial law be declared for all cases provided for by the ordinance dated 6 October 1846 respecting Galicia and to reserve judgement of other crimes injurious to the repose and security of the state to ordinary courts which should in every case proceed summarily.'
28. Ficquelmont to Metternich, Venice, 23 Sept. 1847, H-H.SA.S.P.L-V., K. 23.
    His Imperial Highness expressed a feeling of great confidence in the future of the country assigned to his care when he learned of the decision that had just been taken by the Emperor to authorise the publication of martial law in circumstances foreseen by the ordinance of 6 October 1846 regarding Galicia. The Italian mind, which grows obstreperous by the delays of the judicial process, will recoil before the means of promptest repression. This measure will put paid to the games which these young idlers in Milan love getting up to.
29. Rainer to Metternich, Milan, 21 Dec. 1847, H-H.SA.S.P.L-V., K. 5.
30. Ficquelmont to Metternich, Milan, 3 Dec. 1847, H-H.SA.S.P.L-V., K. 23.
31. Op. cit., H-H.SA.S.P.L-V., K. 23.
32. Pilgram was, in fact, probably referring to Ficquelmont's report of 15 Dec. (H-H.SA.S.P.L-V., K. 23) in which he enclosed his memorandum of 10 Dec. The report included the following passage:
    An extension of the powers of the police authorities as well as a general tightening of punishments for major offences against public order and, in particular, the expediting of business in the police courts when such cases arise, would, in my opinion, under the circumstances which at present obtain here, not merely suffice to maintain law and order, but would prove more effective than stricter measures, which, as things now stand, would be impossible to enforce.
33. Ficquelmont to Rainer, Milan, 10 Dec. 1847, H-H.SA.S.P.L-V., K. 5.
34. Op. cit., H-H.SA.S.P.L-V., K. 5.
35. Op. cit., H-H.SA.S.P.L-V., K. 5.
36. Rainer to Metternich, Milan, 21 Dec. 1847, H-H.SA.S.P.L-V., K. 5.
37. Radetzky to Rainer, Milan, 2 Dec., Vienna, KA.CK. (Präis.), 1848, No. 46.
38. Duhr, op. cit., p. 62.
39. Metternich to Ficquelmont, Vienna, 18 Nov. 1847, H-H.SA.S.P.L-V., K. 23. See also Metternich's memorandum to the Emperor of 18 Nov., Vienna, H-H.SA.S.P.L-V., K. 38.
40. Op. cit., H-H.SA.S.P.L-V., K. 38. Metternich must also have been encouraged by a conversation he had on 20 Nov. with Solomon Rothschild, a conversation he described in a letter to Kübeck (see Maximilian Fr. von Kübeck (ed.), *Metternich und Kübeck. Ein Briefwechsel,* Vienna, 1910, pp. 34–5):
    Sal. Rothschild called on me this morning seeking information about affairs in general. I gave him the true situation in outline. As a result of this, I asked him 'whether he thought it would be better for the Emperor to surrender his Italian states to the Revolution and maintain his position in Lombardy-Venetia?'
    'Good Heavens no!' Rothschild cried out. 'That would be the end of everything.'
    'I think so too,' I said, 'and all reasonable people must think likewise. There is a great difference, however, between thought and action. Action requires means. Means require money.'
    At this point I told Rothschild that I was on the point of proposing to the Emperor that he should order an increase in the number of troops in Italy. 'This requires money and in my view, it is not the time, on account of our difficult financial situation, to distrub the normal running of the exchequer. We have just survived a financial crisis and I would regard a new one as very dangerous. What goes for today goes also for tomorrow. If any claim is made on Austria's finances, it must be done in such a way as not to endanger the secure footing on which these finances have now been placed; extraordinary cases, in my opinion, require extraordinary help; would such help be forthcoming?'
    'You shall have as much as you want,' Rothschild interrupted me. 'Your credit shall not suffer but benefit. I will provide as much as you want.'

'I,' I replied, 'want nothing and if the *Hofkammerpräsident* wants something, he well knows where to find it. I am satisfied with the assurance that if Baron Kübeck should need money without undermining the finances, he can get it from you. I have nothing more to do with it.'

'As much as Baron Kübeck wants,' declared R. 'I will give to him right away. And leave the money market to me. I have made the rate rise and do you know how? I raised it by 2 per cent by allowing 30 m.f. mettalliques to be bought on the exchange.'

'I forbid you to make any offer to Kübeck,' I concluded. 'If he requires you, he will know how to get in touch with you. If he does so, put yourself at his disposal!'

'All I wanted to tell Your Excellency was to do what you see fit.'

41. Ficquelmont to Metternich, Milan, 21 Nov. 1847, H-H.SA.S.P.L-V., K. 23.
42. Rainer to Metternich, Milan, 22 Nov. 1847, H-H.SA.S.P.L-V., K. 5. The original copy of Radetzky's report is not to be found in the archive but its contents can be deduced from other documents referred to here. Composed either on 21 or 22 November on the basis of plans that had already been drawn up in 1840, the report recommended that Radetzky's army be increased to 80,000 men. It also stressed the need to pay attention to developments inside Sardinia.
43. Ficquelmont to Metternich, Milan, 24 Nov. 1847, H-H.SA.S.P.L-V., K. 23.
44. Metternich to Ficquelmont, Vienna, 6 Dec. 1847, H-H.SA.S.P.L-V., K. 23.
45. Metternich to Ficquelmont, Vienna, 6 Dec. 1847, H-H.SA.S.P.L-V., K. 23.
46. Ficquelmont to Metternich, Milan, 16 Dec. 1847, H-H.SA.S.P.L-V., K. 23.
47. Radetzky to Hardegg, Milan, 12 Dec. 1847, H-H.SA.S.P.L-V., K. 23.
48. Radetzky to Ficquelmont, 16 Dec. 1847, H-H.SA.S.P.L-V., K. 23.
49. These quotations are taken from Radetzky's report to Hardegg of 12 Dec. and from his letter to Ficquelmont of 16 Dec.
50. See Note 49 above.
51. Ficquelmont to Metternich, Milan, 18 Dec. 1847, L. 23.
52. Duhr, op. cit., p. 63.
53. Hartig, op. cit., p. 65, fn. and p. 101.
54. Comte de Hübner, *Une Année de Ma Vie, 1848–9,* Paris, 1891, pp. 33–4.
55. See Max. 1.

Notes to Chapter 6

1. Ficquelmont to Metternich, 29 Dec. 1847, H-H.SA.S.P.L-V., K. 23.
2. Carlo Casati, *Nuove Revelazioni su i Falti di Milano nel 1847–48,* 2 vols, Milan, 1885, Vol. II, p. 8, fn. 1.
3. Casati, op. cit., p. 7.
4. Radetzky to Hardegg,KA.CK. (Präs.), 1848, No. 78. For Radetzky's reports on the Tobacco Riots, see Nos, 45, 46, 56 and 90.
5. See *B.F.S.P.,* 1848–9, Foreign Office, 1862, p. 816. Consul-General Dawkins to Palmerston, Milan, 6 Jan. 1848,

> . . . It was natural that the soldiers, finding that when alone or in small parties they were liable to insult and attack, should unite together for protection; but in this case it had too much the appearance of wanton provocation, while it has afforded a pretext to the ill-disposed to assert that they were sent out on purpose to bring on a collision . . . although all reasonable persons admit the attempt to prevent others from smoking to have been unjustifiable and deserving of punishment, and indeed the original cause of all the misfortunes that have ensued, the conduct of the military authorities in thus allowing bodies of armed men, without officers to control them, to parade the town in the midst of an unarmed population, is highly censured.

6. Casati, op. cit., Vol. II, p. 21.
7. Ficquelmont to Metternich, Milan, 7 Jan. 1848, H-H.SA.S.P.L-V., K. 23.
8. Op. cit., H-H.SA.S.P.L-V., K. 23.
9. Radetzky to Hardegg, Milan, 4 Jan. 1848, KA.CK. (Präs.) Nos. 46 and 178.
10. Ficquelmont to Metternich, 7 Jan. 1848, H-H.SA.S.P.L-V., K. 23.
11. Op. cit., H-H.SA.S.P.L-V., K. 23.
12. Ficquelmont to Metternich, Milan, 9 Jan. 1848, H-H.SA.S.P.L-V., K. 23.
13. Ficquelmont to Metternich, 11 Jan. 1848, K. 23.
14. Op. cit., H-H.SA.S.P.L-V., K. 23.
15. Ficquelmont to Metternich, 9 Jan. 1848, H-H.SA.S.P.L-V., K. 23.
16. Op. cit., H-H.SA.S.P.L-V., K. 23.

17. Joseph Alexander Freiherr von Helfert, 'Casati und Pillersdorff und die Anfänge der italienischen Einheitsbewegung', *Archiv. für Österreichische Geschichte*, 91 (1902) 483.

18. Helfert, op. cit., p. 474.

19. Franz Ferdinand Hoettinger, *Radetzky, ein Stück Osterreich*, Leipzig and Vienna, 1934, pp. 13–14.

20. Hoettinger, op. cit., pp. 13–14.

21. Helfert, op. cit., pp. 500–2, Count Wratislaw to Captain Huyn, 1 Feb. 1848.

22. Radetzky to Hardegg, 5 Jan. 1848, KA.CK. (Präs.), 1848, No. 54.

23. Radetzky to Hardegg, 3 Jan. 1848, KA.CK. (Präs.), 1848, No. 45.

24. Radetzky to Hardegg, 14 Jan. 1848, KA.CK. (Präs.), 1848, No. 98.

25. For Radetzky's warnings, see his reports to Hardegg, KA.CK. (Präs.), 1848, Nos. 44, 45, 46, 96, 98, 121 and 276, written between 3 and 28 Jan.

26. Radetzky to Hardegg, 3 Jan. 1848, KA.CK. (Präs.), 1848, No. 44.

27. Metternich to Ficquelmont, Vienna, 8 Jan. 1848, H-H.SA.S.P.L-V., K. 23. But cf. Richard von Metternich and Alfons von Klinkowström (eds), *Aus Metternichs nachgelassenen Papieren*, 8 vols, Vienna, 1880–4, Vol. VII, p. 529, 'from the diary of Princess Melanie': '... It almost seems as if Radetzky has been reproached for having allowed his men to smoke cigars.'

28. Emperor to Hardegg, Vienna, 9 Jan. 1848, KA.CK. (Präs.), 1848, No. 66.

29. Op. cit., KA.CK. (Präs.), 1848, No. 65.

30. Hardegg to the Emperor, Metternich and Radetzky, 21 Jan. 1848, KA.CK. (Präs.), 1848, No. 165.

31. Op. cit., KA.CK. (Präs.), 1848, No. 165.

32. See Federico Curato (ed.), *Gran Bretagne e Italia nei Documenti della Missione Minto*, 2 vols, Rome, 1970, Vol. I, pp. 188–9. Abercromby, British Minister in Turin had written to Minto on 13 Nov. 1847 (see Curato, op. cit., pp. 188–90) that: 'What you say of Radetzky at Milan has been fully confirmed from all other quarters. He is pushing for war in Italy with all his influence, arguing that if the present movement against Austrian influence, is not at once put down with a strong and military hand, the effect of publick opinion will be so greatly increased in the course of a few weeks that it will be impossible ever to regain the position which Austria has hitherto held in Italy.' On 22 January, he again wrote to Minto (Curato, op. cit., pp. 326–8) 'That proclamation, coinciding with other events nearer you looks very much as if it was decided to push matters to extremity and to go the whole hog . . . certainly it will not be Radetzky's fault if something of that sort does not happen . . . I have no doubt now that the cigar row at Milan was intentionally provoked by Radetzky, by means of the soldiers.'

33. Curato, op. cit., pp. 326–8.

34. Curato, op. cit., Vol. II, pp. 5–6, Ponsonby to Minto, Vienna, 6 Feb. 1848, 'I am confident that Metternich's policy has not been abandoned.'

35. Rainer to Ficquelmont, Milan, 14 Jan. 1848, KA.M.K. (Präs.), 1848, No. 1051.

36. Ficquelmont to Metternich, 17 Jan. 1848, KA.M.K. (Präs.), 1848, No. 1051.

37. Hardegg to the Emperor, 30 Jan. 1848, KA.M.K. (Präs.), 1848, No. 1051.

38. With regard to the case of the dragoon mentioned by Ficquelmont, Hardegg pointed out that (*a*) the dragoon could not be judged guilty; (*b*) mitigating circumstances were constituted by the climate of opinion in which he found himself and by the fact that stones were being thrown at him; and (*c*) since the case was at present being investigated, it was one, if anything, of the present legislation working.

39. Metternich to Ficquelmont, Vienna, 23 Jan. 1848, H-H.SA.S.P.L-V., K. 23.

40. Count Hartig, 'Genesis or details of the late Austrian revolution by an officer of state', appended to Archdeacon Coxe's *History of the House of Austria*, London, 1853, pp. 64–5.

41. See below pp. 186–90.

42. See *B.F.S.P.*, 1848–9, Vol. 37, Foreign Office, 1862, pp. 835–6, Consul-General Dawkins to Palmerston, Venice, 18 January 1848. From this it is clear that the arrival of new troops was about the only thing that was impressing anybody in Lombardy-Venetia:

. . . Nothing appears to be done by the government, and it is deplorable to see the dilatory manner in which affairs are carried on. The want of some all-controlling hand is most severely felt and is admitted by the local authorities themselves, who bitterly complain of the delays of the government at Vienna, from whence they can get no answers to their representations. This is most evident at the present moment in Milan where decisive measures are called for, but where no person seems to know who is the head of government. The Viceroy, the Governor, Count Spaur, the Commander-in-Chief, Count Radetzky and the Director General of Police, each exercise authority, while no one appears responsible for the measures that are adopted. The only thing that is actually in progress is the augmentation of the army and notwithstanding the unfavourable season of the year, troops are arriving almost daily in these provinces. I fear these troops arrive for the most part, with a hostile feeling towards the inhabitants generally, which will acquire strength from contact with the regiments already quartered here, between whom and the people the feeling of irritation is very great.

General K. von Schönhals, *Errinerungen eines Österreicheschen Veteranen aus dem italienischen Kriege der Jahre 1848 und 1849*, Stuttgart and Tübingen, 1853, says that at the outbreak of the revolutions Radetzky had only 75,000 men under his command.

43. Ficquelmont to Metternich, Milan, 11 Jan. 1848, H-H.SA.S.P.L-V., K. 23. At the beginning of February, Radetzky realised that yet more troops would be needed: 'We cannot fail to acknowledge that the enemy can field twice our forces against us'; and he reckoned that the enemy, the Sardinians, had 150,000 men, 100,000 of which were capable of moving against him (50,000, he reckoned would be needed for garrisons) and 50,000 of which were well organised. The forces which he had under his command, therefore fell short by some 30–40,000, even on paper, of the number he required. These extra men, he stressed, were just as politically as militarily important. See Vienna, Radetzky to the Emperor, Milan, 1 Feb. 1848, H-H.SA.K., Fascicule 512.

44. Maximilian Fr. von Kübeck, *Metternich und Kübeck. Ein Briefwechsel*, Vienna, 1910, pp. 36–7.

45. See Note 17, Ch. 5 (p. 260).

46. Radetzky to Hardegg, Milan, 9 Feb. 1848, KA.CK. (Präs.), 1848, No. 475.

47. Op. cit., KA.CK. (Präs.), 1848, No. 475. It should be noted, however, that the treasury was able to secure imperial backing for its views. At the end of February the Emperor sent the following instruction to Hardegg: 'In future, no proposition which entails additional financial expenditure is to be presented to me before a preliminary agreement has been reached with the treasury praesidium.' See Emperor to Hardegg, 27 Feb. 1848, KA.CK. (Präs.), 1848, No. 475.

48. The Archduke once made the quip, 'Austria has all the elements of an army but no army.'

49. Radetzky to Hardegg, Milan, 3 Feb. 1848, KA.CK. (Präs.), 1848, No. 32.

50. Ficquelmont to Metternich, Milan, 17 Feb. 1848, H-H.SA.S.P.L-V., K. 23.

51. Benedek to Lugani, Pavia, 11 Feb. 1848, H-H.SA.S.P.L-V., K. 23.

52. Ficquelmont to Metternich, 16 Feb. 1848, H-H.SA.S.P.L-V., K. 23.

53. Op. cit., H-H.SA.S.P.L-V., K. 23.

54. Radetzky to Rainer, Milan, 12 Feb. 1848, H-H.SA.S.P.L-V., K. 23.

55. Ficquelmont to Rainer, Milan, 15 Feb. 1848, H-H.SA.S.P.L-V., K. 23.

56. Ficquelmont to Metternich, Milan, 16 Feb. 1848, H-H.SA.S.P.L-V., K. 23.

57. Ficquelmont to Metternich, Milan, 17 Feb. 1848, H-H.SA.S.P.L-V., K. 23.

58. Ficquelmont to Metternich, Milan, 19 Feb. 1848, H-H.SA.S.P.L-V., K. 23.

59. Metternich to Ficquelmont, Vienna, 8 Feb. 1848, H-H.SA.S.P.L-V., K. 23.

60. Op. cit., H-H.SA.S.P.L-V., K. 23.

61. Metternich to Ficquelmont, Vienna, 17 Feb. 1848, H-H.SA.S.P.L-V., K. 23.

62. Windischgraetz to Metternich, Prague, 23 Feb. 1848, H-H.SA.S.P.L-V., K. 23.

63. See Note 62 above.

64. Oskar Regele, *Feldmarschall Radetzky, sein Leben, Leistung und Erbe*, Vienna, 1957, p. 236. Regele, however, is quoting from the (often unreliable) correspondence of Count Carl Friedrich Vitzthum von Eckstädt, and adds that in any case, reports of resignation threats by the Field Marshal have to be taken with a pinch of salt. See Regele, op. cit., p. 512, fn. 225.

65. Regele, op. cit., pp. 235–6.

66. There is no evidence either in the Haus-Hof- und Staatsarchiv or in the Kriegsarchiv to support the theory of a threatened resignation. The author has carefully combed both these archives and the documents there simply never refer, directly or even indirectly, to such a step having been taken. Metternich on 17 February was still holding out against martial law, although he was beginning to despair; on 19 February, Rainer explained to the daily conference that the decrees were to be published. He must have received instructions, therefore, by telegram for otherwise the Chancellor's letter of 17 February does not make sense. It is possible that what decided the issue was a very indignant letter addressed by Radetzky to Hardegg on 16 February which Metternich might just have seen by 19 February. (If one supposes that even one of the correspondents got his date wrong, even by a day, the chronology becomes much more plausible.) Yet even this in no way hinted at resignation. (Radetzky to Hardegg, 16 February 1848, KA.CK. (Präs.), 1848, No. 447). The letter was another defence of the Austrian troops which the Marshal commanded and of his own position:

... When all energy on the part of the authorities gives way, when every demonstration against the government is viewed as a little playfulness, when every seditious or treasonous poster is seen as an innocent scribble, when [only] the inadequacy of the law is directed against every attempt at sedition, when insults and contempt are taken for popularity, then it is only natural that people seek to paralyse the last support of the government, i.e. the armed forces, in order to have their way entirely.

I am very proud of the complaints which have been made against me, since as long as the spirit here is against the government, I would half consider myself a traitor to the state, were I to retain my one-time popularity. From all parts of Italy, infamous diatribes against my person stream through the usual postal channels. These contemptuous attacks cannot possibly be aimed against my person – what have I in common with the Piedmontese, the Romans, the Neapolitans – they are directed at the representative of the Austrian army, which people hate and fear and which they hope to paralyse by paralysing its activity. Lies and libels are the weapons of these creatures who do not know that if they also remove me from the army, the Emperor, thank God, has generals enough worthy to replace me.

May they thank God that up till now they have only had to deal with patrols and individual officers and soldiers and not with whole corps. Otherwise they would have to celebrate their pompous funerals in honour not of one single student but of hundreds. When I look for something to admire in our army, it is the unexampled patience and moderation with which for months it has calmly borne all sorts of insults and derision. That was not cowardice. That was the force of discipline which was experienced while pens were strained to breaking point.

67. Hohenlohe to Radetzky, Vienna, 27 Feb. 1848, KA.CK. (Präs.), 1848, No. 475.
68. Palffy to Metternich, Venice, 12 Feb. 1848, H-H.SA.S.P.L-V., K. 19.
69. Metternich to Ficquelmont, Vienna, 19 Feb. 1848, H-H.SA.S.P.L-V., K. 23.
70. Op. cit., H-H.SA.S.P.L-V., K. 23.
71. Ficquelmont to Metternich, Milan, 24 Feb. 1848, H-H.SA.S.P.L-V., K. 23.
72. Hübner to Metternich, Milan, 5 Mar. 1848, H-H.SA.S.P.L-V., K. 22.
73. Ludwig, Graf Ficquelmont, *Aufklärungen über die Zeit von 20 März bis zum Mai 1848,* Leipzig, 1850, p. 1.
74. Franz Hartig (ed.), *Metternich-Hartig. Ein Briefwechsel des Staatskanzlers aus dem Exil. 1848—51,* Vienna, 1923, p. 33.
75. Emperor to Hohenlohe, Vienna, 7 Mar. 1848, KA.CK. (Präs.), 1848, No. 584.
76. Schönhals, op. cit., p. 37.
77. Erzsébet Andics, *Metternich und die Frage Ungarns,* Budapest, 1973.

Notes to Chapter 7

1. General K. von Schönhals, *Errinerungen eines osterreichischen Veteranen aus dem italienischen Kriege der Jahre 1848 und 1849,* Stuttgart and Tübingen, 1853, p. 60.
2. Schönhals, op. cit., p. 60.
3. '. . . people no longer doubt the possibility of forcing Austria to give up these provinces'. Radetzky to Hardegg, 28 Jan. 1848, KA.CK. (Präs.), 1848, No. 276.
4. Radetzky to Hardegg, 16 Jan. 1848, KA.CK. (Präs.), 1848, No. 163.
5. Radetzky to Hardegg, 19 Feb. 1848, KA.CK. (Präs.), 1848, No. 473.
6. Metternich to Emperor and Hardegg; Hardegg to Radetzky, 1 Feb. 1848, KA.CK. (Präs.), 1848, No. 267.
7. Op. cit., KA.CK. (Präs.), 1848, No. 267.
8. Op. cit., KA.CK. (Präs.), 1848, No. 267.
9. Op. cit., KA.CK. (Präs.), 1848, No. 267.
10. Ficquelmont to Metternich, Milan, 11 Feb. 1848, H-H.SA.S.P.L-V., K. 23.
11. The diplomatic situation certainly was not favourable and indeed had not been for some time. See Roger Bullen, 'Guizot and the Sonderbund Crisis, 1846–1848', *English Historical Review,* LXXXVI (July 1971), 497–526.
12. See Note 53, Ch. 5 (p. 262).
13. Radetzky to Hardegg, Milan, 6 Jan. 1848, KA.CK. (Präs.), 1848, No. 98.
14. Radetzky to Hardegg, Milan, 9 Jan. 1848, KA.CK. (Präs.), 1848, No. 96.
15. Radetzky to Hardegg, Milan, 15 Jan. 1848, KA.CK. (Präs.), 1848, No. 165.
16. Radetzky to Hardegg, Milan, 24 Jan. 1848, KA.CK. (Präs.), 1848, No. 256. He based his plans on previous ones which had been drawn up in 1829–30.
17. A report of Radetzky's General Staff which he submitted to Hardegg along with his own report, named the three main lines of communication as:

(a) The road from Peschiera via Brescia and Milan to Turbigo;
(b) The road from Goito via Arzi, Novi, Crema, Birnate and Milan to Magenta; and
(c) The road from Mantua, via Cremona and Pizzighetone to Pavia.

The report concluded that if the Austrians lost Milan, they also lost 'the land up to the Mincio and Austria's influence on the whole of Italy'. On the other hand, if Pavia and Milan were saved, so too was Austria's hold over the whole of the Lower Ticino.

18. Schönhals, op. cit., p. 67.

19, 20. Schönhals, op. cit., p. 67. It cannot be emphasised too much just how reliant the Austrians were up until about 1847 on the cooperation of Piedmont. Charles Albert was not only regarded as a reliable ally but it was assumed by the Austrian army that if ever the French attacked in northern Italy, it would be he – not Radetzky – who would head the Austro-Sardinian counter-attack. The Austrians, in fact, had been playing on the King's well-known military ambitions for a long time – indeed ever since he distinguished himself at the siege of Trocadero in Spain in 1823. The French at that time had rewarded Charles Albert with the epaulettes of a grenadier; the Austrians had spectacularly outdone them by awarding him the Maria Theresa Order – their highest military honour. Radetzky himself, who used often to visit the Sardinian court, had readily agreed to act as second to the King and indeed had been courteous enough to give up the proprietorship of his Hussar regiment in order that the King might have it. When it gradually became clear that the latter's ambitions were leading him in a different direction, Radetzky held him to be little better than a traitor (see Schönhals, op. cit., p. 20).

21. No doubt these plans were influenced by that arch-planner the Archduke Maximilian d'Este. One of his plans for the defence of northern Italy had been to turn Milan into a huge military encampment surrounded by fortified towers and to do this on such a grand scale as to be able to reduce the army as a result. If this were done, he wrote (Max. 3) then 30,000 men in these towers could defend the whole of northern Italy. The presupposition was, of course, that such towers would be impregnable, an optimistic one in view of the Archduke's previous experiments. The *United Services Journal* for Jan. 1837 (p. 100) carried a report for British readers on the so-called Maximilian towers which the Archduke had built and tested round Linz in 1836. Apparently, they were demolished at first firing by guns 'which were served imperfectly'.

22. Ferdinand to Hohenlohe, Vienna, 1 March 1848, KA.CK. (Präs), 1848, No. 256.

23. Hohenlohe to Ferdinand, Vienna, KA.CK. (Präs.), 1848, No. 256.

24. See, for example, Radetzky to Hardegg, Milan, 3 Jan. 1848; KA.CK. (Präs.), 1848, No. 44; 'Until now I was always of the opinion that a revolutionary outbreak in our provinces was not to be feared. But if we continue to govern as we do now, there can be no doubt at all that it will come to an insurrection.' On 8 Jan., Hardegg received an opposite opinion (KA.CK. (Präs.), 1848, No. 90): 'Some clashes will take place here and there but I do not believe in a popular uprising.' Radetzky, however, had changed his mind again, by 3 Feb. (Radetzky to Hardegg, Milan, 3 Feb. 1848, KA.CK. (Präs.), 1848, No. 325): 'We stand alone, completely alone against the whole of Italy with two provinces which are only waiting for the moment to break free from us.'

In February his views hardened towards the side of expected revolution. On 19 February he wrote to Hardegg from Milan (KA.CK. (Präs.), 1848, No. 495): 'the slightest push from outside will undoubtedly make the revolution break out throughout the entire Kingdom'. And ten days after that when he had received 'the sad news from Paris' (KA.CK. (Präs.), 1848, No. 538):

> I took it to be a stock-exchange rumour since it was too incredible. I have just received the frightening confirmation of the completely unholy catastrophe, the results of which are still beyond human comprehension . . . I cannot foresee what results this news will have internally; equally uncertain is it whether the weak Italian governments will survive for 24 hours after receiving the news and whether the revolutionary party will not use this moment to realise their old dream of a united Italy. In any case everything is to be feared for our Italian territories. I am threatened on all sides and could find myself engulfed in the struggle in a few day's time.

> My forces are no longer sufficient for my position. Italy is the first forward point of our monarchy against which probably the first attack will be directed. I beg the Praesidium to consider this position and to adopt with haste every measure which my situation demands.

> I will not shrink from the storm whenever it breaks out.

25. See Joseph Alexander, Freiherr von Helfert's 'Radetzky in den Tagen seiner ärgsten Bedrägnis', *Archiv für Österreichische Geschichte*, Vienna, 1906, Vol. 95, pp. 145–62. Radetzky to Ficquelmont, 'a.m., 19 March 1848'.

26. Helfert, op. cit., p. 158. Radetzky to Ficquelmont, 5 p.m. 22 Mar. 1848.

27. Helfert, op. cit., p. 159.

28. Helfert, op. cit., p. 161. Radetzky to Ficquelmont, Montechiari, 30 Mar. 1848.

29. Helfert, op. cit., p. 161.

30. The basic question regarding the 'Five Days of Milan' is why Radetzky retreated when he had superior forces in the city and others at hand not very far away?

The Milanese were not armed. The countryside was relatively peaceful. The Piedmontese army could be seen as a threat but even by 16 March it was still only in a state of mobilization. Moreover, it was very scattered. Only three regiments were in the immediate vicinity of the Ticino. All the others were at least three *étappes* away – twelve to fourteen in the case of those in Nice and Savoy. The initial strategic position was, therefore, favourable to Radetzky.

The insurrection began on the morning of 18 March and went on throughout 18 and 19 March, limiting itself for the most part to the centre of the city (population 170,000). Radetzky's plan, at least on the 19th, had been to keep the citadel at all costs as well as the barracks and other military buildings in the centre. Meanwhile, he would use mobile troops to quell the insurgents inside the city and maintain a defensive posture on the bastions against any external threat. More troops were called to reinforce Milan and nothing as yet was happening on the Piedmontese frontier since Charles Albert was still in the throes of a decision.

On 20 March things got much worse for the Austrians. The insurgents gained ground; the imperial forces began to run short of food and ammunition. Some were also cut off in about fifty-two localities. Morale went down when they had to keep awake all the time and make attempt after attempt to rescue the individual officers or groups of fellow soldiers who had been cut off. On 20 March the foreign consuls in the city attempted to arrange an armistice – Radetzky accepted, but the rebels rejected the offer. The insurgents now sent out balloons with messages for help and the countryside outside Milan rose up in rebellion also.

Inside the city the rebels made for the gates and the bastions, while Radetzky attempted to reconquer lost ground in the centre. The Austrians were beaten back, whereas the rebels got hold of the Tosa and Ticinese gates, thus reaching the periphery of the city. Their success can be variously explained: by this time they were to some extent organised and there was some coordination; they also had shared ideals; but, more important, the barricades were proving enormously effective – by the fifth day there were 1,651 of them, some of which were fixed but some of which were mobile and sheltered mobile columns of insurgents.

After the 20th, Radetzky began to receive reports of the losses and defeats suffered by the garrisons at Como, Bergamo, Cremona and Brescia. There was also more Piedmontese activity on the Ticino. On the night of 21–22 March, therefore, he took the decision to abandon the city.

Probably the least important factor was the activity of the Piedmontese about which Radetzky was not too worried. In any case, Charles Albert did not declare war until 23 March and the first vanguards of the Piedmontese army did not cross the Ticino until the afternoon of 25 March and the morning of the 26th – more than two days after Radetzky had left the city. Had he been able to maintain order in Milan, all the evidence of his previous plans suggests that he would have stood his ground and fought. See Varo Varanini, 'I veri Motivi della Ritirata di Radetzky da Milano', *Atti e Memorie del XXVII Congresso Nazionale 19–20–21 Marzo 1948*, Istituto per la Storia del Risorgimento: Cimitato di Milano, Milan, 1948, pp. 725–30.

31. Varanini, op. cit., p. 205, note 1.

32. Radetzky was not the only one to lose face. Schönhals, for example, told Hübner early in 1848 that 'the imperial army in Italy, 75–80,000 men, is more than sufficient to destroy Charles Albert's in the space of four days'. Comte de Hübner, *Une Année de Ma Vie*, Paris, 1891, pp. 33–4. On the other hand, the 1849 campaign did just that.

33. See Schönhals, op. cit., pp. 71–95. He agrees (p. 81) that the lack of provisions was the main cause of the retreat, but also adds a humanitarian motive (pp. 80–1):

Milan does not know what it owes to the mildness of the Field Marshal during these days of treason and murder. He had submitted to the natural vexation which the treason caused to grip him and his soldiers, he could have repeated Barbarossa's historic tragedy, for, however strongly built it is, Milan has its weak side and we knew its weak side only too well. The Field Marshal as will be understood had no projectiles to deploy – a real bombardment was not possible – but he had 12 howitzers and not a few rockets among his batteries. In any case the Field Marshal had the idea to bring these howitzers together in one battery and have them bomb the city. He gave up the idea because any thought of devastation was far from the human kindness of his heart. In any case it did not solve the problem. He did not want to destroy Milan because he wanted to save for the Emperor and the Empire a city which he hoped one day to see give up its delusions and recognise that it was only the victim and plaything of reckless demagogues and deluded ambition.

All this must be taken with a pinch of salt since (*a*) we know the strategic importance Radetzky placed upon Milan; (*b*) we know that the trouble started because he was 'taken by surprise' – something which is not apparent from Schönhals' description of Radetzky's office when the news of insurrection was received; and (*c*) the Field Marshal had previously told Hardegg that he would indeed bombard the city. There seems to have been some incompetence on the army's part regarding their supplies. Why had they not stocked up with ammunition if they considered their position so grave?

34. Schönhals, op. cit., p. 57 and pp. 101–9.
35. Schönhals, op. cit., p. 57.
36. Radetzky to Hardegg, Milan, 21 Jan. 1848, KA.CK. (Präs.), 1848, No. 201.
37. See, for example, Radetzky to Hardegg, 13 Jan. 1848, KA.CK. (Präs.), 1848, No. 138.
38. Radetzky to Hardegg, 7 Feb. 1848, KA.CK. (Präs.), 1848, No. 355.
39. Op. cit., KA.CK. (Präs.), 1848, No. 355.
40. Radetzky to Hardegg, Milan, 16 Feb. 1848, KA.CK. (Präs.), 1848, No. 439.
41. Zichy to Radetzky, Venice, 18. Feb. 1848, KA.CK. (Präs.), 1848, No. 471.
42. Zichy to Hofkriegsrath, Venice, 19 Feb. 1848, KA.CK. (Präs), 1848, No. 454.
43. Zichy to Radetzky, Venice, 20 Feb. 1848, KA.CK. (Präs.), 1848, No. 486.
44. Ficquelmont to Metternich, 21 Feb. 1848, KA.CK. (Präs.), 1848, No. 631.
45. Radetzky to Hardegg, Milan, 20 Feb. 1848, KA.CK. (Präs.), 1848, No. 471.
46. He also suggested that in future Austrian sailors should be recruited from Dalamatia – the 'old' nursery of the Austrian navy. Apparently before 1848, for reasons unknown to Ficquelmont, Austria had been recruiting her sailors from Lombardy – Milan, Como, Brescia and Mantua. Dalamatia would provide men, he said, who 'could never make common cause with Italy' and who would give Italian thought 'an easterly direction'.
47. Wallmoden to Hofkriegsrath, 22 Feb. 1848, KA.CK. (Präs.), 1848, No. 486.
48. Hohenlohe to Radetzky, 26 Feb. 1848, KA.CK. (Präs.), 1848, No. 471.
49. Zichy to Hofkriegsrath, Venice, 28 Feb. 1848, KA.CK. (Präs.), 1848, Nos. 531–9.
50. Hohenlohe to Zichy, Vienna, 5 Mar. 1848, KA.CK. (Präs.), 1848, Nos. 531–9.
51. Zichy to Hofkriegsrath, Venice, 5 Mar. 1848, KA.CK. (Präs.), 1848, No. 596.
52. Martini to Hofkriegsrath, Venice, 27 Feb. 1848, KA.CK. (Präs.), 1848, No. 539. Martini wrote that 'the main question of the present' was the reliability of the navy.
53. Hohenlohe to Martini, Vienna, 4 Mar. 1848, KA.CK. (Präs.), 1848, Nos. 531–9.
54. Martini to Radetzky, KA.CK. (Präs.), 1848, No. 539.
55. Op. cit., KA.CK. (Präs.), 1848, No. 539.
56. Lombardy-Venetian General Command report, Verona, 27 Mar. 1848, see KA.CK. (Präs.), 1848, No. 997.
57. Op. cit., KA.CK. (Präs.), 1848, No. 997. But see Schönhals, op. cit., pp. 108–9 for the Capitulation. Point 3 reads: 'War materials of any kind will remain in Venice.'
58. Schönhals, op. cit., pp. 108–9.
59. See Schönhals, op. cit., pp. 101 ff.
60. Radetzky to Hardegg, Milan, 20 Jan. 1848, KA.CK. (Präs.), 1848, No. 204.
61. Ferdinand to Hohenlohe, 10 Mar. 1848, KA.CK. (Präs.), 1848, No. 631.
62. Op. cit., KA.CK. (Präs.), 1848, No. 631.

Notes to Chapter 8

1. Federico Curato (ed.), *Gran Bretagne e Italia nei Documenti della Missione Minto,* 2 vols, Rome, 1970, Vol. II, pp. 170–2, Palmerston to Minto, Foreign Office, 28 Mar. 1848.
2. Curato, op. cit., pp. 170–2.
3. A former Governor of Lombardy and, in 1848 a member of the Staatsrath who advised Metternich on Italian affairs.
4. See F(1), pp. 30–4. Full details of titles referred to as F(1) and F(2) are given in the list of Abbreviations on p. 246.
5. F(1), pp. 31–2. Hartig's undated thoughts on a peace with Sardinia. From other documents they appear to have been put on paper during the first week in April 1848.
6. Ficquelmont to Hartig (undated letter), F(1), pp. 33–4.
7. F(1), pp. 33–4.
8. Ficquelmont's thoughts on Hartig's instructions (no date), F(1), p. 34.
9. A full text of Hartig's instructions does not exist. But this is the clear implication of Ficquelmont's discussions in Cabinet and of an undated memorandum of Hartig's on the 'principles' for a compromise with the Lombards. See F(1), pp. 32–4.
10. Hartig to Ficquelmont, Görz, 27 Apr. 1848, F(1), pp. 64–9.
11. F(1), pp. 64–9.

12. Ficquelmont to Radetzky, Vienna, 20 Apr. 1848, F(1), pp. 53–4, for all quotes in this paragraph.
13. See Note 9, above. But these parts of his instructions are contained in Addendum C to Hartig's letter to Ficquelmont of 27 April. Addendum C also includes the covering letter.
14. See Note 13 above.
15. Pillersdorff to Latour (i.e. Home Minister to War Minister), Vienna, 9 May 1848, KA.M.K. (1848), No. 1284.
16. Hartig to Lebzeltern (temporary head of the Foreign Ministry), Udine, 9 May 1848, F(1), pp. 87–90.
17. Op. cit., F(1), pp. 87–90.
18. Hartig to Ficquelmont, Trieste, 19 Apr. 1848, F(1), pp. 45–9. The proclamation is printed in full as Addendum A.
19. Hartig to Ficquelmont, Trieste, 15 Apr. 1848, F(1), pp. 37–40.
20. The Mayor of Milan and head of the Lombard provisional government.
21. Hartig to Ficquelmont, Trieste, 15 Apr. 1848, F(1), pp. 37–40.
22. Hartig to Ficquelmont, Görz, 26 Apr., F(1), pp. 62–4.
23. Hartig to Lebzeltern, Udine, 15 May 1848, F(1), pp. 95–105.
24. Op. cit. F(1), pp. 95–105, for all quotes in this paragraph.
25. Lebzeltern to Hartig, Vienna, 28 May 1848, F(1), pp. 130–1 (Addendum B).
26. Lebzeltern to Hartig, Vienna, 20 May 1848, F(1), pp. 108–11.
27. A. J. P. Taylor, *The Italian Problem in European Diplomacy, 1847–49,* Manchester, 1934, pp. 100–12.
28. Wessenberg to Hartig, Innsbruck, 5 June 1848, F(1), p. 132.
29. Hartig to Wessenberg, Roveredo, 9 June 1848, F(1), pp. 137–43.
30. Hartig to Wessenberg, Roveredo, 7 June 1848, F(1), pp. 133–4.
31. Hartig to Wessenberg, Roveredo, 9 June 1848, F(1), pp. 137–43.
32. Hartig to Lebzeltern, Udine, 13 May 1848, F(1), pp. 95–7.
33. Radetzky to Ficquelmont, Verona, 3 May 1848, KA.M.K. (1848), No. 1098.
34. Radetzky to Latour, Verona, 8 May 1848, KA.M.K. (1848), No. 1278.
35. Radetzky to Latour, Verona, 9 May 1848, KA.M.K. (1848), No. 1370.
36. Op. cit., KA.M.K. (1848), No. 1370.
37. Latour to Radetzky, Vienna, 14 May 1848, KA.M.K. (1848), No. 1370.
38. Radetzky to Latour, Verona, 8 May 1848, KA.M.K. (1848), No. 1278.
39. Radetzky to Ficquelmont, Verona, 3 May 1848, KA.M.K. (1848), No. 1098.
40. Op. cit., KA.M.K. (1848), No. 1098.
41. Radetzky to Latour, Verona, 10 May 1848, KA.M.K. (1848), No. 1375.
42. Radetzky to Latour, Verona, 16 May 1848, KA.M.K. (1848), No. 1942.
43. Radetzky to Latour, Verona, 15 May 1848, KA.M.K. (1848), No. 1942.
44. Op. cit., KA.M.K. (1848), No. 1942.
45. Op. cit., KA.M.K. (1848), No. 1942.
46. Op. cit., KA.M.K. (1848), No. 1942.
47. Radetzky to Latour, Verona, 26 May 1848, KA.M.K. (1848), No. 2126.
48. Radetzky to Latour, Verona, 15 May 1848, KA.M.K. (1848), No. 1942.
49. Radetzky to Latour, Verona, 26 May 1848, KA.M.K. (1848), No. 2126.
50. The *Handschreiben* was one of 10 March the relevant part of which read:
    Should the hostile feeling in my Kingdom of Lombardy-Venetia reach such a pass that the civil authorities can no longer preserve law and order, every single town, every single district, every single province which shall have fallen into this regrettable condition is to be treated like a hostile area occupied in time of war; that is, the preservation of law and order will be maintained by my army in accordance with the articles of war, without however, preventing my civil officials in particular matters from carrying out their functions. *Should the need arise* you are to acquaint F.M. Radetzky with these wishes of mine immediately and to reach an understanding with him regarding their fulfilment. See Note 61, Ch. 7 (p. 268).
51. Pillersdorff to Hartig, Vienna, 31 May 1848, KA.M.K. (1848), No. 2126.
52. Hartig to Wessenberg, Roveredo, 3 July 1848, F(1), pp. 189–94.
53. Hartig to Radetzky, Verona, 6 June 1848, KA.M.K. (1848), No. 2777.
54. Radetzky to Hartig, Verona, 12 June 1848, KA.M.K. (1848), No. 2777.
55. Op. cit., KA.M.K. (1848), No. 2777.
56. Pillersdorff to Latour, Vienna, 12 June 1848, KA.M.K. (1848), No. 2456.
57. Op. cit., KA.M.K. (1848), No. 2456.
58. Latour to Pillersdorff, Vienna, 14 June 1848, KA.M.K. (1848), No. 2456.

59. Latour to Radetzky, Vienna, 14 June 1848, KA.M.K. (1848), No. 2456.
60. Radetzky to Latour, Verona, 19 June, KA.M.K. (1848), No. 2780.
61. Hartig to Radetzky, Roveredo, 16 June 1848, KA.M.K. (1848), No. 2777.
62. Radetzky to Hartig, Verona, 18 June 1848, KA.M.K. (1848), No. 2777.
63. Radetzky to Latour, Verona, 13 June 1848, KA.M.K. (1848), No. 2622.
64. Radetzky to Latour, Verona, 19 June 1848, KA.M.K. (1848), No. 2780.
65. Op. cit., KA.M.K. (1848), No. 2780.
66. Hartig to Wessenberg, Roveredo, 18 June 1848, F(1), pp. 167–8.
67. Wessenberg to Radetzky, Innsbruck, 11 June 1848, F(1), p. 147.
68. The Emperor to Radetzky, Innsbruck, 12 June 1848, F(1), pp. 147–8 (Addendum).
69. Wessenberg to Radetzky, Innsbruck, 13 June 1848, F(1), pp. 151–2.
70. Op. cit., F(1), pp. 151–2.
71. Wessenberg to Radetzky, Innsbruck, 16 June 1848, F(1), p. 165.
72. Wessenberg to Hartig, Innsbruck, 17 June 1848, F(1), pp. 165–6.
73. Hartig to Wessenberg, Roveredo, 14 June 1848, F(1), pp. 158–62.
74. Radetzky to Hartig, Verona, 19 June 1848, F(1), pp. 170–3 (Addendum A).
75. Hartig to Wessenberg, Roveredo, June 1848, F(1), pp. 170–3.
76. Wessenberg to Radetzky, Innsbruck, 19 June 1848, F(1), pp. 168–70.
77. Op. cit., F(1), pp. 168–70.
78. Op. cit., F(1), pp. 168–70.
79. Schnitzer-Meerau to Wessenberg Vienna, 25 June 1848, F(1), pp. 174–8.
80. Wessenberg to Council of Ministers, 26 June 1848, F(1), pp. 180–9.
81. Op. cit., F(1), pp. 180–9 (Addendum C).
82. Wessenberg to Hartig, Vienna, 26 June 1848, F(1), pp. 179–80.
83. Pillersdorff to Latour, Innsbruck (?), 23 June 1848, KA.M.K. (1848), No. 2796.
84. Latour to Radetzky, Vienna, 24 June 1848, KA.M.K. (1848), No. 2772.
85. Hartig to Wessenberg, Roveredo, 3 July 1848, F(1), pp. 189–94.
86. Radetzky to Hartig, Verona, 30 June 1848 (Addendum).
87. Radetzky to Latour, Verona, 18 May 1848, KA.M.K. (1848), No. 1707g.
88. Radetzky to Latour, 13 June, 1848, KA.M.K. (1848), No. 2622.
89. Radetzky to Latour, Verona, 19 June 1848, KA.M.K. (1848), No. 2777. He is referring to Pillersdorff's letter to Latour of 12 June 1848 supporting Hartig (KA.M.K., 1848, No. 2456).
90. Radetzky to Latour, Verona, 21 June 1848, KA.M.K. (1848), No. 2857.
91. Op. cit., KA.M.K. (1848), No. 2857.
92. Latour to Radetzky, 27 June 1848, KA.M.K. (1848), No. 2857.
93. Op. cit., KA.M.K. (1848), No. 2857.
94. Op. cit., KA.M.K. (1848), No. 2857.
95. Windischgraetz to Latour, Prague, 24 June 1848, KA.M.K. (1848), No. 2854/2878.
96. Latour to Windischgraetz, Vienna, 28 June 1848, KA.M.K. (1848), No. 2854/2898.
97. Radetzky to Latour, Verona, 21 June 1848, KA.M.K. (1848), No. 2857.
98. Telegram, KA.M.K. (1848), No. 3733.
99. Radetzky to Latour, H.Q. Alzarea, 25 July 1848, KA.M.K. (1848), No. 3908g.
100. Radetzky to Latour, H.Q. Valeggio, 27 July 1848, KA.M.K. (1848), No. 3908g.
101. Op. cit., KA.M.K. (1848), No. 3908g.
102. Latour to Radetzky, Vienna, 31 July 1848, KA.M.K. (1848), No. 3908g.
103. Welden to Radetzky, Padua, 28 July 1848, KA.M.K. (1848), No. 3836.
104. Op. cit., KA.M.K. (1848), No. 3836.
105. Radetzky to Latour, H.Q. Cigognolo, 30 July 1848, KA.M.K. (1848), No. 3891g.
106. Latour to Radetzky, Vienna, 3 Aug. 1848, KA.M.K. (1848), No. 3891g.
107. Radetzky to Latour, H.Q. Festo, 31 July 1848, KA.M.K. (1848), No. 3913.
108. Radetzky to Latour, H.Q. Lodi, 3 Aug. 1848, KA.M.K. (1848), No. 3997.
109. Latour to Radetzky, Vienna, 9 Aug. 1848, KA.M.K. (1848), No. 4028.
110. Latour to Radetzky, Vienna, 8 Aug. 1848, KA.M.K. (1848), No. 3997.
111. See Note 109 above.
112. Latour to Welden, Vienna, 9 Aug. 1848, KA.M.K. (1848), No. 4028. But see also Radetzky to Welden, Milan, 14 Aug. 1848, KA.M.K. (1948), No. 4345; Radetzky told Welden he had acted without orders and must quit the Legations 'immediately'.
113. Welden to Latour, Bologna, 7 Aug. 1848, KA.M.K. (1848), No. 4069g/70g.
114. Latour to Welden, Vienna, 11 Aug. 1848, KA.M.K. (1848), No. 4069g/70g.
115. Radetzky to Latour, H.Q. San Donato, 5 Aug. 1848, KA.M.K. (1848), No. 4054.
116. See Note 115 above.

117. See Note 115 above.
118. Radetzky to Latour, Milan 6 Aug. 1848, KA.M.K. (1848), No. 4064.
119. Telegram, KA.M.K. (1848), No. 4029.
120. Latour to Radetzky, Vienna, 9 Aug. 1848, KA.M.K. (1848), No. 4029.
121. See below p. 151.
122. Radetzky to Latour, Lodi, 3 Aug. 1848, KA.M.K. (1848), No. 4001.
123. Latour to Radetzky, Vienna, 11 Aug. 1848, KA.M.K. (1848), No. 4064.
124. Radetzky to Wessenberg, Milan, 10 Aug. 1848, KA.M.K. (1848), No. 4294.
125. Op. cit., KA.M.K. (1848), No. 4294.
126. Wessenberg to Radetzky, Frankfurt, 4 Aug. 1848, F(1), pp. 203–5.
127. Op. cit., F(1), pp. 203–5.
128. Wessenberg to Montecuccoli, Frankfurt, 4 Aug. 1848, F(1), pp. 205–7.
129. Op. cit., F(1), pp. 205–7.
130. Op. cit., F(1), pp. 205–7.
131. Wessenberg to Montecuccoli, Frankfurt, 8 Aug. 1848, F(1), pp. 207–8.
132. Montecuccoli to Wessenberg, Verona, 8 Aug. 1848, F(1), pp. 208–10.
133. Montecuccoli to Wessenberg, Milan, 10 Aug. 1848, F(1), pp. 210–13.
134. Wessenberg to Lebzeltern, Frankfurt, 7 Aug. 1848, KA.M.K. (1848), No. 4211.
135. Lebzeltern to Latour, Vienna, 11 Aug. 1848, KA.M.K. (1848), No. 4102.
136. Latour to Lebzeltern, Vienna, 12 Aug. 1848, KA.M.K. (1848), No. 4102.
137. Lebzeltern to Latour, Vienna, 13 Aug. 1848, KA.M.K. (1848), Nos. 4151 and 4154.
138. Wessenberg to Latour, Frankfurt, 16 Aug. 1848, KA.M.K. (1848), No. 4365.
139. Latour to Radetzky and Schwarzenberg, Vienna, 16 Aug. 1848, KA.M.K. (1848), No. 4365.
140. Wessenberg to Radetzky, Vienna, 25 Aug. 1848, F(1), pp. 223–4.
141. Wessenberg to Schwarzenberg, Vienna, 25 Aug. 1848, F(1), pp. 227–9.
142. Radetzky to Latour, Milan, 7 Sept. 1848, KA.M.K. (1848), No. 4941.
143. See Franz Hartig (ed.) *Metternich-Hartig. Ein Briefwechsel des Staatskanzlers ans dem Exil, 1848–1851,* Vienna, 1923, p. 33. Hartig's letter to Metternich dated 19 March 1849 has the observation: 'The harsh judgement delivered to me a year ago by Count Ficquelmont when he returned from Milan, namely, "Radetzky ce n'est plus qu'un nom", I have not found confirmed.'

Notes to Chapter 9

1. Radetzky to Latour, Verona, 9 July 1848, KA.M.K. (1848), No. 3352.
2. Op. cit., KA.M.K. (1848), No. 3352.
3. Op. cit., KA.M.K. (1848), No. 3352.
4. Latour to Radetzky, Vienna, 3 Aug. 1848, KA.M.K. (1848), No. 3891g.
5. Radetzky to Latour, Milan, 7 Aug. 1848, KA.M.K. (1848), No. 5172.
6. Op. cit., KA.M.K. (1848), No. 5172.
7. Op. cit., KA.M.K. (1848), No. 5172.
8. Radetzky to Wessenberg, Milan, 10 Aug. 1848, KA.M.K. (1848), No. 4294.
9. Radetzky to Latour, Milan, 12 Aug. 1848, KA.M.K. (1848), No. 4252.
10. Op. cit., KA.M.K. (1848), No. 4252.
11. Montecuccoli to Wessenberg, Vienna, 10 Aug. 1848, F(1), pp. 210–13.
12. Op. cit., F(1), pp. 210–13.
13. Montecuccoli to Wessenberg, Verona, 17 Aug. 1848, F(1), pp. 216–22.
14. Wessenberg's report to the Council of Ministers, Vienna, 25 Aug. 1848, F(1), pp. 230–2.
15. Wessenberg to Montecuccoli, Vienna, 25 Aug. 1848, F(1), pp. 225–6.
16. Radetzky to Wessenberg, Milan, 17 Sept. 1848, F(1), pp. 254–6.
17. Radetzky to Latour, Milan, 22 Sept. 1848, KA.M.K. (1848), No. 5463.
18. Op. cit., KA.M.K. (2848), No. 5463.
19. Latour to Radetzky, Vienna, 29 Sept. 1848, KA.M.K. (1848), No. 5463.
20. Wessenberg to Montecuccoli, Vienna, 24 Sept. 1848, F(1), p. 258.
21. Wessenberg to Montecuccoli, Vienna, 29 Sept. 1848, F(1), pp. 259–60.
22. Montecuccoli to Wessenberg, Milan, 3 Oct. 1848, F(1), pp. 261–4.
23. Montecuccoli to Wessenberg, Milan, 8 Oct. 1848, F(1), pp. 264–5.
24. Metzburg to Wessenberg, Milan, 10 Oct. 1848, F(1), pp. 265–9.
25. Op. cit., F(1), pp. 265–9.
26. Radetzky to Wessenberg, Milan, 9 Oct. 1848, F(1), p. 271.

27. Radetzky to Zanini, Verona, 29 Apr. 1848, KA.M.K. (1848), No. 958/996.
28. See *Enthüllüngen aus Oesterreichs jüngster Vergangenheit. Von einem Mitglieder der Linken des aufgelösten österreichischen Reichstages*, Hamburg, 1849, p. 64.
29. *Enthüllüngen aus Oesterreichs*, p. 64.
30. *Enthüllüngen aus Oesterreichs*, pp. 66–8.
31. *Enthüllüngen aus Oesterreichs*, pp. 60–70.
32. *Enthüllüngen aus Oesterreichs*, pp. 66–8.
33. Radetzky to Latour, Milan, 30 Sept. 1848, KA.M.K. (1848), No. 6598.
34. Latour to Radetzky, Vienna,? Oct. 1848, KA.M.K. (1848), No. 6598.
35. Metzburg to Wessenberg, Milan, 18 Oct. 1848, F(1), pp. 280–4.
36. Op. cit., F(1), pp. 280–4.
37. Hess to Schwarzenberg, Milan, 21 Nov. 1848, F(1), pp. 338–9.
38. Metzburg to Schwarzenberg, Milan, 5 Feb. 1849, F(1), pp. 393–4.
39. Op. cit., F(1), pp. 393–4.
40. Op. cit., F(1), pp. 393–4.
41. See *B.F.S.P.*, Vol. 44, pp. 393–4.
42. *B.F.S.P.*, Vol. 44, pp. 393–4.
43. Radetzky to Schwarzenberg (no date, no place), F(1), pp. 411–12.

Notes to Chapter 10

1. See *La Vérité sur les Événemens de Galicie*, Paris, 1847, p. 45. The author of this work is anonymous.
2. See Erzsébet Andics, 'Metternich és az 1830 -as évek magyar reformmozgalma', *Századok* (1972), (272–309), 303. This article has since been incorporated into Miss Andics' book, *Metternich und die Frage Ungarns*, Budapest, 1971.
3. Andics, *Századok*, p. 304.
4. Andics, *Századok*, p. 303–4.
5. Andics, *Századok*, p. 304.
6. Andics, *Századok*, p. 304.
7. Andics, *Századok,* p. 304.
8. For a classic statement of these charges, see, *La Vérité*.
9. See Piotr S. Wandycz, 'The Poles in the Habsburg Monarchy', *Austrian History Yearbook*, 1967, Vol. III, pp. 268–70.
10, 11, 12. See *La Vérité* which as well as establishing the charges, also provides the first and some of the key pieces of circumstantial evidence. Wandycz, op. cit. lists a full bibliography on the debate.
13. The documents referred to are the archive of the military praesidium of the Galician civil and military gubernium for 1845–46 which are to be found in O-E.A.(IV), K. 107 and 108, in the Haus-Hof- und Staatsarchiv in Vienna.
14. It is clear from the documents that Breindl had made no sinister suggestions beforehand. However, Benedek on reaching Tarnow was so shocked by what he learned of Breindl's conduct during the jacquerie that he refused to report on it in writing, restricting himself to the comment that Breindl would have to be replaced.
15. For the European 'press war' which followed the news of events in Galicia, see, 'Die gute Press Östreichs und ihr Verhalten bei den galizischen Ereignissen', in *Unsre Gegenwart und Zukunft*, Leipzig, Vol. 3, 1846, pp. 67–107, and, the anonymous *Galizien und die Robotfrage*, Leipzig, 1846.
16. See *Galizien*, p. 51.
17. See Viscount Ponsonby to Viscount Palmerson, Vienna, 2 Apr. 1848, *B.F.S.P.*, Vol. 37, p. 968, No. 214: 'Count Ficquelmont said that I was in error if I believed that all the Italian population was hostile to the Austrians, that, on the contrary, there were large numbers who disapproved greatly of what the Milanese agitators and others had done; that if Austria chose to avail itself of its actual power to raise the peasantry against their superiors it would have perfect facility in procuring the ruin and destruction of those persons; but,' added the Count, 'that is a policy I would rather die than adopt.'
18. Metternich to Apponyi, Vienna, 7 Mar. 1846, Richard von Metternich and Alfons von Klinkowström (eds), *Aus Metternichs nachgelassenen Papieren*, 8 vols., Vienna, 1880–4, Vol. VIII, p. 182, doc. 1543.
19. Metternich to Radetzky, Vienna, 16 Mar. 1846, H-H.SA.S.P.L-V., K. 38.

20. Metternich to Rainer, Vienna, 5 Mar. 1846, H-H.SA.S.P. L-V., K. 5.
21. Palffy to Metternich, Venice, 10 Mar. 1846, H-H.SA.S.P.L-V., K. 6.
22. Rainer to Metternich, Venice, 10 Mar. 1846, H-H.SA.S.P.L-V., K. 5.
23. N.P., Vol VIII, p. 548.
24. Metternich to Ficquelmont, Vienna, 23 Jan. 1848, H-H.SA.S.P.L-V., K. 23.
25. Ficquelmont to Metternich, Milan, 3 Dec. 1847, H-H.SA.S.P.L-V., K. 23.
26. See Joseph Alexander Fruhen von Helfert, 'Casati and Pillersdorf und die Anfänge der italienischen Einheitsbewegung', *Archiv für Österreichische Geschichte*, 91 (1962), 500–2. Lt.-Col. Count Wratislaw to Captain Huyn.
27. Metternich to Ficquelmont, Vienna, 8 Jan. 1848, H-H.SA.S.P.L-V., K. 23.
28. See the *Archivio Triennale della Cose d'Italia dall'Avvimento di Pio IX all'Abbandono di Venezia*, Capologo-Chieri, 3 vols, 1850–5, Vol. 1, p. 491.
29. *Archivio Triennale*, Vol. 1, p. 500.
30. Carlo Cattaneo, *L'Insurrection de Milan en 1848*, Paris, 1848, p. 12.
31. Cattaneo, op. cit., p. 16.
32. Cattaneo, op. cit., p. 16.
33. Cattaneo, op. cit., p. 16.
34. F. A. Gualterio, *Gli ultimi Rivolgimenti italiani*, 2 vols, Forence, 1852.
35. Ficquelmont to Metternich, Milan, 31 Jan. 1848, H-H.SA.S.P.L-V., K. 23.
36. For what follows see the very useful article by Berthold Waldstrum-Wartenberg, 'Österreichische Adelsrecht, 1804–1918', *Mitteilungen des Österreichischen Staatsarchiv*, 17/18 (1964–5), 117–24, 140–2.
37. The following is a list of the city nobilities, confirmed and unconfirmed.

Confirmed		Unconfirmed	
Adria	Feltre	Albona	Nova
Asola	Lendinara	Almissa	Oscero
Bassano	Oderno	Arbe	Pogo
Bergamo	Parenzo	Badia	Pastrovechio
Brescia	Rovigo	Brazza	Perasto
Bellino	Seravalle	Budua	Presichie
Capo d'Istria	Spalato	Cherso	Pola
Cafalonia	Trace	Chioggia	Sacile
Crema	Treviso	Curzola	Scardone
Ceneda	Udine	Este	Sebencio
Cividale	Verona	Lesina	Veglia
Conegliano	Zara	Macarsia	

38. The anonymous author of *L'Autriche et ses Provinces Italiennes*, Paris, 1859.
39. Comte F. de Sonis, *Lettres du Comte et de la Comtesse de Ficquelmont à la Comtesse Tiesenhausen*, Paris, 1911, p. 143.
40. See Joseph Alexander Freiherr von Helfert, 'Zur Geschichte des lombardo-venezianischen Königreichs', *Archiv für Österreichische Geschichte*, 98 (1908), 195.
41. Helfert, 'Zur Geschichte', p. 195.
42. Ficquelmont to Metternich, Milan, 3 Dec. 1847, H-H.SA.S.P.L-V., K. 23.
43. Franco Arese, 'La Lombardia e la politica dell'Austria: un colloquio inedito del Metternich nel 1832', *Archivo Storico Lombardo*, LXXVII (1950), 5–57, 9.
44. Arese, op. cit., p. 24.
45. Helfert, 'Zur Geschichte', pp. 18–19.
46. See Helfert's 'Casati und Pillersdorff', pp. 463–4. The judiciary, he emphasised, constituted the main bone of contention, since most judicial appointments went to bilingual Germans from the South Tyrol. This, in fact, was a consequence of the introduction in 1814 of the Austrian Civil Code into Lombardy-Venetia.
47. See General K. von Schönhals, *Erinnerungen eines österreichischen Veteranen aus dem italienischen Kriege der Jahre 1848 and 1849*, Stuttgart and Tübingen, 1853, pp. 23–4.

Notes to Chapter 11

1. Phillipsberg to Metternich, 3 Apr. 1847, H-H.SA.S.P.L-V., K. 40.

2. Op. cit., H-H.SA.S.P.L-V., K. 40.

3. See N. Bianchi Giovini, *L'Autriche en Italie*, 2 vols, Paris, 1854, Vol. I, pp. 176–7.

4. See Carlo Casati, *Nuove Rivelazioni su i Fatti di Milano nel 1847—48*, 2 vols, Milan 1885, Vol. I, p. 169.

5. Carlo Cattaneo, *L'Insurrection de Milan en 1848*, Paris, 1849, pp. 4–5.

6. Di Capitani to Metternich, see Franco Arese, 'La Lombardia e la politica dell'Austria: un colloquio inedito dell Metternich nel 1832', *Archivo Storico Lombardo* (1950), p. 9.

7. *L'Autriche et ses Provinces Italiennes*, anonymous pamphlet, Paris, 1859, p. 9. Curiously enough, the lack of interest in a military career was shared by one pseudo-Lombard aristocrat, the Archduke Rainer, son of the Archduke-Viceroy. Writing to his brother Ernst from Verona on 20 March 1848, he lamented that he could no longer get a post in the civil government thanks to recent events. He added:

> But what can I do? Nothing! I can take nothing in the civil profession and therefore must enter the military and get myself killed on the first occasion. All this we owe to our government of old women – an idiot for an Emperor – a worm for heir presumptive – an overbearing boy for the prince and as a tail to them the Empress-Mother Sophia – and all belonging to them are—. In this manner and by these people the Empire which was so strong has been demolished.

This letter was intercepted by revolutionaires and later printed in *The Times*. See D. Wemyss Jobson, *Metternich and the Austrian Rule in Lombardy*, London, 1848, pp. 79–82.

8. General K. von Schönhals, *Errinerungen eines österreichischen Veteranen aus dem italienischen Kriege der Jahr 1848 und 1849*, Stuttgart and Tübingen, 1853, p. 34.

9. Schönhals, op. cit., p. 34.

10. See Count Ficquelmont, *Lord Palmerston, L'Angleterre et le Continent*, Paris, 1852, p. 66.

11. See Joseph Alexander Freiherr von Helfert, 'Casati und Pillersdorf und die Anfänge der italienischen Einheitsbewegung', *Archiv für österreichische Geschichte*, 91 (1902), 289.

12. Quoted by Helfert, 'Casati und Pillersdorf', p. 292.

13. Helfert, 'Casati und Pillersdorf', p. 468. Captain Rossbacher to Captain Huyn.

14. Casati, op. cit., Vol. I, p. 147.

15. See Franz Ferdinand Hoettinger, *Radetzky, ein Stück Österreich*, Leipzig–Vienna, 1934, pp. 87–9.

16. Hoettinger, op. cit., pp. 87–9. But see A. Lucchini, 'Memoriale del Maresciallo Radetzky sulle condizioni d'Italia al principio del 1848', *Nuova Rivista Storica*, XIV (1930).

17. See Max. 1.

18. Max. 1. The Duke of Modena recognised the 'psychological importance' of having the people behind him. Of the militia, he wrote: '. . . sometimes the one, sometimes the other [company] is called out for garrison duty or field manœuvres or reserve service, or sometimes the alarm bell is merely rung to see how quickly they can form ranks. They always turn up, happily and voluntarily and do whatever is asked of them.' Parma operated a similar system and 'thanks to this, the two Duchies stand completely secure against any revolutionary uprising whatsoever'.

19. See Max. 1, 2, 3, 4 and 5.

20. Max. 1. The Archduke despised the timid, should-be outspoken defenders of the government in the towns. They showed too much *paura* – the Italian word for 'fear' – 'a feeling unknown to the German race and therefore the word is untranslatable' (Max. 4). 'Hence the indisputable conclusion arises that if the Austrian government understands how to support its loyal peasantry and to set them against the ever less trustworthy city populations, if it shows confidence in the first and takes strict measures against the latter and makes them afraid, if it goes ahead with this . . .' all would be well.

21. Max. 1: '. . . Only the volunteering sons of well-respected families of real peasants, namely the so-called Mezzadri, are to be accepted, if the community leader and priest certify them as loyal men; as soon as they show themselves to be something else, they will be immediately thrown out of the militia.' Max. 2. In his second essay, the phrase *nur wahren Bauern (Feldarbeiter)* appears underlined. He did not want *jedes anderen Menschen*. That phrase was also underlined.

22. Ten bullets per man would also be kept in the company arsenal which would be under the supervision of a captain.

23. See Max. 2.

24. See Max. 2.

25. Max. 2. 'However, also as a means of maintaining proper order, it should be established that, should a militiaman be expelled from the militia by a court-martial on account of bad behaviour of a certain kind, or because he no longer belongs to the peasantry, from that moment on, the man who he freed from conscription is liable again, regardless of age.'

26. See Max. 2.

27. See Max. 1.

28. See Max. 2.

29. Max. 2. But see his comments in Max. 1: 'The hatred of the Italian against his neighbours hailing from a different [Italian] stock, is so great that he just loves to get into a brawl with them; indeed he prefers to fight with his neighbours than with foreigners.' He cites the example of Modena's militia: 'The militia of the Modenese part of Lunigiana and of the Duchy of Mahsa were extraordinarily keen to try their strength against the Tuscans and rendered excellent service, their ardour being in no way cooled despite the difficulties they had to experience in their deployment along the border.'

30. See Max. 1 and 2.

31. Maximilian also wrote that from time to time the militia units should be called out at the discretion of their captain to be instructed about service obligations and drilled in simple formations. He was quite adamant, however, that they should not be paid for doing so.

32. See Max. 4: 'Since this militia would give all civil authorities in the land an ever ready means of force to hand, so the third of the above-mentioned causes on account of which so many people think it necessary to keep so many troops in Italy falls away and in the case of war breaking out in another theatre a great number of troops stationed in Italy could be used there without the fear that in the meanwhile the civil government would completely collapse . . . if the theatre of war should be Italy itself, the militia could be well employed in occupying the forts along with the troops of the line and thereby a greater part of these troops could be freed for the active army.'

33. Max. 4 has the National Guard in charge inside the towns.

34. Max. 3.

35. Casati, op. cit., p. 21.

36. Casati, op. cit., pp. 21–3. Ziboldi's wife told her employers what had happened and this report ended up in the local archives, the Director of which made it available to Casati.

37. Ficquelmont to Rainer, Milan, 10 Dec. 1847, H-H.SA.S.P.L-V., K. 23.

38. Ficquelmont to Metternich, Milan, 27 Dec. 1847, H-H.SA.S.P.L-V., K. 23.

39. Metternich to Ficquelmont, Vienna, 8 Jan. 1848, H-H.SA.S.P.L-V., K. 23.

40. Radetzky to Hardegg, Milan, 3 Jan. 1848, KA.CK. (Präs.), 1848, No. 44.

41. Ficquelmont to Metternich, Milan, 7 Jan. 1848, H-H.SA.S.P.L-V., K. 23. See also Bianchi Giovini, op. cit., Vol. II, pp. 23–4.

42. See Franco Della Peruta, 'I contadini nella rivoluzione lombarda del 1848', *Movimento Operaio* (1953), 525–75, 543.

43. Metternich to Ficquelmont, Vienna, 25 Jan. 1848, H-H.SA.S.P.L-V., K. 23 (second letter of that day).

44. Metternich to Ficquelmont, Vienna, 8 Jan. 1848, H-H.SA.S.P.L-V., K. 23.

45. Bianchi Giovini, op. cit., Vol. II, p. 21.

46. See Della Peruta, op. cit., pp. 539–40.

47. Della Peruta, op. cit., pp. 542–3.

Notes to Chapter 12

1. Franco Della Peruta, 'I contadini nella rivoluzione lombarda del 1848', *Movimento Operaio* (1953), 549.

2. See Pio Pecchiari, 'Caduti e feriti nelle Cinque Giornate di Milano: ceti e professioni cui appartenaro,' *Atti e Memorie del XXVII Congresso Nazionale. Milan, 19—20—21 Marzo 1848*, pp. 533–37, p. 535.

3. *Archivio Triennale delle Case d'Italia dall'Avvimento di Pio IX all Abbandono de Venezia*, 3 vols, Capolago-Chieri, 1850–5, Vol. II, p. 247. For the special role of the Bergamaschi see Tullia Franzi, 'I volontari bergamaschi nel Quarantotto', *Atti e Memorie*, pp. 227–32, as well as Ippolito Negrisoli, 'Bergamo all riscossa, *Atti e Memorie*, pp. 495–504.

4. *Archivio Triennale*, Vol. II, p. 450.

5. Della Peruta, op. cit., p. 550.

6. *Archivio Triennale*, Vol. II, p. 469.

7. *Archivio Triennale*, Vol. II, p. 208.

8. Della Peruta, op. cit., p. 551.

9. Della Peruta, op. cit., p. 552.

10. Della Peruta, op. cit., p. 558.

11. Della Peruta, op. cit., p. 559.

12. Della Peruta, op. cit., p. 559.
13. See F. A. Gualterio, *Gli Ultimi Rivolgimenti Italiani,* 2 vols, Florence, 1852, Vol. II. pp. 278–9.
14. See Achille Marazza, *Il Clero Lombardo nella Rivoluzione del '48,* Florence, 1852, Vol. II, pp. 278–9.
15. Marazza, op. cit., pp. 278–9.
16. General K. von Schönhals, *Errinerungen eines osterreichischen Veteranen aus dem italienischen Kriege der Jahre 1848, und 1849,* Stuttgart and Tübingen, 1853.
17. Marazza, op. cit., pp. 10–13.
18. Marazza, op. cit., p. 15.
19. Marazza, op. cit., pp. 14–15.
20. Marazza, op. cit., p. 87.
21. Marazza, op. cit., pp. 95 and 99 and pp. 113–14.
22. Marazza, op. cit., p. 56.
23. Marazza, op. cit., p. 57.
24. Marazza, op. cit., p. 57.
25. See Della Peruta, op. cit., pp. 562–6.
26. See Della Peruta, op. cit., pp. 562–5.
27. See Della Peruta, op. cit., pp. 562–5.
28. See Della Peruta, op. cit., pp. 562–5.
29. See Della Peruta, op. cit., pp. 562–5.
30. The Lombard peasantry in the north of the country continued to fight the Austrians until the armistice (see Della Peruta, op. cit., pp. 569–71). But it was apparent, especially to the Sardinians, that there was little enthusiasm for the war on the Lombard plain. Indeed, a controversy had arisen in Italian historiography concerning the extent of the Lombard contribution to the war, a controversy which has its roots in the literature of the time. See *inter alia*: L. C. Bollea, 'Il contributo dei Lombardi alla prima guerra dell "Independenza" ', *Il Risorgimento Italiano,* XVIII (1925); Antonio Monti, 'Il contributo dei Lombardi alla prima Guerra dell "Independenza"', *Nuova Rivista Storica,* X (1926), 241–6 (with successive replies on pp. 409–13, and pp. 589–90; Ettore Rota, 'Del contributo dei Lombardi alla prima Guerra del 1848: il problemo del Volontarismo', *Nuova Rivista Storica,* 12 (1928), 1–52; L. Marchetti, 'I moti di Milano il problema della fusione col Piemonte', in E. Rota (ed.), *Il 1848 nella Storia Italiana ed Europa,* Milan, 1948, pp. 653–723. Also Piero Pieri, 'Il Generale Eusebio Bava nelle sue Carte Inedite del 1848–9', in P. Vaccari and P. F. Paulumbo (eds), *Studia di Storia Medievale e Moderna in onore di Ettore Rota,* Rome, 1958, pp. 499–548. But see too, Emilio Dandolo, *The Italian Volunteers and Lombard Rifle Brigade,* London, 1851, and *Memorie ed Osservanzioni sulla Guerra dell' Independenza d' Italia nel 1848. Raccolte da un Ufficiale Piemontese,* Turin, 1849.
31. Ausano Labadini, *Milano ed alcuni Momenti del Risorgimento Italiano,* Milan, 1909, p. 32.
32. Radetzky to Latour, Fresto, 31 July 1848, KA.M.K. (1848), No. 3913.
33. See Radetzky to Zanini, Verona, 30 Apr. 1848, KA.M.K. (1848), No. 1059. The Counts arrested were Thun, Manci, Lizzo and Festi, all of whom Radetzky characterized as 'the leaders of the Italian Party'.
34. Brandis to Radetzky, Innsbruck, 24 Apr. 1848, KA.M.K. (1848), No. 1059 (Addendum I); Brandis to Radetzky, Innsbruck, 28 Apr. 1848, KA.M.K. (1848), No. 1059 (Addendum III); Radetzky to Brandis, Verona, 30 Apr. 1848, KA.M.K. (1848), No. 1059 (Addendum IV).
35. Op. cit., KA.M.K. (1848), No. 1059 (Addendum III).
36. Op. cit., KA.M.K. (1848), No. 1059 (Addendum III, original letter).
37. Radetzky to the Archduke John, Verona 28 Apr. 1848, KA.M.K. (1848), No. 1059.
38. Radetzky to the Archduke John, Verona, 28 Apr., 1848, KA.M.K. (1848), No. 1059 (Addendum II).
39. Op. cit., KA.M.K. (1848), No. 1059 (Addendum II).
40. Op. cit., KA.M.K. (1848), No. 1059 (Addendum II).
41. Op. cit., KA.M.K. (1848), No. 1059 (Addendum II).
42. Latour to Radetzky, Vienna, 6 May 1848, KA.M.K. (1848), No. 1059 (Addendum II).
43. Radetzky to the Archduke John, Verona, 5 May 1848, KA.M.K. (1848), No. 1370.
44. Labour to Radetzky, Vienna, 14 May 1848, KA.M.K. (1848), No. 1370.
45. *Raccolta,* Vol. 1, pp. 139–40. Full details of this title are given in list of Abbreviations on p. 246.
46. *Raccolta,* Vol. 1, pp. 139–40.
47. *Raccolta,* Vol. I, p. 156.
48. *Fonti per la Storia Italiana, III Series, 1848–60,* Abercromby to Palmerston, Turin, 30 Sept., 1848, C(1), pp. 385–6. Full details of titles referred to as C(1) and C(2) are given in the list of Abbreviations on p. 246.

49. N. Bianchi Giovini, *L'Autriche en Italie*, 2 vols, Paris, 1854, Vol. II, p. 65.
50. Branchi Giovini, op. cit., Vol. II, p. 65.
51. Doblhoff to Latour, Vienna, 2 Oct. 1848, KA.M.K. (1848), No. 5674.
52. Op. cit., KA.M.K. (1848), No. 5674.
53. Op. cit., KA.M.K. (1848), No. 5674.
54. Op. cit., KA.M.K. (1848), No. 5674. Doblhoff concluded that Pachta was scarcely fit to wear a decoration. The test was whether the public could be expected to applaud the Emperor's decision.
55. Bianchi Giovini, op. cit., Vol. II, p. 102.
56. Bianchi Giovini, op. cit., Vol. II, p. 59. See also *Raccolta,* Vol. I, pp. 45–7.
57. *Raccolta,* Vol. I, p. 232.
58. *Raccolta,* p. 33 and pp. 218–19.
59. Bianchi Giovini, op. cit., Vol. II, pp. 59–60.
60. Bianchi Giovini, op. cit., Vol. II, pp. 66–7.
61. Radetzky to Latour, Verona, 23 June 1848, KA.M.K. (1848), No. 2861.
62. Abercromby to Palmerston, Turin, 30 Sept. 1848, C(1), pp. 385–6.
63, 64, 65. See Vice-Consul Campbell to Palmerston, Milan, 24 Nov. 1848, *B.F.S.P.,* Vol. 44, pp. 823–4.
Campbell's statement read as follows:

1848		Austrian L.
20 Sept.	Rate of ordinary tax in advance	1,200,000
20 Sept.	Tax on tradesmen and merchants	175,000
5 Oct.	First rate of extra tax	493,000
26 Oct.	Second rate	550,000
7 Nov.	First rate of provincial extra tax	991,000
20 Nov.	State of predial tax paid in advance	1,100,000
Remaining rate of provincial tax due 4 Dec. 1848		991,000
Total paid by the city of Milan:		5,500,000
Ordinary predial tax for the whole province of Milan paid to the end of Dec. 1848		4,500,000
Loan from the city of Milan		2,836,000
Raised on mortgages guaranteed by the provincial congregation of Milan		700,000
Total sum paid by city and province of Milan		13,536,000
Paid by the provinces of:		
Lodi and Crema about		5,000,000
Pavia		2,000,000
Brescia		5,500,000
Como		2,000,000
Bergamo		2,000,000
Sondrio		1,800,000
Total paid by the city and province of Milan and the above-mentioned provinces:		31,386,600
Or in pounds sterling:		1,061,200

N.B. The sums raised in the provinces of Mantua and Cremona are still unknown at the Chamber of Commerce here.

66. Campbell to Palmerston, Milan, 5 Dec. 1848, *B.F.S.P.,* Vol. 44, pp. 842–3.
67. *Raccolta,* Vol. 1, p. 359. It went on to say that this did not apply to ordinary direct taxes or extraordinary ones not connected with the upkeep of the army.
68. See Antonio Monti, 'Il Contributo dei Lombardi alla prima Guerra dell'Independenza', *Nuova Revista Storica,* X (1926), 245.
69. Metzburg to Wessenberg, Milan, 7 Nov. 1848, F(1), pp. 307–11.
70. Metzburg to Wessenberg, Milan, 13 Nov. 1848, F(1), pp. 324–6 (author's italics).
71. Op. cit., F(1), pp. 324–6 (author's italics).
72. Abercromby to Palmerston, Turin, 13 Nov. 1848, C(1), pp. 442–3.
73. Abercromby to Lord John Russell, Turin, 19 Nov. 1848, C(1), pp. 450–3.
74. Palmerston to Ponsonby, Foreign Office, 20 Nov. 1848, *B.F.S.P.,* Vol. 44, pp. 770–1.
75. Abercromby to Palmerston, Turin, 13 Nov. 1848, C(1), pp. 442–3.
76. *B.F.S.P.,* Vol. 44, pp. 812–14. For the reactions of the Consulta Lombarda at this time in more

detail, see Federico Curato, *1848–49. La Consulta Straordinaria della Lombardia (2 August 1848—20 March 1849)*, Milan, 1950.

77. Metzburg to Wessenberg, Milan, 13 Nov. 1848, F(1), pp. 324–6.
78. Radetzky to Wessenberg, Milan, 16 Nov. 1848, F(1), pp. 331–2.
79. Op. cit., F(1), pp. 331–2.
80. Op. cit., F(1), pp. 331–2.
81. Op. cit., F(1), pp. 331–2.
82. Campbell to Palmerston, Milan, 24 Nov. 1848, *B.F.S.P.*, Vol. 44, pp. 825–6.
83. Metzburg to Wessenberg, Milan, 20 Nov. 1848, F(1), pp. 332–6.
84. Op. cit., F(1), pp. 332–6. F(1), pp. 336–7. See also *B.F.S.P.*, Vol. 44, pp. 825–6.
85. Montecuccoli to Wessenberg, Milan, 21 Nov. 1848, F(1), pp. 339–40.
86. Bianchi Giovini, op. cit., Vol. II, p. 89.
87. *B.F.S.P.*, Vol. 45, pp. 255–7.
88. Campbell to Palmerston, Milan, 26 Jan. 1849, *B.F.S.P.*, Vol. 45, pp. 308–9.
89. Bianchi Giovini, op. cit., Vol. II, p. 92.
90. Metzburg to Schwarzenberg, Milan, 17 Jan. 1849, F(1), pp. 383–5.
91. Metzburg to Schwarzenberg, Milan, 29 Jan. 1849, F(1), pp. 388–9.
92. Abercromby to Palmerston, Turin, 13 Dec. 1848, C(1), p. 476.
93. Op. cit., C(1), p. 476.
94. Bianchi Giovini, op. cit., Vol. II, p. 92.
95. Bianchi Giovini, op. cit., Vol. II, p. 95.
96. *B.F.S.P.*, Vol. 45, pp. 310 and 362.
97. Campbell to Palmerston, Milan, 16 Feb. 1849, *B.F.S.P.*, Vol. 45, p. 362.
98. Op. cit., *B.F.S.P.*, Vol. 45, p. 362.
99. Campbell to Palmerston, Milan, 25 Feb. 1849, *B.F.S.P.*, Vol. 45, pp. 389–90.
100. Campbell to Palmerston, Milan, 25 Feb. 1849, *B.F.S.P.*, Vol. 45, pp. 389–90.
101. Abercromby to Palmerston, Turin, 2 Apr. 1849, C(2), pp. 169–72.
102. Radetzky to Schwarzenberg, Milan, 13 Apr. 1849, F(2), pp. 34–5.
103. Op. cit., F(2), pp. 34–5. It must also have been fairly well known. See Appendix 16.
104. Campbell to Palmerston, Milan, 21 Apr. 1849, P.R.O., F.O. 7/371.
105. See *Raccolta*, Vol. II, pp. 328–32. Also Campbell to Palmerston, Milan, 13 Aug. 1849, P.R.O. F.O. 7/371.
106. Bianchi Giovini, op. cit., Vol. II, p. 103.
107. Campbell to Palmerston, Milan, 22 Aug. 1849, P.R.O., F.O. 7/371.
108. Bianchi Giovini, op. cit., Vol. II, pp. 111–12.
109. Bianchi Giovini, op. cit., Vol. II, p. 112.
110. Bianchi Giovini, op. cit., Vol. II, pp. 115–16.
111. Bianchi Giovini, op. cit., pp. 115–16.
112. *Raccolta*, Vol. I, p. 100.
113. *Raccolta*, Vol. I, pp. 607–8. See also Vol. V, pp. 78–9, which shows that periodic extensions continued at least until 31 March 1851.
114. *Raccolta*, Vol. I, pp. 6–7.
115. Latour to Emperor, Vienna, 9 Sept. 1848, KA.M.K. (1848), No. 447j.
116. That is, the number of years for which the troops were required to serve.
117. Latour to Radetzky, Vienna, 9 Sept. 1848, KA.M.K. (1848), No. 4779.
118. *Raccolta*, Vol. I, pp. 18–19.
119. Radetzky to Latour, Milan, 27 Sept. 1848, KA.M.K. (1848), No. 5563.
120. Radetzky to Latour, Milan, 27 Sept. 1848, KA.M.K. (1848), No. 5563g.
121. Op. cit., KA.M.K. (1848), No. 5563g.
122. Op. cit., KA.M.K. (1848), No. 5563g.
123. Latour to Radetzky, Vienna, 4 Oct. 1848, KA.M.K. (1848), No. 5563g.
124. Campbell to Palmerston, Milan, 26 Jan. 1849, *B.F.S.P.*, Vol. 45, p. 309. Cf. *Raccolta*, Vol. I, pp. 326–7.
125. *Raccolta*, Vol. I, pp. 248–9, 348.
126. *Raccolta*, Vol. I, pp. 400–1.
127. *Raccolta*, Vol. I, pp. 476–80.
128. *Raccolta*, Vol. I, pp. 476–80.
129. *Raccolta*, Vol. I, pp. 476–80.
130. Campbell to Palmerston, Milan, 7 May 1849, P.R.O., F.O. 7/371.
131. *Raccolta*, Vol. II, pp. 29–33, 108–110 (cf. pp. 53–4).
132. Campbell to Palmerston, Milan, 7 May 1849, P.R.O., F.O. 7/371.

133. *Raccolta,* Vol. II, pp. 154 and 167–70.
134. *Raccolta,* Vol. II, p. 186.
135. Abercromby to Palmerston, Turin, 26 Jan. 1849. *B.F.S.P.,* Vol. 45, pp. 301–3.
136. The existing correspondence of Schwarzenberg and Radetzky for the year 1849, although considerable, contains practically nothing on the internal administration of Lombardy-Venetia. Hence the above conclusion. See Karton XK/64 of the Politisches Archiv of the Haus-Hof- und Staatsarchiv in Vienna.
137. The documentation for what follows is from the works by Franco Valsecchi (ed.), referred to here as V(1) and V(2). Full details of these titles are given in the list of abbreviations on p. 246.
138. Schwarzenberg to Apponyi, Vienna, 15 Dec. 1849, V(1), pp. 36–7.
139. Schwarzenberg to Radetzky, Vienna, 13 Dec. 1849, appended to Schwarzenberg to Apponyi, Vienna, 15 Dec. 1849, V(1), pp. 36–7.
140. Op. cit., appended to V(1).
141. Apponyi to Schwarzenberg, Turin, 18 Dec. 1849, V(1), pp. 42–5.
142. Op. cit., V(1), pp. 42–5.
143. Op. cit., V(1), pp. 42–5.
144. Montecuccoli to Zulauf, Verona, 15 Dec. 1849. Appended to V(1).
145. Schwarzenberg to Apponyi, Vienna, 14 Jan. 1850, V(1), pp. 61–3.
146. Op. cit., V(1), pp. 61–3.
147. Schwarzenberg to Bach, Vienna, 29 Dec. 1849, appended to Schwarzenberg to Apponyi, 14 Jan. 1850, V(1), pp. 64–8.
148. Op. cit., V(1), pp. 64–8. Bach's report is undated.
149. Op. cit., V(1), 64–8.
150. See Schwarzenberg to Apponyi, Vienna, 8 Aug. 1850, V(1), pp. 135–8.
151. Sir James Hudson to Lord John Russell, Turin, 9 Feb. 1853, P.R.O., F.O. 67/192.
152. See Leopoldo Marchetti, 'Il decennio di resistenza', Part 5 of Vol. XIV (*Sotto L'Austria*) of the *Storia di Milano, Fondazione Treccani degli Alfieri per la Storia di Milano,* Milan, 1960, pp. 502–4. Also B. Caizzi, 'La crisi economica nel Lombardo-Veneto nel decennio 1850–59', *Nuova Rivista Storica* (1958), 208 ff.
153. Cf. F. Della Peruta, 'I democratico il problema della rivoluzione Italiana dal 1849 to al 1852', *Movimento Operaio,* Jan./Feb. 1955.

Notes to Conclusion

1. In time of war commanders in the field could promote up to the rank of major. Radetzky made so many promotions that there were fears voiced after 1848 that he had devalued the status of service nobility. See Antonio Schmidt-Bretano, *Die Armee in Österreich Militar, Staat und Gesellschaft, 1848–67,* Boppart am Rheim, 1975, p. 449.
2. Radetzky to the Archduke Rainer, Verona, 4 Apr. 1848, KA.M.K. (1848), No. 302. The fall of Venice and the uprisings everywhere, he added, 'have hit me like a bolt from the blue'.
3. The Austrian general who in 1741 had lost Silesia to Frederick the Great of Prussia was actually consoled by the Empress Maria Theresa with the words: 'you are not the first of my generals to have met with such an accident'. See Manfred Rauchensteiner, *Kaiser Franz und Erzherzog Carl, Dynastie und Heerwesen in Österreich, 1769–1809.,* Münich, 1972, p. 6. Then cf. Zanini to Radetzky, Vienna, 20? March, 1848, KA.M.K. (1848), No. 141, in which Zanini tells the Field Marshal that no one is to blame for events in Italy.
4, 5. See in particular, Radetzky to Schwarzenberg, Milan, 7 Apr. 1849, V(1), pp. 416–18 and Radetzky to Schwarzenberg, Monza, 28 July 1849, V(2), pp. 459–64. For Radetzky's refusal to send troops to Hungary, see Radetzky to Schwarzenberg, Milan 17 Apr. 1849, V(2), pp. 48–50
6. This view would not be accepted, I note, by Paul Ginsborg who has recently published an article entitled 'Peasants and revolutionaries in Venice and the Veneto, 1848', *The Historical Journal,* XVII, 3 (1974), 503–50. Dr Ginsborg arrives at the same conclusion as myself regarding the peasantry in 1848, but assigns the leadership of the revolutionary movement to the rising bourgeoisie. It must be said, however, that he can do this only by ignoring the role of the nobility and by involving himself in glaring contradictions. Thus while we learn on p. 518 that 'those who had recently acquired land and the rural "intelligentsia", priests, doctors, lawyers and any other professional or business men, were often to be found at the head of the National Guard', we are told on p. 524 that 'there was a shortage of officers' [in the National Guard] because 'so many of the middle class had bought their way out of conscription'. Likewise, on pp. 517–18 we learn that 'most

of the noble landlords undoubtedly remained hostile to the Italian cause' and on p. 519 that they 'facilitated the Austrian withdrawal' and provided Radetzky with the key city of Verona. But on p. 526 we are told that they 'controlled' the peasantry which according to Ginsborg was revolutionary! One is tempted to refer Dr Ginsborg to the introduction by Romeo of the revised edition of Kent Roberts Greenfield's *Economics and Liberalism in the Risorgimento, A Study of Nationalism in Lombardy, 1814–48,* Baltimore, 1965, pp. xvii and xii. There he writes:

> It would be natural to infer that Italian liberalism reflected amovement by the middle classes to gain control of society. The defect of this thesis is that the liberal programme was initiated, expounded and propagated, not by an aspiring and self-conscious bourgeoisie, with strong economic interests to serve, but by landed proprietors and a group of intellectuals, many of whose leaders were of the aristocracy. . . . There is no evidence to colour the view that the liberal publicists were being pushed by a rising capitalistic class or were prompted to act as its mouthpiece. . . .

> It may be, of course, that the social structure in Venetia was entirely different from that in Lombardy but if so, nobody at the time believed so.

7. See R. John Rath, 'The Habsburgs and the Great Depression in Lombardy-Venetia, 1814–18', *Journal of Modern History,* XIII (1941), 305–20.

8. See *I Prezzi dei Generi Alimentari in Milano dal 1789 al 1918,* Milan, 1919, pp. 15–20.

9. B. Caizzi, 'La crisi economical nel Lombardo-Veneto nel decennio 1850–59', *Nuova Rivista Storica* (1958), p. 221.

10. See G. Luzzatto, 'L'Economia Venezia dal 1796 al 1866', in *La Civilta Venezia nell'Eta Romantica,* Venice, 1961, pp. 105–8.

11. See Luzzatto, op. cit., pp. 105–8.

12. Edward Heller, *Fürst Felix zu Schwarzenberg, Mitteleuropas Vorkämpfer,* Vienna, 1933, p. 265.

13. Heller, pp. 265–6.

Bibliography

The following is a select bibliography; it lists only those works which were found to be of particular value in the writing of this book. It is by no means a complete record of works consulted by the author.

Primary sources

(a) Unpublished

Vienna, Kriegsarchiv:
  (i) Centralkanzleiakten, Präsidialreihe 1848. All Kartons.
 (ii) Ministerium des Kriegswesensakten, Präsidialreihe, April 1848–March 1849. All Kartons.
(iii) Feldakten, 1847. Kartons 213 and 214.
 (iv) Memoiren Abteilung; Radetzky Nachlass; Nachlass FML. Freiherr D'Aspre; Nachlass Erzherzog Maximilian d'Este.

Vienna, Haus-Hof- und Staatsarchiv
  (i) Staatskanzleiakten, Provinzen, Lombardei-Venezien.
 (ii) Kabinettsarchiv, Geheimakten, Schwarzènberg Nachlass.
(iii) Politisches Archiv, Karton XL/64.
 (iv) Österreichisch-Estensisches Archiv (IV), Kartons 107 and 108.
  (v) Staatskanzleiakten, Kriegsakten, Karton 512.

London, Public Record Office:
Foreign Office: 7/371 and 67/192.
British Museum: Documents relating to Lombardy-Venetia during the Revolutions of 1848. (Catalogue No. 804 k. 13.)

(b) Published sources

(i) Collections of documents
The following collections of documents, published by the Istituto Storico Italiano per L'Età Moderna e Contemporanea in the series *Fonti per la Storia d'Italia*, were most helpful:
(*a*) **Curato, Federico** (ed.), *Le Relazioni Diplomatiche fra la Gran Bretagna e il Regno di Sardegna*, 2 vols, Rome, 1961.
(*b*) **Curato, Federico** (ed.), *Gran Bretagna e Italia nei Documenti della Missione Minto*, 2 vols, Rome, 1970.
(*c*) **Filipuzzi, Angelo** (ed.), *Le Relazioni Diplomatiche fra l'Austria e il Regno di Sardegna e la Guerra del 1848–49*, 2 vols, Rome, 1961.
(*d*) **Valsecchi, Franco** (ed.), *Le Relazioni Diplomatiche fra l'Austria e il Regno di Sardegna*, 2 vols, Rome, 1963.
Also very useful were the following:
Archivio Triennale delle Cose d'Italia dall'Avvimento di Pio IX all'Abbandono di Venezia, 3 vols, Capolago-Chieri, 1850–5.
British and Foreign and State Papers, Vols, 37, 44 and 45.
Carte Segrete della Polizia Austriaca in Italia Estratte dall'Archivio di Venezia e pubblicate per Commissione di D. Manin, 3 vols, Capolago, 1851.

Curato, Federico (ed.), *1848–49. La Consulta Straordinaria della Lombardia (2 August 1848–20 March 1849),* Milan, 1950.

Raccolta degli Atti ufficiali, dei Proclami ecc. emanati e pubblicati in Milano delle diverse Autorità durante l'I.R. Governo Militare. 1848–53.

(ii) Memoirs, accounts, diaries, etc.

Anonymous, *Enthüllungen aus Oesterreichs jüngster Vergangenheit. Von einem Mitglieder der Linken des aufgelösten österreichischen Reichstages,* Hamburg, 1849.

Cattaneo, Carlo, *L'Insurrection de Milan en 1848,* Paris, 1848.

Duhr, Bernhard (ed.), *Briefe des Feldmarschalls Radetzky an seine Tochter Friederike, 1847–57,* Vienna, 1892.

Gualterio, F. A., *Gli ultimi Rivolgimenti italiani,* 2 vols, Florence, 1852.

Hartig, Count, 'Genesis of the Revolution in Austria', appended to Archdeacon Coxe's *History of the House of Austria,* London, 1853.

Hübner, Le Comte de, *Une Année de Ma Vie,* Paris, 1891.

Metternich, Richard von and **Klinkowström, Alfons von** (eds). *Aus Metternichs nachgelassenen Papieren,* 8 vols, Vienna, 1880–4.

Schönhals, General K. von, *Errinerungen eines österreichischen Veteranen aus dem italienischen Kriege der Jahre 1848 und 1849,* Stuttgart and Tübingen, 1853.

Sonis, Comte F. de, *Lettres du Comte et de la Comtesse de Ficquelmont a' la Comtesse Tiesenhausen,* Paris, 1911.

Torrelli, Luigi, *Pensieri sull'Italia di un Anonimo Lombardo,* Paris, 1848.

Secondary sources

Published

(i) Books

Anonymous: *La Vérité sur les Événemens de Galicie,* Paris, 1847; *L'Autriche et ses Provinces Italiennes,* Paris, 1859; *I Prezzi dei Generi Alimentari in Milano dal 1789 al 1918,* Milan, 1919.

Andics, Erzsébet, *Metternich und die Frage Ungarns,* Budapest, 1973.

Benedikt, Heinrich, *Kaiseradler über dem Appenin. Die Österreicher in Italien, 1700 bis 1866,* Vienna and Munich, 1964.

Bianchi Giovini, N., *L'Autriche en Italie,* 2 vols, Paris, 1854.

Casati, Carlo, *Nuove Rivelazioni su i Fatti di Milano nel 1847—48,* 2 vols, Milan, 1885.

Greenfield, Kent Roberts, *Economics and Liberalism in the Risorgimento. A Study of Nationalism in Lombardy, 1814–48,* rev. ed., Baltimore, 1965.

Hajnal, István, *A Batthyány-Kormány Külpolitikája,* Budapest, 1957.

Hoettinger, Franz Ferdinand, *Radetzky, ein Stück Österreich,* Leipzig and Vienna, 1934.

Kiszling, Rudolf (ed.), *Die Revolution im Kaisertum Österreich,* 2 vols, Vienna, 1948.

Marazza, Achille, *Il Clero Lombardo nella Rivoluzione del'48,* Milan, 1958.

Marchetti, Leopoldo, 'Il decennio di resistenza', Part 5 of Vol. XIV (*Sotto L'Austria*) of the *Storia di Milano, Fondazione Treccani degli Alfieri per la Storia di Milano,* Milan, 1960.

Pieri, Piero, *Storia Militare del Risorgimento,* Turin, 1962.

Rath, J. R., *The Fall of the Napoleonic Kingdom of Italy,* New York, 1941.

Rath, J. R., *The Provisional Austrian Régime in Lombardy-Venetia, 1814–15,* University of Texas, 1969.

Regele, Oskar, *Feldmarschall Radetzky, sein Leben, Leistung und Erbe,* Vienna, 1957.

Sandonà, Augusto, *Il Regno Lombardo-Veneto, 1814–59. La Costituzione e l'Amministrazione,* Milan, 1912.

Srbik, Heinrich Ritter von, *Metternich, der Staatsmann und der Mensch,* 2 vols, Munich, 1925.

Taylor, A. J. P., *The Italian Question in European Diplomacy, 1847–49,* Manchester, 1934.

(ii) Articles

The following collections were very rewarding:

Atti e Memorie del XXVII Congresso Nazionale, 19–20–21 Marzo 1948, Istituto per la Storia del Risorgimento.

La Civiltà Venezia nell'Età Romantica, Venice(?) 1961.

Rota, Ettore (ed.), *Il 1848 nella Storia Italiana ed Europea,* Milan, 1948.

Also:

Andics, Erzsebet, 'Metternich és az 1830 – as évek magyar reformmozgalma', *Századok*, **105** (1971).

Arese, Franco, 'La Lombardia e la Politica dell'Austria: un Colloquio inedito del Metternich nel 1832', *Archivio Storico Lombardo*, LXXVII (1950).

Arno, Col. Freiherr Wolf-Schneider von, 'Feldmarschall Radetzky', *Militärwissenschaftliche Mitteilungen*, **65** (1934).

Caizzi, B., 'La crisi economica nel Lombardo-Veneto nel decennio 1850–59', *Nuova Rivista Storica*, **45** (1958).

Campanini, N., 'I Proclami latini diretti dagli Italiani ai Soldati ungheresi', *Rassegna Storica del Risorgimento* (1919).

Della Peruta, Franco, 'I Contadini nella Rivoluzione lombarda del 1848', *Movimento Operaio* (1953).

Della Peruta, Franco, 'I Democratici e il Problema della Rivoluzione Italiana dal 1849 al 1852, *Movimento Operaio* (1955).

Helfert, Joseph, Alexander, Freiherr von, 'Zur Geschichte des lombardo-venezianischen Königreichs, *Archiv für österreichische Geschichte*, **98** (1908)

Helfert, Joseph, Alexander, Freiherr von, 'Casati und Pillersdorff und die Anfänge der italienischen Einheitsbewegung', *Archiv für österreichische Geschichte*, **91** (1902).

Helfert, Joseph, Alexander, Freiherr von, 'Radetzky in den Tagen seiner ärgsten Bedrängnis', *Archiv für österreichische Geschichte*, **95** (1906).

Magda Jászay, 'L'Italia del Quarantotto nella Stampa ungherese del Tempo', *Rassegna Storica del Risorgimento* (1968).

Kiszling, Rudolf, 'Habsburgs Wehrmacht im Spiegel des Nationalitätenproblems 1815 bis 1918' in *Gedenkschrift für Harold Steinacker*, **16**, Munich, 1966.

Kiszling, Rudolf, 'Das Nationalitätenproblem in Habsburgs Wehrmacht, 1848–1918', *Der Donauraum*, **4** (1959).

Monti, Antonio, 'Il contributo dei Lombardi alla prima guerra dell'independenza', *Nuova Rivista Storica*, X (1926).

Pierazzi, Giuseppe, 'Studi sui rapporti italo-jugoslavi, 1848–49', *Archivio Storico Italiano*, CXXX (1972).

Rath, R. J., 'The Habsburgs and public opinion in Lombardy-Venetia, 1814–15', in E. M. Earle (ed.), *Nationalism and Internationalism, Essays Inscribed to Carlton J. H. Hayes*, New York, 1950.

Rath, R. J., 'The Habsburgs and the Great Depression in Lombardy-Venetia, 1814–18', *Journal of Modern History*, **13** (1941).

Rothenberg, Gunther E., 'The Habsburg Army and the Nationality Problem in the Nineteenth Century, 1815–1914', *Austrian History Yearbook*, III (1967).

Rothenberg, Gunther E., 'The Austrian Army in the Age of Metternich', *Journal of Modern History*, **40** (1968).

Rothenberg, Gunther E., 'Jellacić, the Croatian Military Border and the intervention against Hungary in 1848', *Austrian History Yearbook*, I (1965).

Urbán, Aladár, 'A Magyarországi Osztrák Hadszervezet és a Hazánkban Allomásagó Katonság 1848 Aprilisban', *Hadtörténelmi Közlemények* (1963).

Waldstrum-Wartenberg, Berthold, 'Österreichische Adelsrecht, 1804–1918', *Mitteilungen des österreichischen Staatsarchiv*, **17/18** (1964–5).

Wandycz, Piotr S., 'The Poles in the Habsburg Monarchy', *Austrian History Yearbook*, III (1967).

Index

Notes have been indexed only where they add signifigantly to the text.

Abbreviations used in the index:

Capt.	Captain	FML.	Fieldmarschalleutnant
Col.	Colonel	Gen.	General
Dr.	Doctor	Lieut.	Lieutenant
FM	Field Marshal	US	United States of America